Yizkor Book of
Ostrow Mazowiecka
(Number 2)

Translation of *Ostrow Mazowiecka*

Translator and Editor: Gary S. Schiff, Ph.D.

Original Book Written and Edited by: Yehuda Leib Levin

Published in Hebrew in Jerusalem-Tel Aviv 1965/1966

Published by JewishGen Press

**An Affiliate of the Museum of Jewish Heritage - A Living Memorial to the Holocaust
New York**

Yizkor Book of Ostrow Mazowiecka (Number 2)
Translation of *Ostrow Mazowiecka*

Copyright © 2017 by JewishGen, Inc.
All rights reserved.
First Printing: July 2017, Tamuz 5777
Second Printing: August 2019, Av 5779

Translation Project Coordinator: Michael B. Richman (Rockville, Maryland)
Translator and Editor: Gary S. Schiff (Kennedyville, Maryland)
Image Editor and Layout: Lynn Mercer (Morrisville, North Carolina)
Cover Design: Nili Goldman (Ramat Gan, Israel)

Published by JewishGen, Inc.
An Affiliate of the Museum of Jewish Heritage
A Living Memorial to the Holocaust
36 Battery Place, New York, NY 10280

Printed in the United States of America by Lightning Source, Inc.

Library of Congress Control Number (LCCN): 2017934031
ISBN: 978-1-939561-51-0 (hard cover: 392 pages, alk. paper)

Cover Photographs: Selected from the Appendix of Photographs
Back Cover Credit: From a postcard dated 1914, colorized by Nili Goldman

JewishGen and the Yizkor-Books-in-Print Project

This book has been published by the **Yizkor-Books-in-Print Project,** as part of the **Yizkor Book Project** of **JewishGen, Inc**.

JewishGen, Inc. is a non-profit organization founded in 1987 as a resource for Jewish genealogy. Its website [www.jewishgen.org] serves as an international clearinghouse and resource center to assist individuals who are researching the history of their Jewish families and the places where they lived. JewishGen provides databases, facilitates discussion groups, and coordinates projects relating to Jewish genealogy and the history of the Jewish people. In 2003, JewishGen became an affiliate of the **Museum of Jewish Heritage - A Living Memorial to the Holocaust** in New York.

The **JewishGen Yizkor Book Project** was organized to make more widely known the existence of *yizkor* (memorial) books written by survivors and former residents of various Jewish communities throughout the world. Later, volunteers connected to the different destroyed communities began cooperating to have these books translated from the original language—usually Hebrew or Yiddish—into English, thus enabling a wider audience to have access to the valuable information contained within them. As each chapter of these books was translated, it was posted on the JewishGen website and made available to the general public.

The **Yizkor-Books-in-Print Project** began in 2011 as an initiative to print and publish *yizkor* books that had been fully translated, so that hard copies would be available for purchase by the descendants of these communities and also by scholars, universities, synagogues, libraries, and museums.

These *yizkor* books have been produced almost entirely through the volunteer effort of researchers from around the world, assisted by donations from private individuals. The books are printed and sold at near cost, so as to make them as affordable as possible. Our goal is to make this important genre of Jewish literature and history available in English in book form, so that people can have the personal histories of their ancestral towns on their bookshelves for themselves and for their children and grandchildren.

A list of all published translated *yizkor* books in the project with prices and ordering information can be found at:
http://www.jewishgen.org/Yizkor/ybip.html

Lance Ackerfeld, Yizkor Book Project Manager

Joel Alpert, Yizkor-Books-in-Print Project Coordinator

JewishGen
Yizkor Book Project

This book is presented by the
Yizkor Books in Print Project
Project Coordinator: Joel Alpert

Part of the
Yizkor Books Project of JewishGen, Inc.
Project Manager: Lance Ackerfeld

These books have been produced solely through volunteer effort
of individuals from around the world. The books are printed and
sold at near cost, so as to make them as affordable as possible.

Our goal is to make this history and important genre of Jewish
literature available in English in book form so that people can have
the near-personal histories of their ancestral towns on their bookshelves for themselves and for their children and grandchildren.

Any donations to the Yizkor Books Project are appreciated.

Please send donations to:
Yizkor Book Project
JewishGen
36 Battery Place
New York, NY 10280

JewishGen, Inc. is an affiliate of the
Museum of Jewish Heritage
A Living Memorial to the Holocaust

Translator/Editor's Foreword

In undertaking the translation and editing of this *yizkor* book of Ostrow Mazowiecka, I realized that for me it was not going to be just another scholarly project. Yes, it was the hitherto mostly untold story of the large orthodox community of an important, two hundred year-old *shtetl* on the cultural border between Polish and Lithuanian Jewry. True, it was the product of a survivor of that community who had done much research into its origins and development and who may have uncovered facts that might not have appeared elsewhere. And it did record the stories of many of the renowned rabbis and others who had led that community over time up to its destruction in the Holocaust and the history of its many great institutions. In that sense, it constituted yet another brick in the re-constructed wall of testimonies embodied in the over one thousand memorial books of destroyed Jewish communities, more of which are now being translated into English to be more readily accessible to general readers and researchers alike.

But at the same time it was also my own and my family's story. My father's mother's clan, the Feinzeigs, had been among the first twenty families that had been officially allowed to settle in the town in the mid-1700s. Since that time they had grown to become one of the largest Jewish families in town, the name being the fourth most common among the ten thousand or more Jews in Ostroveh, as it was called by the Jews, around the turn of the twentieth century. A number of them are mentioned in the text here and in the other, larger, more general *yizkor* book of articles on the town published in English translation by JewishGen in 2013. So this was also very personal to me, a story of my "hometown." I had long heard about the Amshinover *rebbe*, for example, and the famous story about Mendel Feinzeig and his coat.

So I undertook the task with care, not only to get it right translation-wise, and to supply additional information to broaden the perspective for the reader where appropriate, but also to communicate the flavor and tone of the text as well. The author, Yehuda Leib Levin, who wrote and published his book in Israel in the mid-1960s, wrote in an educated, fluent modern Hebrew. But given his background and subject matter, he at times utilized a respectful--even reverential--tone that I tried to reflect and respect.

From a technical point of view I translated Hebrew words, terms and names using modern Israeli Sephardi Hebrew, giving the Ashkenazi equivalents in parentheses in early mentions, e.g., Agudat Yisrael [Agudas Yisroel]. Similarly, I did not distinguish between the guttural letters of *het* and *chaf*, as some purists might have it, transliterating both as *ch*, except in cases where the word is already commonly used in the English language, e.g., Hassidim. Nor did I distinguish between the letters *alef* and *ayin*, or separate out the definite article *ha* from the word it modified. Foreign words of whatever language were italicized and lower cased if not proper names or titles. I have also made the word "orthodox" lower case, even though it is commonly capitalized today in order to distinguish it from other "denominations" of Judaism, such as Conservative or Reform. However, in the context of the community that this book depicts, no other such denominations are germane. Given the plethora of spellings of names of people and places in the area (Yiddish in its various iterations, German, Polish, other Slavic languages, etc.), for consistency's sake I have shown a preference for a single spelling throughout, providing the alternatives in parentheses where possible, for example, the town of Ger [Gur or Gora Kalwaria]. Names of major cities that are widely known in English, like Warsaw or Cracow, are utilized in their Anglicized formats. In translating Yiddish surnames, I have generally preferred the Germanic spellings long commonly used by American Jews (e.g., Feinzeig), rather than their Polish (Fajncajg) or other equivalents (except perhaps in footnotes that were drawn directly from Polish records, where the order is reversed). Finally, where there were captions in the original, they appear in translation; where there were no captions, there are none. But their placement in the text (they consist mostly of portraits of individuals) should make it clear who they are.

While the entire book was translated directly by me--and I take full responsibility for it all--I did have a few back-up resources at my disposal. For the odd Hebrew word or phrase that defied my powers and best efforts at translation, my friend and colleague, Dr. Anat Gilboa of UCLA, was always there for assistance. For the even rarer Yiddish word, rabbinic expression, complex abbreviation or acronym, my nephew, Rabbi Dov (Rephael Baruch) Schiff of Lakewood, New Jersey, was of great help.

But perhaps the greatest source of ongoing support was Michael Richman, Esq. He not only served as the administrator of the project *per se*, keeping in touch with the publishers and removing the burden of fund raising from my shoulders. (The generous donors, who are listed separately, deserve a warm thank you as well.) But as a founder of the Ostrow Mazowiecka Research Family, his own deep knowledge of the subject matter, including names, dates and places, as well as his eagle eye for editing, all helped shape the work in a very real way, including by compiling the photographic and other addenda material. I am greatly indebted to him. Lance Ackerfeld, Yizkor Book Project Manager of JewishGen, and Joel Alpert, Yizkor-Books-in-Print Project Coordinator, were also very helpful.

I hope that this work will add to our growing knowledge and understanding of the world of our forbears that is now gone, but not forgotten.

Gary S. Schiff, Ph.D.

Kennedyville, Maryland
Erev Rosh Hashanah, 5777

October 2, 2016

Acknowledgements for Contributions to the Translation

We wish to the following people whose donations enabled the completion of this translation:

Harold S. Berzow	Ross Malaga
Regina Bracher	Jennifer Mohr
Gerald Cook	Shirley Ranz
Alan Droz	Michael Richman
Deborah Frey	Ruth Rosenberg
Richard H. Hoffman	Joel Sharkey
Barbara Krasner	Barry Sieger
Robinn Magid	Steven Wolmark

Special thanks to the National Yiddish Book Center in Amherst, Massachusetts and the New York Public Library for supplying the high resolution images used in this book.

Brief Summary of the Book

This is one of the two *yizkor* or memorial books for the Jewish community of Ostrów Mazowiecka, Poland.

This translated edition of the Yizkor Book of Ostrów Mazowiecka (Number 2) is nearly 400 pages long. Unlike the earlier, 1960 *yizkor* book, this one (published in 1966) is focused on the rabbis of the town and others who were prominent in its orthodox (heavily Hassidic) community. It includes all the photographs and illustrations from the original *yizkor* book itself.

Records of the earliest history show Jews living in Ostrów Mazowiecka as early as 1765. At the beginning of the twentieth century there were about 10,000 Jews or about 60% of the population. When the Nazi forces occupied Ostrów Mazowiecka in 1939, many fled; the remaining Jews were executed. Of those who fled, many went to Bialystok and Slonim and suffered the fate of those communities; those who survived did so mainly as a result of being deported to Siberia or other areas deep within the Soviet Union. Today there are many descendents of the Jewish community of Ostrów Mazowiecka living around the world, especially in the United States, Israel, Canada and Latin America. There are no Jews remaining in Ostrów Mazowiecka, Poland.

Geopolitical Information

Ostrów Mazowiecka, Poland: 52°48' North Latitude, 21°54' East Longitude

Alternate names for the town are: Ostrów Mazowiecka [Polish], Ostrov-Mazovyetsk [Yiddish], Ostroveh, Ostrova [Yiddish], Ostrów, Ostrov, Ostrove, Ostreve, Mazovyetska, Ostrov-Mazovetskiy
Region: Lomza

	Town	District	Province	Country	
Before WWI (c. 1900):	Ostrów	Ostrów	Łomża	Russian Empire	
Between the wars (c. 1930):	Ostrów Mazowiecka	Ostrów	Białystok	Poland	
After WWII (c. 1950):	Ostrów Mazowiecka			Poland	
Today (c. 2000):	Ostrów Mazowiecka			Poland	

Jewish Population in 1896: 10,471 (out of a total population of 16,431)

Notes: Russian: Остров / Острув-Мазовецка. Yiddish: אסטראוו-מאזאוויעצק/ אָסטרעווע
28 miles SSW of Łomża.

Nearby Jewish Communities:

Brok 7 miles SSW
Kosewo 8 miles N
Małkinia Górna 9 miles SSE
Prostyń 10 miles SSE
Zaręby Kościelne 10 miles ESE
Wąsewo 11 miles WNW
Poręba-Kocęby 11 miles SW
Poręba Średnia 12 miles SW
Andrzejewo 12 miles ENE
Szumowo 12 miles NE
Czerwin 12 miles NNW
Długosiodło 13 miles W
Goworowo 16 miles WNW
Śniadowo 17 miles NNE
Brańszczyk 17 miles SW
Stoczek 17 miles S
Kosów Lacki 17 miles SE
Czyżew-Osada 17 miles E
Łopianka 19 miles SSW

Baczki 19 miles SSW
Zambrów 19 miles NE
Nur 20 miles ESE
Kamieńczyk 20 miles SW
Różan 21 miles WNW
Jabłonka 22 miles ENE
Sterdyń 22 miles SE
Wyszków 23 miles SW
Ostrołęka 24 miles NW
Gać 24 miles NE
Miedzna 24 miles SSE
Jadów 26 miles SSW
Wysokie Mazowieckie 27 miles ENE
Ciechanowiec 27 miles ESE
Łomża 28 miles NNE
Piątnica 28 miles NNE
Węgrów 28 miles S
Liw 29 miles S
Nowogród 30 miles N

BALTIC SEA

LITHUANIA

RUSSIA

Vilnius ●

POLAND

BELARUS

Ostrów Mazowiecka
●

GERMANY

● Poznan   Warsaw ●

● Lodz

● Prague

CZECH REPUBLIC

● Krakow

UKRAINE

SLOVAKIA

250 miles
0

0   250 Km   500 Km

POLAND - Current Borders

Map of Poland with Ostrow Mazowiecka indicated

Title Page of Original Yizkor Book

מגילת פולין	יד יהדות פולין
מפעל להנצחת יהדות	ארגון עולמי של יוצאי
פולין, גאליציה וליטא	פולין, גאליציה וליטא

סידרת
קהלות ישראל

אוסטרוב מאזובייצק

יו"ל ע"י
"יד יהדות פולין"

| תשכ"ו | ירושלים – תל-אביב |

Translation of the Title Page of Original Hebrew Book

The Memorial to Polish Jewry:
The World Organization of Emigrants
from Poland, Galicia and Lithuania

The Scroll of Poland:
The Project to Memorialize Polish,
Galician and Lithuanian Jewry

The Jewish Communities Series

Ostrow Mazowiecka

Published by
The Memorial to Polish Jewry

Jerusalem – Tel Aviv   5726 [1965-1966]

כתב וערך

יהודא לייב לוין

נדפס בישראל

Translation of previous page

Author and Editor

Yehuda Leib Levin

Printed in Israel

"Daat" Press, Meah Shearim, Jerusalem

Additional Notes to the Reader

The original book can be seen online at the NY Public Library site:

http://yizkor.nypl.org/index.php?id=2512

In order to obtain a list of all Shoah victims from Ostrow Mazowiecka, the reader should access the Yad Vashem web site listed below; one can also search for specific family names using family name option. These lists are continually updated by Yad Vashem, so it is worthwhile to periodically search these lists.

There is much valuable information available on this web site, including the Pages of Testimony, etc.

http://yvng.yadvashem.org

A list of this book and all books available in the Yizkor-Books-in-Print Project along with prices is available at:

http://www.jewishgen.org/Yizkor/ybip.html

Table of Contents

Notes

With the help of God, Kislev 5726 [November-December 1965]

The Memorial to Polish Jewry, the World Organization of Emigrants from Poland, Galicia and Lithuania, was established last summer in Tel Aviv at a well attended assembly of emigrants from that glorious Diaspora for the purpose of setting up a permanent memorial to Polish, Galician and Lithuanian Jewries, to perpetuate the eternal values of that glorious Diaspora, and to preserve its heritage.

Within that framework of activity we have dedicated an honored place to the perpetuation of the memories of the Jewish communities of Poland, Galicia and Lithuania by means of publishing appropriate memorial books that will eventually include all the Jewish communities of that Diaspora that were destroyed and uprooted to their very foundations.

A significant number of the Jewish communities that were destroyed have already had the benefit of memorial books being published about them. Nevertheless, despite all the efforts invested in these works, there still remains room for--and an obligation to--augment them, especially in regard to memorializing the orthodox segments within these communities which, for whatever reason, have been somewhat neglected.

In the context of the Scroll of Poland project we are publishing the first books of the series dedicated to those communities whose names begin with the letter *aleph*.

In order to produce a complete series it is our intention not to skip over any community in that august Disapora, so that we may be faithful to the historical truth and the establishment of a memorial to that Jewry as it was when it was still extant, both in its all its glory and splendor and in the decline and destruction that befell it.

Polish-Galician-Lithuanian Jewry brought glory to God through its vibrant life. It wrote glorious chapters in bright flaming letters in the history of our eternal people. As survivors of that great Diaspora we see it as an obligation and a religious commandment to record the history of these communities for future generations.

We will make every effort to establish a memorial to each and every community, large and small, sparing no effort to assemble the necessary material to accomplish this task. We have begun with those communities whose names begin with *aleph*. So after the book about the community of Ostroh [Ostrog] we are now publishing the second book in the Scroll of Poland series on Ostrow Mazowiecka.

[signed]
The President and Administration in Israel of the Memorial to Polish Jewry

This book has appeared with the assistance of the
Yosef Glazer-Simcha Horowitz Fund
In memory of their parents
The late Rabbi Meir Glazer died on the fourth of Tevet, 5705
[December 20, 1944] in Bari (Italy) and was buried in Israel
Rabbi Yaakov David, son of the late Rabbi Yitzhak Isaac Halevy
Horowitz, died in the Lodz Ghetto in 5702 [1941-1942]

With the assistance of IRSO

Introduction

Ostrow Mazowiecka was not among the oldest of Jewish communities in central Poland, or one of its largest either. Nevertheless, by the time of the outbreak of the Holocaust, it had already managed to achieve a key and respected place in that Diaspora. In Ostroveh [as it was called by Jews] there was a lively Jewish life. This community stood out in a number of spheres, and its influence far exceeded its numerical size. Ostroveh did not achieve its fame as a result of any particular institutions that functioned therein, nor as a result of any historical events that took place there, but rather as a result of its unique characteristics that emanated from its inhabitants and founders.

The history of this community is rather brief, actually only beginning with the abolition of the prohibition on Jews residing in Mazovia. Because of its central location it developed rather quickly. Differing from other fairly new communities, however, it succeeded in establishing its unique ways of life and character. "Ostrovite" became a defined concept or type of Polish Jew, whether orthodox or not, whether Hassidic[1] or Mitnagdic.[2]

It is difficult in a few short pages to portray a complete memorial to this great community. Its history was never fully or accurately recorded in such a way as to enable us to present it in a chronological and fully objective fashion. The limited raw material that we have barely permits us to provide a partial monument to represent this Jewish community.

Ostroveh no longer exists. Even far more complete memorial books cannot adequately represent the brilliant personages that functioned within this community. We can only portray the briefest of sketches of the giants who left their imprints on this community, whether it be Rabbi Ben-Zion Rabinowitz, the rabbi of the Hassidim, or Rabbi Berish Shapira, rabbi of the scholars and Mitnagdim, or other famous rabbis of Ostroveh like Hassidic *rebbe* Rabbi Gershon Chanoch of Radzyn or the Gaon [literally, genius][3]

---

[1] Hassidism (literally pietism) was a mass religious and social movement that began in the mid-late 18th century in southeast Poland and spread throughout most of Eastern Europe, stressing the mystical and emotional bases of orthodox Judaism. Opposed to the traditional religious establishment and its classic *yeshivot*, it later broke into numerous sub-groups revolving around particular rabbinic dynasties.

[2] The Mitnagdim (or Misnagdim, literally opponents of the Hassidim) arose in the late 18th century, notably in Lithuania, site of the leading *yeshivot*, who accused them of various forms of heresy and fought them for control of many Jewish communities.

[3] Honorific title usually attributed to a distinguished rabbi recognized for his exceptional status as a leader, author and decisor in matters of Jewish law.

Rabbi Yehuda Leib Gordin[4] or the Gaon Rabbi David Shlomo Margaliot [whose acronym was the Maharshdal] or the Hassidic Rabbi Yosef of Ostroveh, the Gaon Rabbi Feivel Sokolower, or the Gaon Rabbi Meir Dan Plotzky [Plocki].

No, this dry pen can hardly portray a living memorial to Rabbi Yaakov Velvel the porter, who taught a class every evening between the afternoon and evening prayers in the study hall, or to Rabbi Mordechai Mendel Markusfeld, the ritual slaughterer, the rabbi of the working men at the old study hall, who was always performing righteous acts.

We recall Ostroveh with sorrow and pain, much as we do every other community in the Diaspora of Poland, Lithuania and Galicia. Will there ever again be Jews such as these? Will there ever walk among us Jews like Reb Zelig the *shames* [beadle], whose services the rabbis of the city refused to exploit given his great knowledge and respect for the Torah, or will there ever live among us again a Jew like Mr. Salzberg from Ostroveh, who served for twenty-five years under horrific circumstances in the army of Tsar Nicholas but who remained unremittingly faithful to everything related to Judaism until his final day?

Yes, Ostroveh was blessed with outstanding scholars, some of whom served her in various capacities. Take, for example, Reb Aharkeh the *shames*, who was well learned in the Torah, or the aged Reb Tanchum the *shames*, whose Torah knowledge was both broad and deep, who was friendly to all people, and whose said, when his wife was weeping as he lay dying, "Why are you crying? As long as I am alive they won't yet take me."

Ostroveh is now sleeping its final sleep before the Great Day [of Judgment] comes. The voice of Reb Leizer Loew, who lacked even bread, is no longer heard at two in the morning disturbing one's sleep with a call to arise and serve God with morning prayers. There are no longer rich or poor [Jews] in Ostroveh. The house of Reb Mendel Feinzeig (Elke's)[5] no longer serves as a gathering place

---

[4] The author and others spell the name in Hebrew Gordon, while the obituaries at the time of his death in Chicago in 1925, as well as his mausoleum in the *Tiferet Zion* section of the Waldheim Jewish Cemetery there, use Gordin in English, a spelling that we utilize.

[5] The name Mendel, the Yiddish diminutive for Menachem, was widely used in the large Feinzeig clan, which was among the first twenty "legal" families to settle in Ostroveh ca. 1765, during a period of political and constitutional liberalization. See below, footnote 24, p. 49 and footnote 183, p. 270, and Gary S. Schiff, *In Search of Polin: Chasing Jewish Ghosts in Today's Poland* (New York: Peter Lang Publishing, 2012), pp. 146-147. Holders of that name were therefore often given "nicknames" to distinguish them for other relatives with the same first name, in this case that of his mother-in-law, Elke.

for all those who are needy. No longer does he make his way on foot to the synagogue of the Gerer *rebbe*, stopping on his way back at every house where there is someone ill or otherwise suffering to provide aid and support.

Ostroveh is desolate. There is no longer a *yeshiva* [school of higher Jewish learning] or *cheder* [Jewish elementary school], no institutions of education or teaching. The old study house on the road to Komorowo is no longer filled with worshippers, much as were many other synagogues and Hassidic prayer houses. It is closed forever. The society for endowing poor brides, the society for providing shelter to the needy, and the society for supplying prayer shawls and phylacteries, whose members prayed and studied until noon wrapped in their prayer shawls and phylacteries, all no longer exist.

There is also no longer the prayer house of the Gerer Hassidim or that of the Amshinov Hassidim, or of the Alexander or Strikov Hassidim either. There are no longer Agudists[6] or Zionists, nor is there heard the blessing of some great Hassidic rabbi. Fire had never before overtaken Ostroveh. Its houses had never been burned, until there descended a gigantic flame from on high that destroyed everything.

We will deal with the city and its history, its people and personalities, its institutions and its enterprises in the upcoming chapters.

Yehuda Leib Levin

---

[6] Members of Agudat Yisrael [Agudas Yisroel, the Association of Israel], an orthodox religious, social and political movement established in 1912 to counter the Zionist movement and its orthodox wing, Mizrachi. See Gary S. Schiff, *Tradition and Politics: The Religious Parties of Israel* (Detroit: Wayne State University Press, 1977) (to be made available online and re-printed in hard copy on demand by Wayne State under a grant from the National Endowment for the Humanities and the Andrew W. Mellon Foundation by the end of 2017), especially Chapter 3.

Chapter One
The History of the Community

Eastern Mazovia

In the several centuries before the Holocaust, the districts of Mazovia were witness to a vibrant Jewish life, so much so that one would have imagined that these were pure Jewish areas where Jews had lived forever. However, these areas were settled by Jews only much later than other areas of Poland. At a time when Jewish communities in eastern and western Galicia, in Pomerania and Volhynia, already had a distinguished past and a tradition going back hundreds of years, it was still forbidden for a Jew to settle in Mazovia. While Jews traveled the roads of Mazovia, peddled in its villages, knew its byways, most of the cities in this region were bereft of any Jews. Special laws that were renewed periodically absolutely prohibited Jews from living anywhere in old Mazovia, which sprawled over major portions of central Poland.

Mazovia retained a certain level of political independence since the establishment of the Kingdom of Poland, at which time central political institutions--weaker or stronger--had been set up. Its rulers and the few citizens who had special rights meticulously preserved these special rights, and viewed any attempt to settle Jews in Mazovia under royal edicts as a threat to their efforts. The clergy of the Catholic Church, which was very influential in this region, perhaps even more than elsewhere, was particularly vigilant in observing the ban on Jewish settlement in the territory of Mazovia. The clergy was consumed with flaming anti-Semitism and never ceased to take pride in its attainments in this realm, and in its success in preventing the settlement of Jews in any place where its influence was decisive, especially in eastern Mazovia.

The fact that Mazovia, despite its fertile lands, was weaker economically than other regions of Poland, very likely because of the absence of Jewish initiative and trade, did not influence the firm position of the Church or the rulers of Mazovia. They were more interested in the independence of the region than in its prosperity.

Up until 1360 the kings of Poland were not even recognized by the dukes of Mazovia. While legally subject to the kings of Poland, in fact the dukes were semi-independent. Only from this period on did the dukes of Mazovia swear allegiance to the Kingdom of Poland at the time of the coronation of its new kings, but ties with the institutions of the monarchy were weak. The kings of Poland worked diligently to bring Mazovia under their rule. When a duke of Mazovia died without sons or legal heirs, the kings of Poland would rush to incorporate his realm into the state. In 1462 when a noble who ruled the County of Rawa died, the kings of Poland absorbed the areas of Rawa and Gostynin into their kingdom. Two years later they took Sochaczew [Sochachow] and its environs, and thirty years later Plotzk [Plock] and Ostroveh. It was only from this period on that the kings of Poland would crown themselves as the being the rulers of Mazovia as well, a Polish region populated by Poles located in the very heart of central Poland.

From the time Mazovia was absorbed into Poland, the latter's laws applied. The *szlachta*, members of ruling noble families, received the same rights as their counterparts in other parts of Poland. But over and above this, the province maintained a series of special laws, in particular as regards the Jews, who had been given privileges by the kings of Poland.

Mazovia was divided into three counties (*voivode*ships) [literally, circuits], Rawa, Plotzk and Czersk. But their rulers continued to

view themselves as a united authority representing all of Mazovia. Ostroveh already enjoyed the status of a city. Boleslaw IV, Duke of Mazovia, had conferred upon the town the status of a city in 1410. But it was a small city of no particular importance, located in the midst of a great, dense forest sprawling over hundreds of kilometers.

The Three Counties of Mazovia

While in the County of Plotzk and in parts of the County of Rawa Jewish communities had already established themselves, despite the official bans, in the County (or *voivode*ship) of Czersk, which included Ostroveh, there was not a single Jew to be found except for the few who ran country inns.

The rulers of Mazovia briefly succeeded in maintaining a certain degree of independence and in retaining special laws that applied only in Mazovia. Two compendia of the laws of Mazovia were compiled that were also authorized by the kings of Poland. But in 1578 Stefan Batory, the brave King of Poland, decided once and for all to abolish the autonomy of the duchy of Mazovia, and to implement within its borders all the laws that were applicable across the Kingdom of Poland.

The rulers of the region, especially members of the *szlachta*, were unsuccessful in opposing the brave, victorious and much lauded king. They unwillingly submitted to all the laws that applied to the status of the monarchy and the royal house, the rights of the officers of the king, and so forth. But they continued to fight for the continued existence of various special laws, a battle which is known in Polish history as *Excepta Ducato Mazovia*.[7] In relation to these laws, for over two hundred years the representatives of the *szlachta* (privileged families who enjoyed full rights) continued to demand in their *sejmikis* (regional councils) that the Jews be expelled from all the counties of Mazovia.

While for all practical purposes these laws were now only applied to the residents of the County of Czersk, demands were made to apply them to all the counties of Mazovia, especially to the County of Plotzk. Members of the Catholic clergy, who by and large led the battle against the Jews and who for all practical purposes encouraged all anti-Jewish efforts, organized the members of the *szlachta* in the districts outside Mazovia to support these requests and demands.

The laws of Mazovia about which these battles raged were more like customs rather than signed and sealed laws. In those legal compendia there were no specific paragraphs that prohibited Jews from living in those places. Moreover, even according to those sources, an edict that had been issued by Boleslaw II, Duke of Mazovia, expelling all the Jews was never implemented. So Jews did in fact live in the counties of Plotzk and Rawa and in other places with no clear or permanent boundaries defining them. But the rulers of Mazovia continued to press for the expulsion of the Jews from all its territories. Even after the *G'zerot Tat v'Tach*[8] and the Polish-Swedish wars [of 1655-60], when the Polish kingdom was teetering on the brink, the region's representatives stridently demanded that all Jews without exception be expelled from all of Mazovia. This demand was once again forcefully put forth in the regional conference at Drobnin. There was in fact a good chance that these demands would succeed. Only the great efforts of the Council of the Four Lands[9] and the payment of large bribes prevented passage of the edict.

---

[7] A Latin phrase referring to the exceptions made for the Duchy of Mazovia from laws applicable elsewhere in the kingdom of Poland; the exact spelling is not clear from the Hebrew characters.

[8] The 1648-49 massacres of Poles and Jews led by the Ukrainian Cossack Bogdan Chmielnicki.

[9] The autonomous governing body of Polish (and separately Lithuanian) Jewry from the mid-1500's through 1764.

Prohibition and Excommunication for the Jews

As these demands did not cease, the leaders of the Council of the Four Lands saw a need to restrict the movement towards the settlement of more Jews in the Mazovia region. In the year 1660, on the day of the Fast of Gedaliah, the following declaration was read aloud in the synagogue of Tiktin [Tykocin] in the name of all the leaders of Council of the Four Lands: [cited from the Record Book of Tiktin in Yiddish, then translated into Hebrew]

"Attention members of the Holy Community. We, the officers, heads and leaders hereby aver that it is well known that according to previous rules no Jews are permitted to live in the province of Mazovia. But recent news indicates that some people have established their residences there. As these incidents have passed without any reaction, we were silent and did not respond. However, now that the bitter problems of the Diaspora have increased and the evil ones have re-awakened and are gnashing their teeth at us every day, we reiterate that the rules established by our predecessors were appropriate as stated and that the prohibition remains in place. We hereby proclaim and declare that from this day forward no Jews shall take up residence in the province of Mazovia. Anyone who shall dare to do so against our will should know that the opinion of the wise will not be pleased with him and that he will be deemed a sinner, thereby separating himself from the community of Israel, which will exclude him. And if something should occur to him, or if there should arise some baseless accusation where such attacks are common, we will not expend a single penny or any other effort to come to his aid. He is on his own, since as of this notification due warning has been given that he is responsible for his own actions. And we will further pursue him through Jewish law, using all the means of compulsion available to us as agreed upon by the assembly of officers and nobles of the community, who have agreed to maintain the prohibition against Jews living in the province of Mazovia as per the previous regulations."

From this sharply worded declaration we learn that the Council of the Four Lands issued a ban on living in the province of Mazovia, and that apparently the target thereof was specifically the County of Czersk, where over the years quite a number of communities had arisen, among them that of Ostrow Mazowiecka.

But it was clear that neither these bans and excommunications, on the one hand, nor the evil laws of the Polish authorities, on the other, prevented Jews from settling in this county, whether as individuals in the villages or as small communities, despite the great anti-Semitism that expressed itself specifically in this area, which was blessed neither with good fortune nor with a vigorous economy.[10]

These threats of the heads of the communities that they would not come to the aid of Jewish settlers in the event that they were falsely accused and that they would not help them at all; the extreme decisions that they would view the Jewish settlers in this area as having excluded themselves from the wider Jewish community, would all indicate that the heads of the Jewish community in Poland at the time were under great pressure from the veteran communities in the counties of Plotzk and Rawa. They felt that they were in serious danger of expulsion by the enemies of the people of Israel thanks to the Jews in the County of Czersk, who were dragging the other [Jewish] residents of Mazovia down along with them.

But Mazovia was not completely off limits, especially to Jews of means. Thus, there arose large and elaborate communities in this area. And only a few years after the threats of excommunication and prohibition the beautiful community of Ostrow Mazowiecka also arose.

The Beginnings of Ostrow Mazowiecka

The efforts of the authorities in Mazovia, and the ceaseless incitement of the Catholic clergy, who were consumed with hatred for the Jews, and even the prohibitions and regulations to prevent the settlement of Jews in the County of Czersk, all failed. The rules of prohibition and the special regulations remained on paper only. Jews streamed into this area and set up settlements and communities all over.

The *szlachta* in Mazovia did not give up on their war against the Jews. But as their rule weakened along with undermining of the status of Polish institutions in general, so too did the rules of exclusion vis-a-vis the Jews. No one spoke of the ban on the settlement of Jews in Mazovia any longer. The most extreme ones among them demanded only maintenance of the exclusion of Jews from certain cities and towns.

Ostrow Mazowiecka was one of those cities. In 1789 a royal court issued a final decision that absolutely prohibited Jews from

---

[10] The author's bleak view of the Mazovian economy is corroborated by one of the leading contemporary historians of Poland: "Mazowsze (Mazovia) on the middle Vistula has always been relatively backward. Gravelly soils, morainic deposits, and poor drainage have inhibited agriculture, leaving wide expanses of heath and scrubland. The province has no natural resources of note, and its poverty-stricken nobles and peasantry traditionally provided large numbers of emigrants and colonists." Norman Davies, *God's Playground: A History of Poland, Vol. I, The Origins to 1795*, New York: Columbia University Press, 2005, p. 27.

living in Ostroveh. For more than seventy years until 1862[11] this ruling was technically in force. But in practice it had no effect whatsoever. Jews arrived and settled in this ancient city, and in the towns and areas of settlement nearby, to such extent that, despite the law, the entire area became a lively and active Jewish one. Neither the non-Jewish residents nor the Jews even remembered its official legal status as a district that "prohibits entry to anyone of the Jewish faith."

Ostroveh was an ancient city. Back in 1410 Boleslaw IV, the Duke of Mazovia, conferred upon Ostroveh the status of a city, granting the rights of urban dwellers to its residents. The non-Mazovian duchess substantially extended the rights of Ostroveh shortly thereafter.

The kings of Poland, who had vigorously suppressed the independent status of Mazovia, nevertheless maintained the special rights granted to the city of Ostroveh. It had its own *starosta* (district ruler), as well as a rest stop or temporary residence for the king. Six fairs were held every year. And by 1660 the population of the city and its surrounding villages totaled 5,509 souls.

The Polish authorities had attempted over the course of hundreds of years to prevent the admission of Jews to this place. But in the early 1600's, even before the law prohibiting Jews to live there was abolished, Ostrow Mazowiecka already had 2,486 Jews among a total population of 4,119. Thus, there was a Jewish majority in the city proper, while only a few Jews lived in the surrounding villages.

In this period there were already ten functioning communities in the vicinity of Ostroveh: in Anarzow [Andrzejewo] 586 Jews (among 1,448 residents), in Brok 1,296 Jews (among 2,657 residents), in Vonseva [Wasewo] 196 Jews (among 516 residents), in Dlugow [Dlugosiodlo] 800 Jews (among 1,249 residents), in Zaremba [Zareby Koscielne] 1,063 Jews (among 2,401 residents), in Malkinia [Malkinia Gorna] 348 Jews (among 1,439 residents), in Nur 1,212 Jews (among 3,345 residents), in Parzemba [Poremba] 14 Jews (among 615 residents), in Sitzukhi [Suchcice] 88 Jews (among 610 residents), and in Czeziva [Czyzewo] 1,596 Jews (among 3,391 residents).

---

[11] On June 4, 1862, the Jews of the "Kingdom of Poland," i.e., that part of the Russian Empire in central Poland in which the tsars (who were also the kings of Poland) had granted some autonomy to the Poles, were officially granted emancipation by the tsar's viceroy, Polish Count Aleksander Wielpolski, rendering them more or less equal citizens. Among other things all restrictions on residence were abolished. Ostrow Mazowiecka was in the Kingdom of Poland.

The fact that Ostrow Mazowiecka was situated at the very heart of central Poland undoubtedly contributed to its development. It was eighty kilometers from Warsaw the capital, thirty-five kilometers from Lomza, seventy kilometers from Bialystok, and just a bit over ten kilometers from Malkinia, where the main railroad line between Warsaw and St. Petersburg stopped. The main road between Warsaw and Bialystok and to Polish-ruled Upper Lithuania passed through Ostrow Mazowiecka as well.

The area around Ostroveh was not especially blessed with fresh water rivers, as were other, surrounding areas. In the northern part of the district there were no rivers at all. Water had to be drawn from the wells that were commonly found in those areas. Only in the southern part of the district was there flowing water, the Brok River and a few other smaller streams that flowed into the great Bug River in the adjacent region.

The Majority of Ostroveh Residents Were Jews

For many years the Bug River served as an inexpensive and popular means of transportation for the area and contributed greatly to its development. The main Warsaw-St. Petersburg railroad traversed twenty-five kilometers in the Ostroveh area, with two stations, one in Malkinia and one in Czeziva [Czyzewo]. Roads were also paved to Ostrolenka and other communities. The County of Czersk now ceased to be a laggard, thanks in large measure to the hard work and initiative of the Jews, whose numbers continued to grow year by year. The Jewish majority in Ostroveh established itself and grew. In 1886 some 7,800 residents lived there, including 5,088 Jews and only 2,712 non-Jews. Ten years later a number of villages were incorporated into Ostroveh and the city had 16,431 residents, of whom 10,471 were Jews and 5,690 non-Jews. In 1921, after the independence of Poland, the population was 13,425, among whom were 6,812 Jews. In 1934, five years before the destruction and disaster, Ostrow Mazowiecka, which had been joined with Komorowo, had over 20,000 inhabitants, among whom were only 8,000 Jews.

Despite the establishment of the communities in Ostrow Mazowiecka and its environs in general, the Jews of the city and its surrounding areas never succeeded in achieving a well established economic status. There never developed any serious industry in the city or its hinterland, except for a few miscellaneous and rather small enterprises. Only a few Jews attained any degree of wealth that would have rendered them to be thought of as people of substantial means, but these were rare instances. Most of the Jews of Ostrow Mazowiecka (known during Russian rule as Ostrow Lomzinski) were poor or semi-poor. They eked out their livings from small scale trade or artisanship, from peddling or portering and the like. Only several tens of merchants operated fixed places of business.

The most important businesses in which some of the local Jews engaged were the trades in grain and in lumber. A number of flour mills in the area made the development of the first of these fields possible, even if these were of modest scale. The forests in the region became the source of income for some Jews in the area, who even built two lumber mills. Lumber merchants from Ostroveh did business with all of the cities in Poland and beyond. Before the development of the railroad in a major way the trees were transported down the rivers on rafts. After that the trains replaced them.

However, the principal trade and source of such limited income of the area's Jews was purely local and internal. Every Monday and Thursday peasants from near and far would stream into the city.

A street in Ostrow Mazowiecka

They sold their produce and bought what they needed at the shops of the local Jews. (This was so until the intensification of the anti-Semitic movement in independent Poland, the establishment of shops by non-Jews and the setting up of co-operatives with government encouragement with the aim of causing Jewish businesses to fail.)

Once a month, on the Monday of the fourth week, a monthly market or fair was held. At that time masses of peasants from hundreds of villages near and far would come, as would hundreds of Jewish peddlers from tens of towns in the area. Several times a year "annual fairs" were held. The basic trade at these fairs was relatively modest, but at times it reached a more or less considerable level. Jews bought grain from the peasants and sold them everything they needed. A peasant would come to town with a cart laden mostly with produce, and would return with a cart even more heavily laden with goods. In an earlier period the peasants would acquire their needs from itinerant peddlers who would travel among the villages fairly often. But over time this practice ended. In the market or at the fair he had a choice of obtaining goods from hundreds of peddlers and merchants, which strengthened his resolve to buy at the fair.

Many roads connected Ostroveh with its surrounding areas both near and far and facilitated access to the city. The main road, which over time became the main highway between Warsaw and St. Petersburg, passed right through Ostroveh. It went from Warsaw by way of Radzymin and Wyszkow to Zambrow, Bialystok, Grodno and Vilna, and from there it reached St. Petersburg, the summer capital of the Russian Empire (today Leningrad).[12]

At the entrance to Ostroveh on the right was a road that led to the town of Brok, which sits alongside the Bug River. On the left of the entrance to the city was a road that led to Goworowo, Rozan, Makow and Pultusk.

In the middle of Ostroveh was a road that led to Malkinia, and on the other side a road that went past Komorowo (three kilometers beyond Ostroveh, which was later integrated into Ostroveh) to Ostrolenka.

The fact that Ostrow Mazowiecka sat at the crossroads of central Poland between its capital, Warsaw, and Polish-ruled Lithuania, was a contributing factor to the settlement of Jews in the city, who came from various places in Poland. This gave a unique character to the inhabitants of the city and its surrounding areas. The particular Yiddish dialect that was used by Jews in central Poland was mixed by residents of Ostroveh and its environs with the Lithuanian Yiddish dialect, thereby creating the unique dialect of the region's residents that distinguished its Jewish inhabitants.

---

[12] Ironically, today, after the fall of communism, the city is once again called St. Petersburg.

Hassidim and Mitnagdim in the City

As mentioned, the residents of the locale and its environs came to Ostrow Mazowiecka from other areas of Poland and Lithuania. Thus, there were to be found among them both ardent Hassidim and committed Mitnagdim. From the very establishment of the community and its institutions the conflict between Hassidim and Mitnagdim was still alive long after once the sharp battles between Hassidim and Mitnagdim in general had long been forgotten.

When the Mitnagdim sought to dominate the institutions of the community--to select rabbis whom they approved of, or to appoint *dayanim* [religious judges] or *shochtim* [ritual slaughterers] who were in accord with their traditions--the Hassidim fought against them, trying to give the city an authentic Hassidic aura. When it came to the selection of rabbis, *dayanim* or *shochtim*, and so on, from the Hassidic camp, in the early days of the establishment of the community in Ostrow Mazowiecka the opposing forces were about equally weighted. Sometimes the Hassidim won out, at other times the Mitnagdim. But over time the Hassidim came to dominate the religious establishment of the city, except for those synagogues which had a distinctly Mitnagdic character.

In Ostrow Mazowiecka, as every place else, this conflict between Hassidim and Mitnagdim morphed into a conflict between orthodox and non-orthodox, and among various parties and movements with different political or ideological beliefs. Revolutionary labor movements arose, as did educational institutions with differing or even conflicting goals. The traditional *cheder*, in which generations of Jews were educated and which became the foundation stone of Jewish education in the Diaspora, lost its dominance to more modern and organized educational institutions, some of which had a religious character, some an anti-religious one.

The new period of chasing innovation and modernization also changed the traditional way of life that had been accepted for generations in Polish Jewry. Being satisfied with little, aspiring to a modest and restrained life, being happy with the little that the Jew had, and opposing luxuries and a life of ostentation, lost out to a modern life that is lacking in truly joyous occasions, a life centered on the pursuit of luxury and especially the conflict between man and his neighbor to see who could outdo one another with luxuries and in the display of wealth. None of this had ever existed before.

Ostrow Mazowiecka and its surrounding towns, which, like most towns in Poland, Galicia and Lithuania, were not all that big, preserved the beautiful old traditions in this realm until the very day of her destruction. With increasingly greater efforts over the years Jews eked out their limited and modest living with hard work and sweat and were satisfied with their lot. They continued in the beautiful lifestyle of modesty and austerity until their dying day.

From its founding as a community Ostrow Mazowiecka was not prosperous. Of course there were a few wealthy people, but they did not leave their stamp on the community as a whole, nor did they determine its way of life. In fact, poverty conferred a certain charm, an aura of holiness to the life of restraint and modesty of the local residents.

Ostroveh was not a gay city, nor did it ever have such a reputation. But the joys of life were not lacking either. There was no end to the amount of hard work the peddler exerted to earn his few coins. Nor was there any limit to the wearisome toil that the merchant had to exert in his store to support his household modestly, without ostentation. The artisans poured forth rivers of sweat in order to earn a few crusts of bread from their oppressive and difficult manual labor.

The Jews of Ostrow Mazowiecka did not come upon a community that was fully formed. In a relatively short time they established all the institutions of the community. Neither poverty nor lack of resources deterred them from this mission. While a spare penny may not have been available to some individuals, when it came to the general needs of the community nothing was lacking. And as in every Jewish community in Eastern Europe at the time, the homes were modest and meager, but the community buildings were large and beautiful.

Warsaw Street in Ostrow Mazowiecka

There were synagogues, houses of study and Hassidic prayer houses, and societies for every need: to provide dowries for poor brides and to visit the sick, to benefit the Jewish soldiers who served in the tsar's army, and for every other charitable purpose. Each of these tasks found a leader who was willing to dedicate his life to that worthy cause without any need for honor or recognition, without reward in any form whatsoever, each of whom worked devotedly in his area or areas.

Only in a later period, when "European modernization" penetrated into public and private life, did each society learn that it had to choose presidents and committees. The first Jews of Ostrow Mazowiecka knew that a *mitzvah* [religious commandment] is supposed to be carried out heart and soul. It should be done wholeheartedly, with pure, unsullied and honorable intentions for its own sake and not for the sake of any tainted intentions, with modesty and with no personal motivations or desire to stand out or to call undue attention to anything.

The founders of the community of Ostrow Mazowiecka were poor Jews who did not have a penny in their pocket. But they were also wonderful and rare people, who excelled in their values of giving, whose exemplary actions would serve as a model for generations to come. Such Jews, scholars and Hassidim, had no personal needs. The very little that they had, their modest meals, even they seemed extravagant.

Ostroveh did not resemble those older communities where all or most of the members considered themselves family, who had become familiar with one another over the course of the generations and were used to one another. As mentioned, the residents of the town came to Ostroveh from various other counties and regions. Yet, there developed in this community, as in all the older Jewish communities, a feeling of concern and responsibility for one another.

In this period in the Polish Diaspora there was no lack of Jews with charitable values, whose doors were always open, whose hearts were always open to all who those who needed or who asked for help. Moreover, they were on the lookout for any instance of need or trouble. Even though they themselves might have lacked for food, their sole concern was for the poor widow who was caring for orphans or for the sick or the depressed. Every wanderer found shelter and every starving person succor for his soul.

Jews in Ostroveh Studying Mishnayot

The Best and Most Honored People of the City

Ostroveh was no different from other communities in maintaining this beautiful heritage. The narrow dwellings of the residents of the city and of the founders of the community in the early years of its existence were always open for assistance. Poverty gave sort of a certain charm to the city and its inhabitants. It did not prevent the residents from doing all they could for one another or for any stranger who knocked on its gates.

As in Israel of old, the face of the city and those who represented it were not the representatives of one class or another, the advocates of one particular ideology or another, or the representatives of parties or movements, but rather the finest people of the city. A Jew who was outstanding in his characteristics and deeds, in his knowledge of the Torah, and so forth, attained the highest rank. Of course, there is no light without a shadow. There were rare instances where the strong ruled and the wealthy advanced themselves thanks to their sharp elbows, but these were few and far between.

The traitor who sidles up to a repressive government was the symbol of degradation. A person who ingratiates himself to people not of his own kind, to the "magistrate," the non-elected city government that was appointed by the authorities of the Russian tsar, be it Nathan Zelig or Hershel Balbier, who registered dates of birth and of weddings in the official registers, came into direct contact with the world of non-Jews. But the world of the Jews was a world unto itself, a special world.

The small, narrow wooden houses, whose floors squeaked mightily from every step tread upon them, became an integral part of their residents, who practiced a life of austerity and modesty. It was said that thanks to the blessings of a righteous person fire never overcame Ostroveh, that flames never broke out within its gates. Thus, hundreds of ancient houses, of all shades and colors, remained intact.

The residents got so used to their small, modest houses that it was difficult for them to move to larger, more spacious homes, stone houses that were built over the years. These were of greater dimensions containing large and spacious living spaces. But alas they did not bring good fortune to their residents. They introduced a jumbled appearance into Ostrow Mazowiecka, a mixture of old and new that was unlikely to live together in harmony.

Chapter Two
Crystallization of the City

The Jewish community of Ostrow Mazowiecka lasted nearly two hundred and fifty years. At first it was on a small scale, with one Jew at a time arriving there and building or renting a small house. Gradually an established, permanent community arose. There are no monuments to be found in the Jewish cemetery in town from this early period.

As mentioned, this settlement of Jews in Ostrow Mazowiecka in this initial period was "illegal." Official prohibitions and warnings on the part of the leaders of the Council of the Four Lands accompanied the settlement of these first settlers. They did what they did not out of any particular love for the immense forests of the area, but rather out of a lack of any other option for survival and in the course of endless wandering to find economic sustenance.

Polish Jewry in this period experienced a spiritual efflorescence and growth that had continued on from the bright and glorious period since Poland had become the center of Torah. But along with this was a life based on starvation and deprivation, on poverty and the absence of even the most limited means of sustenance. This was because of the extremely limited economic areas in which Polish Jews were permitted to engage in order to eke out their meager livings.

This was also a tumultuous period in which the highways and byways of Poland ran with blood. In the southeast of the country, in Volhynia and its neighboring areas, the Chmielnicki murderers left hundreds of communities destroyed and devastated. Countless victims, the elderly and the youth, women and girls, children and babies died terrible deaths. Masses of Jews, lacking everything, took up their wandering staffs in search of a place to lay their heads.

No sooner had the battles with the bloodthirsty Chmielnicki rebels ended when the soldiers of the Polish General Czerniecki began to rampage with incomparable cruelty in western Poland following the war between Poland and Sweden. Jewish life became chaotic. Jewish blood flowed endlessly. Both large and small communities were devastated and destroyed mercilessly. So to the masses of Jewish refugees from eastern Poland were now added refugees from western Poland.

During this period veteran communities like Pinczow or Opatow turned to the leaders of the Council of the Four Lands with a request and a demand to ban Jewish refugees from either western or eastern Poland from settling in their communities. Major impediments were stacked up in the paths of these homeless people, burdened with large families, from settling in the largest communities in Poland that in effect became virtual closed ghettos.

This was due to the fact that the residents of those veteran communities were also seriously impacted by the bloody events. They worked under great difficulty just to maintain themselves, burdened as they were with supporting their local poor. The veteran and highly regarded community of Opatow was crowded into one single, not very large street, under extremely difficult housing conditions. The Polish authorities and residents, local and regional, absolutely refused to expand the Jewish residential borders by so much as even one meter.

It was not possible for the majority of communities in Poland to absorb the masses of homeless. Nevertheless, their difficult financial situation--and the burden of debt that hovered over the Council of the Four Lands and over every community, small or large--did not prevent them from providing major financial assistance to the homeless refugees and to come up with succor and aid to them as they wandered the roads of Poland. A few, those with the means and the strength, went to Germany, Moravia, Bohemia or Hungary. But the majority sought a new home in Poland.

Thus, while Jews were originally loath to become "infiltrators" into the Czersk region and other areas of Mazovia into which the entry of Jews was prohibited by law, the need to find a home and shelter overcame other considerations and other official bans of the Council of the Four Lands and the leaders of the communities. People no longer looked upon these new residents of Mazovia as "criminals" as they had been officially labeled from the rostrums of the communities, but rather as unfortunate ones who lacked any alternative.

But settling in Mazovia entailed serious risks. The most dangerous weaponry was in the hands of the Jew baiters, as the bloody libels against them were accompanied by wild incitement. This was especially true in those areas where these enemies were just looking for an excuse to work against the Jews or to expel them from their places of residence and to steal their meager property. Great efforts and unlimited initiatives were invested by the Jews of Poland against such false accusations.

But Jews came and took that risk. They settled in Ostrow Mazowiecka and in tens of towns around her near and far. Did they actually suffer serious difficulties? Did they actually pay a price in blood for this step? The later generation of residents of

Ostroveh and its environs were unable to tell, as there remained in the hands of the community no written record that could uncover the treasures of the past or that could recount the events of the first settlers.

Nevertheless, there is no doubt that great suffering was the lot of the first Jews of Ostrow Mazowiecka, much as the authorities of Mazovia had known how to embitter the lives of the Jews of Plotzk and its environs. They knew how to oppress them, but were oblivious to the fact that due to the initiative and hard work of the Jews this region ceased to be the prime example of a failed and undeveloped one.

From partial records it is clear that the first Jews of Ostroveh were the pioneers in exploiting the enormous forests in the area. They developed business ties with the owners of the great estates and developed the natural resources. The Jews worked very hard and made a modest living, with only a few amassing any wealth, while the owners of the estates and the rulers of the area prospered. Therefore, they prevented or did not allow the expulsion of these early Jews from the city and its surrounding area.

Well established and chosen communal institutions of the kind that were typical for other communities in Poland were in fact lacking in Ostrow Mazowiecka until after World War I. During the very long period of Russian rule in Poland the community had no legal basis, serving merely as a committee of the municipal council, which was never elected but rather appointed by officials of the Russian authorities.

The officers of the community were the wealthy of the city, those who paid substantial taxes or who took out important commercial licenses. Their appointment was made in accordance with the list of those who paid the *etat* (the community tax) and those who attended the *galewka*, the celebration held on the birthday or other major event of the family of the Russian tsar. Such celebrations were held at the old *beit midrash* [study hall] on Komorowo Road, with the participation of the rabbi, the *dazars* (the officers of the community), and some government official.

The *Chevrah Kadisha* [literally "Holy Society," i.e., the burial society], which was the oldest and without doubt one of the first in the city, strictly observed an internal protocol. This protocol proved that among the founders of the community or among its first settlers were those who came from Volhynia and other communities in southeast Poland. The protocols of the society, which were maintained until the destruction of the city, were copied from the protocols of similar societies in those regions.

For example, one of the provisions of the society relating to acceptance of new members was that each new member had to undergo a certain period of "internship." In this period, called *salozhveh* (service) from the word *melodzi* (youth), he had to perform every difficult duty that was asked of him by the veteran members. He had to serve all the members having full privileges at all their banquets and to carry out all their instructions.

Such banquets were held by the *Chevrah Kadisha* of Ostrow Mazowiecka as a group every *Rosh Chodesh* [new month] eve after the *Yom Kippur Katan*[13] service in the old *beit midrash*. The principal annual banquet was held on the fourth day of Adar, the day of the death of Moses Our Teacher, peace be unto him, according to the custom of all *Chevrot Kadisha* [pl.] throughout the Jewish Diaspora. The many other banquets that were held every month were paid for by the society and were conducted in Ostroveh as a local custom.

From the records of the society from the early period of its existence we learn nothing about any additional functions that may have devolved upon them beyond their limited scope of operation. In various other communities, especially in eastern Poland, the *Chevrah Kadisha* would in effect function as the community council and as the body that represented the entire community in all realms, even though the income of the society came exclusively from the burial of the dead and from the sale of burial plots in the local cemetery.

The protocols of the *Chevrah Kadisha* of Ostrow Mazowiecka did not contain any special provisions or customs that were not customarily followed in other places, which would indicate that the society was founded and functioned along the lines of other societies in the area. And while drastic fires had not beset the city in later generations, no document was extant that would have indicated the manner of the formation of the society or its character.

The communities of Crakow, Lwow [Lviv, now in Ukraine], Lublin, Ostroh [Ostrog], Poznan and Brisk [Brest-Litovsk] had different protocols and customs that were meticulously preserved over the course of many generations. Many communities had special holidays or memorial days to commemorate events or overt miracles that had occurred in those communities. Ostroveh in this sense was considered a new community without any particular traditions or special provisions or unique or interesting customs in general.

---

[13] It was customary in some communities to designate the eve of each new month as a day of fasting and atonement, thus a "small" (*katan*) or "minor" Yom Kippur.

The residents of Ostroveh in the last period before the Holocaust did not themselves know very much about their distant past. While the residents of other cities were proud of their golden eras and their glorious pasts, the Jews of Ostrow Mazowiecka were proud of their present and of the reality that they created in the two hundred fifty years of the existence of the city and community, and especially in the course of the later generations that preceded that destruction and devastation.

The Rabbis of Ostroveh

While the pride of Crakow and Lublin lay in the rabbis who served in those communities in earlier times, the pride of Ostroveh lay in the rabbis who served with distinction in their community specifically in the later generations. They transformed the rabbinate in this community into a very important position that brought honor to the community and its supporters.

Like the residents of Ostrow Mazowiecka itself, its rabbis came from various different camps and movements. The Gaon Rabbi Yehuda Leib Gordin and the Gaon Rabbi David Shlomo Margaliot (whose acronym was the Maharshdam) represented the camp of the Mitnagdim and Torah scholars in the city, while the Hassidic *rebbe* Rabbi Gershon Chanoch of Radzyn or the Hassidic *rebbe* Rabbi Yosef of Amshinov, who were elected as a result of the hard work of the Hassidim of the city, represented the Hassidic camp in Ostroveh, and the great, highly regarded and ardently Hassidic Gaon Rabbi Meir Dan Plotzky, who also represented the Hassidic camp.

Who was the first rabbi of the city? Who held that position in the first period of its existence? The residents of Ostrow Mazowiecka were unable to answer this question. It was clear, however, that the position of *av beit din* [chief of the rabbinical court, often also the town rabbi] did not go unfilled. The first rabbi that the people of Ostroveh remembered was "the Rabbi from Koil" (Kolo, near Kalish), without even remembering his name or when he served in the city.

When this rabbi from Koil, whose name was not even etched in the memories of the people of Ostrow Mazowiecka, arrived was no longer known by the locals. Various stories about the rabbi of Koil, his deeds and his works were bandied about by the locals, especially about his position in Ostroveh. Apparently he left the city and the position and went somewhere else. Where? Even to this question the local residents had no answer.

They said that he was the son of a wealthy and respected family, and that he himself was also wealthy, and therefore did not need the salary from the people of the community. He did not receive any compensation from the residents, nor any financial benefits whatsoever. On the contrary, he supported the people of the city from his own funds, and made long-term loans to those residents of Ostroveh who came to study with him. It was particularly the latter who paid him more than the usual honor.

The residents of Ostrow Mazowiecka mentioned the "rabbi from Koil" as the first rabbi whose memory was preserved among the residents of the city. Among the many rabbinical books of questions and answers that were published in this period throughout Poland there is no mention of the rabbi of Koil who served as the rabbi of Ostroveh, nor is there any mention in any other document.

The second rabbi that was remembered by the residents of the city was Rabbi Feivel, who was referred to by the locals as "Rabbi Feivel Sokolker." He was a Lithuanian *gaon* who apparently also served in the rabbinate of Sokolka, but it is not clear whether he came from Sokolka to Ostrow Mazowiecka or the reverse, from Ostroveh to Sokolka. The period of his service in the city is not known either, when he arrived and when he left. Nor was his gravestone to be found in the cemetery of Ostrow Mazowiecka.

The third known rabbi of Ostrow Mazowiecka was the Gaon Rabbi Yehuda Yudel from Brok, one of the Hassidim and students of the Hassidic *rebbe* of Ger [Gur or Gora Kalwaria], author of *Chidushei Harim* [*The Novellae of the Rim*].[14] He was both a *gaon* and a fervent Hassid who did much to raise the level of Hassidism in Ostroveh. He had first served as rabbi in Sokolow Podlaskie, and from Ostroveh he went on to serve as the rabbi in the larger and longer established community of Plotzk.

Why did he leave Ostroveh and move to Plotzk? There were no relevant documents left in the hands of the city's residents. But undoubtedly the difficult battle that was then being waged between Hassidim and Mitnagdim in Ostrow Mazowiecka over hegemony in the city found its full expression in the stands of the rabbis and their work there. It is quite likely that work of the [future] rabbi of Plotzk--as recalled by residents of the city [of Ostroveh] after he left--to fortify the Hassidic movement there directly caused the controversy that resulted in his leaving Ostroveh.

Thus, there came to fill his place as chief of the rabbinic court the Gaon Rabbi David Shlomo Margaliot, who was well known and remembered locally by the acronym the Maharshdam because of his book, *Chidushei Hamaharshdam* [*The Novellae of the*

---

[14] Acronym of **R**abbi **Y**itzchak **M**eir Rothenberg Alter (1799-1866), the first *rebbe* of Ger.

Maharshdam]. Much as his predecessor Rabbi Yehuda Yudel was appointed with support of the ardent Hassidim, so too was the Maharshdam appointed with the support of the extreme Mitnagdim.

The Maharshdam arrived in Ostroveh in the year 5643 [1882-1883]. His name preceded him as a brilliant *gaon* and a man of high standing. Two volumes of his book *Chidushei Hamaharshdam* had already been published, at the beginning of which appeared enthusiastic endorsements from giants of the Torah in those days, who described the author as a great *gaon*, a right hand and the descendant of holy people. Prior to his coming to Ostrow Mazowiecka he already held the position of rabbi in Kalwaria, Lithuania, in Lukow, in Dzialischzeh [Dzialoszyn, Zaloshin], and in Neustadt near Crakow.

In his youth the Maharshdam had studied with the Hassidic *rebbe*, the *gaon* and righteous one Rabbi Abraham of Ciechanow, about whom he wrote in the introduction of his book: "...and I studied with the late *gaon* and *tzadik* [righteous man, often a title for a Hassidic *rebbe* as well], leader of the Diaspora, the chief judge of the rabbinical court of Ciechanow, when he taught at the higher *yeshiva*. He placed upon me the heavy yoke of the Torah and accustomed me to both study in depth as well as to homiletics by which one can broaden one's knowledge." (Introduction to Volume I of *Chidushei Hamaharshdam*, Vilna: 5637 [1876-1877].)

Despite the fact that this teacher of his was one of the pillars of Hassidism in that period, the Gaon Rabbi David Shlomo Margaliot was an extreme and sworn Mitnaged [s.] his entire life. So it is most likely that this very fact caused an intensified struggle against him on the part of the Hassidim of the city, who were undoubtedly very insulted after their rabbi, the Gaon Rabbi Yehuda Yudel, was forced to leave the community as a result of his affiliation with the Hassidic movement.

And so in the year 5646 [1885-1886], just three years after his arrival in Ostroveh, the Maharshdam was forced to leave the city because of the sharp opposition of the Hassidim to his appointment. At this point the hand of the Hassidim grew in strength over that of the Mitnagdim, whom they paid back in kind for their attacks on their movement. Added to this internal battle in the city were now added groups of Maskilim [enlightened ones or modernists]. And while they did not scrupulously observe the *mitzvot* [religious commandments], nevertheless they, too, began to involve themselves in matters of religion and in the issue of the selection of the rabbis of the city.

A few months after the departure of the Gaon Rabbi David Shlomo Margaliot from the city the various local factions--with the exception of a few ardent Hassidim--united and decided to choose the Hassidic *rebbe* Rabbi Gershon Chanoch Leiner of Radzyn as the rabbi of the city. But this *rebbe* and *gaon* only served as chief of the rabbinic court for half a year. At the beginning of the year 5647 [1886-1887] he left.

Chapter Three

Hassidic Rebbe Rabbi Gershon Chanoch of Radzyn as Chief of Ostroveh's Rabbinical Court

Hassidic *rebbe* Rabbi Gershon Chanoch[15] served in this position for only a brief period. In addition he also served as the *rebbe* and leader of thousands of Hassidim of Izbica [Izhbitz]-Radzyn, as he was the son of and successor to Hassidic *rebbe* Rabbi Yaakov of Izbica, author of *Beit Yaakov [House of Jacob]*, who in turn was the son of and successor to Hassidic *rebbe* Rabbi Mordechai Yosef of Izbica, author of *Mei Hashiloach [The Waters of the Pool of Siloam]*, who had broken off from the Kotsk Hassidim and began to lead a sect of his own.

Rabbi Gershon Chanoch was a wonderful and unique *gaon*, wise and knowledgeable about everything, and possessor of great energy and initiative. No one knows what motivated him to abandon his court in Radzyn to accept the responsibility as rabbi of the not very large Ostroveh, and to invest in it--albeit for not very long a period--his energy and time. The brilliant rabbi from Radzyn always operated according to his own personal considerations without taking into account the opinions of others.

He was born in the year 1839 in Izbica, at a time when his grandfather Rabbi Mordechai Yosef was leading his large flock. At an early age he began to manifest his exceptional brilliance, his great acuity, his incomparable wisdom, the forcefulness of his ideas, and his great piety. At the age of twenty-nine he evoked great surprise and enthusiasm in the entire Torah community with the publication of his great book, *Sidrei Taharot [The Orders of Purity]*, a collection along the lines of the Talmud on the laws of purity in the Mishnah that was assembled from both the Babylonian and Jerusalem Talmuds, the Sifra, the Sifrei, the Mechilta, and from Midrashim, generally accompanied by an interpretation along the lines of Rashi,[16] in which he exhibits remarkable knowledge and penetrating insight into all the subject matter of the Talmud. He was already considered an exceptional *gaon*, who amazed people with his wide ranging knowledge in all

---

[15] Rabbi Gershon Chanoch Leiner (1839-1890).

[16] Rashi, acronym for **Ra**bbi **Sh**lomo **Y**itzchaki [ben Yitzchak] (b. Troyes, France, February 22, 1040, d. Troyes, July 13, 1105, having also lived in Worms, Germany), preeminent medieval Franco-German commentator on the Hebrew Bible and Talmud.

branches and areas of life, his startling memory, and his
exceptional shrewdness.

A main street in Ostrow Mazowiecka

He went into great depth in every sphere in which he worked,
and fought bravely for every ideal that he set for himself despite
any difficulties and obstacles. So it was when he decided that he
had discovered the *chilazon*[17] and that therefore it was necessary
to include a blue yarn in the *tzitzit*, a view that was in opposition
to the opinions of virtually all of the leading rabbis of the time. The
Hassidim of Radzyn abide by this ruling of their *rebbe* and wear
tzitzit containing a blue yarn to this day.

He was dressed like a Hassidic *rebbe*, surrounded by
thousands of Hassidim, but would also always leave his house
alone, without aides or escorts. He was kind to all and received
everyone pleasantly. There were no barriers between him and his
guests. He was concerned with all people, was interested in them,
and was beloved by all who came into contact with him.

During his brief period of service in Ostroveh he continued to
lead own his large community. Hassidim would continue to knock

---

[17] A certain marine snail from which a kind of blue (called *t'chelet*) or purple dye was
derived in ancient times and which was used in the garments of High Priest in the Temple
and in part of the *tzitzit* (fringes) on the four corners of a man's *talit* (prayer shawl) or
smaller under garment, as per Biblical mandate. With the loss of the knowledge about
the creature and how to derive the dye from it, the practice had been largely abandoned.

at his door. But he brought about real revolutionary change in the town, too.

As soon as Rabbi Gershon Chanoch arrived in Ostroveh as chief of the rabbinical court he began to work energetically to organize the affairs of the town. Unlike other rabbis the *rebbe* of Radzyn was not satisfied with dealing just with the rabbinical and religious affairs of the town, but began to deal with all the problems and issues of the city as well. And without ignoring any current matters, his influence and initiative were apparent in everything that was going on.

Rabbi Gershon Chanoch presided in Ostrow Mazowiecka only about half a year, but in that time he managed to subject it and its residents to his rule. Many admired him. Others valued his personality. Even those opponents who had gotten used to breaking away from tradition began to fear the rabbi and to harken to his instructions and his words. It came to the point where no one in town would dare not to fully implement the rulings of this religious head of the town or any directive that came from him.

The *rebbe* of Radzyn was forceful in his ideas and full of energy. He issued instructions and laid down rules generally without consulting anybody or informing anyone in advance. These steps were taken in order to advance the issues of the community and to deal with the problems of its residents. He was not satisfied only with what was or what already existed, but quickly turned to establish and maintain institutions and societies that were non-existent until his arrival in Ostrow Mazowiecka.

Education in Ostroveh, as in every community in Poland in those days, was in the hands of *melamdim* [religious teachers], whether teachers of small children or teachers at more advanced levels. Only anti-religious circles who were interested in assimilation into other nations within Russia and Poland advocated for the establishment of "modernized" schools along the lines established by the founders of the Reform movement in Germany, which only brought in their wake the destruction and wreckage of the Jewish community in Germany and other places.

Whether it was spoken of as a "modernized" *cheder,* or as a more organized educational institution altogether, the practical intent was to change the content and objective of the education of the children. The ultra-orthodox and others loyal to the Torah and the eternal tradition struggled mightily against any effort to change the face of education and its content in any way. They viewed these efforts as destructive aspirations that would result in the destruction of the wall surrounding the House of Israel.

A Model Talmud Torah

One of the first who decided, following in the footsteps of the edict issued by Rabbi Yeshayahu Halevi Horowitz,[18] author of the *Shelah*, to establish an organized *Talmud Torah* [religious elementary school], a Torah-oriented institution of education, was Rabbi Gershon Chanoch. And he implemented this decision immediately upon his arrival in Ostrow Mazowiecka. He established a *Talmud Torah* consisting of five grades of study. And he also saw to it to obtain a full budget for this institution, which already then totaled some 1,000 rubles a year, a considerable sum in those days.

He also dealt with setting up appropriate conditions for this institution. The teachers did not receive their salaries from the parents, but rather received their fixed wages from the treasury of the *Talmud Torah* itself. The parents, in turn, paid tuition into that fund. The poor paid nothing, as the Rabbi Gershon Chanoch did everything necessary to find the money necessary to cover the first year's budget by soliciting people of means and the wealthy of the area.

The rabbi also was concerned with establishing an orderly method of teaching in the *Talmud Torah*, which of course would all be according to sacred norms, and that the studies would be entrusted to teachers who were religiously observant and schooled in the age-old methods of teaching, while at the same time incorporating testing and supervision into the mix.

In this effort Rabbi Gershon Chanoch preceded the orthodox Jewish movement Agudat Yisrael that was later involved in organizing education for the orthodox and in establishing organized educational institutions. It is said that the rabbi was thinking about instituting fundamental change even in regard to education for girls that would have set up similar *Talmud Torah*s for girls of a certain type. However, in the interim he left the city and returned to Radzyn.

Even before he left his work in establishing a *Talmud Torah*, the rabbi had also immediately undertaken to set up yet another institution, the *Hachnasat Orchim* [Welcoming Guests] society, which existed from its inception until the destruction of the community. The society and its by-laws, maintained up until the Holocaust, were organized and established by Rabbi Gershon Chanoch during the period of his service.

---

[18] (b. Prague, ca. 1565, d. Tiberias, Israel, March 23, 1630); his principal work, *Shnei Luchot Habrit* (*The Two Tablets of the Covenant*, abbreviated *Shelah*, which is often used as his *nom de plume*), was a compilation of ethics, ritual and mysticism that had influence on the later rise of Hassidism.

The purpose of the *Hachnasat Orchim* society was to care for poor guests and wanderers who arrived in Ostrow Mazowiecka, to provide an appropriate place for them to rest their weary heads, whether for a day or several days, and not to leave a single poor guest without a decent place to stay overnight in the city, no matter how many wanderers or poor people arrived.

Rabbi Gershon Chanoch did not favor the establishment of a special synagogue just for such guests with special rooms and beds for them there. This was because every house that was designated for such guests would only have a set specific, fixed number of sleeping places for guests, and that it was not clear as to whether the number of accommodations of any one house would be sufficient to warrant setting up such a separate synagogue. But he was not against the idea in principle.

The rabbi gathered a number of local residents and informed them of the establishment of this new institution and told them in advance about its specific fixed rules. Officers of the society were chosen, as well as a director, who would deal directly with the guests and wanderers who might be in need of his services and care. There was no shortage of wandering poor people who arrived in town looking for a few pennies during that period, or in the following one either, or in fact up until the Holocaust and the great destruction.

The income of the society came mainly from membership dues. Jews with sufficient income and means would donate a fixed annual sum to the society. In addition, the director of the society would circulate around town every Friday in order to collect money for it as well. Another source of income came from those who had weddings or other happy occasions celebrated in the town. These donations would be made in a very special manner that would uplift the entire atmosphere of their celebrations and that also brought in substantial sums to the society.

When they would appear at weddings members of the society would wear special costumes that resembled those of officers or generals, with special gleaming buttons and hats, as well as masks on their faces that would elicit laughter. They danced and sang, and would order people to give money, as if they were people of authority. The Jews enjoyed this act and did contribute. They would especially solicit local residents for these needs on Purim, when they would go to houses all around town decked out in such costumes.

In the period of Russian rule the society issued its own special scrip, tickets with the stamp of the society on them worth half a penny each. This ticket was always considered by the Jews of the city as real currency, as a full penny was considered too much of an amount to give to any poor person just passing through, given the conditions of poverty then prevailing. The tickets were used by recipients to give "change" to the donors, who were themselves of limited means, which were in turn redeemed back to the donors by the society.

From the time of its founding up until the destruction of the community the officers of the society were simple, unpretentious Jews who went about their work with no expectation of reward. For the most part they were artisans who themselves barely made a living from the work of their own hands. For many years Reb[19] Hersh Mordechai, the *mularz* [bricklayer], who built kitchens and chimneys, an artisan who by profession was engaged in heavy and difficult labor, donated his spare time to this holy work for the society.

There were also a number of directors of the society, who performed many difficult tasks on its behalf with a religious fervor. Among them were Reb Yankel Nacher, Reb Beinish Betchke [Beczka] (a teacher of small children, who eked out a meager living from his teaching fees), and Reb Avraham Markus. They did not view their work on behalf of the society as some kind of official job, but rather as holy work that should be performed with a warm heart and full devotion without asking for any thanks for their work or their deeds.

Caring for such wandering guests was no easy task. Many embittered souls were wandering around cities, lacking adequate clothing and in total poverty. Many had lost all emotional balance. There were those who walked around in rags, caked in mud and mire from their wanderings. They would arrive in small or large numbers, sometimes in the tens, without anyone knowing in advance that they were coming. The people of the *Hachnasat Orchim* society never became exhausted or tired, even though there was hardly a day in the year on which such guests did not visit the city.

Those guests who remained in town for the Sabbath were also taken care of by the officers and directors of the *Hachnasat Orchim* society, who divided them up among various synagogues and prayer houses. Each group prayed in a different place. And at each synagogue or Hassidic prayer house members of the society or other volunteers would perform the *mitzvah* of making sure that every guest would have a home in which he could eat the Sabbath meals in comfort. No guest or wanderer went hungry on the Sabbath or on a holiday, no one was left out on the street.

---

[19] Honorific for a respected layman, like Mr., as opposed to Rav, or rabbi.

Welcoming Guests and Visiting the Sick

Rabbi Gershon Chanoch was not complacent. Within two months of his arrival he assembled a large meeting and announced the establishment of a *Bikur Cholim* [Visiting the Sick] society, whose purpose was to attend to the sick and the frail, to be concerned with medical assistance for them, to provide them with appropriate medicines, and especially to aid them during their illness with the good food they needed and to provide a night watch for the seriously ill so that they would not go without care and supervision.

The rabbi drafted fifty men and women who accepted the responsibility to work within the framework of the society, whether in acquiring medicine, or whether in obtaining food for poor patients who needed it during this period. There were many cases of consumption or diseases that derived from the lack of adequate nutrition or ongoing starvation. There was no lack of sick people living under harsh conditions to be seen in town. The activists of the society always had plenty of work to do.

Up until World War I and even during the war, when Ostroveh was full of refugees from tens of cities and towns in the immediate area and beyond, these functions were performed by the *Bikur Cholim* society. They were subsequently inherited by the *Linat Hatzedek* [Righteous Respite] society, which essentially continued the holy tradition of the *Bikur Cholim* society that had been founded by Rabbi Gershon Chanoch during his period of service as chief of the rabbinical court in the town.

The basic function did not change at all: concern for every sick person, and first and foremost, the effort to enlist a number of people who were prepared to stay awake at night next to the beds of the seriously ill who needed help and care. There was no lack of volunteers in Ostrow Mazowiecka who, tired and worn out after a long day of work, hurried off to the house of the afflicted and were willing to work hard all night to serve the patient, and to stand in for the members of the sick person's family who were tired after working with the patient during the daytime hours.

The functions of *Linat Hatzedek* branched out. There was a need to call doctors to the hospitals and to pay the doctors for their visits, while at the same time relieving poor patients from having to make any payments. Another function of the society was to supply various medical devices, as well as medicine, needed by the sick without any charge to them.

The many volunteers of the society received no financial remuneration whatsoever for their work, except the secretary who was eventually engaged and who worked full-time for the society and its programs. A special effort of the society was made in the transport of sick people to the hospital. In the city [of Ostroveh] and especially in the smaller towns there was no hospital at all. In the larger places there were hospitals, whether governmental, municipal, or Christian, but the food was not kosher and the services not under Jewish auspices.

The large majority of the residents of Ostrow Mazowiecka were religious Jews, who absolutely refused to seek the services of non-Jewish hospitals, or to be tainted by their non-kosher food, even if they needed to be in a hospital for an operation or other service. A major Jewish hospital functioned in distant Warsaw on Czysta Street, a hospital that operated at a high standard.

When they were sick Jews from hundreds of towns and villages in the Warsaw region, whether near or far, did everything to be admitted to this hospital, which was always crowded and where it was difficult to gain admittance. The activists of *Linat Hatzedek* worked hard to obtain beds in this hospital. But many sick people remained in their homes in Ostroveh, unable to be admitted to the Jewish Hospital in Warsaw, which only made the work of the *Linat Hatzedek* society all the more difficult.

Nevertheless the Jews of Ostroveh were neither exhausted nor worn out by this sacred work. With dedication and sacrifice, working class people--even porters, themselves poor and weak--did everything for the sick day and night under the society's auspices. No effort, no activity was seen as too much to do.

Sometimes the efforts of these volunteer activists, who did what they did without reward or any desire to publicize their deeds, evoked admiration. In recounting their sacred unselfish service today, these precious Jews who sought no reward or honor, who did everything to sacrifice themselves for their fellow human beings, one should mention these spiritual loved ones in truly worshipful terms.

There were those among them who stood out exceptionally. There was a Jew in Ostrow Mazowiecka who was called Efraim the hat maker. He was a simple and pure Jew who worked very hard in an oppressively, physically demanding way in order to support his large family in a most modest fashion.

But he had a heart of gold. On those nights when he had no other religious obligations he would sit and sew hats for peasants. During the day he would travel to various markets and fairs to sell his wares in order to earn a few cents for his household. Competition among Jewish hat makers was intense, and it was not easy for him to earn even a modest sum. At times he had to starve along with the members of his large family.

Nevertheless, as soon as he would return to Ostroveh he would go home, eat his modest meal quickly, and rush over to *Linat Hatzedek* to determine what had occurred during the day when he was outside the city limits. Without ever being asked he was the first to volunteer his assistance, despite his being very tired, having sat up all night making hats and having spent the day traveling the roads with his merchandise. But he never said anything about that. He was weak, his strength was very limited, but in relation to the holy work and the sick there was no limit or measure to the strength of the courage of his soul and the capability of his efforts. No work in this realm was too difficult for him. He knew every person who was sick in town. He knew every instance where medical assistance was required, such as whether it was necessary to recruit a volunteer for night duty with a sick person. Reb Efraim would rush out to find such a person. And if he could not find one, he himself would go and stay with the patient and care for him with dedication and without any signs of weariness on his part. He visited every seriously ill patient, offered advice, and gave encouragement to members of the family. If there was need to transport the sick person to the hospital in Warsaw, Reb Efraim Rybka always volunteered first for such tasks. He put aside his hats and his living and went on the road to Warsaw accompanying the patient until his admission to the hospital.

He related with great warmth to all seriously ill patients, who were for him the most important people. No effort was too great for him in order to bring respite and provide aid to the ill person. He was even prepared to awaken the mayor or other municipal officials in the middle of the night to obtain a permit from them that would allow a seriously ill patient to be admitted to the hospital. Thanks to such efforts of his, he more than once he saved people who were seriously and perilously ill.

There was no lack of activists on behalf of this society, which in effect continued in the tradition established by Rabbi Gershon Chanoch during the very brief period of his service.

For example, Reb Leib Olshaker, who had heart disease, never ceased his work on behalf of the society. His job was to watch over the medical devices owned by the society that were lent out upon the receipt of a deposit from the borrower so that they would take good care of the devices and would remember to return them. Reb Leib was a good Jew who undertook this work with love and devotion. Like a soldier he stood guard over the medical devices as well as the sanitary equipment belonging to the society. He required and insisted upon the return of the society's equipment. There were not just a few people who were always fully prepared to help others, good Jews with big hearts. There was never any lack of such people in Ostroveh.

The *Hachnasat Kalah* Society

The initiative of the *rebbe* of Radzyn never waned. He always appeared before the community with new proposals. He suggested the establishment of the *Hachnasat Kalah* [Supporting the Bride] society in order to extend help and support to poor brides, to supply them with all the needs for their weddings. However, this society did not develop over time because of the extensive financial demands it required in order to carry out its mission.

The people of Ostroveh believed that had the *rebbe* stayed in their midst for a more extended period of time he would have established a longer list of wonderful institutions in the community, and that Ostrow Mazowiecka would have become an outstanding model community with an entire network of various notable and model institutions and programs. But the period of service of the *rebbe* of Radzyn was all too brief.

Had another rabbi served for such a short period, which lasted only seven-eight months, he would not have left any impression on the city or its infrastructure. But his period of service was viewed solely as temporary. Nevertheless, what Rabbi Gershon Chanoch managed to accomplish in that short time as religious leader many other rabbis could not have achieved over decades, this in a city that was neither a particularly large nor wealthy one.

Therefore many of the veteran residents of Ostrow Mazowiecka never forgot Rabbi Gershon Chanoch of Radzyn as the chief of the rabbinical court of the community all the way up until the destruction of the community more than fifty years later. They pointed to his unmatched wisdom, his ability to get to the bottom of complex and difficult issues in all areas of life, whether in business or other matters, or even in matters of medicine and health.

Therefore many came to learn from him, both Hassidim and Mitnagdim, and even those who were already far removed from religion and Judaism. Hassidim saw him as their sainted *rebbe*, the head and leader of their sect; the residents of the city as their great rabbi, a mover and shaker; the masses as a wise sage from whom one should derive advice and innovative ideas; while the learned came to partake of his knowledge of Torah and Jewish law in all their diverse branches.

At this time in the much larger and older community of Lomza, a center of those who were opposed to Hassidim and Hassidism, a sharp conflict broke out in the community. Many came out in opposition to the chief of the rabbinical court, the distinguished *gaon* and Torah scholar, Rabbi Eliezer Simcha Rabinowitz. A minister of the tsar and other royal Russian officials had also joined with the opponents of the rabbi to the point where his life was at risk. Feeling besieged, the Gaon Rabbi Eliezer Simcha Rabinowitz, despite his being an opponent of the Hassidim, decided to turn to the *rebbe* of Radzyn, who was then serving as chief of the rabbinical court in Ostrow Mazowiecka, to seek his advice and assistance. He came to Ostroveh and, as per his request, Rabbi Gershon Chanoch went back with him to Lomza, where he remained for several days. With his great wisdom and under his unusual oversight he rapidly succeeded in calming the conflict down, bringing the two sides to together to a single table and restoring peace to the community. The Gaon Rabbi Eliezer Simcha peacefully remained in his position.

To the distress of the vast majority of local residents, he left Ostrow Mazowiecka early in 5647 (late 1886). There was no possibility of his acquiescing to requests that he remain and continue to serve as chief of the rabbinical court there. As per usual his decision was firm and final, not open to any change whatsoever.

When he left Ostroveh, the *rebbe* of Radzyn got more involved in his idea about the *chilazon* and the wearing of the *t'chelet* in the *tzitzit*. To this end he left for Italy, to the shores of the Mediterranean, in order to find the *chilazon* and to use it to dye a yarn that color. Given his stubbornness with regard to matters of religion and his limitless enthusiasm, he worked hard and, according to him, actually found the *chilazon*. He derived *t'chelet* from it and with it dyed a yarn of the *tzitzit* that color, which he wore. And all the Hassidim of Radzyn followed in his footsteps.

The sharp opposition of a decisive majority of leading rabbis to his position did not dampen his spirits. On the contrary, he fought a stormy battle against them and stood his ground regarding his idea and position. He published special books for this purpose in which he attempted to find grounds for his idea and his teaching. After that he never returned to the seat of the rabbinate either in Ostroveh or anywhere else for that matter. He occupied himself with the battle for his idea and teaching, as well as with the leading of his large Hassidic sect, which numbered in the thousands.

The *rebbe* of Radzyn did not lead a long life. On the fourth of Tevet 5651 (December 13-14, 1890) he passed away at the age of only fifty-one. His death produced an echo that resounded across the Jewish, Hassidic and Torah worlds. Many of his adherents and opponents alike mourned him. Much of his teaching was printed in his many publications on all areas of Torah study and in his profound books on Hassidism. His words, so full of wisdom and wit, became the heritage of all.

Ostrow Mazowiecka did not forget this rabbi. Up until the very last day of the existence of the community many of the residents of the city still quaked in awe when they recalled the name and period of service of Rabbi Gershon Chanoch.

Chapter Four
The Gaon Rabbi Yehuda Leib Gordin,
Chief of the City's Rabbinical Court

The Gaon Rabbi S. D. Anolik

The Hassidic *rebbe* of Radzyn Rabbi Gershon Chanoch had left the city. And once again the Mitnagdim of the town attempted to prevent the selection of someone from the Hassidic community. Only after the service of a Mitnagdic rabbi could someone from the Hassidic community serve and vice versa. This time the Mitnagdic circles prevailed and, against the wishes of the Hassidim, a Mitnagdic rabbi, who was called locally "the Rabbi from Piotrkow," came to Ostroveh.

The Hassidim did not acquiesce. They did not accept the authority of the new rabbi. They brought a young Hassidic rabbi to town and appointed him as *shov*,[20] and decided only to eat meat that he had slaughtered. The rabbi sharply criticized this action by the Hassidim, but the latter remained firm in their position and defended their *shochet*, who did not function under the supervision of the Mitnagdic rabbi. And so the community was divided into two hostile camps.

The matter was offensive to the Rabbi of Piotrkow. The Hassidim harassed him at every turn. They gave him no respite. And while the core of the conflict centered about the Hassidic *shochet*, in fact it was intended to undermine the very mandate of the Mitnagdic rabbi as the rabbi of the city. The conflict only intensified. So one fine day the Rabbi of Piotrkow packed up his things and permanently left the city, which remained mired in disagreement.

The Mitnagdic camp in Ostrow Mazowiecka never forgave the Hassidim for their deeds. At their head stood Rabbi Dov Berish Shapiro, a distinguished scholar and man of means who had great influence locally. He was the son of the renowned Gaon Rabbi Isaac *Charif* ("the Sharp One"), the rabbi of Slonim. Rabbi Berish himself

---

[20] The contraction *shov* (for **shochet ubodek**) encompassed the two basic functions of a Jewish ritual slaughterer, the first as actual slaughterer of the animal and then as the examiner of the health of its interal organs which, if not healthy, could render the meat *treif* (not kosher). In some communitites the two functions were divided among two separate functionaries, but in many they were combined into a single position, usually held by an ordained rabbi. He, plus the synagogue or pulpit rabbi , along with the chief of the rabbinical court, who was often also the town's official rabbi, would constitute the *beit din* or rabbinical court of three.

was worthy of the mantle of rabbi and to serve as chief of the rabbinical court, which he vehemently refused to do. Instead he ran a trading business and was considered to be a wealthy man.

Rabbi Berish proposed to choose the Gaon Rabbi Shimon Dov Anolik, a protégé of Rabbi Isaac *Charif*, as well as a childhood friend of Rabbi Berish, as chief of the rabbinical court of Ostroveh. Rabbi Shimon Dov had become known in Lithuania since his early youth as a *gaon*, and was dubbed "the black genius" because of his black hair. His fame preceded him as one of the giants of the Torah, as being both sharp and profound, and as an excellent educator.

Rabbi Shimon Dov Anolik presided as the rabbi of the small Lithuanian town of Shaki. He enjoyed his position and the members of the community enjoyed him. He lived there in peace and tranquility and was able to engage in the study of the Torah, as the small number of congregants he had did not disturb him in his studies and made few demands on his time. This was a relatively small rabbinical position that did not pay all that much, but was peaceful and tranquil, without much conflict, quarrel or trouble.

At the initiative of Rabbi Berish Shapiro, head of the Mitnagdim and one of the important people of the city, a delegation set out from Ostroveh to Shaki to invite the rabbi to come and serve as chief of the rabbinical court of their community. In addition to Rabbi Berish two other wealthy and prominent citizens went along as well. They presented him with a letter of rabbinic appointment signed by the most important Mitnagdim of Ostrow Mazowiecka and many of its householders, promising him a fitting salary from which he could live most respectably.

When the arrival of the delegation from Ostrow Mazowiecka became known in Shaki, the majority of its residents streamed to the rabbi's house and informed him that under no circumstances would they permit him to leave town. But when Rabbi Shimon Dov disclosed that he had in any event wanted to move to a larger and more important community, the people of Shaki began to put pressure on the rabbi's wife that she not allow her husband the rabbi to leave Shaki and move to Ostroveh.

The people of Shaki had some reasonable arguments. They were able to recount how the Hassidim of Ostrow Mazowiecka had harassed the Rabbi of Piotrkow because he was a Mitnaged, to the point where he had to pack up his things and abandon the city. The Hassidim in Ostroveh would likely continue to pursue the new rabbi as well, given that he was opposed Hassidim and Hassidism. Why would he want to leave a life of repose and tranquility to enter into one of conflict and dispute?

Nevertheless the members of the delegation did not back down. But the rabbi's wife did not agree to move to Ostroveh. So it was decided that Rabbi Shimon Dov would travel to Ostroveh by himself, without his family. He would stay in the city for a time and look into matters for himself. Only then would he make a final decision as to what to do. The Mitnagdim of Ostroveh had prepared an excellent reception for the new rabbi, but were very disappointed when they learned that the rabbi's family was not coming with him.

During the week that Rabbi Shimon Dov Anolik appeared in Ostroveh there was a wedding in town made by Feige Zissel Bromberg, the wealthiest woman among all the city's residents. She married off one of her six children into another extremely wealthy family.

The members of the wealthy Bromberg family decided to give the new rabbi one hundred fifty rubles for officiating at the wedding, a very considerable sum in those days. Of that sum seventy-five was presented to him in cash, and the balance was held as a deposit by the family, which they committed to remit once the rabbi's wife and her family came to town. This was an expression of dissatisfaction by the backers of Rabbi Anolik with the failure of his family to appear.

This fee (for the rabbi, cantor and *shochet*) for officiating at the nuptials was given at every wedding. Its size was always determined on the basis of the wealth of the respective families and their relationship with the officiating rabbi.

But even this pressure did not suffice. The rabbi's wife and his family stood their ground. They were opposed to his acceptance of the new position in a city where there were many Hassidim opposed to a Mitnagdic rabbi, and who would eventually make his life miserable and bitter. According to the rabbi's wife, she preferred the poverty in tranquil and quiet Shaki over the wealth and greater income in Ostrow Mazowiecka that would only be accompanied by conflict and disagreement.

The rabbi's wife won out. She never set foot in Ostroveh. Rabbi Shimon Dov was forced to give in to her will and decision. He returned to his town of Shaki, where he remained for a long time. He was later appointed as chief of the rabbinical court of Tiktin [Tykocin],[21] Lithuania. After serving there for years he moved to

---

[21] While Tiktin was culturally more part of Lithuanian (Litvishe) than Polish Jewry per se, it was in fact legally part of the province of Bialystok, Poland, and was originally a far older and larger Jewish community than the latter's eponymous city, which later grew enormously in the industrial era. Reflecting its past glory, today Tykocin is the site of one of the few large, magnificently restored Baroque synagogues of Poland, built in 1642.

Siedlce, where he was appointed chief of the rabbinical court in that important community and where he remained until his final days. He died in the year 5667 (late 1906) at the age of fifty-nine.

After Rabbi Anolik had left Ostroveh the Gaon Rabbi Weingott, a great rabbi of Torah from Poland, who was neither an avid Mitnaged nor a Hassid, came to replace him. But neither side, Hassidim or Mitnagdim, supported him. So as soon as he received a letter of rabbinical appointment to the much smaller Lipno he quickly left Ostrow Mazowiecka and moved there. The residents of Ostroveh once again began to search for a suitable candidate who would accept the seat of the rabbinate in their town.

And once again the heads of the Mitdnagdim in the city got together and chose the rabbi of Partzeva [Parczew] as the city's rabbi. He was a Mitnagdic rabbi far removed from Hassidim and Hassidism, with whom he fought, and who fought with him. They did not allow him to function in accordance with his views and wishes. They took a very aggressive stance, not accepting any of the rabbi's decisions on any matter that they did not agree with or like.

The new rabbi adhered to his own ideas, and fought hard for his views. But the many Hassidim in Ostrow Mazowiecka frustrated his plans and stymied his efforts, while the Mitnagdic camp in the city stood by his side and supported him. But none of this was sufficient to calm the storm and enable the rabbi to sit peacefully in his place and to conduct the affairs of the community as he wished, which in any event was against the wishes and aspirations of the many Hassidim of the town.

During this period the numbers of Hassidim in Ostroveh only grew. Many of the younger Mitnagdim joined various Hassidic sects. There was in fact no possibility for the rabbi to conduct the rabbinate in the city against their will. Thus, with deep sadness, the Rabbi of Partzeva, weak and ill for some time, left Ostroveh. In 5654 [1893-1894] he fell ill for a final time and died that year. He was perhaps the first rabbi of the city who found his final rest in the cemetery in Ostroveh.

The problem of choosing a new rabbi once again came to the fore. It became clear to all sides that it was impossible to choose a rabbi that was acceptable only to one segment of the population of the city. Rather every effort had to be made to find a prominent rabbinic personality whose rule both Hassidim and Mitnagdim, as well as regular residents, the plain people, artisans and working men, would be accepted by all and whose authority would not be undermined. The Mitnagdic circles had given up on the idea of choosing a rabbi acceptable only to them and in their spirit.

After an extensive search, the dignitaries of Ostroveh found a rabbinic personality who would be acceptable to all factions in the city, who was unanimously chosen as chief of the rabbinical court by all residents without exception. He was a Mitnagdic rabbi who did not belong to the Hassidic camp, but who understood and appreciated Hassidism and even defended it, whether vis-a-vis the hostile rulers of Russia or in any other context.

The Gaon Rabbi Yehuda Leib Gordin Is Acceptable to All

The Gaon Rabbi Yehuda Leib Gordin was born in Rezhitsa near Drozkenik in the year 5613 [1853]. He manifested exceptional abilities from his earliest youth, and therefore even as a boy studied like a veteran student with the city's rabbi, the Gaon Rabbi Yerachmiel Ziskind Katz. He did not go off to study in *yeshivot* until first rounding out his studies with the rabbi of the town of Svir, the Gaon Rabbi Moshe Danishevsky, one of the distinguished giants of that generation.

Rabbi Gordin was incomparably diligent in his studies from the days of his youth. He did not desist from them day or night, nor did he neglect delving into or working in any area of Torah study, be it *kabbalah* [Jewish mysticism] or Hassidism, not to mention the Talmud or the works of the great decisors of Jewish law, whether of the earlier or later periods. Nor did he neglect the study of the Russian language, which he learned chiefly on his own and over which he attained great mastery. He was a true prodigy in all areas and a possessor of great abilities, while having great perception and memory as well.

When Rabbi Yehuda Leib Gordin was twenty-four years old it happened that Rabbi Yehuda Leib Hacohen Kurlitzer, one of the renown older rabbis of the day, chief of the rabbinical court and teacher in the small Lithuanian town of Michalishok, passed away. In his will he ordered that the young Rabbi Yehuda Gordin be appointed to his position. He had been a great admirer of the young *gaon* who was so knowledgeable in all areas of the Torah and who was also sage and wise, who delved into the depths of issues, and yet whose piety exceeded even his wisdom.

In the year 5637 [1876],[22] after nine years of service in that small town, Rabbi Gordin was invited to accept the seat of the rabbinate in the larger Augustow. The small town of Michalishok was no longer appropriate for the exalted abilities of the well known *gaon*, who had become famous for being a speaker who attracted the masses, and for being a rabbi who was blessed with

---

[22] Other sources indicate 5646 [1886].

qualities and gifts like few others in the country. He was agreeable to the request and accepted the new appointment.

In Augustow, Lithuania, Rabbi Gordin found a wider field for his successful activities, news of which spread far beyond the limited boundaries of his not too large city and community, which adhered to its rabbi with true admiration and love. He was not only the official chief of the rabbinical court of the city, but also the rabbi and spiritual leader of all the circles and classes of the residents of Augustow without exception. There was not a person who was not at home in the house of the rabbi.

The learned and scholarly people of Augustow found in him an outstanding *gaon*. There was no area of the Torah in which he was not an expert. The Hassidim enjoyed his exceptional knowledge of the lore of Hassidism and its foundations, and his positive attitude to this worldview. The simple people could not sufficiently praise the rabbi's talks which, while they were profound, were nevertheless understood by them in part thanks to his great oratorical abilities.

Even the Maskilim [literally "enlightened ones," meaning more modernized, secularized intellectuals], who among themselves were less invested in tradition and were involved in different ideas and ways of thought as regards the nature of Judaism and its future, spoke in admiring and appreciative terms about their great rabbi, who did not omit any subject at all from the scope his expertise. The officials of the authorities in Augustow and those who happened to be passing through it could not stop praising the rabbi for his rare knowledge of the Russian language and the rich and varied expressions that he used. Even the Russians marveled at the richness of the rabbi's language.

In the Defense of Hassidism and Judaism

In this period, as in previous ones, there was no lack of converts who were brimming with anti-Semitism. They did everything they could against the Jews in order to ingratiate themselves with anti-Semitic Russian circles, mainly so that they would not be suspected as still being Jews or still having ties to Judaism. There were those who had no shame in performing any repugnant act that would help them to advance up the anti-Semitic ladder and among anti-Jewish organizations.

One of these converts found himself a unique hobby: writing memoranda against Hassidim and Hassidism and circulating them among the heads of the anti-Semitic tsarist government. Like his predecessors in this disgusting work, he portrayed Hassidim as an ignorant sect whose adherents hated the Russian government and frequently cursed the Russian Crown. There were no more traditional haters of Russia or its government than the Hassidim.

These lies had their effect. Little by little the tsarist Russian authorities began to take concrete steps against these "dangerous" Hassidim. The Jews of the Enlightenment in Russia, profound antagonists of the Hassidim, did much to re-awaken the tsarist authorities to take action against Hassidism. They unhesitatingly encouraged the officials of the regime to take steps against the aura of rebellion that surrounded the Hassidim, those enemies of true light.

In fact the persecution of the Hassidim and their leaders began immediately as soon as Hassidism spread across Russia. The heads of the Hassidim were arrested and Hassidim were persecuted. Only with great efforts were they able to refute the accusations against them and to free the great leaders of Hassidism. These new activities against the Hassidim once again spurred hostile views among the authorities against Hassidim and Hassidism and encouraged them to do everything to renew their persecution.

The Gaon Rabbi Yehuda Leib Gordin

These many calumnies ultimately bore fruit among ruling circles in St. Petersburg, the capital of tsarist Russia, and they began to put them into action. They first turned to the Minister of Education, asking him to undertake a fundamental examination of the entire issue of Hassidim and Hassidism and to decide once and for all whether it was time to arrest all the Hassidic rabbis, to close down centers of Hassidim in all of Russia and her conquered territories, and to completely ban this movement.

After extensive research, the Minister of Education decided to appoint Rabbi Gordin, the rabbi of Augustow, who was not a Hassid but rather a Mitnaged, to clarify in a fundamental manner the nature and substance of Hassidism and to present a complete report on this subject to the government of the tsar. Rabbi Gordin accepted this assignment and promised to write and edit a detailed, fundamental and comprehensive survey on the question of "What Is Hassidism?"

In a high caliber book entitled, *What Is Hassidism?*, Rabbi Gordin was able to recount the entire history of Hassidism, its philosophy and fundamental beliefs, the bases of its worldview, the entire mystery surrounding Hassidism, the philosophy of Hassidism as expressed in its various streams, and the practical implications that Hassidim had brought about in the Jewish world at large.

The book, written in a pure literary Russian and in an exquisite style, made a deep impression on all the intellectual circles in Russia and its capital. The question of persecution of the Hassidim and Hassidism was removed from the public agenda entirely. Rabbi Gordin's name soon became well known all across Russia. Even the opponents of Hassidism and its sworn enemies were forced to praise the book and its gifted author, who had succeeded once and for all in quashing the malicious calumnies and false accusations against Hassidim and Hassidism.

There was no lack of enemies of Israel in Russia at that time. Some aimed their poison arrows at Hassidim and Hassidism. But there were others who fought against Jews in general, against the religion and the Talmud. From time to time there appeared posters against the Talmud and Jewish law in which blatant words of incitement against the Jews and Judaism were expressed, citing miscellaneous quotes from the Talmud.

In the anti-Semitic Russian press there occasionally appeared antagonistic pieces about the Jews and against Jewish law based largely on the Talmud, to the effect that Jews were likely to kill non-Jews, to poison them, and to use their blood, whether for Passover or other purposes. In fact all this venomous anti-Semitic propaganda was based on the "authority of the Talmud," which was portrayed as a "truly terrible and poisonous" work.

Acceding to the demands of many people, Rabbi Gordin decided to publish a book in defense of the Talmud, to prove that all the accusations and calumnies were based on lies. It was a high caliber and substantive book written in polished Russian entitled, *What Is the Talmud?* It was a balanced and serious reply to all the accusers with their malice and falsehoods. As a scholar and brilliant *gaon* imbued with the Talmud, which he knew by heart, he cited pearls from the treasury of the Talmud that made a great impression upon wide circles in tsarist Russia. It transformed those who railed against the Jews and the Talmud and Jewish law into mere superficial instigators lacking any substance or seriousness. Thanks to this book he became well known across Russia and one of the leading Russian writers of the era. Leo Tolstoy began a correspondence with him. Ardent Jew haters did not harass Rabbi Gordin, nor were they able to threaten or debate him. They simply ignored him and continued to spread their poison about the Jews. In the famous Beilis Trial[23] in Kiev the defense used this book to undermine the blood libel.

Amidst admiration and honor Rabbi Gordin presided in Augustow at the time when the people of Ostroveh were seeking a fitting rabbi for themselves, one who stood head and shoulders above others, one who could unify all segments and movements in the community and who could restore the honor and glory of the rabbinate to its former luster. The Mitnagdim sought a candidate of stature, as did the Hassidim, recognizing that they should not once again engage a rabbi who was not acceptable to all sides.

From Augustow to Ostroveh

In Ostrow Mazowiecka there lived at that time a wealthy and honored man by the name of Noach Feinzeig,[24] a contractor to the

---

[23] In 1913 Mendel Beilis, a Jewish brick factory worker, was accused of the ritual blood libel, i.e., of killing a Christian boy and using his blood for making *matza*. Despite extensive anti-Semitic publicity, the trial, which garnered worldwide attention, resulted in a not guilty verdict. The story was the basis of Bernard Malamud's later novel, *The Fixer*, which won the Pulitzer Prize for fiction in 1967, and which was later made into a film.

[24] The Feinzeig [Fajncajg] family, of which this editor is a descendant, was one of the oldest, largest (it was the fourth most common Jewish surname in town) and most prominent Jewish clans in Ostrow Mazowiecka, with roots there going back to the mid-1700's. The name itself derives from some of its early members' most common occupation, the tailoring of fine clothes from fine fabrics (the words "fein zeug" mean "fine cloth" in German), one of the few professions originally permitted under the 1750 Revised General Code for the Jews by King Frederick the Great of Prussia, which ruled parts of Poland at that time. Many of the clan subsequently also became government suppliers and contractors to the military of whatever power ruled the area at the time (Prussian, Russian or Polish). Among them was this editor's paternal great-grandmother and partial namesake, Leah Gittel Feinzeig, who ran just such a business in Ostroveh until her departure for America in 1923 to join her husband, Chezke, in New York, where he had arrived in 1911.

Russian army, and one of the leading citizens of the city. In the course of his business he frequently visited Augustow, where he became friendly with and close to its famous rabbi, the Gaon Rabbi Yehuda Leib Gordin. Full of admiration for this extraordinary rabbi, he began to think about having him as the rabbi of Ostroveh and as an appropriate candidate for that position.

Reb Noach Feinzeig assembled a group of people in his home, to which he invited all the factions in the city, both the Hassidim and the Mitnagdim. He presented to them the attributes of the rabbi of Augustow: a brilliant Torah scholar, one who was knowledgeable in Hassidism, a man of broad-based knowledge, and a wonderful speaker. He was one of only a handful of such rabbis. Ostroveh could not even imagine having a more capable and fitting rabbi.

Word of the rabbi had reached the people of Ostroveh from time to time. The Hassidim knew of his work in denying the accusations made against the Hassidim and of the publication of his book, *What Is Hassidism?*, which was sympathetic to Hassidism.

The Mitnagdim had heard of the greatness of his knowledge of the Torah. Plain Jews had heard of his wonderful lectures. Thus, it was decided unanimously and by all circles in the town to choose Rabbi Gordin as the rabbi of the city.

A special delegation, comprised of the head of the Hassidim in Ostroveh, the Hassidic Gaon Rabbi Ben-Zion Rabinowitz, and Rabbi Berish Shapiro left for Augustow. They met with the rabbi for a long time, discussing the Talmud and the works of the great rabbinic decisors with him. Both were impressed with the rabbi's greatness, with his wisdom and the depth of his intelligence, and with his radiant and attractive personality. They decided to ask him to move to Ostroveh and accept the position of chief of the rabbinical court.

When Rabbi Rabinowitz moved on to discuss Hassidism, the rabbi revealed an exceptional knowledge of the teachings of *Chabad*[25] within Hassidism. As a Hassid of the Kotsk and Ger sects, Rabbi Ben-Zion displayed a somewhat disparaging attitude towards that approach. But the rabbi of Augustow stood his ground and enthusiastically defended the *Chabad*-Lubavitch

---

[25] An acronym for *chochmah*, *binah* and *da'at* (wisdom, understanding and knowledge), the fundamental principles of the Lubavitch sect of Hassidism, founded in 1775 by Rabbi Shneur Zalman of Ladi (1745-1812) and headquartered in the Belorussian town of Lubavichi for a century. Lubavitch is now the largest Hassidic sect and known for its assertive outreach to non-observant Jews around the world.

viewpoint. Thus Rabbi Ben-Zion thought he was a *Chabad* Hassid. But it soon became clear that he was a Mitnaged who appreciated all outlooks in Hassidism and Judaism.

When the delegation returned to Ostroveh the community sent a letter of rabbinical appointment to Rabbi Gordin. It was signed by all residents of the town without exception.

Despite his unanimous selection as rabbi of Ostroveh, Rabbi Gordin still had doubts about accepting the position in a city full of Hassidim, given the fact that he was, and conducted himself as, a Mitnaged. It has been said that he decided to consult with his neighbor, the Gaon Rabbi Yisrael Meir Hacohen[26] of Radin, author of the *Chafetz Chaim* [*Desirer of Life*], and to accept his decision on this matter, be it positive or negative.

The author of the *Chafetz Chaim* listened to Rabbi Gordin's question and immediately replied: "I do not understand the question. Why are you afraid of the Hassidim? What is the worse they can do? To gulp down some drinks and toast one another with *l'chaim* ["to life"] or what? Drink some liquor with them and say *l'chaim* back and you'll get along. How can it hurt?"

Rabbi Gordin listened to the advice of his brilliant and saintly neighbor and accepted the offer from Ostroveh. So in the year 5657 [1896-1897] he arrived in Ostroveh to the joy of all its residents. They felt that the burning question of the rabbinate that had divided the city more than once was finally coming to an end. Ostroveh had a rabbi who was appropriate for the position and was able to unite all the city's residents and bestow upon them his authority, thereby solving all the questions of religion locally.

From that time forward the influence of the rabbi was infused into everything in Ostrow Mazowiecka. Hassidim and Mitnagdim, the mass of people, workmen and Jews of all circles and classes admired their rabbi. On the day of his official appointment by the Russian government authorities, when the rabbi was supposed to give a lecture at the house of study, Russian military and civil officials thronged the study hall in order to hear the rabbi's words in his engaging Russian.

Such speeches, lectures that he gave first in Augustow and then later in Ostroveh, were not ones designed merely to flatter the Russian government, however. Rather they were substantive and impressive speeches in which he exposed the glory and beauty in Judaism. He also gave full expression to the suffering of the Jews in the bitter and difficult Russian Diaspora of those times. These

---

[26] Rabbi Israel Meir Hacohen Kagan (b. Dzyatlava [now Belarus], February 6, 1838, d. Radin [now Belarus], September 15, 1933).

speeches were later printed in a separate book in the Russian language entitled, *Saluba,* for which he received a special expression of appreciation from Tsar Nicholas II.

In those speeches he fully expressed his condemnation of anti-Semitism. Rabbi Gordin did not conduct disputations with either the clergy of the Catholic Church or the White Russian [Orthodox] one. But he did consider what would have happened had he done so with these spreaders of anti-Semitic viruses, who were directly or indirectly responsible for the bloody pogroms against the Jews of Russia and Poland.

But the essence of the greatness of Rabbi Gordin did not lay in his knowledge of Russian or in those lectures. Rather they resided in his absolute brilliance in the Torah. He especially excelled in teaching. Many rabbis from near and far turned to him with questions, which he answered in great number with practical solutions in his characteristic clarity and his deep and straightforward intelligence, eschewing sophistry and complicated thinking, and getting down to the essence of matters and resolving them.

A large number of Rabbi Gordin's responsa in Jewish law were printed in his notable book of responsa, *Divrei Yehuda* [*The Words of Judah*], which became well known in scholarly and rabbinical circles. Many used it in dealing with practical problems. A few years later he published another book of responsa entitled, *Teshuvot Yehuda* [*The Responsa of Judah*], at the time when he was chief of the rabbinical court in Smorgon. But not all of the responsa that he sent to rabbis and *dayanim* [religious judges] far and wide were printed in his books.

Rabbi Gordin presided as rabbi of Ostroveh for only seven years, which many in the city later called "the Seven Fat Years." He enjoyed honor, admiration and even affection on the part of the residents. It was approximately at the beginning of 5664 [1903-1904] that he then decided to move to Smorgon,[27] which caused great sorrow to many of the residents of Ostroveh.

It was there that he published his homiletic book, *Degel Yehuda* [*The Flag of Judah*], a classic book that raised the level homiletics among the Jewish people. His books sold out quickly (though for some reason most of his writings were never

---

[27] Smorgon was also the birthplace of Chazzan Moshe Koussevitzky, one of the greatest cantors of the 20th century (b. June 9, 1899, d. New York, August 23, 1966), with whom this editor had the privilege of singing in New York. Koussevitzky had served as the last cantor of the Great Synagogue of Warsaw (the "Tlomackie Shul," named for the street on which it was located), where he succeeded the great Gerson Sirota (1874-1943), who died while officiating at the last Jewish service on Passover in a bunker beneath the Warsaw Ghetto.

published). Rabbi Gordin established a *yeshiva* in Smorgon, something he was unable to do previously. He appointed the Gaon Rabbi Zalman Ashinovsky to be its head. More than two hundred students studied there under Rabbi Gordin's overall supervision. He even occasionally gave a lecture there as well.

Rabbi Gordin had wanted to stop moving around and to remain in Smorgon. But in 5673 [1912-1913] the rabbinate in the city of Lomza, the provincial capital, became available. The residents sought an appropriate rabbi that would be able to administer this large community, as well as represent it vis-a-vis the authorities, to quash libels and to prevent harsh edicts. They could find no more suitable candidate than Rabbi Gordin, whose fame had preceded him.

Thus Rabbi Gordin moved to Lomza and remained there until his later years. But he never forgot the communities in which he has served with distinction as chief of the rabbinical court and continued to do much on their behalf. The people of Ostroveh remembered their great lofty rabbi, who was a Mitnaged both in fact and in principle, but one with a warm soul, a Hassidic soul, one that expressed his deepest thoughts and his true enthusiasm for the sacred. He maintained warm friendships with all of the local residents, including the head of the Hassidim, Rabbi Ben-Zion Rabinowitz, and the head of the Mitnagdim. Even when he was presiding over the rabbinate in Lomza he said, "I still have strong feelings for Ostroveh until today. I still feel love for the people of that city, and their love for me. I have great affection for Ostroveh, where I was able to author my best books that were of use to so many."

The Rabbi of Lomza

The community of Lomza was much larger and of far greater importance, far and above that of Ostrow Mazowiecka, Augustow or Smorgon. It was the provincial capital where some of the greatest rabbis, giants of the Torah and performers of great deeds, whose names were well known far beyond the borders of their city, had served.

In 5673 [1912-1913][28] Rabbi Gordin arrived in Lomza. But even before he could get settled into his rabbinate, World War I broke out. Difficult and dark days soon arrived. The large Jewish communities in Russian Poland began to suffer the pains of Job from the harshness and cruelty of the Russian commanders, who were anti-Semitic and full of hatred towards the Jews.

---

[28] Other sources indicate 1914.

They were incited principally by the Poles, poisonous enemies of the Jews. Many of the Poles were pro-German. Many of them hated their occupiers from the east, who had forcefully suppressed all nationalistic feelings among the Poles and even prevented them from emerging. But in order to hide their tracks and to harass the Jews at every step, the Poles continually informed on the Jews and pointed to them as some sort of dangerous spies.

This duplicitous Polish activity was very effective. The Russians paid close attention to the accusations of the Poles. Jews were arrested, were brought before unauthorized "field courts," and were sentenced to death for spying and treason, or were even just hanged, on orders from cruel Russian officers. Entire communities were expelled, while the Russian soldiers carried on at will, pillaging and robbing the Jews.

The exalted Rabbi Gordin, who viewed it as his mission and task to defend his captive and persecuted people, stood tall during this difficult battle. He worked day and night on behalf of the Jews of Lomza and hundreds of other cities and towns around her, both near and far. No task was too much for him. More than once he put his own life in danger in order to save Jews. Often Jews were arrested and the rabbi got them freed, mostly on his own personal recognizance.

For the Benefit of All

Not too long after the outbreak of World War I, the ongoing retreat of the Russians began under pressure from the German forces, which successfully conquered extensive territories in Russian Poland. As the battle lines neared the city of Lomza, the Russian command, believing the Polish accusations that every Jew was a German spy, issued an order for the expulsion of the Jews of Lomza.

The commander of the Russian army in the Lomza sector at that time was General Baziladnov, a Ukrainian, a sworn anti-Semite, who was glad for the opportunity to expel the Jews and to harass them at every step. When Rabbi Gordin came to his command post, General Baziladnov shouted, "Hands up, Jew. Who knows if there is a bomb of some type in your pocket...."

The rabbi was not afraid and raised his hands in a scornful way, and said loudly in reply, "We Jews have no bombs, not in our pockets nor in our homes. We do not shed blood. I am responsible for the people of my community and assure you that they are innocent of any blame. I would be pleased if you would take me as a hostage."

When General Baziladnov refused to cancel the edict, Rabbi Gordin turned to his commander, General Danilov, and succeeded in getting the decree nullified. But the battle lines drew even closer. The defeated Russian commanders were angry and their assignments were frequently changed. Now a General Miasvidov arrived in Lomza who was even more anti-Semitic and hateful of the Jews than his predecessor. This enemy threatened the rabbi that he would kill him if he continued to interfere in "the performance of his duties." The rabbi was not intimidated and continued in his efforts, not paying attention to the threats of this antagonist, who was carrying on without restraint and who was likely to carry out a death sentence and kill the rabbi.

The difficult winter months of 5774 [1914-1915] went by, with the Jews of Lomza living under threats and suffering. Throngs of Jews from the nearby areas and further afield filled the streets of the city when they were cruelly expelled from their homes and places of residence. Every day brought with it new decrees and new suffering. Incited by the Poles and unrestrained by their anti-Semitic officers, Russian soldiers frequently carried on, pillaged, attacked Jews and even made false accusations against them. Rabbi Gordin knew no rest during this period. He turned into a defender, a shield and a fighter. Day and night he was available for every assignment, even the most dangerous, in order to save a Jew, to prevent looting, or to free a Jew from imprisonment.

It was Passover time. The Russian army began to strengthen its positions against the German spring offensive that was well under way. Hurriedly the Russian army began to create fortifications and trenches around Lomza. Shortly before the holiday was to arrive, on the eve of Passover, forty-one Jews were picked up by the Cossacks and were assigned to the heavy labor of building fortifications. Immediately Rabbi Gordin appeared before the commander of the regiment of the Cossacks and asked him to free the Jews. He argued that the Poles were suffering from unemployment and would be only too glad to undertake the construction of fortifications and the digging of trenches if they were given appropriate compensation for their work. Why, then, pull Jews out of their houses on their holiday?

At first the Russian commander refused to listen to the advice of the rabbi. But after he was promised a large sum of money with which he could hire many Polish workers, while also keeping a not inconsiderable sum in his own pocket, he accepted Rabbi Gordin's recommendation. But he made it clear that only after he would receive the entire sum that he demanded would the last Jew be freed. But by the time the rabbi finished this negotiation with the officer over bribery it was getting near evening.

The rabbi hurried from the headquarters of the Cossacks to the Magen Avraham synagogue, where the wealthiest Jews in Lomza prayed. The rabbi delayed the service and placed his own private contribution to free the captured Jews on the table. He demanded that the congregants hurry back to their homes and that each to bring back his own contribution on the very eve of the holiday. Only when they would collect the entire amount needed would he allow the evening service to proceed.

The congregants scattered to their homes, while the rabbi sat at the table. Gradually the wealthy congregants returned, each with his own contribution. The rabbi did not move from his place until the entire required sum was collected. He then sent the money to the commander of the Cossack brigade. The rabbi did not deviate from this plan until the last Jew was released from the hands of the Russians and had returned to his home in order to celebrate the holiday of Passover in the embrace of his family and in his own home.

In the wake of the war, the expulsions and the edicts, the acts of pillage and the pogroms, the effects on business and employment were great. Many Jews were impoverished. Most of the refugees went about lacking everything. Some were even starving for a mere crust of bread. Rabbi Gordin never forgot about these matters. He saw it as his duty to care for them, about their pressing needs and in general. It was said by those around him that the rabbi loved the poor and visited them even more than the rich. There was a story about one of the wealthy people of Lomza whose poor tenant in one of his houses complained to the rabbi that he had struck him hard. The rabbi lost his temper and ordered that the wealthy man be punished and labeled a criminal in public. But in the end it became clear that the entire story was false. People complained to the rabbi that he had acted too rashly on behalf of the poor and their complaints. But Rabbi Gordin did not flinch. "It is better to err and later to apologize to a rich man than to witness the humiliation of a poor man and stand by silently," he said.

The German Occupation

Lomza was captured by the Germans,[29] but the rabbi did not know a word of German. So the rabbi holed up in his house for a while and learned perfect German. Given his extraordinary abilities he was able to attain this goal in a very short time. Henceforth he had a command of pure German with all its intricacies, as if he had been born in Germany. He appeared before the German commander of the district, Wilkens, to represent his community. The German commander liked the rabbi

---

[29] The "fort" of Lomza fell to the Germans on or about August 8, 1915. See W.C. King, ed., *King's Complete History of the World War*, The History Associates: 1922, p. 174.

and was impressed with his knowledge of the east and of philosophy. Wilkens enjoyed debating with the rabbi about matters of religion and faith. Whenever he had free time he would meet with the rabbi. Thus the influence of the rabbi with the German commander grew, and he used that influence for the benefit of his suffering brethren.

During the German occupation in World War I the Poles tended to lay low. They did not know German, and did not succeed in communicating with them or in understanding the language of their conquerors. So they always had to use Jews as interpreters. By contrast the Jews somehow managed to master German and were considered close to the authorities, even though among themselves they felt that German anti-Semitism was no less severe than the Russian, perhaps even more so, albeit covered in a silken wrapper.

The Jews, who had suffered endlessly during the period of the Russian occupation, especially during its latter days, breathed a sigh of relief during the German occupation. They received permits to import various needed supplies and were not limited in their ability to travel. They were freed from the nightmare of Polish tale telling. The latter tried to explain to the Germans that these very people, whom they had previously accused of spying on behalf of the Germans, were now spies on behalf of Russia. The masses of Poles, who saw the Jews frequently conversing with the Germans, saw them as sidling up to the rulers, who in turn viewed them as superior to the Poles. To the traditional and ancient hatred of the Poles towards the Jews were now added feelings of jealousy and revenge because of this insult to their honor.

So when the German occupation authorities decided to organize a local militia to oversee law and order within the bounds of the city of Lomza, once the Germans had to transfer most of their forces to the front, the German commander appointed a Jew as commander of the militia with broad powers. The rabbi understood that this would only intensify the feelings of hatred and incitement of the Poles towards the Jews, and that the Germans would not rule Poland forever. Thus Rabbi Gordin made every effort to change the decision of the German command and to appoint two commanders to the local militia, a Pole who was acceptable to the local Polish community, and a Jew.

The rabbi succeeded in his mission. Alongside the Jewish commander of the militia was appointed a Polish commander, to the great satisfaction of the Poles. This was a wise step that bore fruit a few years later, when Poland received complete political independence.

After World War I, when the independent Republic of Poland was established, the rabbi, despite his advanced age, decided to learn perfect Polish, after having mastered Russian and German. It was his view that it was one of the responsibilities of a rabbi to represent the Jewish population to the authorities, to be a representative of the Jews, and therefore it was incumbent upon him to know the language of the state. Otherwise he could not successfully fulfill his duties properly. His abilities once again came to his aid. And although he never knew Polish previously, he quickly succeeded in mastering Polish and even in orating in that language in public.

As an excellent speaker he captured the hearts of all his listeners with his lectures and speeches even in Polish, which became widely known. Unlike other rabbis, Rabbi Gordin was not satisfied in giving the lectures traditionally presented by the rabbis of Israel, i.e., on the Great Sabbath or the Sabbath of Repentance.[30] He expressed his views much more frequently, at every opportunity. He would say, "In the past, in the 'good old days,' it was sufficient for clocks to ring only twice a year. Life flowed along in a quiet and predictable way. Today, in these crazy and bizarre times, when a person does not even know what day or what time it is, clocks need to chime more often."

In the early days of the independent Republic of Poland the Jews suffered many shocks, pogroms and shortages. Rabbi Gordin stood at his post and represented the large community of Lomza brilliantly. He cared for its institutions and for the situation of every poor person and sufferer. When things settled down, life began to flow along more calmly, on a more steady and regular course. The rabbi now came to experience a brief period of rest and tranquility. But as a veteran fighter he did not suffer this period of tranquility and inactivity lightly. The status of the *yeshiva* of Lomza,[31] which had been developing nicely, was now in a bad way. Its debts were overwhelming, and its leaders had no

---

[30] The Sabbath before Passover and the Sabbath between Rosh Hashanah and Yom Kippur respectively, which were traditionally occasions where rabbis delivered major sermons.

[31] The *yeshiva* of Lomza was founded in 1883 by Rabbi Eliezer Shulevitz. This editor's grandfather, Rabbi David Tzvi (Hershel, later Harry) Schiff, studied and was ordained there, and served for some years as the editor of the publications of its faculty, including Rabbi Gordin. It was an unusual *yeshiva* in that while it followed the highly intellectualized and analytical educational model of the classic Mitnagdic Lithuanian *yeshivot*, it allowed the majority of its students, who were from Hassidic backgrounds, to continue their Hassidic family traditions in regard to style of prayer, etc. It was also the first Lithuanian-style *yeshiva* to adopt a favorable attitude towards Zionism, establishing a branch in Eretz Yisrael as early as 1926 in Petach Tikvah that still exists. See Gary S. Schiff, *In Search of Polin: Chasing Jewish Ghosts in Today's Poland*, pp. 169-170.

prospect of funding its budget. In Lomza the rabbi did everything he could to strengthen the status of the *yeshiva*, but its modest income could not guarantee the existence of this great *yeshiva*.

The Last Stop

The rabbi decided to respond positively to the requests of the heads of the *yeshiva* to embark for America on its behalf. He also had a personal family reason for this trip, despite his advanced age. His brother and two of his sons had immigrated to America and had cut all ties to Judaism and to the rabbi. Rabbi Gordin hoped to try to influence them to change their attitude and behavior.[32]

In 5685 (1924-1925) the rabbi departed on his long and exhausting journey. He arrived in Chicago, where his family lived. He met with them and was very sad. Chicago at the time had a very large Jewish community, but one that was chaotic in matters of religion and Judaism. The rabbi envisioned a vast field of operations for himself. When the rabbis of the city and the presidents of the synagogues appeared before him and proposed to him that he accept the position as chief rabbi of the city, a post that had not existed previously, he immediately agreed to accept this assignment.

Before he left for the United States the rabbi devoted some of his time to learning English perfectly, so that the knowledge of the language of the land could assist him in his work in America. The observant and traditional Jews of Chicago saw before them a well known and distinguished *gaon*, a brilliant speaker and a wise man, to whom all the intricacies of the rabbinate were clear. He was experienced in the running of a community, and also spoke fluent English. He had great influence on all who came into contact with him. They hoped that Rabbi Gordin would be able to bring about a fundamental turn around in the life of the Jews of the city.

For his part the rabbi believed that through his work as chief rabbi of Chicago he would be able to assist the *yeshiva* in Lomza and could also help change the ways of his relatives and their attitude towards Judaism. But while the rabbi was preparing to enter into his new job, and while still living in a hotel, he suddenly became ill and in a few days his great and pure soul was returned to its maker. This

---

[32] Passenger list records indicate that Rabbi Gordin also made a trip to the U.S. in 1921, arriving in New York on August 1 of that year reportedly for a period of three months.

occured on the tenth of Iyar, 5685 [April 11, 1925].[33]

The death of the rabbi evoked great sorrow in Chicago. An enormous funeral was held for him, and he was buried in one of the city's Jewish cemeteries. The news of the passing of Rabbi Gordin shocked the Jews of Lomza and the other cities in which he had worked during his long years of life, including the Jews of Augustow, Ostroveh and Smorgon. In all these places there were emotional eulogies in his memory. The light and glory of the Jews of Lomza was extinguished. At the initiative of the rabbi's admirers in Chicago a fund was set up for his orphaned family in Lomza, which later immigrated to Israel. (His grandson, the son of his daughter, was Mr. David Raziel, the first head of the *Irgun Tzvai Leumi*.[34] His son-in-law, Rabbi Regensburg, later moved to Chicago, where served as a lecturer at its rabbinical college.)

At the Lomza *yeshiva* a free soup kitchen, called *Beit Lechem Yehuda* [Judah's House of Bread], was established in the rabbi's memory. And up until the last day of the glorious Polish Diaspora many cherished the blessed memory of this devoted rabbi, who had so much impact and who did so much for the residents of the communities in which he worked and for Polish Jewry as a whole as one of the great rabbis that brightened the name of the Torah in Poland.

---

[33] Chicago-area newspapers give Rabbi Gordin's date of death as April 11, 1925, which corresponds with the seventeenth day of Nisan, rather than the tenth day of Iyar. He is buried in the *Tiferet* (or *Tipheret*) *Zion* section of the Waldheim Jewish Cemetery. *Tiferet Zion* was the name of the synagogue he had been asked to lead.

[34] The *Irgun Tzvai Leumi* (or National Military Organization, sometimes referred to as just the *Irgun* or by its acronym, *Etzel*) was an underground military organization in the pre-state period that fought against the British Mandate outside the scope of the mainstream Zionist movement. It was headed by Menachem Begin (b. Brest-Litovsk, 1913; d. Tel Aviv, 1992), who later headed the Herut (subsequently Likud) party, served as Prime Minister of Israel from 1977 to1983, and won the Nobel Peace Prize in 1978 jointly with President Anwar Sadat of Egypt for their peace treaty.

Chapter Five

Hassidic Rebbe Rabbi Yosef of Amshinov, Chief of Ostroveh's Rabbinical Court

New Songs

The Gaon Rabbi Y. L. Gordin had left Ostroveh and the question of choosing a new rabbi, one of stature and real influence, was once again on the agenda. It was a stormy period, as the Russo-Japanese War had broken out in the Far East. Thousands of families were dying of hunger as their breadwinners were sent as soldiers to the other side of the world to fight under extremely difficult conditions in a foreign war to which they had no real connection.

On the Jewish street new winds started blowing, fundamental changes were taking place. Many Jewish youth were caught up in revolutionary movements on whose flags were inscribed slogans of making war on everything that represented the past and the present. Such movements, which operated mostly underground, frequently developed quite deep and extensive roots in the Jewish community, including in Ostrow Mazowiecka.

There were some revolutionary movements whose entire aim was to uproot everything old, to put an end to the Jews' way of life over many generations, to change everything. This revolution in the Jewish community was viewed as being linked to the greater revolution to which they aspired directed against the bloody, rotten and corrupt government of the Russian tsar, a government of injustice, cruelty and hard heartedness, of exploitation and slavery.

Many Jewish youth were caught up in these ideological movements. They began to believe that a future full of complete goodness could be expected in the days following the great revolution. There would be equality for all people with no distinction as to nationality or race, happiness and prosperity for all. There would be a new world without poor and without rich and without chains. Man would be freed from every yoke and every type of subjugation. All the good of the world would be his.

These movements splintered into various and sundry streams and operated vigorously within the Jewish community. Among them were extremists who demanded implementing the revolution through blood. There were also those who advocated more moderate changes, a different life, but one that was improved. But they all fought against that which was old, the eternal tradition that had operated for generations in the Jewish community. It was a spirit of rebellion against the Torah and the Halacha [Jewish law], against the life of the Torah according to the Halacha, which threatened the status quo.

The old conflict between the Hassidim and Mitnagdim declined, pushed aside in the face of the new revolutionary force in the Jewish community. The Zionist movement, too, did its best, for its part, to advocate for its ideas and principles, including anti-religionism, fighting against the old ways and tradition. Whereas in the past Ostroveh, like other cities and towns in Poland, witnessed conflicts between Hassidim and Mitnagdim, now these two camps were up against new forces that quickly arose and that threatened to eliminate both the Hassidic movement and the Mitnagdic camp and to inherit their place. The abandoning of the obligations of the Torah and commandments became an all too widespread vision that caused the hearts of the religious people, be they Hassidim or Mitnagdim, to tremble. It was clear that a new era was coming and with it a fundamental change in the conduct of public life.

The older generation rejected these movements and, except for a few individuals, did not get swept up by them. But the younger generation was actually split. One group followed the religious people, continuing in the tradition of generations; while the other turned to these new movements, rebelling against their parents and teachers, and beginning to behave according to their own will and spirit. This new stream grew increasingly stronger and caused fear among the religious people, both Hassidim and Mitnagdim.

It was now clear that once again there was no room for conflict between Hassidim and Mitnagdim when it came to the selection of a new rabbi, and that it would be necessary to organize all the religious people against the new movements. The Hassidim were the first to organize themselves for the battle against the revolutionary movements. They were extremely fearful for the youth and stressed the danger that hovered over Jewish youth. The Mitnagdic camp was more moderate, but adhered in part to the position of the Hassidim.

The attempt of the revolutionary workers to overthrow the Russian tsar failed, drowned in the blood of masses of laborers. Great suffering also befell the Jews. After many Jewish youth had enthusiastically joined the revolutionaries, organizing demonstrations and fomenting unrest, many of them were arrested and exiled. Others hid and were pursued relentlessly. Not a few families were destroyed in the wake of these events. A vast chasm appeared between fathers and sons and between mothers and daughters. It became apparent to those who continued to observe the religion in Ostroveh that what they needed was not only a rabbi to represent them vis-a-vis the authorities and to wall himself in within the confines of the Halacha, but also a rabbi who had a charming and attractive personality who could halt the decline amongst the youth, or at least prevent the revolutionary movements from taking hold over the entirety of Jewish youth.

On the recommendation of the Amshinov Hassidim in Ostroveh, a delegation of prominent citizens left for Amshinov to meet with the son of the Hassidic *rebbe* of Amshinov, Rabbi Yosef, to assess his nature and substance and to determine whether he was able and worthy of serving in this position at such a serious time. The delegation returned from Amshinov full of praise about the charm and personality of this young candidate. The community of Ostroveh immediately sent him a letter of appointment.

A *Tzadik* Son of a *Tzadik*

The Hassidic *rebbe* Rabbi Yosef was born in the year 5637 [1877-1878] in Amshinov.[35] His father was the *rebbe* Rabbi Menachem, son of the *rebbe* Rabbi Yaakov Dov of Amshinov, the oldest son of the *rebbe* Rabbi Yitzchak the elder of Warka [Vurka, Vorki]. He was educated and grew up in the court of his father. The Hassidim said that he closely resembled his grandfather, the *rebbe* Rabbi Yaakov Dov of Amshinov, and his great-grandfather, the elder *rebbe* of Warka.

This family of *tzadikim* [pl., righteous men; Hassidic *rebbe*s] had a special appeal and an incomparable charm about them. They were famous as great lovers of their fellow Jews like few others, as possessors of fine and generous character traits, being the very symbols of a refined heart and soul. Curly black hair was

---

[35] Rabbi Yosef Kalish, the third Amshinover *rebbe* (b. Amshinov [Mszczonow], 1878, d. 1935 [other sources indicate 1936]). His brother, Rabbi Shimon Shalom Kalish (b. 1882 [other sources indicate 1883], d. New York, August 18, 1954), was also considered the Amshinover *rebbe*, but headquartered in Otvotsk near Warsaw. During the war he fled to Lithuania, where he was instrumental in saving many *yeshiva* students and others by getting them permission to cross the Soviet Union to Japan, and thence to Shanghai, China, as did he. After the war he settled in Borough Park, Brooklyn, New York, where this editor's great uncle, Mendel [Wolf] Feinzeig, was a close friend and supporter. The two died within a day of each other. The leaders of the family/dynasty/sect, which still exists in Israel and the United States, bore the name of the town of Kalish (Kalisz) in western Poland where, for the first time, a Polish ruler, Boleslaw the Pious, Duke of Greater Poland (Wielpolska), issued a broad-based charter of rights for Jews, sometimes referred to as the Statute of Kalish, in 1264, a charter that was expanded and re-affirmed by Polish kings over the subsequent centuries. He invited them to immigrate to Poland from German-speaking territories further to the west. See Gary S. Schiff, *In Search of Polin: Chasing Jewish Ghosts in Today's Poland*, pp. 52-54.

the identifying mark of this prominent family. Their aristocratic beauty shone from their faces, while a veritable sea of love for their fellow man and an unlimited compassion for every fellow creature of God was reflected in their large dark and gleaming eyes.

The elder *rebbe* from Warka, Rabbi Yisrael Yitzchak, was one of the leading students of the Hassidic *rebbe* Rabbi Simcha Bunim of Peshischa [Przysucha]. After the death of the *rebbe* of Peshischa his son, the Hassidic *rebbe* Rabbi Avraham Moshe, was chosen by the mass of Hassidim as the *rebbe*, who inevitably accepted this appointment. He settled in the town of Warka near Warsaw, from where he began to conduct the affairs of his community that in those days was both large and influential in Polish Jewry.

His Hassidim were renowned for their devotion to God. For many of them their whole world was wrapped up in Hassidism. The strict Peshischa method accepted no compromises and demanded the complete devotion of a person with no exceptions and no limitations. They saw in Rabbi Yitzchak an exalted holiness, as if he were one of the angels from above, filled as he was with the love of his fellow Jews in an exceptional manner. Many stories and legends circulated among the Hassidim about his generous character traits and his devotion to every human being, near or far, and about the wellsprings of mercy and righteousness that emanated from his every deed.

His father had been called Rabbi Shimon, the "Master of Mercy," characterizations which also befit his rare traits even back then. His teacher and educator from his youth was Rabbi David of Lelov,[36] one of the giants and great lights of Hassidism, who in his own lifetime became a living legend of righteousness and love for one's fellow Jew without parallel. The elder *rebbe* of Warka followed in their footsteps.

Not only was Rabbi Yitzchak a *rebbe* and leader, teacher and rabbi to the masses of his Hassidim. He was also a man of stature who took responsibility for the Jewish people as a whole. There was no matter, no public issue in which he was not interested and did not touch his big heart. No effort or undertaking was too hard for him in his public activities. Even in the last years of his life, when he was weak and ill, he did not cease his holy work for even a day.

Almost every week he traveled to Warsaw, a distance of some forty-three kilometers from Warka by wagon. Along with the Hassidic *rebbe* Rabbi Yitzchak Meir of Ger, author of *Chidushei*

---

[36] Rabbi David Biderman (1746-1814), known as the Lelover *rebbe*.

Harim,[37] he labored on behalf of the congregation and the community. Among these issues were the reforms that the German Jewish community attempted to infuse into Polish Jewry, which the Russian tsarist government authorities favored; and the many decrees that were imposed upon religious Jews and their traditional religious way of life, the official declared aim of which was, "to change the face of the Jews, to take them out of their caves of darkness and to let some light into their tents."

Edict followed edict. There was no limit to the pressure that was used to narrow the pathways of Jews loyal to the Torah and to the traditional way of life. It was forbidden for Jews to go outside in the streets of the cities dressed in traditional garb or to wear *peyot* [sidelocks]. Veteran traditional teachers of small children now had to obtain licenses, and so on.

The elder *rebbe* of Warka worked day and night on efforts against this wave of decrees, trying ceaselessly to guard the walls of religion and tradition of Polish Jewry jointly with Rabbi Yitzchak Meir of Ger. These battles succeeded after indescribable efforts. Traditional Jewry in Poland managed to retain its uniqueness, thanks in no small part to the devotion and self-sacrifice of the *rebbe*s of Ger and Warka.

In the year 5608 [1848] the *rebbe* of Warka died. His great community of Hassidim splintered. One faction chose his oldest son, Hassidic *rebbe* Rabbi Yaakov David, who established his residence in the town of Amshinov, whence he launched the long line of *rebbe*s of the House of Amshinov. The other faction chose the youngest son of the elder Rabbi Yitzchak, the Hassidic *rebbe* Rabbi Menachem Mendel, who remained in Warka near Warsaw.

---

[37] See above, p. 26.

The Hassidic Rebbe Rabbi Yosef
of Amshinov

While the second *rebbe* of the House of Warka, Rabbi Menachem Mendel, devoted himself to the spreading and deepening of Hassidic learning, his older brother, Rabbi Yaakov David of Amshinov, followed in his father's tradition and ran the affairs of his Hassidic sect, while not neglecting his duties on behalf of the wider community. He established the hallmark of this version of Hasidism, a refined Hassidism, full of sacrifice and devotion, but one also wrapped up entirely in the love of one's fellow Jews and in immeasurable mercy.

Rabbi Yaakov David ran his sect for thirty years and worked for the public good. He died in the year 5638 [1878]. His place was taken by his son, Rabbi Menachem, who followed closely in the footsteps of his great father, both as a lover of his fellow Jews and as a public servant. His home and his heart were always open to everyone. His aristocratic appearance engendered unending respect and admiration. He captivated all who came into his presence.

It was in this manner that he raised his children. His oldest son, Rabbi Yosef, who resembled his father and his illustrious grandfather in every way, was married in his youth to the daughter of the Gaon Rabbi Chaim Elazar Wachs, chief of the rabbinical courts of Piotrkow and Kalish, author of *Nefesh Chaya*

[*The Living Soul*], and one of the greatest rabbis and decisors of his generation, and the son-in-law of one of the greatest *geonim* [pl. of *gaon*] of Polish Jewry, Rabbi Yehoshua,[38] chief of the rabbinical court of Kutno. From the day of his marriage forward Rabbi Yosef spent day and night studying Torah and doing good works. He studied eighteen hours a day and lived entirely in a spiritual world, surrounded by admiration on all sides, as an offshoot and continuity of this great tradition.

When he was twenty-seven, the representatives of Ostroveh appeared and offered the position of rabbi in their city. At the behest of his father Rabbi Menachem, Rabbi Yosef accepted the invitation and moved to Ostroveh as chief of the rabbinical court and its rabbi. From his first appearance his wonderful image engendered an attitude of respect and admiration in the city. Both the Mitnagdic circles and the Hassidim, as well as plain Jews, were charmed by contact with the rabbi, by his relations with every person, and by the great love of fellow Jews that emanated from him.

It is told that thirty years before Rabbi Yosef became the rabbi of Ostroveh his grandfather, Hassidic *rebbe* Rabbi Yaakov David, happened to arrive in Ostroveh in order to collect money for the redemption of captives. The power of the Hassidim in Ostrow Mazowiecka was as yet small and weak, while the power of the Mitnagdim over Hassidism was very strong. The latter forcefully demanded of the Hassidic *rebbe* that he leave the city before the start of the Sabbath and that he not celebrate the Sabbath there. With great difficulty Rabbi Yaakov David succeeded in finding an inn on the outskirts of the city and spent the Sabbath there. Thirty years later all the people of Ostroveh prepared a tumultuous welcome for his grandson, Rabbi Yosef, who continued in his ways.

In a relatively brief time Rabbi Yosef succeeded in endearing himself to all the people of the community and in capturing all their hearts. Like the love of a father for his son such was his love for the people of his community, without distinction as to class or group, and they reciprocated his great love. His home was always open as a safe place for anyone who needed or asked for it. Every poor person and bitter soul found refuge with him, and he never refused to offer his full assistance to any person.

His conversation with or his discussion of the affairs of every person was full of sincere love for his fellow Jews, which emanated from the very depths of his heart. Even the residents who were more worldly and distant from religion could not deny the love that

---

[38] Rabbi Yisrael Yehoshua Trunk, 1820-1893.

emanated from his open heart. No one dared to refuse the rabbi or deny his authority. The rabbi's house became the permanent address for anyone with a request or need, for any bitter soul. Whether during the daytime hours or the nighttime ones, the people of Ostroveh knew that it was always possible to turn to the rabbi at any time, and that he would never refuse to help, to offer advice, to do everything on behalf of the community.

The rabbi devoted every free moment to Torah and good works and to the strengthening of the study of the Torah. He invested much effort into the city. He vigilantly presided over the development of the city's *Talmud Torah* [religious elementary school], taking interest in every detail of that institution. He invested his efforts and time into the development of the local *yeshiva* [school of higher religious studies], and worked to establish societies for the regular study of the Torah. In all the Hassidic houses of worship and study the voices of those studying Torah grew louder. Numerous new classes were set up with the encouragement and at the initiative of the rabbi.

The thrust of his efforts was to attract the youth to the Torah and Hassidism. He brought every young person close to him and loved him as if he were his own son. These efforts bore fruit. Soon the benches of the old study house on the road to Komorowo, which had once been full of young men studying Torah, were once again no longer vacant. With the assistance of the heads of the Hassidim in the city who wholeheartedly supported the rabbi's actions, a turning point was reached in the character of the city. The revolutionary and anti-religious youth movements no longer threatened to capture the next generation. The process of disengaging from the life of the Torah and tradition was slowed, if not completely halted. The hopes of the religious people of Ostroveh for the future of the city were not proven false.

The Kosher Food Company

The rabbi did not concentrate his efforts on only one area. He initiated and established the Kosher Food Company for Jewish soldiers, an institution which functioned up until the outbreak of World War I. In Ostroveh two regiments of Russian infantry were stationed permanently, amounting to thousands of soldiers, located at a distance of just a kilometer from the city. In Komorowo military camps were set up, and half the Russian Sixth Division was encamped there. In the summer months the other half of the Sixth Division would also usually arrive in Komorowo, for the purpose of joint exercises and so on. Among the thousands of soldiers who encamped in this area there were always two to three hundred Jewish soldiers. The Russian Army did not provide kosher food for the Jewish soldiers, and usually pressured these soldiers to eat in the general *treif* [non-kosher] mess hall. These soldiers had no other alternative, as they had no means of obtaining kosher food.

At the initiative of Rabbi Yosef Kalish a Kosher Food Company was established in Ostroveh for the Jewish soldiers. Among its aims was to supply kosher food to Jewish soldiers. The rabbi invested a great deal of energy in the initial establishment and securing of this company. The residents of the city volunteered to pay a certain monthly sum towards the company. The students of the study hall undertook to collect the needed funds for this purpose on a regular basis.

Another source of funding for the company was the collection of money at every wedding that took place in the city and its environs. The young volunteers put on masks and special costumes that were stored in a special warehouse in the basement of the house of Reb Moshe Schwartz, one of the public figures of the city. These fund raisers, with their special masks, elicited laughter, brought joy to the crowd, and injected an air of gaiety into the weddings, along with raising substantial sums for the needs of the company.

The rabbi did not limit his efforts to obtaining food for the Jewish soldiers, however. Before every holiday or other special occasion he would work to obtain leave for the Jewish soldiers, so that the soldiers spend time in the company of and among Jews, free from the military yoke and the oppressive atmosphere of the Russian military camp. It was not easy for the rabbi to achieve his goal. He sometimes had to invest substantial sums of money in these efforts in the form of bribes to officers, hungry for pay-offs, so that they would not withhold leaves from the soldiers.

The soldiers who were granted leave from the army for the holidays were put up in the homes of Jews. Every self-respecting householder invited one or several soldiers to his table and provided him with every amenity. The Kosher Food Company, headed by the rabbi, saw to it that not a single soldier would be without a home in which to stay and eat. The rabbi especially liked to host Jewish soldiers in his own home, and did everything to make them happy and to draw them near. Jewish soldiers from great distances for many years remembered the rabbi who welcomed them with such love and took care of them with such true devotion.

Rabbi Yosef of Amshinov served for thirteen years as the chief of the rabbinical court of Ostroveh. About ten of those years were a period of relative calm, even though there was no lack of hardship, suffering or sadness for many. It was the fate of the rabbi that he took part in the problems of every individual and every resident of his community as if it were his own. But once World War I broke out in the year 5674 [1914], a terrible period of period of unimaginable shock and suffering came upon the community of Ostroveh and on the whole of Polish Jewry.

The Teachers of the Talmud Torah and Its Students

With exemplary devotion the rabbi stood at his post even in this difficult period. Whether he was present in Ostroveh or elsewhere he never forgot about his city and its residents. He neither stinted nor tired from his work on behalf of the Jews of his city. Sometimes it seemed as if he saw himself responsible for their suffering.

At the end of World War I the Hassidic *rebbe* Rabbi Menachem of Amshinov died. The majority of the Amshinov Hassidim chose his son, Rabbi Yosef, as the successor to his great father. He moved to Amshinov, where he served as *rebbe* and chief of the rabbinical court until the day he died in the year 5697 [1935-1936].

Chapter Six
The Gaon Rabbi Meir Dan Plotzky

The Prodigy of Kutno

Ostrow Mazowiecka was fortunate to have the Gaon Rabbi Meir Dan Plotzky [Plocki] presiding there with distinction for several years. He was one of the great lights in the constellation of the rabbinate in recent generations, a *gaon* and a Hassid, a *tzadik* with superlative virtues, a man of action and a man of Halacha. He was a rare and multi-faceted figure like few in his generation, a personality that was elevated above his contemporaries, a spiritual giant who merited admiration in the worlds of the Torah, the rabbinate and Hassidism combined, who became a legend in his time.

"Rabbi Meir Dan," as he was called and known among the Jews of Poland, was a giant among rabbis. He served as the rabbi of the community of Dvart [Warta], the rabbi of the community of Ostrow Mazowiecka, and in his last days as head of the *Metivta* [or *Mesivta*] *yeshiva* in Warsaw, the capital of Poland. But holding these positions per se did not add luster to his name; rather it was because of his great personality that these communities themselves became renowned. This personality sprouted and grew in the very heart of Hassidic Poland. He was educated in the lap of pure Hassidism to become a pillar of Torah and education.

Rabbi Meir Dan was born in Kutno in the year 5627 [1866-1867] to his father Rabbi Chaim Yitzchak Plotzky, a scholar and ardent Hassid, one of the followers of the Hassidic *rebbe* Rabbi Chanoch Henich of Alexandrow.[39] After the latter's death he became one of the important followers of the *rebbe* of Ger, the author of *S'fat Emet* [*The Language of Truth*],[40] and was among his inner circle. His mother, Mrs. Gela, was a distinguished woman and one of the most righteous and well known women of Kutno, who implanted in her beloved son the love of Torah and the fear of God from the moment he could understand, even before he went to *cheder*.

When he was only eleven months old Rabbi Meir Dan came down with a mortal disease. The doctors in Kutno refused to treat him any further, as they saw no possibility of saving his life. His

---

[39] Rabbi Chanoch Henich Hacohen**Error! Bookmark not defined.** Lewin (b. Lutomiersk, 1798, d. Alexandrow Lodzki, 1870).

[40] Rabbi Yehuda Aryeh Leib Alter, the second Gerer *rebbe* (b. Warsaw, 1847, d. Ger, 1905).

father Rabbi Chaim Yitzchak rushed to the house of his teacher, Rabbi Chanoch Henich Hacohen of Alexandrow, and bitterly poured out his heart about his terrible trouble. The *rebbe* gave him a blessing for a complete recovery, but Rabbi Chaim Yitzchak remained there, immersed in pain. He knew what the doctors of Kutno had said before he left his house. He had left his baby son at the very edge of death.

"Why are you worried? You will yet derive much pleasure from him. He will be a great rabbi in Israel," the great *rebbe* said. Rabbi Chaim Yitzchak pulled himself together at that moment, and no longer hurried to get back to the bed of his sick child. He stayed for a while in Alexandrow in the presence of his teacher and rabbi. Then the little Rabbi Meir Dan gradually regained his strength. When he grew up and gained understanding, he was found to have exceptional abilities, an unusual acuity of mind. He was already thought of as a prodigy even before he was brought to the *cheder*.

His father Rabbi Chaim Yitzchak was never a wealthy man. He barely made a living as a clerk and trusted employee, a bureaucrat for wealthy Jews who owned great woodlands in western Poland. Generally his work, whether in the forest or in a village, was located close to where they felled trees. Rabbi Chaim Yitzchak wandered from place to place along with his family and his brilliant son. But his mother was concerned about his studies. So she went out and sold her jewelry and engaged exceptional teachers, who stayed in the villages with her family and taught the little Rabbi Meir Dan. He rapidly progressed in the levels of Torah study to the point where he was considered a great prodigy. When Rabbi Meir Dan eulogized his mother after her death he highlighted the greatness of her spirit, her rare moral qualities and the extraordinary deeds of a young woman who would sell her jewelry in order to have higher caliber teachers, who shared their high level of knowledge.

When Rabbi Meir Dan was nine years old he was no longer in the hands of wandering teachers. Even the best of them had nothing more to teach the young prodigy. So despite his young age his parents sent him to Kalish, to the *yeshiva* of the Gaon Rabbi Chaim Eliezer Wachs, the rabbi of the city and author of *Nefesh Chaya* [*The Living Soul*]. At first visitors to the rabbi's house had doubts about what such a young child was doing there and attending the rabbi's lectures, even if he were gifted. But once Rabbi Wachs examined Rabbi Meir Dan he immediately included him in the group of his best students. From that time on he never stopped loving him and caring for his needs. After a few years Rabbi Meir Dan moved to Sochachow [Sochaczew], to the *yeshiva* of the Hassidic *rebbe* Rabbi Avraham, author of *Avnei Nezer*

[*Stones of the Crown*],[41] a place where exceptional scholars and giants of the Torah tended to congregate. The lectures of the *gaon* of Sochachow were replete with such sharpness and depth that even adult students with great abilities at times found them difficult to comprehend. Nevertheless, the young Rabbi Meir Dan quickly succeeded in becoming part of this elite group. When he was thirteen years old his father arranged a Bar Mitzvah celebration in Kutno and invited all the leaders of the city to the event. Rabbi Meir Dan himself composed a discourse, which overwhelmed all those who heard it with its acuity and profundity. Word of the talk reached his teacher and rabbi, the *rebbe* of Sochachow. When Rabbi Meir Dan returned to his yeshiva he was asked to reprise his discourse that had become known. This veteran prince of the Torah listened to his young student and said, "One can debate what he said, but he built a beautiful structure and it would be a shame to bring it down when it is just as likely that it will stand...."

Head of the Yeshiva of Dvart

In Dvart, located in this district, a city full of wise men and *sofrim* [scribes; authors], great Hassidim and excellent scholars, there lived at that time Rabbi Mordechai, a Hassid and a learned man, a wealthy man and a man of good deeds. His wife was Mrs. Sheina Reizel, a righteous woman who grew up in the house of her uncle, the Gaon Rabbi Chaim Auerbach,[42] chief of the rabbinical court of Linschitz [Leczyca].

Rabbi Mordechai had three daughters. The two older of them were married to great scholars who eventually served as rabbis. The first was Rabbi Yosef, chief of the rabbinical court of Kletcheva [Kleczew], and the second the Gaon Rabbi Menachem, chief of the rabbinical court of Kozminka [Kozminek]. For the youngest of his daughters, the talented and outstanding Tziril, Rabbi Mordechai sought an exceptional young man who was known as an outstanding *gaon* of note. In Sochachew at the *yeshiva* of the *rebbe* Rabbi Avraham he found the young Rabbi Meir Dan and took him as the groom for his daughter.

Rabbi Mordechai spent much money on the dowry and gifts. In the year 5642 [1882] Rabbi Meir Dan married his bride when he was just fifteen years old. His father-in-law Rabbi Mordechai spent a great deal of money so that Rabbi Meir Dan could acquire a large library and also took care of all his needs. For ten years Rabbi

---

[41] Rabbi Avraham Borenstein (b. Bendin, 1838, d. Sochachew, 1910).

[42] (1755-1840), author of *Divrei Mishpat* [*Words of Judgment*].

Meir Dan worked at studying Torah and became a great scholar, having no worries about his subsistence or that of his family, being reliant on the support of his father-in-law. In his book, *Chemdat Yisrael* [*The Delight of Israel*], Rabbi Meir Dan says, "I am morally obligated to mention for good and blessing at the beginning of my book the name of my dear rabbinical, righteous and just father-in-law, who walked a straight path and loved Torah and its students, Rabbi Mordechai, may his memory be a blessing, and my dear and righteous mother-in-law, Mrs. Sheina Reizel, may she rest in peace, who supported me for ten years, when all my needs were dependent upon them in all matters, and I was able to study and teach worthy students."

The grandfather of Rabbi Meir Dan, his father's father, was an outstanding *gaon* and Hassid and multi-talented man, named Rabbi Yisrael. He died in the year 5643 [1882-1883] when Rabbi Meir Dan was seventeen. On the day of his death the grandfather called for his grandson, asked him to put his hand on his heart and to swear that he would study with all his heart and soul and that he would cultivate innovative and profound ideas about the Torah. His grandfather's request never left the memory of Rabbi Meir Dan up until his final day. (This information is found in the introduction to his book, *Chemdat Yisrael*, Volume I, where he adds that he named his book after his esteemed grandfather.)

For a short time Rabbi Meir Dan studied in Dvart by himself. But soon a number of young men came to him, and he began to deliver his lectures to them. From that time on there was never an absence of a *yeshiva* around him. In the house of his rich father-in-law, surrounded by love and devotion, Rabbi Meir Dan dedicated himself to learning and teaching, day and night. He was always found in the midst of his studies. His *yeshiva* grew, and it became famous in the surrounding area and beyond. Its students were deeply attached to their teacher, the young *gaon*, whose name became well known in the entire world of Torah as one of the sharpest minds of his generation, a genius in Halacha and a genius in understanding. He diligently and rapidly went through both of the two Talmuds[43] and the early and later commentators. He was a *gaon* whose sharpness of mind did not detract from the breadth of his knowledge and whose breadth of knowledge did not diminish his acuity.

Sharp and Broadly Knowledgeable

His method of study, like that of his teacher, the *rebbe* of Sochachow, author of *Avnei Nezer*, was to go into depth in his

---

[43] The Babylonian Talmud and the Jerusalem Talmud.

studies. But this was not for the sake of finding the logic or the beauty of this penetration or depth, but rather to find the very truth of the reasoning and of the Halacha. For even more than one has to work hard to understand the reasoning, one has to work hard to understand the Halacha and everything that emanates from it. Rabbi Meir Dan did not reject the method of sharp *pilpul*,[44] built layer upon layer, full of sparks of acuity and based on the sharpness of the mind, in the manner of the *rebbe* of Ostrovtse [Ostrowiec], Rabbi Meir Yechiel.[45] He only used it only if the *pilpul* would point to the truth and would not distract from the topic under consideration. The main thing was that it would contribute something of substance to the clarification of a particular Halacha, or that it would point out some pathway in the sea of the Talmud or the early commentators, but not *pilpul* for its own sake, whose only purpose is to highlight the sharpness therein per se, when such acuity only distracts from the understanding of the essential plain meaning.

Rabbi Meir Dan did not object at all to the mixing of Halacha with Agadah [legend; non-Halachic parts of the Talmud], or of *pilpul* with plain meaning, if the purpose was to advance the student towards the truth in his studies. In his view the entire Torah, whether in its literal sense, its allusions or in its hidden meanings, comprises one single structure. Only through systematic study--when at first it might appear that the simple meaning contradicts the legend or vice versa--does one who delves deep discover that there is no contradiction or difference between the different paths and ways of understanding the Torah. In his books and in his teaching he began to use both sharpness and breadth of understanding, deep study and *pilpul.* He sailed directly towards the target with all the weapons of the Torah at his disposal, something which only an outstanding *gaon* like him is able to do and carry through. The prodigy in him combined with the scholar laden with knowledge thanks to his extensive studies. The search for a clear outcome in Halacha combined with his desire to clarify the complexities of the issue that are hidden from superficial view.

Rabbi Meir Dan was a Hassid in every fiber of his being. He adhered to pure Hassidism with all his heart and soul and to his studies with enthusiasm and awe, with holiness and purity. He related to every iota of the Torah with fear and trembling, but also with love and soulful devotion. Study was never for him a matter

---

[44] A kind of close, often hairsplitting form of analysis that some may deem to be sophistry.

[45] Rabbi Meir Yechiel Halstock (1852–1928).

of pleasure, but rather a holy undertaking. The Torah obligates every part of one's body, not just the mind and intelligence. Therefore he worked in the field of Torah with literally with all his strength. He approached the study of the Torah with a real hunger, as if he had never studied it before. Every day he would set aside time to infuse into his heart the love of Torah. Thus, there was no limit or parallel to his love of the Torah.

Gaon and Hassid

He was one of the devoted and sharpest Hassidim of Ger. He had a permanent place at the house of prayer of the Hassidim of Ger in Dvart, which was full of extraordinary men of learning and Hassidim, both old and young, enthusiastic in their service to God. His limitless devotion to Hassidism was planted in his heart by his father, Rabbi Chaim Yitzchak, and by his grandfather, Rabbi Yisrael. And so he maintained this precious heritage in every aspect. From a very young age he would frequently visit the holy ambience to be found at the court of the Hassidic *rebbe* Rabbi Aryeh Leib of Ger, author of the *S'fat Emet* [*The Language of Truth*]. After the latter's death he accepted the authority of the Hassidic *rebbe* Rabbi Avraham Mordechai of Ger.

The *rebbe*s of Ger had a deep love for this young and exceptional *gaon*. There were very few like him in his generation. At the same time, every word that came out of the mouth of the *rebbe* was like a law for him, and every demand or request an obligation for which he was prepared to go through fire and water to fulfill. Rabbi Meir Dan viewed Hassidism as an integral part of the obligations incumbent upon every Jew of recent generations. Only Hassidism would prevent deviations in thought and action in our bereft generations, assuming that Hassidism was directed by a true *tzadik*, a saint of Israel.

Every person needs some real submission, and not only of the heart. Just as prayer needs to be expressed with your mouth, so, too, every submission needs to be expressed in actions. A person who has no teacher, no rabbi, and does not submit to anyone only diminishes his own stature. No matter who he may be there is a higher power above him and God helps him, Rabbi Meir Dan posited. Thus, he viewed in Hassidism an activity which supplemented his study of Torah and good work, and without which everything is deficient. Later in his life, when he was on a mission in America, he was asked by one of the Mitnagdic rabbis, "A *gaon* like you, who has mastered every aspect of the Torah, why do you need to travel so much and why do you need to submit to the *rebbe* so much?" Rabbi Meir Dan replied, "We learn that 'thunder was created in order to straighten out the crookedness of the heart.' This teaching seems surprising and incomprehensible. For a person who infuses into his heart much Torah, his work consists of prayer, fear and love of God, the fear of sin and adherence to the blessed Creator. Is he not yet able to rid the crookedness from his heart with the strength of his Torah and fear of God? Must he wait until a day of rain, thunder and lightning storms in order to be able to expel the crookedness?"

"From this analogy we understand," Rabbi Meir Dan went on, "that this crookedness, which is the fertile source of all poison and bitterness, cannot be cured by the person himself. Rather he needs help. The Hassid does not wait until a stormy day. He travels to the *rebbe*, who guides and directs him and prunes the wild growths that envelop the heart and soul of a person. He learns to know submission, its nature and substance. He absorbs his *rebbe*'s Torah and teachings like a pupil before his master. He learns from his manner, his conversation and his conduct of affairs. His Torah knowledge is not diminished thereby, but rather his stature is only straightened."

The Rabbi of Dvart

While Rabbi Meir Dan was in Dvart, serving there at the time as rabbi and chief of the rabbinical court in his later years was the Gaon Rabbi Yosef,[46] son of the Gaon Rabbi Moshe, the Maggid [famed preacher] of Zalozhits [Dzialoszyce], author of *Mishpat Tzedek* [*Righteous Judgment*], a commentary on the Book of Psalms. Rabbi Meir Dan became fond of the elderly rabbi and sought out his company, basking in his Torah. The rabbi appointed the sharp *gaon* to be a *dayan* [religious judge] and teacher, and as his substitute in the rabbinate. In the year 5651 [1890-1891], after the passing of Rabbi Yosef, Rabbi Meir Dan was chosen as the chief of the rabbinical court of Dvart, when he was but twenty-four years old.

After a year Rabbi Meir Dan no longer accepted support from his father-in-law. But for some reason he waived any income from the meat slaughtering fund, even though it was the usual entitlement of the rabbi to receive income from slaughtering. Contrary to the opinion of many of the great lights of Israel of his generation, he opposed the transfer of funds from the slaughtering fund for purposes of running the community. The salary of the *shochet* should come rather from the community's funds. Rabbi Meir Dan favored such an arrangement. In his view the rabbi, as

---

[46] Rabbi Yosef Gershon, who served as rabbi of Warta from 1851-1891. He was the son of Rabbi Moshe of Zaloshits [Dzialoszyce], author of *Tikunei Shabbat* [*Regulations of the Sabbath*].

well as the *shochet*, should in every community receive his salary from communal funds. All income, including the slaughtering fund, should be centralized in the hands of the communal fund. He therefore refused to receive any money from the slaughterers' fund, but rather made do with the limited salary that came from the community itself, all of whose limited income came from taxes on the residents.

After many years, after World War I and the rise of the Republic of Poland, while Rabbi Meir Dan was serving as rabbi of Ostrow Mazowiecka, the community decided, with his encouragement and under his influence, to transfer the funds of the slaughtering fund to its own authority. The rabbi was gratified by the decision, and viewed it as an important sign post in guaranteeing complete *kashrut* [keeping kosher] and in providing organized communal governance in the city. The *shochtim* [pl. of *shochet*] in Ostrow Mazowiecka sharply objected to this decision. They solicited a number of great rabbis to side with them. They even called a strike. But Rabbi Meir Dan was not intimidated, despite his very friendly ties with the slaughterers of the city. He asked the leaders of the community not to yield. Finally both sides agreed to arbitration, which was held under the auspices of the Gaon Rabbi Moshe Shatzkes in Lomza, who decided in favor of the community. The *shochtim* had to acquiesce.

As his family and his expenses grew markedly, Rabbi Meir Dan agreed to conduct arbitrations in the surrounding areas, both near and far, in order to balance his personal budget. Despite his limited income he spent considerable amounts on *tzedakah* [charity] out of all proportion to his income. He always gave generously and willingly, and sometimes gave his last penny to charity. And if he were asked but did not have anything to give at that time, he became very sad. He did not rest or sit silently by until he could get a loan with which to contribute to *tzedakah*. Even as a young rabbi he was open to any debate on Halacha, for ideas and information to combat and to stand his ground. But while there was a bit of aggressiveness in all this, he could never let a poor man leave without alms.

Once when he was presenting his set morning lecture to his students, a needy visitor appeared. Rabbi Meir stopped his lecture and took his visitor into a separate room. The visitor left and the rabbi returned to his discourse. But his heart and soul were not in it. The students discerned that he was full of sadness and pain and found it difficult to deliver his words.

Charity and Righteousness

Every day at the same time the postman brought letters for the rabbi, which remained unopened until the afternoon. Once he finished his lecture he turned to dealing with the mail. But this one time he deviated from his custom, and stopped his teaching and quickly went to open the letters. And lo and behold but in one envelope there were twenty-five rubles, fees for an arbitration that one of the parties was paying him. He immediately sent two of his students to look around town for that needy visitor and give him this money. Only then did he return to his teaching with joy and enthusiasm, his face understandably aglow.

Rabbi Meir Dan suffered much. Countless torments were visited upon him without breaking his spirit or detracting from his enthusiasm for matters of holiness, without diminishing his burning faith or the light in his face. When he was immersed in Torah he was able to recover from his troubles. He often approached his lectures broken and crushed with his eyes red from crying, after tragedies afflicted his family, but he ended his lecture with a glowing face, full of faith and hope that all would be well. To his pious and righteous wife, Mrs. Tziril, who cried bitterly after the death of their eldest son, the outstanding Gaon Rabbi Eliezer Yehuda,[47] who had barely turned eighteen, Rabbi Meir Dan said, "It is said that just as one should recite a blessing for good things, so, too, should one recite a blessing for the bad. For one who recites a blessing on the good is convinced that the good came upon him because he deserves it, that it is his due. So, too, should the one who recites a blessing on the bad should know that he deserves the bad as well."

The tragedies that afflicted his family did not depress his spirit, although he mourned the death of children deeply. As was mentioned his oldest son, Rabbi Eliezer Yehuda, died as just a young man, eighteen years old, without leaving behind a son. Rabbi Meir Dan deeply grieved the loss of his beloved son, a young *gaon* who resembled him in every way. He was sharp and broadly knowledgeable, exacting in his great diligence, an enthusiastic Hassid who did not avail himself at all of any of the pleasures of this world, and never in his short life did he enjoy any material things. Despite his young age he assisted his father in the writing of his first book, *Chemdat Yisrael [The Delight of Israel]*, which contains many of his own novellae.[48]

---

[47] (d. Dvart, 1902).

[48] *Chidushim* in Hebrew, novel interpretations of sacred texts.

Chemdat Yisrael

Rabbi Meir Dan appended to his book, *Chemdat Yisrael*, novellae on the Torah that came from his son, the young prodigy, in a special pamphlet, *Beit Yehuda* [*The House of Judah*]. Afterwards he published a second volume of his son's teachings also called, *Beit Yehuda*. In the few pages of these pamphlets, written by a young man who had not even lived eighteen years, the greatness in Torah of Rabbi Eliezer Yehuda, his broad knowledge and especially is great acuity, were apparent. Rabbi Meir Dan had hoped that this son would be his continuity. His premature death shocked the *gaon* to the point where he never forgot about his wonderful son for a single day of his life. He was once asked why, twenty years after his passing, he still spoke of his tragedy as if it had occurred only yesterday. He replied that when a father walks behind's his son's coffin and brings it to be buried he finds comfort for the tragedy in his mind. It is as if he is making a sacrifice to the Creator of the World. We are commanded to make daily sacrifices. So when I recall my great tragedy, when it recurs to me, it seems as if I am making a new sacrifice.

But this was not the only tragedy that afflicted his family. Two of his daughters, Mrs. Chana and Mrs. Sarah, died young, leaving behind young orphaned boys and girls. And it fell to the *gaon* and his wife to educate and support them. Rabbi Meir Dan and his righteous wife accepted these afflictions with love. They carried these burdens in silence until their final days. The issue did not influence the great rabbi's teaching or prayer or his work on behalf of the public.

In the year 5663 [1902-1903] Rabbi Meir Dan published his book, *Chemdat Yisrael*, to which some of the greatest rabbis of the generation gave their enthusiastic endorsements. Among them were his teacher, Rabbi Avraham of Sochachew, the Gaon Rabbi Chaim Soloveichik, chief of the rabbinical court in Brisk [Brest-Litovsk], the Gaon Rabbi Eliyahu Chaim Meisel, the rabbi of Lodz, and others. They adorned the rabbi-author with the greatest of titles, they crowned him as being an awesome *gaon*, a prince of the Torah. But Rabbi Meir Dan, in printing their endorsements, edited out all the compliments that were directed at him, but made do only with references to "the rabbi."

Most of the hours of the day he devoted to his holy work. He delivered several lectures to the students in his *yeshiva* per day. But in addition to this he was aware of everything that was going on in his community, Dvart. He served as the address for every bitter soul and every trouble that afflicted the people of the city or its environs, and never stinted in any effort to assist anyone who asked for help. He saw himself as responsible for the well being and health of all the poor and suffering, the widows and orphans in his community and the surrounding area. He never ceased in his devotion to the downtrodden.

Defending Religion

But he viewed his most important duty as defending Halacha and the ramparts of Judaism. Even in Dvart in those days there arose groups of "progressives," outright secularists and partial secularists, who sought to change the entire face of Judaism, who sought to introduce improvements and changes in the traditional vineyard of the House of Israel. There were also those who sought such disintegration by means of games and public plays to encourage Jewish youth to enter into the circle of their activities and ideas which negated the bases of Judaism. Rabbi Meir Dan viewed his battle against these groups as an integral part of his rabbinate.

In Dvart a Zionist circle arose, comprised primarily of people who had already discarded the obligations of Judaism. Some people joined who, while their lifestyle was religious, their approach to religion was very compromising and tepid. Rabbi Meir Dan, who rejected the political Zionist movement from the very day of its founding, was not afraid to come out openly in opposition to this group. He did not negate the aspiration to immigrate to Zion. On the contrary, he was a lover of the Land of Israel and always cared about her situation. He was concerned as much as possible with the Jewish communities in the Land of Israel, and with the Fund of Rabbi Meir Baal Haness.[49] Every request that came to him that was related to the Land of Israel he related to in a most positive way. But he viewed political Zionism as a negative and dangerous force that would ultimately likely undermine the ramparts of Israel and bring about a spiritual and moral catastrophe to our people, one worse and more dangerous than any other calamity.

In his lectures, which also found expression and an echo in his books, Rabbi Meir Dan argued that there is no other basis for the survival of our people than the Torah, the Halacha and Judaism that is tied to it exactly as it is with no changes at all. Those who seek to change the spiritual basis of our people resemble those who seek to destroy the economic basis of the Jews, or the right to their physical existence. They are like an enemy who seeks to destroy a holy nation. In general, the concern for assuring the

---

[49] A charitable fund established in 1796 that supports the basic needs of orthodox Jews in Jerusalem.

physical existence, economic well being or political existence of a nation cannot in any way come at the expense of the destruction of its spiritual and essential existence. Rabbi Meir Dan offered this analogy: a vineyard owner attempts to save one of his plants that is being knocked over by storms and winds. The vineyard owner finds the roots of the plant. He saws them off and uses them as supports for the other vines, without realizing that he is condemning the one he came to save to destruction.

An Approach and a Pathway

His attitude towards anti-religious Zionism was the same in regard to religious Zionism. For in his mind there is no place for religious life if the Torah is not at the center, controlling all ways of life. He who places religion in second place is as bad as one who puts it outside the realm of activities altogether. One who battles against pure religion at least enables its defenders to defend themselves. But those who put religion in the shade as some kind of appendage actually destroy the bases for religious life--or even the concern for Judaism--under the guise of compromise. Rabbi Meir Dan, who was flexible and moderate and who loved peace, was not afraid to do battle without compromise on behalf of Torah, to fight for every jot and tittle of the Torah, for custom and tradition. For those who determined that "a custom in Israel is like a law" are those who assured the survival of Judaism and the people of Israel.

The Gaon Rabbi Meir Dan

In those days there arose among the Jews socialist and revolutionary popular movements. Hunger, want and discrimination that were the lot of the masses of Jews served as motivating factors for joining those new movements. Rabbi Meir Dan felt the pain of every miserable and depressed person, as he viewed with trepidation the war for survival of the exploited workers and the overburdened artisans. But he absolutely rejected the new movements which came as if to free the masses from darkness to light, to assure them of a rosy and beautiful future, a tomorrow full of light. The agitation increased and created conditions for a mass uprising and revolutionary acts, especially among Jews who were opposed to the cruel and oppressive tsarist regime in the year 5664 [1903-1904]. Rabbi Meir Dan continued to speak out in public against those movements, and was not intimidated by the threats of the revolutionaries.

He did not advocate loyalty to tsarist rule. He more than once took a risk in leveling withering criticism against the oppressive regime, which he hated with all his heart and about which he had not a good word to say. He was disgusted by all those who could sit side-by-side with those who represented that evil government at any level. It was not loyalty to the rule of the tsar that motivated him. On the contrary, it was his loyalty to the masses of Jews, to their future and well being.

We are among non-Jews, we are in exile, the rabbi repeated again and again. These non-Jews are corrupt to their very souls, cruel, callous, evil hearted, bloodthirsty and seeking sacrifices, anti-Semites. When things are bad for the non-Jew and he is distracted, he is not preoccupied with and has no time for the Jew. But when the non-Jew is otherwise sated, he can turn his full cruelty upon the Jew. If a revolution would bring prosperity, it would bring it to the non-Jews, while the Jews would remain negatively discriminated against. Why are we Jews getting involved in their ways of life and governance?

In order to free man from his suffering one needs a change in values, restraint by the one who rules, the extraction of the animal of prey from within him, the negation of the animal instinct that has penetrated into him. Man must first repair himself before he can repair others. And until people correct their own actions they cannot correct the world, countries and states. Without Torah, without Judaism a person is not able to correct his flaws or to restrain himself. Revolutionary movements that strip Jews of all holiness, from every spark of Judaism, will only lead its followers to the brink of disaster. They will empty him of all content. One can never satisfy a person who has no values.

The Profound and the Sharp

Rabbi Meir Dan was a *gaon* who like to delve deeply into matters, to examine all sides of the coin. He read all the propaganda of the socialists and Zionists, perused their books and publications, so that he might know how to reply to them. He felt that it was first and foremost the obligation of a rabbi in Israel to propound the views of Halacha about all issues so that he might make relevant rulings concerning them. In order to counter the opposition one must know the essence of what he says. Such material was to be found in his house for short periods of time. He would hide it on the upper shelves of his bookcase and instruct his students not to go there. So when he went out to do battle at the gates he would know what his enemies, the enemies of Torah Judaism, were saying. There were those young men who may have glanced into this secular literature and who were harmed, but Rabbi Meir Dan restored them to health, as he knew how to remove every thorn that penetrated the heart of a naïve young man who was unable to understand matters in depth.

In his battle against the movements that were attempting to destroy the ramparts of the House of Israel Rabbi Meir Dan was not satisfied in conducting a war of ideas alone. He was not deterred from any activity that would assure that the anti-religious, revolutionary or even partially secular movements would not sink deep roots in Dvart, or that they would not take over the community, but rather that they would remain within a limited framework. But even their limited influence would not let the rabbi rest. He was ready and willing to attack them, and would ignore no opportunity to do so. Once, on the eve of the holiday of Shavuot [the Feast of Weeks], the rabbi was walking in the street in Dvart when he came upon a poster announcing that a traveling artisans' choir was going to be visiting the city, and that on the holiday of Shavuot it would be presenting a play entitled, *L'vavot Sh'vurim* [*Broken Hearts*], to the public at large, which was invited to attend. The rabbi immediately sent his students all over town to announce that on the day of the holiday the rabbi was going to lecture on the synagogue on the topic of *L'vavot Sh'vurim* between the morning (*shacharit*) and supplementary (*mussaf*) services. As he was the religious leader of the community people felt that it was obligatory to attend. So it was ordered that all the synagogues and houses of prayer would be closed at that time and the entire community was asked to come and listen to the sermon of the rabbi.

The next day the majority of the residents of the city gathered at the synagogue, some surprised to hear the lecture, other curious as to what its meaning was. The rabbi mounted the pulpit, raised his voice and broke out in tears. "Today is the memorial day for King

David, peace be unto him, who in the Book of Psalms presented to us a portrait of the broken and depressed heart, with which we have approached the Creator for thousands of years, before whom we present our pleadings and supplications. The Creator will not mock the broken and depressed heart of King David. And today, the very day we remember him, people come and make a mockery of and scorn this broken heart, rendering it a mere display of laughter and frivolity. The one thing that we have of him as a keepsake, the broken heart, they make into a morbid game."

The tears of the rabbi, his shouts of pain shocked the local residents. The organizers of the play kept trying to explain themselves, that it was not their intention to hurt the feelings of anyone who was broken hearted. They canceled the play, and gave in to the rabbi. Sometimes the rabbi, for lack of an alternative, would organize a group of learned people of Dvart, from among those who were his adherents and friends, and would lead them to the place where a play was being put on. And because of the presence of the rabbi and dignitaries of the city the organizers of the plays would generally cancel them, albeit reluctantly. They did not dare to dishonor the rabbi.

Clean Hands

The community of Dvart was not among the largest or most important in Poland. But the reputation of the rabbi reached the far corners of the country and beyond. Many boasted and took pride in this famous *gaon*, a prince of the Torah, the definitive decisor, the true Hassid who fought the good fight, who was active in all areas and who was not afraid of doing anything that would accord honor and glory to the rabbinate and to Polish Jewry. Many saw him as the very symbol and the role model for a rabbi in Israel, whose shoulders towered above those of others, one who was ready and willing to sacrifice, who eschewed glory but rather was one whom glory pursued, who detested graft in any form.

There was a case where two well known lumber merchants got into a dispute with one another. One of the parties invited Rabbi Meir Dan to serve as an arbitrator for him. The rabbi agreed to do so. His salary from the community of Dvart was extremely limited and he would therefore do arbitrations. After a number of sessions the arbitration fell apart. One of the sides rescinded his willingness to participate. The other merchant presented Rabbi Meir Dan with a respectable sum of money to pay for his efforts, even if they had come to naught. He further promised to help him and to stand by his side and that "whatever the rabbi thought in his heart or mind about having he would provide." Rabbi Meir Dan heard this and refused to accept the money, saying "I am not looking to acquire anything." The wealthy man then offered a much smaller sum, arguing that the rabbi had dispersed money for his travel and lodging, which he was entitled to under any circumstances. But Rabbi Meir Dan refused this money as well, asserting that, "In each ruble of yours there are embedded kopeks of bribery." Two years later, when he was again asked to sit as an arbitrator for another wealthy merchant, whose opponent was the very same merchant who had try to "acquire" him, the rabbi refused, saying who knows if there is still not a tinge of resentment in my heart against that merchant? Therefore I recuse myself, as I might not be able to decide the matter truthfully.

In the year 5672 [1911-1912] the Hassidic *rebbe*s and leading rabbis of Poland assembled to deal with the fund for poor Polish Jews in the Land of Israel, as complaints and criticism on the part of the poor who came from Poland and were living in Jerusalem about the administration of the fund and the activities of its directors had mounted. The participants in the assemblage decided to send a delegation of prominent rabbis to the Land of Israel that would investigate matters in Jerusalem and decide on any necessary measures. So in that year Rabbi Meir Dan Plotzky left on that mission along with the Gaon Rabbi Shaul Moshe Zylberman, the rabbi of Vyershuv [Wieruszow], and the Gaon Rabbi Chaim Naftali Zylberberg of Warsaw. They worked hard to bring about peace and to prevent a rift between the funders and the recipients of the distributed funds. Upon his return to Poland Rabbi Meir Dan refused to speak about the nature of the dispute and its origins. He argued that after the delegation of the rabbis did what it did there was no point in rehashing the complaints and replies to them. To do so would only serve to slander the Land of Israel, or to say that there were people in Jerusalem who were involved in conflict, and that it was equally forbidden to tell that tale.

The Torah of the Land of Israel

His novel interpretations of the Torah, which he came up with during his stay in the Land of Israel, were very dear to him. He recorded them in his book, *Klei Chemdah [Instruments of Delight]*, after his return to Poland. He wrote, "The ideas that I came up with when I was in our Holy Land are very precious to me. I wrote them down when I returned from the Holy Land...." In the Land of Israel Rabbi Meir Dan came into contact with all the giants of the Torah in Jerusalem, and established ties of friendship among them which lasted for years long after his return home. He was particularly fond of the scholars of Jerusalem, who sat and learned despite the difficult circumstances they were under. They got by on the very minimum, but never left the confines of their religious studies and work. "There are among them," he wrote, "exceptional scholars the likes of whom you would be hard pressed to find in the Diaspora."

In that same year [in May 1912] there gathered in Kattowitz [Katowice] rabbis and communal leaders from many countries in Eastern and Central Europe with the goal of establishing an international organization of orthodox Jews that would work in a united fashion for the rule of the Torah in all spheres of activity of the Jewish people and would rebuff the assaults on the faithful of the House of Israel. Rabbi Meir Dan joined this new organization with enthusiasm, for which, he said, he had waited for a long time. He was prepared to do everything he could to insure its success and firm establishment. But before this new movement, Agudat Yisrael [or Agudas Yisroel, the Association of Israel], could strike deep roots in Poland, World War I broke out, which prevented any organizational work.

As early as the first few months of the war the imperial German Army succeeded in capturing Dvart and its environs. Compared to the suffering that the Jewish people in central and eastern Poland underwent as a result of the actions of the Russian army and its officers, those Jew haters, Dvart and its surrounding area were relatively quiet. Rabbi Meir Dan was in Dvart, cut off in fact from the vast majority of Jewish communities in Poland. He then wrote his book, *Klei Chemdah*, on the Torah, which received wide attention in the entire Torah and rabbinic worlds, and prepared the second volume of his book, *Chemdat Yisrael*, for publication.

During this time there appeared in Poland a book of the Jerusalem Talmud dealing with matters of holiness that had never hitherto even been known to exist. The author of the book, one Shlomo Friedlander, presented himself under false circumstances. He claimed that the book was authentic and that it was uncovered by him. He succeeded in obtaining the endorsement of some leading rabbis in Galicia and Hungary for its printing as a book of the Jerusalem Talmud, and to which he added a gloss of his own. He presented a garbled and counterfeit volume, and continued to deceive the rabbis from whom he extracted endorsements without their having examined the character of the author and his work.

Rabbi Meir Dan published a special booklet in which he proved the author's fraud beyond a doubt. At first the fraudster still tried to defend himself, but he quickly disappeared when he could not stand up to the withering criticism of this great *gaon*, who exposed his true identity and the nature of his deeds. The rabbis who had endorsed him quickly retracted their endorsements.

Before the last world war ended the position of the rabbinate in Ostrow Mazowiecka became vacant. The rabbi of the community, Rabbi Yosef Kalish of Amshinov, was chosen as the Hassidic *rebbe* and chief of the rabbinical court of Amshinov in place of his father, the Hassidic *rebbe* Rabbi Menachem, who had just died. The people of the community of Ostrow Mazowiecka chose the Gaon Rabbi Meir Dan as their rabbi and teacher. As usual, Rabbi Meir Dan took no final step until he had consulted with his teacher and rabbi, the Hassidic *rebbe* Rabbi Avraham Mordechai of Ger. When the rabbi came to ask his question, the *rebbe* replied, "For a few years, why not?"

Rabbi Meir Dan no longer hesitated. He left Dvart and went to Ostrow Mazowiecka, where his reputation was as a great *gaon*, a prince of the Torah, a devoted rabbi and courageous fighter, one of the greatest rabbis of his generation, and a paver of the paths to Torah Judaism. In Ostrow Mazowiecka, as in Dvart, he immediately took the lead in all communal activities. He stood at the gates as a father and patron, responsible for everything that occurred within. He did not flinch before anyone, nor did he put up with anyone. He saw in the rabbinate a holy mission whose responsibilities must be fulfilled with devotion.

These were days of chaos and confusion. The Russian tsardom had fallen. An independent Poland arose and anti-Semites again reared their ugly heads. They attacked the Jews and carried out bloody pogroms. Many Jews became impoverished. They lost all their property. Their source of income was gone. Rabbi Meir Dan did not see himself as limited to matters of Jewish law, but rather as an address for all who needed help and support and all who were depressed. He never turned anyone away, nor did he ever evade giving assistance to anyone who asked for it. In the first months of his presence in Ostrow Mazowiecka he devoted days and nights to helping the poor and the suffering.

As the situation in Poland calmed down, the question of the organization of traditional Judaism once again rose to the fore. Rabbi Meir Dan was co-opted to this service, and was appointed as one of the leaders of Agudat Yisrael. The founders of this new movement were faced with a difficult problem, that of establishing a budget for the organization's activities. Without adequate financial resources it was clear that it would be impossible to establish a mass movement, with centers, hundreds of branches, and thousands of educational and other institutions.

For the Good of All

Therefore it was by decided by the organizers of the Organization of the Faithful of Israel (a/k/a Agudat Yisrael) to send a high level delegation to England and the United States to encourage orthodox Jews to organize and offer their full support to the new movement. Chosen as head of the delegation was Rabbi Meir Dan Plotzky. Its members consisted of the Gaon Rabbi Asher Lemel Spitzer, chief of the rabbinical court of Kirchendorf [Kirchdorf], Rabbi Dr. Meir Hildesheimer of Berlin, Germany, Dr. Nathan Birnbaum, Rabbi Yosef Lev, who later served as rabbi in London, and Rabbi Yitzchak Meir Levin, may he live and be well, who headed the delegation only in England.[50]

Rabbi Meir Dan was everywhere received royally. Rabbis and those knowledgeable about the Torah trembled before this great *gaon*, who was rightfully thought of as a prince of the Torah and a pillar of education. But the delegation did not succeed in raising the needed sums. Rabbi Meir Dan, who had a kind and gentle soul, did not succeed, as he was not adept at the games of honorifics by which fundraising was accomplished in America in those days. He did know how to flatter people, especially the nouveau riche, who were ignorant of Torah, did not have the fear of Heaven, and did not have the same charitable impulses to which Rabbi Meir Dan was accustomed.

Many communities in the West had offered him the position of rabbi and promised him very generous salaries. One community competed with the other in offering the rabbi compensation. But Rabbi Meir Dan rejected all the offers, even though his income in Ostrow Mazowiecka was very limited, not sufficing to support his family and himself, given his open-handedness to charity. But the rabbi refused to consider emigration to the wealthy countries of the West. As he told one delegation that had offered him a very remunerative position:

> "As we learn in *Pirkei Avot* [*The Ethics of the Fathers*],[51] a story is told of Rabbi Yosi ben Kisma, who met a man who suggested that he live in his locale, for which he would give him a thousand thousands of gold dinars. He replied that even if you give me all the silver and gold in the world I would not live any place other than in a place of Torah. This story, Rabbi Meir Dan said, is incomprehensible. How did Rabbi Yosi ben Kisma know that the place which the man had proposed that he move to in exchange for a great fortune was not a place of Torah so that he quickly

---

[50] For more about Rabbi Plotzky's trips to the United States in 1921 and 1926, see Appendix I to this chapter.

[51] A volume of the Mishnah (the earlier part of the Talmud, a collection of rabbinic traditions redacted by Rabbi Yehuda Hanasi in Israel at the beginning of the third century of the Common Era) that is devoted principally to ethical teachings.

rejected his offer? He passed up a thousand thousand dinars so lightly?"

"However, the rabbi went on to explain, everything necessary in the world, without which you cannot live and cannot do without, like air and water, bread and so on, is cheap or free. Otherwise it would be impossible to live in the world. So if a man came to Rabbi Yosi and offered a thousand thousand gold dinars for his Torah knowledge, it is a sign that the Torah is not considered necessary, like air to breathe, to the residents of that place, otherwise it would not be so expensive."

Thus, he rejected their proposal, saying that all the gold and silver in the world cannot compare with the value placed on the Torah by those who deem it as a necessary thing, like air to breathe.

Rabbi Meir Dan then returned to Poland. But a great shock now befell the state that had just attained its new political independence, after more than a hundred years of subjugation to Russia, Germany and Austria. The Bolshevik Red Army invaded Poland and attempted to conquer her anew. The Polish Army quickly retreated westward. In a relatively short time the soldiers of communist Russia had arrived at the gates of Warsaw.

Pain and Suffering

The undisciplined Polish Army retreated. It was commanded by corrupt, Jew-hating officers. It attacked Jews without restraint in the cities and towns. The Jews were accused of treason, were portrayed as Russian spies as exemplified by Leon Trotsky, who was of Jewish origin and who was the Commissar in command of the Red Army. The communist soldiers robbed and pillaged everything there was to steal and plunder, and did not spare the Jews at all. When the Polish Army mounted a counter attack and the Red Army withdrew back in chaos to the Russian front, the communist soldiers emptied entire communities in the course of their retreat. And the Polish Army, when it returned and re-captured the cities and towns, once again began to launch wild attacks on the Jews. Soldiers cut the beards off Jews who fell into their hands. They made up accusations against them. Any Pole who wished to would now fabricate an accusation against a Jew that he was acting as a spy. The testimony of a single Pole, no matter how flawed, was sufficient for officers of the Polish Army, hungry for Jewish blood, to convict the poor sacrificial lamb to death by hanging or shooting. All efforts to save those condemned to death for no reason failed. The Poles were interested in killing

Jews without any justification. The wild, riled up Polish mobs rejoiced at the sight of a hanged Jew.

In Ostrow Mazowiecka the Poles captured a young Jew named Moshe Zlatovsky, a native of Siedlce, and accused him of criticizing the Polish government in its pursuit of the war with the Bolsheviks. To no avail the Jews endeavored to prove that the whole story was based on a lie. Without success the leaders of the community appealed to the representatives of the authorities that there was no law that prohibited criticism of the government. Neither were the tears and wailing of the relatives of the poor innocent of any use either. A few junior officers sat as judges, acting as a field court, and quickly issued a death sentence by hanging for the young man.

In the forest on the road to Komorowo thousands of Poles gathered, exultant and rejoicing, as they came to witness the lynching of a Jew. Moshe Zlatovsky, may God avenge his blood, was brought to the site and with him was Rabbi Meir Dan, who did not abandon him in his last moments. He recited with him the confessional, *Sh'ma Yisrael* [*Hear, O Israel*], and the prayer for justification of God's judgment until his holy soul departed. Broken and depressed, the rabbi returned to the town. The dreadful scene shook the rabbi to his core. Upon his return home he could not even stand upright. He took seriously ill and for several months could not arise from his bed.

When he recovered Rabbi Meir Dan returned enthusiastically to his studies, his work and his efforts on behalf of the community. He published his book, *Klei Chemdah*, on the Torah, which quickly captured the hearts of the Torah community in Poland and beyond. Major endorsements were given to this book by leading contemporary Torah scholars. Among them were the Gaon Rabbi Yosef**Error! Bookmark not defined.** Rosen, the Gaon Rabbi Meir Simcha of Dvinsk, the Gaon Rabbi Yosef Engel and others. The book was quickly sold out and made the name of its author famous as one of the sharpest *geonim* [pl. of *gaon*]. He also published the second volume of his book, *Chemdat Yisrael*, which included rabbinic responsa, lectures and moral discourses that Rabbi Meir Dan had delivered since he was appointed as rabbi and chief of the rabbinical court. These were only a few of the thousands of responses that the rabbi had sent to communities near and far, to hundreds of rabbis and *dayanim* [pl. of *dayan*] who had turned to him with all manner of serous issues and complicated questions. He responded quickly, precisely and clearly to every inquirer. He did not avoid deciding difficult matters of Jewish law, although he occasionally surrounded his replies with other topics, meandering through the Talmud and the early and later decisors in the course of clarifying the law.

He was thought of in those days, while serving as rabbi in Ostrow Mazowiecka, as one of the first rank of decisors of his generation. In addition he was deemed one of the giants of the Torah who helped carry the burden of responsibility in the Torah community, and his heart was aware of every communal problem.

Among the Greats of the Generation

The rabbis of Poland had organized themselves into a nation-wide association in order to cooperate in raising the level of the rabbinate, to strengthen religion, to alleviate the plight of *agunot*,[52] and to operate in every other sphere of the rabbinate. At its first convention in 5682 [1921-1922], at which hundreds of rabbis took part, Rabbi Meir Dan was elected as chairman of the executive committee of the Association of Rabbis of Poland. He functioned in this framework principally in matters revolving around issues of Halacha. He refused to get involved in any activity that involved improving the economic status of rabbis. He left this matter to other rabbis.

The Jewish communities in Poland were organized on a democratic basis. The government of Poland officially recognized the communities and established regulations for their functioning. Every Jew was obliged to pay a special tax to the community in which he lived. Every five years there were general elections under the supervision of the authorities. The number of officers was determined by the number of members of the community. In the larger communities a council was elected, which in turn chose an executive body. The law gave the rabbi of the community the right to participate in the meetings of the executive as an equal member. Rabbi Meir Dan was opposed to this law. The rabbi is not an elected representative; his place was not among the representatives, he contended. The salaries of rabbis were also determined according to special regulations. The level of salary was determined by the size of the community. According to this governmental regulation the community of Ostrow Mazowiecka was required to add 1,800 zlotys to the rabbi's salary per year. When the community of Ostrow Mazowiecka presented its budget for 5684 [1923-1924] to the government for approval, the government official demanded that the discrepancies in the salary of the rabbi that he was entitled to be added as per the law. But Rabbi Meir Dan refused to accept the raise just so that he could

---

[52] "Chained women" who had been abandoned by their husbands or whose husbands were missing and who, lacking a *get* or divorce document, were therefore unable to remarry.

balance his own personal budget. He stated clearly that he was not a rabbi of the government, but rather of the community. The arrangements of government bureaucrats were of no interest to him. His limited income did not prevent the rabbi from being the first among the donors to charity and among the largest.

In Agudat Yisrael

The Gaon Rabbi Meir Dan was active and involved in the organization of the Agudat Yisrael movement in Poland. Its firm establishment was important to him, and he did much on its behalf. The rabbi saw Agudat Yisrael, then known as The Organization of the Faithful of Israel, as very serious force for the strengthening of the ramparts of religion, for saving future generations for Judaism, for the prevention of the domination of anti-religious movements in the Jewish community, and for the rule of Torah in the life of the nation. Therefore he sharply opposed and totally rejected the wish of certain rabbis to appear politically unaffiliated. "At a time when full loyalty to the Torah has become a political party matter, how can a rabbi who fulfills his Torah mission see himself as unaffiliated? What rabbi can remain indifferent to the question of whether the Torah is that which determines all the ways and means of the life of the nation, or whether other factors, national or class ones, do?" he asked.

Even within the orthodox Agudat Yisrael movement Rabbi Meir Dan had his own distinct ideas and approach. A fundamental debate was then being undertaken in the new movement on the following question: who has the right to join Agudat Yisrael? The debate originated in Germany, Slovakia and Hungary, where separate orthodox communities existed [independent of the general Jewish community]. There were those who argued that only members of such separate communities could join Agudat Yisrael, since following the rulings of the giants of the Torah of the previous generation separate orthodox communities had been established. This would oblige every orthodox Jew to join these separate entities. There were even those who forbade joining the general communities, which included the non-religious and even the anti-religious, and whose provisions did not comply at all with the explicit Halacha. As opposed to them there were those who argued that it would be inappropriate to limit the world organization to the framework of the separate communities, and that it was incumbent upon Agudat Yisrael to include all Jews who observed the word of God, and not to prevent any Jew who indentified with its principles to join. Rabbi Meir Dan joined in this debate. As soon as he returned from the Agudat Yisrael mission to England and the United States he ceaselessly demanded that the gates of Agudat Yisrael should be opened to the maximum extent in order to attract the masses to its ranks. Everything should be done so that the masses would join the movement in every locale, without being overly concerned with the minutiae of their observance. The very fact of their joining and being active within the framework of Agudat Yisrael under the authority of the leaders of the Torah would bring about a turning point in their lives and in all their actions. He voiced this opinion on every occasion, whether in the conferences of Agudat Yisrael or in the meetings of the *Moetzet G'dolei Hatorah* [The Council of Torah Greats],[53] to which body he was elected on the very day of its founding.

Alongside the establishment of Agudat Yisrael in Poland was also founded the *Tz'irei Agudat Yisrael* [Young Agudat Yisrael]. Clubs were set up for young orthodox [men], along with libraries for its members and other religious youth. Many of the leading Hassidic *rebbe*s and other rabbis in Poland were strongly opposed to the very idea of setting up of religious libraries. A religious youth should study Torah. So, too, should the working youth devote every free hour to Torah and its works, and not waste time reading books of literature, meaningless stories, which may contain poison dangerous to the soul.

But the young orthodox activists, who worked to establish clubs and libraries for the religious working youth, found a champion in Rabbi Meir Dan**Error! Bookmark not defined.** Plotzky, who saw this as an imperative of the times. "The libraries for youth will prevent the reading of forbidden and dangerous books that corrupt the soul, and do not, Heaven forefend, prevent the study of the Torah," he ruled.

When in 5682 [1922] the national convention of Agudat Yisrael in Poland convened in Warsaw, Rabbi Meir Dan delivered an enthusiastic and fiery speech. He demanded of the masses to sanctify the name of Heaven by committing themselves to this undertaking. He energized the thousands who attended the convention who applauded enthusiastically. At the conclusion of his words a resounding sound blasted forth from the mouths of thousands, *Sh'ma Yisrael Adoshem Elokeinu Adoshem Echad* [*Hear, O Israel, the Lord Our God the Lord Is One*]. This scene uplifted Rabbi Meir Dan. This lecture found particular favor in his eyes, to the point where it was printed in his book, *Klei Chemdah*

---

[53] The supreme governing body of Agudat Yisrael consisting entirely of leading orthodox rabbis.

(in the section dealing with the weekly biblical portion of *Nitzavim*).[54]

The Death of the Rabbi

During his decades at his *yeshiva* in Dvart, to which many young men streamed, and during his service as rabbi of Ostrow Mazowiecka, he nurtured thousands of students. As he approached sixty he began to pine for the days of his youth, before he had burdened himself with the onus of the rabbinate and when his time was completely free for spreading the Torah, for learning and teaching. When he was approached to accept the post as head of the *Metivta yeshiva* in Warsaw, at which hundreds of young men studied, he responded positively. He even agreed to travel once again to the United States to raise the money needed to expand the *yeshiva*, to absorb hundreds of additional students, and to secure its existence. Thus, in the year 5686 [1926] the Gaon Rabbi Meir Dan left on this mission to the United States and remained there for many months.

Upon his return from the United States Rabbi Meir Dan resigned his position as rabbi of Ostrow Mazowiecka, to the distress of many of its residents who were tied to the rabbi with strong bonds of love and friendship. A spacious apartment was rented for him at 7 Marianska Street in Warsaw. The rabbi began his new job as head of the *Metivta yeshiva* and began to give his opening lectures on the Laws of the Sanctification of God's Name of the Rambam[55] [Maimonides]. The rabbi hoped that in Warsaw, the capital of Poland and the largest Jewish community in those days, he could contribute to the Jewish and religious community, whether in the framework of Agudat Yisrael or the Association of Rabbis, etc.

Rabbi Meir Dan refused at first to have a synagogue in his home. He would attend one of the many Hassidic houses of prayer of Ger in Warsaw, as just one Hassid among many. "From now on I am no longer a rabbi and am free from any of the requirements of praying at any one particular place," he said gratefully. He was fortunate in his new position, and planned to expand the framework of the *yeshiva*, to raise its status, and to transform it into a center of Torah learning in Poland. Thus, many young men began to stream to Warsaw, applying to the *Metivta*, the reputation of whose head was widely spoken of. Hundreds of young men,

---

[54] Deuteronomy, 29:9-28; 30.
[55] Acronym for **R**abbi **M**oshe **b**en **M**aimon, preeminent Sephardi Jewish philosopher, rabbi and physician (b. Cordoba, Spain, ca. 1135 [or 1138], d. Egypt, December 12, 1204).

sharp and excellent, from all over Poland wanted to study Torah directly from the mouth of the leading *gaon* of the generation.

But the happiness of Rabbi Meir Dan did not last long. Just a few months after his arrival in Warsaw he fell ill with a disease from which he never recovered. The disease got worse day by day, to the distress of his many admirers, students and friends.

Even has he lay in his sick bed the *gaon* did not stop learning with enthusiasm, innovating ideas about the Torah. In the *Compendium of Sermons* that was published by the Association of Rabbis in Poland, Volume IX, in the year 5690 [1929-1930], page 16, the Hassidic *rebbe* Rabbi Yitzchak Zelig of Sokolow wrote, "Our colleague, the Hassid and Gaon Rabbi Meir Dan, chief of the rabbinical court of Ostroveh, just a few days before his death wrote me a letter reminding me to pray with him that he would be cured of his illness. He also wrote a note to clarify the text of the Mechilta on the weekly Bible portion of *Vayakhel*.[56] I replied to him briefly to gladden him with words of Torah, knowing that words of Torah would make him feel better and that the light of the Torah will make him live. My reply did not reach him before he went up to heaven, to our great regret. I greatly loved his words of Torah that he innovated when he was beset with pain (may we not know of such), and this was Torah that he taught despite all this and remains to his credit."

It is told that shortly before his death an expert physician, one of the great doctors of Poland, stood at his bedside. The doctor said to him that if you invest all your desires in a particular matter, and you derive maximal unlimited pleasure from it, it will stimulate strength within you that will help fight the disease and you might be able to overcome it.

When the doctor left, the Gaon Rabbi Meir Dan said, "In fact I have been fortunate to be counted among the type of rabbis who are sufficiently knowledgeable to deal with very serious and complex questions. So if I invest all my strength in this, it is clear that I will derive great pleasure from it, that I will be strengthened. But this will not be strength but rather pride, conceit, egoism. It is better to die than to fall into the morass of pride...."

In his last days he even wrote a will, saying that it might even help to lengthen his days. In his will he asked his sons, the Gaon Rabbi Yisrael Natan and the Gaon Rabbi Chanoch Henich, to publish the lectures that he gave on the observance of the Sabbath and to print his many Torah novellae. His pain grew from day to day, but it did not detract from his great concentration until the last moment of his life.

---

[56] Exodus, 25-28:20.

On the sixth day of Nissan 5688 [March 27, 1928], the Gaon Rabbi Meir Dan departed for on high, not quite attaining the age of sixty-two. There was much mourning after the death of this *gaon* and honored one of his generation. Many eulogies were given about him all across the Jewish world.

Appendix I -
Rabbi Plotzky's Visits to the United States

U.S. passenger ship list records confirm that Rabbi Plotzky made two trips to the United States:

1. He arrived in New York City on the S.S. Adriatic from Southampton on May 27, 1921 (under the name Majer Don Plocki, age 54, Rabbi [written over "Priest"], from Ostrowo, Lomza Gubernia, Poland), traveling with Rabbi Josef Srul Lew, another member of the Agudat Yisrael delegation (see below). They were both marked as non-immigrants on three-month visits, with their trips being financed by the "Israel World Organisation" [sic]. Their destination was 194 Henry Street, New York.
2. He arrived on the S.S. Mauretania from Cherbourg on May 14, 1926 (under the name Majer-Don Plocki, age 58, Rabbi [written over "Rev'd."], from Ostrow, Poland, Warszawska 22). He was marked as planning to remain permanently, with his destination being Congregation Beth-Chasidim of Poland. He was also listed as having a medical condition, a hernia.

The 1921 visit is described in several sources, including the book, *The Struggle and the Splendor*, by the late Rabbi Moshe Sherer (published by Agudath Israel of America, 1982), which is a history of that organization. Rabbi Sherer writes that in 1921 "a distinguished European Agudath Israel delegation came to the United States seeking to strengthen Torah allegiance and organize an Agudah movement here. Led by one of the outstanding gaonim of Poland, the Ostrover Rav, Rabbi Meir Don Plotzky, the group included Rabbi Asher Spitzer of Kurdorf [Kirchdorf], Slovakia, Rabbi Dr. Meir Hildesheimer of Berlin, Dr. Nathan Birnbaum, and Rabbi Joseph Lev." The book includes the photograph below of these five individuals, with Rabbi Plotzky at the center.

Left to right: Rabbi Asher Spitzer, Rabbi Dr. Meir Hildesheimer, Rabbi Meir Don Plotzky, Rabbi Joseph Lev, and Dr. Nathan Birnbaum, upon their arrival in America in 1921

Reproduced with permission from Agudath Israel of America

According to one source, on one of his visits to America, Rabbi Plotzky pronounced Manischewitz matza to be thoroughly reliable ("there is none more faithful to be found"). See Rebecca Kobrin, ed., Chosen Capital: The Jewish Encounter with American Capitalism, New Brunswick: Rutgers University Press, 2012.

Appendix II - The Plotzky Family

The Jewish records of Dvart (Warta) indexed by Jewish Records Indexing (JRI)-Poland record the following births for the children of Rabbi Plotzky:

Lajb Lajzer (name given in the above chapter in Hebrew as **Eliezer Yehuda**), birth recorded in 1884, death recorded in 1902.

Binem, birth recorded in 1886.

Genoch (name given in the above chapter as **Chanoch Henich**), birth recorded in 1892; perished in the Holocaust with his wife **Yiska**, as recorded by a Page of Testimony at Yad Vashem in Jerusalem and in the Yizkor book of the town of Turek.

Izrail Nason (name given in the above chapter as **Yisrael Natan**), birth recorded in 1894; perished in the Holocaust with his family.

Chana Genendel, birth recorded in 1894; described in the above chapter as having married and died young.

Sura, birth recorded in 1894; described in the above chapter as having married and died young.

Mordka, birth recorded in 1902.

Ginda, birth recorded in 1902.

Rabbi Plotzky is buried in the huge Okopowa Street Jewish cemetery in Warsaw, sharing a *matzevah* (headstone) with his father, **Rabbi Chaim Yitzchak** son of Yisrael (d. September 5, 1909). His Hebrew name is given as **Meir Dan Refael**. The name Refael, Hebrew for "God has healed," may have been added during his final illness as a prayer for his recovery.

The death of Rabbi Plotzky's wife, **Tziril (Cyrla)**, was recorded in Ostrow Mazowiecka in 1930.

Chapter Seven
The Gaon Rabbi Yaakov Shraga Singer

The Gaon Rabbi Zalman Sorotzkin

After the Gaon Rabbi Meir Dan Plotzky resigned his rabbinical seat in Ostrow Mazowiecka, the question of appointing someone to fill this exalted position arose in the community. The decisive majority of the members of the administration and council of the community were members of the Agudat Yisrael movement. So at the meeting of the central committee of that movement, which took place in the year 5688 [1927-1928] in Warsaw, it was decided to put forth the candidacy of the Gaon Rabbi Zalman Sorotzkin[57] as rabbi of Ostrow Mazowiecka. The members of Agudat Yisrael in Ostroveh took it upon themselves to carry out this decision. Rabbi Sorotzkin was invited to the city, spoke in the synagogue, and quickly became liked by everyone. In his brief stay in the city he founded a society for the study of Talmud in the new study hall. In fulfilling its aim of establishing a permanent daily lecture, this society, which later counted some one hundred fifty members, functioned up until the destruction of Ostrow Mazowiecka.

In a joint session of the executive and council of the community, Rabbi Sorotzkin was elected unanimously as rabbi and chief of the rabbinical court. At the same time the community of Lutzk, much larger and older than Ostrow Mazowiecka, also chose Rabbi Zalman Sorotzkin as its rabbi and teacher. The rabbi preferred the position in Lutzk and moved there. The community of Ostrow Mazowiecka remained without a rabbi and chief of the rabbinical court. The residents of the city began searching for a candidate, a well known personality, a brilliant and lofty *gaon*, who would be worthy of filling the place of the famous rabbis of Ostrow Mazowiecka, who were renowned for their accomplishments.

Meanwhile Rabbi Meir Dan Plotzky had died in Warsaw. His heirs, his sons and son-in-law, each of whom was worthy of the rabbinate, claimed the right of inheritance. But many members of the community opposed the idea, which was customary then in Poland. The leaders of the community agreed to deal with the heirs of the rabbi. After long discussions it was decided to choose the Gaon Yisrael Natan Plotzky, son of the Gaon Rabbi Meir Dan Plotzky, as a *dayan* and teacher in the city, while the members of the rabbi's family conceded their demand for the rabbinate itself.

---

[57] Then rabbi of Zhetyl [Zhetl in Yiddish, Dziatlava in Polish, in Grodno *gubernia*, now in Belarus].

The Candidacy of the Gaon Rabbi Yaakov Shraga Singer

There then appeared in Ostrow Mazowiecka the Hassidic *rebbe* Rabbi Yosef of Amshinov, who had served for many years as chief of the rabbinical court of the city and who had great influence on its residents. He proposed the candidacy of his well known son-in-law, the Gaon Rabbi Yaakov Shraga Singer, as rabbi of the city. At first many of the residents refused to accept this proposal. The candidate rabbi appeared too young to occupy the seat of the revered Gaon Rabbi Meir Dan Plotzky. The residents split into a number of factions, some of whom supported the proposal of the *rebbe* of Amshinov, while other vigorously opposed it, while still others took a passive position.

This internal controversy in the community went on for about two years, until a decision was made under the direction of the Hassidic *rebbe* of Ger, Rabbi Avraham**Error! Bookmark not defined.** Mordechai**Error! Bookmark not defined.** Alter, whose many local adherents proved to be a decisive factor. The large community of Ger Hassidim joined the camp favoring the candidacy of Rabbi Yaakov Shraga Singer.[58] A joint meeting of the executive and council of the community convened, and by a majority vote Rabbi Yaakov Shraga Singer was elected as the last rabbi of this glorious community.

Rabbi Singer quickly succeeded in capturing the hearts of all the residents of the city. Even those who were opposed to his selection became his friends and admirers. In the ten years of his service from the year 5690 [1930] until the destruction of the community, all the groups of residents, irrespective of their many and diverse affiliations, united around the rabbi, who succeeded in fulfilling his mission with honor, to the credit of his community. His loyalty and honesty, his devotion and willingness to sacrifice proved that Rabbi Singer was indeed worthy of this honored position.

Rabbi Yaakov Shraga Singer was born in Alexander [Alexandrow Lodzki] in the year 5659 [1898-1899] to his father the Gaon Rabbi Yitzchak Meir Singer, the rabbi of Alexander and the son of the Gaon Rabbi Eliahu Singer, rabbi of Peshischa and chief of the rabbinical court of Kalish. Rabbi Yitzchak Meir was the son-in-law of the Hassidic *rebbe* Rabbi Shmuel Tzvi of Alexander,[59]

---

[58] Note that the author's text repeatedly and erroneously gives the rabbi's name as "Silber" ["Zilber"], rather than "Singer" ["Zinger"] in this paragraph, but we have corrected it accordingly. Other sources occasionally add the common middle name of "Feivel" to "Shraga" as well.

[59] Rabbi Shmuel Tzvi Danciger (1840-1923), the third Alexander *rebbe*.

author of *Tiferet Shmuel* [*The Glory of Samuel*]. He was raised and educated in the court of his grandfather, where there were many Hassidim. When he was still young he transferred to the *yeshiva* of his father's father, the Gaon Rabbi Eliahu, in Kalish.

The Gaon Rabbi Yaakov Shraga Singer, may God avenge his blood

There he continued to learn with great intensity and excelled in his knowledge of Torah and in his faith, in his Hassidism and in his superlative personality.

The Great Wedding in Ostroveh

In the year 5677 [1916-1917] he married the daughter of the Hassidic *rebbe* Rabbi Yosef of Amshinov, who was then serving as the rabbi of Ostrow Mazowiecka. The wedding took place in that city in the presence of the grandfather of the groom and the grandfather of the bride, the Hassidic *rebbe* Rabbi Menachem of Amshinov and the Hassidic *rebbe* Shmuel Tzvi of Alexander. Throngs of Hassidim arrived at that time in Ostroveh and celebrated the nuptials for seven full days, as the residents of the city participated in the celebration of the *rebbe*s with great joy.

Rabbi Yaakov Shraga remained in Ostrow Mazowiecka about a year staying close to the presence of his father-in-law. When Rabbi Yosef left the seat of the rabbinate in the city and went to serve as *rebbe* and chief of the rabbinical court in Amshinov, all the members of his family went with him, among them Rabbi Yaakov Shraga. For years he was close to his father-in-law and spent all his time studying Torah and doing good deeds. After that he moved to Alexander, to the court of his uncle, the Hassidic *rebbe* Yitzchak Menachem[60] (may God avenge his blood), devoting his time to advancing himself in terms of Torah and Hassidism. He completed his studies in the teaching of the law and became expert in both the early and later decisors.

Upon his elevation to the seat of the rabbinate in Ostrow Mazowiecka, Rabbi Yaakov Shraga devoted all his energies to raising the level of Torah and the rabbinate in the city, to the strengthening of the ramparts of religion and to Torah education. In the early years of his tenure his father-in-law, Rabbi Yosef of Amshinov, stood closely by him. He would frequently visit the city and help the young rabbi to strengthen his position. The influence of the rabbi of Amshinov on the residents of Ostrow Mazowiecka in general, and on his many Hassidim there, was great. Residents of all classes and movements recalled his years of service in the city, and his loving concern for all, his devotion to every human being. The *rebbe* of Amshinov had many loyal and devoted friends and they did not abandon their ties of friendship with him. Whenever Rabbi Yosef appeared in Ostrow Mazowiecka he was received with royal honors. Many people would light candles and place them in the windows facing the street. Many streamed to greet him and to receive his personal blessing. These were days of holiday and spiritual uplifting for the local residents.

Rabbi Yaakov Shraga quickly strengthened his position as rabbi of the city. His authority extended over everyone. He had superlative traits and related to all people with heartfelt warmth and honesty. Gradually even those who were distant from him grew nearer to the rabbi.

Sometimes they were invited to his home and were charmed by his words and his teaching. The young rabbi infused honor and worthiness into this glorious community.

For the Sake of the Honor of the Torah

While his approach towards secular, day-to-day matters was flexible, his stand on matters of religion, Torah, Halacha and respect for the divine was assertive and non-compromising. Since the days of its founding, Ostrow Mazowiecka had never known any public desecrations of the Sabbath within its boundaries. All the merchants and peddlers, storekeepers and artisans rested from their labors on the Sabbath and holidays. Until there appeared the

---

[60] Rabbi Yitzchak Menachem Mendel Danciger (1880-1943), the fourth Alexander *rebbe*.

owner of a barber shop who, on the Sabbath of Repentance, opened the doors of his barber shop for business for all to see.

Orthodox Ostroveh was shaken to its core. When the matter was reported to the rabbi, he ceased his prayers and went out into the street of the city accompanied by the *dayan*, the Gaon Rabbi Yisrael Natan**Error! Bookmark not defined.** Plotzky. Hundreds of residents joined them in protest near the barber shop. The rabbi was prepared for anything. He said to himself that he was determined to prevent this breach in the wall of the Sabbath at all costs. Rabbi Yaakov Shraga, accompanied by hundreds of activists, entered the barber shop and requested of the barber that he close the doors of the shop. But the man lashed out derisively, laughing at the rabbi and the *dayanim*. He insisted that he would not close the barber shop, come what may.

Meanwhile the crowd that had gathered at the place grew even larger. The windowpanes of the shop were broken because of the crush of people, the door was unhinged. The rabbi stood inside, fully prepared to stay all day in the barber shop, even to celebrate his Sabbath there, in order to prevent any violation of the Sabbath. The owner of the barber shop, who had begun to fear the anger of the crowd, raised his voice in an hysterical cry, saying that people were attacking him, were about to kill him. Soon the police arrived, but they were not able to control the crowd. The commander of the local police, a sworn anti-Semite, called on the army for help. He quickly alerted his superiors in Lomza, the district capital, saying, "An uprising has broken out in Ostrow Mazowiecka, led by the rabbi and his cohorts." A unit of fully armed soldiers rushed to the city from nearby Komorowo. The soldiers shot into the air, and the crowd quickly dispersed. The police immediately arrested the rabbi, the *dayan* Rabbi Yisrael Natan**Error! Bookmark not defined.** Plotzky, and several prominent residents: Reb Mendel Lichtenstein, Reb Moshe Grudka, Reb Moshe Yosef Suravich [Surawicz] and others.

For the Sake of Sabbath Observance

For the rest of that Sabbath day the rabbi and the other prisoners remained in the local jail, immersed in fasting. At the close of the Sabbath the council of the community and representatives of the Jews in town met in a special meeting. They decided to do everything in order to free the prisoners and to prevent the escalation of the event by the police, who were antagonistic towards the Jews. The district attorney, based in Lomza, had discretion in the case. The leaders of the community contacted the leaders of the community in Lomza and succeeded in setting up a meeting with the district attorney on Sunday, the official day of rest in all of Poland. The next morning representatives of the community of Ostroveh left for Lomza.

The representatives of the community of Ostroveh and the people of the community of Lomza explained the background of the entire matter to the district attorney, that it was not an illegal uprising or demonstration against the authorities, but rather an internal matter among Jews based on purely religious criteria that were of no interest whatsoever to the authorities. The attorney was convinced, and issued an order to the commander of the police in Ostrow Mazowiecka to release the prisoners immediately, in consideration of bail of two hundred zlotys per person. It was on the Sunday before Yom Kippur that Rabbi Yaakov Shraga and his associates were freed from prison, after a fast that in fact lasted some twenty-four hours, having refused to taste the non-Jewish food that was given to them. The residents of Ostrow Mazowiecka prepared for the fast, happy about the release of the rabbi but angry about the breach of the fence that took place among them that was forced by the man's refusal to retract his evil deed. Thus, the wall of the Sabbath in the city was never breached until the last day of its existence.

In the Days of the Holocaust

The days of the terrible Holocaust had arrived. A few days after the outbreak of the war the German hordes entered Ostrow Mazowiecka, after bloody battles in the surrounding area. Germans were now seen galloping in the streets. Immediately the sad news spread among the confused and frightened Jews that the murderers had arrested sixteen Jews at random, taking them out to be killed. The bodies of these martyrs were hanging in the street, surrounded by members of their families crying over their tragedy.

At the risk of his life, Rabbi Yaakov Shraga, along with Rabbi Moshe**Error! Bookmark not defined.** Rosenzweig, Reb Shimon Hersh Goldwasser and Reb Yaakov Farbiarz, rushed out to collect the bodies of the martyrs and to give them a Jewish burial. They proceeded to the Jewish cemetery, as the families of the victims, widows and orphaned children, accompanied them. In the cemetery the rabbi and his followers opened the graves and prepared to bury the bodies. Suddenly Nazi troops appeared, laughing at their misfortune and ordering the rabbi and his helpers and the family members of the murdered ones to descend into the graves. "We will take care of the burials of the dead," the bloodthirsty murderers said laughing cynically.

The rabbis and his aides immediately knew the meaning of what was happening. The women and children raised their voices in a horrific scream that pierced the heavens. The murderers now "softened up," satisfied with merely a few blows that they inflicted upon the group and left. Mournful and sad the rabbi and his helpers and the afflicted families returned to their homes. The horrendous and fearsome period of the Holocaust had begun, a period of loss, suffering, destruction and murder leading to the great sacrifice of Polish Jewry.

The Jews of Ostrow Mazowiecka once again knew not a moment of respite. The bloodthirsty German dogs carried on, killing and wounding, angrily crushing the unfortunate Jews into the ground. On the second day of Rosh Hashanah the men of the Gestapo arrived. They arrested the rabbi, Rabbi Yaakov Shraga, and the secretary of the community, Rabbi Tuviah Makover, and imprisoned them in the old study hall. With torture and maltreatment they transported them around the streets of the city. Rabbi Tuviah was forced to cut off the beard of Rabbi Yaakov Shraga, chief of the rabbinical court, and the rabbi was forced to cut off the beard of the secretary of the community, as the sound of laughter at their plight was heard from the murderers and from Poles who had gathered to view the suffering of the Jews.

The Escape to Slonim

Broken and crushed the rabbi returned to his home. After two more days he was arrested again. This time he was faced with demands to supply the Gestapo with five kilograms of gold within twenty-four hours, whether in the form of jewelry or wedding rings of Jewish women. These wild beasts imposed the task of collecting the gold on the rabbi. He had to go from house to house removing the rings and taking items of value out from their hiding places and giving them over to the murderers, lest he be punished severely.

Children of the Gaon Rabbi Yaakov Shraga Singer, Avraham Eliezer and Shmuel Tzvi, and their cousin, Shmuel Tzvi, may God avenge their blood

Rabbi Yaakov Shraga did not want to abandon the people of his community in these bitter and mad times. But he had no means of standing up against this German blackmail. Most of the Jews of the city had run away. There remained in Ostrow Mazowiecka only a small number of the poor and the sick. So lacking an alternative the trusted and devoted rabbi was also compelled to escape with his family to the border under cover of darkness, slipping away to the Soviet zone of occupation to evade the terrible enemy. Before Yom Kippur Rabbi Yaakov Shraga and his wife and ten children arrived in Slonim, which was then in the hands of the Soviet forces of occupation.

The rabbi had intended to continue on to Vilna, but he did not succeed in doing so. Only his son Rabbi Yechiel Menachem[61] reached there. His life was saved thanks to his subsequent escape to the United States, and remained the only survivor of this distinguished family.

Many refugees from Ostrow Mazowiecka were concentrated in Slonim.[62] The rabbi of the city, the Gaon Rabbi Yehuda Leib Fein (may God avenge his blood), died when the Nazis had captured the

[61] Rabbi Yechiel Menachem Singer (1919-1988), who at the end of his life was the Alexander *rebbe* in America.

[62] Among them was this editor's great-aunt, Dina Feinzeig Weinzimmer, her husband Meir, and their four children, Feigeh, Zalman, Avraham and Moshe.

city, before they handed it over to the Soviets in accord with their treaty of friendship and its division of captured Poland between Nazi Germany and the Soviet Union. From that point on Rabbi Yaakov Shraga served as the *de facto*, if not the *de jure*, rabbi of the members of the community in general, and the patron of the many of the refugees from Ostrow Mazowiecka in particular.

The Sanctification of God's Name

For about a year and half Rabbi Yaakov Shraga and his family suffered terribly in the communist-occupied part of eastern Poland. During this period he occupied himself with Torah and good works, with the uplifting of Hassidism and pure fear of God, until the war between Germany and Russia broke out. Within a few days the Nazis captured Slonim before the Jews had had the opportunity to escape. Once again the masses of refugees from Ostroveh, headed by Rabbi Yaakov Shraga, were caught up in a horrific bloody trap, in a dark ghetto established by the bloody German dogs after violent attacks on the Jews of Slonim.

The suffering went on about a year, in terrible and frightful conditions. The Jews walked around like human skeletons in the dark ghetto. In the summer of the year 5702, on June 29, 1942, Belorussian police surround the large ghetto in Slonim, where some 10,000 Jews were concentrated, the remnants of three previous *aktion*s that were conducted by the murderers against the Jews. It was four in the morning when they broke into the ghetto like cruel wild animals, terrible bloody dogs, shooting in all directions. With the raging fury of cannibals they removed the poor, starving, broken and crushed Jews. And under a hail of bullets and murderous beatings thousands of Jews were swept along towards the fields of Petralevich. That same morning Rabbi Yaakov Shraga Singer and his family were taken out of their bunker and moved to the prison in Randinsky, where they were held for a day and night in frightful conditions.

The next day Rabbi Yaakov Shraga and his wife, the *rebbetzin* [the wife of a rabbi] Yuta, and their children Roza, Pesya, Efraim, Eliezer, Shmuel Tzvi, Rivka Chaya, Shifra Devora, Sarah Golda and Yosefa, were taken to the site of the destruction of the martyrs of Slonim, the tree-lined streets of Cheplova [Chepelev], and along with thousands of other martyrs they ascended in a whirlwind to the heavens. May God avenge their blood.

Chapter Eight
From World War I to World War II

At the Outbreak of World War I

For all intents and purposes, the final phase of the Jewish community of Ostrow Mazowiecka began with the outbreak of World War I. These twenty-five years were under the disintegrating government of the harsh Russians and under the government of the Polish enemies, who excelled in their oppression of the Jews, in the undermining of their economic status, and in the absence of any continuous period of calm. The foreign and alien Polish land that tolerated the presence of the eternal people over hundreds of years suddenly began to burn beneath the feet of the Jews, so well versed in suffering.

The dark clouds that covered the sky of the Jews of Europe in general, and the skies of the Jews of Poland in particular, with the arrival of the Holocaust, could already be seen from afar at the outbreak of World War I. The Poles, who were never known for their love of the Jews, despite the loyalty shown to them at every opportunity, increased their hatred of the Jews. The hatred of the Poles towards toward the Jews was unparalleled during this period.

The understandable enmity of the Poles towards the Russians, derived from their subjugation and oppression, was transformed into hatred for the Jews. The bitterness that had accumulated within Polish nationalism caused their leaders to turn on the weak Jews, as it is always easier to attack the weak, to express their hatred vis-a-vis the Jews rather than toward the Russians, the powerful rulers. The average Pole, the farmer and the worker, the clerk and the landowner, readily accepted the narrative that said that all the troubles that had befallen the Poles were because of the traitorous Jews.

In the eyes of the Pole the Jew was to blame for everything. The influential Catholic clergy stirred up incitement against the Jews at every turn. They portrayed the Jew in the eyes of those Poles, who were loyal to the clergy, as an inferior creature, for whom treason was a basic and natural characteristic. He only came to Poland to suck the good blood of the Poles and to poison the pure Polish environment. Because of the Jews the natives of the land had lost their independence. And meanwhile they were not able to free themselves from the great powers that suppressed them.

Therefore, it was not the harsh, cruel, violent Russian policeman who was the principal enemy of the Poles, nor the

German Junker who thirsted after conquests and sought to oppress his neighbors, nor the Austrian officer, who sought from afar to rule lands that did not belong to him, who was conceited and who mocked the Pole and all Poles, and who despised their culture in Galicia. No, the true foe was the Jew, and only when the Jewish Diaspora in Poland was destroyed would the Pole succeed.

Anti-Semitism above All Else

Anti-Semitism was not only the province of those loyal to the Catholic clergy or of the broader nationalist circles. Rather it was also a part of the labor and farmers' movements, the revolutionary organizations and even of the left. Writers and fighters for freedom who worked hard for the independence of Poland were unable to conceal their anti-Semitism, which found full expression at every opportunity. The constant worship of the Poles, of Polish culture, and of everything Polish by the assimilationists and partial assimilationists of Jewish origin did not change matters one iota. The Jew remained a Jew in the eyes of the Pole, one whom he hated with all his heart. Hatred of the Jews became second nature to the Poles, an integral part of their existence and their core character. The Polish child suckled anti-Semitism already in his cradle. The ignorant Polish lad knew that "thief meant the Jewish merchant, cheat the Jewish artisan, child killer the Jewish doctor, and rabbi, the one who collected the blood of Christian children for the baking of *matzot* [unleavened bread] for the Jewish holiday of Passover."

Even when the Poles needed the assistance of the Jews they were unable to conceal their strong anti-Jewish feelings that beat within their hearts, and this was even before the anti-Semitism of the Poles increased even more in the decades before the Holocaust. As early as the year 1863, when Polish nationalists rose up against the cruel Russian oppressor, the Polish commanders of the rebellion issued enthusiastic calls to the Jews asking them to join the ranks of the fighters, calling upon them as "brother" residents fighting against a foreign occupier that must be expelled. Many Jews responded to these calls, fighting heart and soul. But the Poles did not hesitate to re-pay the Jews in kind. Immediately after the suppression of the revolt by the Russians, there were pogroms against the Jews in Warsaw and other cities. The Russians, who were angry about the help given by the Jews during the rebellion, stood aside and did not prevent the Polish mobs from carrying on. The Polish clergy, which stood behind the rebellion and preached ceaselessly on behalf of nationalism, also benefited. If it did not achieve the main goal of freeing Poland from the Russians and from the Orthodox Church, at least another goal was accomplished, namely that pogroms against the Jews were conducted.

Accusations against the Jews

When World War I broke out, and the possibility of liberating themselves from the yoke of Russian occupation first arose for Polish nationalists, the anti-Semitic Poles nevertheless saw it as their first duty to incite the Russian authorities against the Jews, "those perpetual traitors, those spies on behalf of the Germans and the Austrians." The Russians were never philo-Semites, so they readily accepted the Polish accusations. There was no lack of extremely committed anti-Semites among them who were only too glad for the opportunity to carry on and oppress "the Jewish spies," and to inflict pogroms upon them.

During the early days of the war a large Russian army passed through Ostrow Mazowiecka. Made up of divisions that resulted from the great draft, it was under the command of General Samsonov, and was assigned to penetrate into East Prussia. They succeeded in capturing a number of cities and towns, to the glory of tsarist Russia as a whole. Not long passed, however, before it became clear that these were illusive victories, a trap thought out in advance by the commander of the German troops in East Prussia, Marshal Hindenburg. He tricked the huge army of General Samsonov into a steel trap in order to wipe out this force and then to attack the Russian rear behind the Russian lines along the Vistula River.

The Russians figured out the German trap too late. The Russian defeat in this first stage of the war was total. Masses of confused soldiers began to flee. Gigantic columns of soldiers in tatters, many of them lacking weapons, some with shoes and some barefoot, retreated via Ostrow Mazowiecka further inland towards Russia. Suddenly it was revealed to the Russian command that which many knew beforehand, that the Russian army was riddled with spies, and that the Russian officer corps--which lacked any Jews, as they were prohibited from being admitted--did not lack for traitors. These were mostly Poles or Germans who were residents of Russia, Ukrainians, as well as Russians who did not shrink from taking bribes.

The Russian command, consumed as it was with hatred of the Jews, did not seek out those who were guilty where it was possible to find them. It rather preferred to follow in the footsteps of Polish incitement, to see the Jew as the spy, as the guilty one. The Jew was selling out Russia and Poland to Germany. The Poles knew how to explain to Russian soldiers how they had found a telephone in the synagogue that connected the rabbi to the

German command at the front. The Jews were collecting information and transmitting it to their rabbi, who would immediately ring up the German commander. The largely ignorant Russian soldiers believed these accusatory stories with all their hearts. They saw the Jews as the cause of their retreat and of the deaths of their comrades. So it was no wonder, therefore, that they pounced on every Jew that they encountered.

The Danger of Total Expulsion

In Ostrow Mazowiecka, located at the crossroads of the main highways from East Prussia, the impact of the great Russian disaster was fully felt. Hatred of the Jews on the part of the defeated Russian commanders and officers grew day by day. Jewish leaders were arrested for no reason and exiled to Siberia. Jews who were evicted from nearby towns that were closer to the German front filled the houses in Ostroveh. And the shadow of an expulsion order against the Jews of Ostrow Mazowiecka hovered in the air. Fear beset the city that was full of refugees who were lacking in everything and without any means of support, fear that was well founded as people looked forward to a future that was obscured by an ominous fog.

The taste of war was already felt in Jewish Ostroveh in the first days after the outbreak of World War I, when a German bomb exploded in the municipal horse market, directly causing the death of three Jewish teamsters, Chaim Hersh, Yitzchak and Avika (the father). As the failures of the Russians increased, so did the suffering of the Jews. The battle lines shifted from East Prussia to Poland itself, between the Rivers Narew and Bzura. Ostroveh increasingly filled with refugees from the surrounding area. All the Jews of Rozan, Chorzel [Chorzele], Myszyniec, and other towns were expelled. The Jews of the city were concerned that an order of evacuation of the city would be proclaimed any day.

Under Siege and in Distress

The merchants were pauperized, the artisans had no work, many suffered the humiliation of hunger at extreme levels. But many of the residents exhibited devotion and resourcefulness. They helped the refugees and took care of the poor. Trusted leaders did everything for the expellees, who had arrived naked and lacking everything. The heads of the community obtained large quantities of tobacco and cigarettes, and distributed them generously to the soldiers who passed through Ostrow Mazowiecka in their retreat so that they would not carry on too much, so that they would not pillage the Jews. For who can trust an embittered soldier who is subject to unremitting incitement?

Most of the houses of Ostrow Mazowiecka in those days were made of wood, hence were highly flammable. Therefore the Jews were afraid lest there was truth to the rumor that the Russians would burn the entire city down the moment that they would have to retreat from the area and abandon the place. Sad news that came from various places indirectly seemed to confirm these worries. The fact that many Jews of substance in Ostroveh had been expelled to the interior of Russia and even to Siberia depressed the remaining leaders, but did not weaken their hands.

The leaders of the community did everything to avert a disaster. The military commander of the area, General Dudenko, was one of the more liberal officers who served in the Russian army. He related to the Jews with some sympathy, and promised a Jewish delegation that he would save Jewish Ostroveh, and actually stood by his promise. In the winter of the year 5675 [1914-1915] a relative calm came over the front. The Germans fortified themselves along their new lines, re-organizing their positions in anticipation of a summer offensive. The Russians sent forces to the new lines, and prepared for the next stage. The Jews looked forward with dread to what would come.

In the summer of 5675 [1915] bitter battles broke out. The great, well planned German attack began. Once again the weakness of the Russian army became apparent, consumed as it was by rot, full of spies and traitors. The Germans knew all the weak spots in the Russian front. They were updated on all the movements of the tsarist command and knew in advance all its movements. The Russian espionage service was shown to be worthless, lacking any information of significance. The little information that it did have was in fact prepared by the German intelligence service in order to send the Russian forces into snares and traps.

The Years under Imperial German Rule

The fact that some Russian commanders and officers, governors and civil servants, were found to be spies did not prevent the defeated Russian authorities from casting the blame on the Jews, and from killing hundreds, even thousands of Jews who were completely innocent, in order to satisfy their murderous desires or to cover up their failures and helplessness. The situation of the Jews grew worse from day to day. The supreme Russian command ordered that Jews be expelled from the battle zone, but General Dudenko kept his promise. The Jews of Ostrow Mazowiecka remained in their homes and breathed more easily when the first soldiers of the imperial German army appeared at the gates of the city.

But the German occupation, which brought with it relative security, also brought starvation and want, and in their wake illnesses and plagues. As soon as German rule was established locally the new occupiers began to systematically requisition every supply of value. Commerce was completely shut down. Immediately a complete lack of everything was felt. Even bread was not to be had. In exchange for ration coupons every resident was given two hundred twenty grams of bread per day. Long lines were seen every day near the bakeries, which found it difficult to supply even the reduced rations. The bread was baked with cheap flour, sometimes mixed with waste. Everything of value was taken by the Germans and sent to Germany, which was already hungry for everything.

In difficult, abnormal circumstances, albeit in relative personal security, the Jews of Ostrow Mazowiecka lived through three years of German occupation. The condition of the Germans got more serious day by day. Scarcity of everything was felt. They requisitioned everything of value. The hunger resulted in illnesses and plagues, while the imperial German authorities were not concerned with the situation of the residents of the occupied areas in general, and of the Jews in particular.

As always, the Germans were harsh and cruel, given to strict discipline, but did not have a specifically anti-Jewish policy. On the contrary, the Jew, whose Yiddish "jargon" was his mother tongue, was able to speak to the German by adding some German or German-like words into his Yiddish. By the same token the Poles did not understand German, and the Germans had never heard Polish. The sounds of Slavic were completely alien to the ears of the descendants of the Teutonic tribes. The Jew usually served as interpreter and intermediary between the German ruler and the Pole, which was a benefit to the Jew.

In Independent Poland

In the beginning of the year 5679 [fall 1918] the entire German front broke down and the militaristic rule of the kaiser completely disintegrated. Confused and afraid, the Germans retreated back to Germany. The Poles received full political independence in accordance with the Treaty of Versailles, which was signed at that time. A large Republic of Poland arose, which stretched from Silesia and Pomerania in the west to Ukraine and Belarus in the east. The Poles rejoiced as they freed themselves from the chains of captivity of the Germans, the Austrians and the Russians. But the fullest expression of their joy was to be found in their wild carryings on against the Jews. Priests incited their church goers and officers and their soldiers. It was dangerous for a Jew, especially a Jew with a beard, to pass by a military base. The draftees from the districts of Poznan and Pomerania, under the command of the hostile General Haller, were particularly noted for their wild behavior.

The head of state, Marshal Pilsudski, the fighter and dreamer of Polish independence, was not among the virulent anti-Semites in the military service. In his youth he was member of the Polish socialist party, and many of his friends and colleagues were Jews. But neither was he particularly concerned with the fate of the Jews, which was at times unbearable. He did not intervene against criminal acts that his officers carried out against the Jews. He was preoccupied with the restoration of the Polish state and the establishment of the Polish army that would successfully defend the borders of the state. Only in very rare cases did he intervene on behalf of the Jews, to put down incitement and blood libels against them.

The Bolshevik Invasion

The western borders of Poland were with the defeated Germany, which had to accept the international terms that were set down in the Treaty of Versailles. On the other hand, independent Poland never came to an agreement about borders with Soviet Russia, which had signed a peace treaty with imperial Germany immediately after the revolution against the tsar.[63] Having been based on very temporary armistice lines, independent Poland, with the support of the West, was interested in establishing borders deep inside Belarus and Ukraine, arguing that these territories were once Polish and were appropriately placed under Polish rule. On the other hand, the Bolshevik Soviets did not agree with this aspiration. Attempts to resolve the dispute peacefully went nowhere. In the summer of the year 5680 [1920], the Red Army invaded Poland. After very brief battles it began to conquer broad territories and to gallop towards Warsaw, the Polish capital. The Polish armies under the command of Marshal Pilsudski quickly fell back to battle lines set up along the Vistula River, which crosses the entire length of Poland.

Serving as Commissar for Military Affairs and as commander of the Soviet Russian troops at the time was Leon Trotsky. He had no ties whatsoever to Jews or Judaism, from which he stemmed. But in the eyes of the masses of Poles, Trotsky symbolized the Jews, Jewish rule. The anti-Semites in Poland had no doubt in their assumption that the millions of Jews in Poland were loyal to

---

[63] The Treaty of Brest-Litovsk of March 3, 1918, which had ceded vast territories of the western part of the former Russian Empire, including Poland, to Germany.

Trotsky without hesitation. They were representatives of the communist regime in Russia, were serving as spies on his behalf and saboteurs against the Polish army, and committing every crime and providing every assistance to the Bolshevik occupation forces.

There was no limit or end to the bloody accusations that usually ended tragically for the Jews of Poland. There were only a few communities where Jews were not hanged without justification as Poles exulted. False witnesses, malice and wickedness were never lacking. The Polish authorities never investigated very much when a Jew was accused of espionage or sabotage, and quickly came to a judgment of death without much discussion.

Jewish Blood Spilt in the Streets

Once two members of the Polish provisional assembly, who were representatives of Agudat Yisrael, the Gaon Rabbi Avraham Tzvi Perlmutter and the Gaon Rabbi Moshe Eliahu Halperin, appeared before Marshal Pilsudski and pleaded before him to vacate one such an evil judgment. It had been based entirely on falsehoods and resulted in a death sentence against a young Jew, the only son of his parents. The head of the Polish general staff replied with great anger, "Today two Christians accused of treason were hanged, and not a single priest came to argue on their behalf. And now one Jew is about to be hanged for the crime of treason and two rabbis come to intervene on his behalf...."

The soldiers of the Red Army did not last long in Poland. They reached the gates of Warsaw, which is on the other side of the Vistula River. But they did not succeed in organizing their forces for a final attack on the sections of Poland to the west of the Vistula. They had quickly captured vast territories, but their supply lines remained long, some five-six hundred kilometers or more. The Russian forces were scattered across great distances. And before they were able to organize appropriately, the Poles launched a counter-attack. After brief battles, in which the Red Army lacked arms and ammunition and organized contact with their command positions, the startling great retreat of the Russians began. Hundreds of thousands of soldiers ran away in confusion, some lacking clothing and exhausted. They ran for their lives, abandoning any attempt to slow the pace of the Polish advance. Large territories were re-captured by the Poles, who called these victories "the Miracle on the Vistula."

Bolshevik Russia was forced to recognize these expanded borders of Poland, though it did succeed in restoring its rule over central Ukraine. Peace now prevailed at the borders between

Poland and Russia. The victorious Poles once again carried on out of joy, and once again turned against the Jews. Much Jewish blood was spilt. On August 17, 1920, the Poles returned and captured Ostrow Mazowiecka and the entire area from the hands of the soldiers of Red Army, which had ruled there for only a few weeks. Immediately seven innocent Jews were arrested and without much ado were hanged before a rejoicing crowd of Poles. The legal authorization for such murders always arrived after the poor Jews were taken out to be killed. The Poles had all kinds of excuses: that the Jews cooperated with the Bolsheviks and that leftists circles assisted the Bolsheviks during their brief rule.

A Brief Period of Tranquility

Much time elapsed before things calmed down, and life entered upon a more or less normal track under anti-Semitic Polish rule. The economic condition of the Jews of the city was difficult. Many had become impoverished as a result of the war and the pogroms. Not a few merchants and people of means lost their assets and were not able to recover. A new class of modest wage earners and small scale entrepreneurs now arose, but this was a very thin stratum. Most of the residents found it hard to make a living in independent Poland since the new state was established. A policy of discrimination and bigotry against the Jews was carried out. Many emigrated abroad.[64] A few managed to get certificates of entry and went to Palestine.

The authorities of independent Poland worked hard to establish organized municipal institutions and organized communities that began to operate within the framework of the law, as elections were held on the basis of full democratic rule. Since Ostroveh had been established the leaders of the municipality had never been elected by the residents, but rather had been appointed by the Russian occupation authorities. And despite the fact that about half of the residents were Jews they had no representation in the institutions of the municipality. The law on municipalities and local councils that had been passed by the Polish parliament officially guaranteed the right to vote to every resident and to democratic elections. But secretly the Poles in fact worked to discriminate against Jewish candidates, to

---

[64] Among them was this editor's great-grandmother, Leah Gittel Feinzeig, who had run a successful military supply business in Ostroveh. She left in 1923 for New York with the younger of the surviving eleven of her seventeen children to re-join her husband, Chezke, who had left in 1911; as well as his grandfather, Rabbi David Tzvi (Hershel, later Harry) Schiff, a *shochet*, who left in 1922, followed by his wife, Malka Feinzeig Schiff, and their seven children (two more were born in New York), including his father Jacob, (Yaakov/Yankel) in 1924.

minimize their representation, and to favor their own representatives.

Prejudice and Discrimination

In the year 1919, immediately after the establishment of the Polish republic, municipal elections were held, the first in the city's history, after having had the mayor and his assistants being appointed by the Russians. The Jews did not participate in these elections out of fear of antagonizing the Poles, who were carrying on against the Jews anyway. The municipal institutions remained closed to the Jews, and the city government took on a distinctly anti-Semitic character until 1927, when new elections were held for the city council, in accordance with the law. At that time the Jews participated in an active way. Ten Jews were elected among the twenty-four elected members of the council. Thanks to the Jews a Polish socialist was elected as mayor of the city, one of the few who was not known for his hatred of the Jews. The local anti-Semites did not give up and declared war against the new city council. After a year or so the mayor was removed by the central authorities, along with about half of the members of the council. By-elections were held. The authorities carefully oversaw them to minimize the Jewish representation, despite the fact that the official law provided the right to vote to every resident. They found the means to accomplish this anti-Jewish objective. Only five Jews remained on the city council of twenty-four. From then until the destruction of the city the Jewish representation never grew any larger, which as mentioned did not reflect the percentage of Jews among the residents of Ostrow Mazowiecka.

Elections in the Jewish Community

On the other hand the Poles were also concerned with there being more or less honest and democratic elections in the Jewish communities of Poland. Officially recognized communities functioned under the Russian occupation, but these community institutions were not elected in a democratic fashion. Officially there were election protocols here and there. But in fact each district or community had its own election rules as they saw fit or in accordance with the regulations that the Russian rulers of the district issued. The right to vote, whether active or passive, was accorded to every Jew who paid the community tax (or *etat*).

This is how the community elections were organized under Russian rule: an officer of the authorities would appear in the old study hall on the day of the elections, holding in his hands the list of all those who had the right to vote which had been presented by the heads of the community. Every voter wrote four names on a piece of paper, candidates for the administration of the community. The Russian or Polish official would place these ballots in the ballot box, and those who received the greatest number of votes were elected. Participation in the vote was always very limited. The masses generally did not have the right to vote. And for some reason people who were recommended by the leaders of the community themselves were always elected.

The election law that was passed by the Polish authorities, however, required secret and democratic elections, proportional elections according to lists of candidates that were submitted in advance to the official authorities. Every local Jew had the right to vote. In the larger communities a council was elected, the size of its membership determined by the number of members of the community. The elected members of the council themselves then chose the executive. In the smaller communities an executive of at least eight members was chosen directly.

The Battle for Control of the Community

In the year 5684 [1923-1924] the first general elections for the community of Ostrow Mazowiecka took place in accordance with democratic election procedures. In effect it became the first confrontation between the parties and movements within the Jewish community. A bitter battle was conducted between the three lists that appeared in the elections, the Zionist and Mizrachi [religious Zionists], the non-partisan artisans' list, and Agudat Yisrael. The Agudat Yisrael list won a decisive victory, receiving an absolute majority, this despite the difficult battle waged against it by all of the Zionist and artisans' movements.

Twelve members of the council were elected, seven from the Agudat Yisrael list: Reb David Lichtenstein, Reb Meir Leszcz, Reb Avraham Yaakov Fridman, Reb Moshe Pokrzywa, Reb Yaakov Schwartz, Reb Yosef Wolf Rekant, and Reb Meir Gabinet. There were two representatives of the Zionists and Mizrachi, Reb Michael Teitel and Mr. Yitzchak Yaakov Podbielewicz, and three representatives of the artisans, Mr. Chaim Dessel, Mr. Mendel Kozuchowicz and Mr. Reuven Wengerka. The Agudist leader Reb David Lichtenstein was elected chairman of the council.

The council elected an executive committee of eight members. From the Agudat Yisrael faction the following were elected: Reb Aharon Yashinsky, Reb Yosef Suravich, Reb Eliahu Lach, Reb Baruch Silberstein, Reb Yitzchak Elbaum and Reb Yitzchak Yechiel Emert. From the Zionist and Mizrachi list, Reb Aryeh Margolis (Margoliot) and Reb Mordechai Cohen. Reb Aharon Yashinsky, one of the leaders of Agudat Yisrael in the city, was chosen as chairman of the executive committee. Up until the destruction of the community general elections were held twice, but Agudat Yisrael maintained its absolute majority until the end. Its representatives ran the community and its institutions until the outbreak of the Holocaust, when the group of elected leaders changed from time to time. In place of Reb Aharon Yashinsky, Reb Anshel Knorpel was elected chairman. He, too, was a leader of Agudat Yisrael and one of the heads of the Ger Hassidim.

The community of Ostrow Mazowiecka ran an organized and diversified range of programs until the day of its destruction. The institutions of the community were exceptionally well organized and successfully administered. As with other Jewish communities in Poland, the community of Ostrow Mazowiecka did not limit itself to matters of religion and religious services. In accordance with the law, it became the address for every Jewish problem and for every Jew, whether in the realm of hospitalization and care for the sick or the concern for the poor, the orphaned or the suffering. The executive of the community served as the representative of the Jews in all internal as well as external matters. The heads of the community of Ostroveh carried out this mission honorably and successfully up until the very last day of its existence.

Institutions and Projects

Despite the dominant and very influential status of the elected community, there remained a number of public institutions in the city that enjoyed full autonomy. The most notable was the kosher meat slaughtering enterprise, which originally was run by the slaughterers themselves, but which was transferred to the authority of the community in 1924 under continual pressure from the Gaon Rabbi Meir Dan Plotzky, the rabbi of the community, who demanded that the slaughtering fund be transferred to the ownership of the community. Since then the community did not add any other institution to the network of its projects.

Thus, the *Chevrah Kadisha* [literally, "Holy Society," in fact the burial society] operated independently up until the destruction of the community, not changing any of its customs or traditions. Every member had to undergo a period of *salozhveh* (service), during which period there were no real privileges. One's status was that of *melodzi*, which meant intern. Only after a certain period of time--after he had carried out various difficult tasks--was the candidate accepted as a member with full privileges. The members of this society were the most important of the city's residents.

This society was always wealthy and had substantial income. It demanded and generally received substantial sums as burial fees.

And if a wealthy person died, the members of the society demanded money for the burial ground. If refused, the heads of the *Chevrah Kadisha* would deny the dead person a place of honor for burial. People would frequently grumble about the practices of the society, but always accepted its control over the dead. The income was invested by the members of the society first and foremost in the maintenance of the graves, in the care of broken gravestones and in the acquisition of additional land. Any overage they distributed to charity as the officers of the society saw fit.

Similarly there operated in the city the *Linat Hatzedek* [Righteous Respite] society, which had a long tradition of extensive activities. Its purposes included providing every kind of aid to the sick: sending a doctor to the home of a poor ill person at no cost to them, supplying the needed medicines, making sure that there was someone to attend the sick person at all times, especially at night, so that members of the family of the ailing person could get some rest. The heads of the society also made every effort get the person hospitalized in Warsaw or elsewhere.

Linat Hatzedek

The activists of the society, simple Jews, performed their tasks as volunteers, with no expectation of reward. Among them were those who worked heart and soul, with unparalleled self-sacrifice, to perform this holy work. One of its leaders in the later years, Reb Efraim Rybka, became a symbol through his actions. A poor artisan, he made his living selling hats to peasants, which necessitated his traveling from city to city wherever there was a fair for peasants, whether near or far. Reb Efraim would go there with his merchandise and spread it out on the counter and wait patiently for a peasant to buy something. More than once he would return home the way he left, with no sales at all. This was especially true in the last years before the Holocaust, when feelings of anti-Semitism grew and the majority of the peasants began to boycott Jewish peddlers and artisans. More than once he would return home tired, exhausted after distant wanderings with nothing in his hand to show for it. Then he and his wife and ten children would taste the flavor of real hunger and deprivation.

But the heart and soul of Reb Efraim was not wrapped up in hats for peasants and their sales, but rather in the *Linat Hatzedek* society. He would barely finish his meager meal after a tiring trip and the hard work of sewing hats that preceded that trip and would immediately direct his steps to the office of *Linat Hatzedek*. He was interested in knowing what was happening in the society, had anyone had taken ill that needed its help? Was there another task that needed to be done? Reb Efraim was prepared to do anything. If someone was needed to serve on watch next to the bed of an ill person, Reb Efraim was the first to volunteer. His tiredness never bothered him. He was always prepared to fulfill any task that was asked of him with enthusiasm and good will.

There was no connection between the efforts of the Jews to assist the sick and the poor and the official Polish institutions, whose responsibilities including providing welfare and assistance to the sick. The latter took no interest in the fate of poor and sick Jews. They used all government and municipal welfare funds for Poles who needed welfare and help, albeit in a limited, distant and cold manner. The Pole did not know about sacrifice and devotion for the other. The concern and burden for the Jewish poor, sick, and so on was placed squarely on the shoulders of the Jews, without consideration of the fact that the Jew, as a Pole, was a citizen with equal rights, and it was his right to benefit from the government or municipal budget. The Jews no longer complained about the reality of such discrimination, as this policy was not limited to any one field.

A Common Disaster

Just once in the last decades before the Holocaust and destruction were the Jews and Poles partners in mourning and pain over an accident which befell the city and its residents. A bus that was traveling from Warsaw to Ostroveh and the surrounding cities overturned when it crossed over a narrow bridge over the River Bug and fell into the water at a depth of eight meters. All twenty-one passengers were killed in this horrific accident, among them seventeen Jews, some of them residents of Ostrow Mazowiecka and some residents of Lomza. Volunteers, soldiers and policemen worked very hard until they were able to recover the bodies from the river. With tears and wailing the Jews of the city accompanied the victims. All the stores and workshops were closed during the funeral. Traffic and worked ceased everywhere. All the residents, Jews and non-Jews, without exception participated in the gigantic funeral.

The Old Study Hall

The central place of prayer for the Jews of Ostrow Mazowiecka was without doubt the old study hall [beit midrash]. It was there that during the days of Russian rule elections were held for the heads of the community. And in those days the representatives of the government and its officers came to participate in the official prayers for the welfare of the monarchy. It was to the old study hall that Russian officers came to listen to the beautiful and enchanting lectures in rich literary Russian by the Gaon Rabbi

Yehuda Leib Gordin, where he frequently spoke when he served as rabbi of the city.

The congregation of the old study hall was very diverse. There were among them great scholars, honored ones of the community who sat along the eastern wall, heads of the community and leaders sitting alongside artisans and butchers, teamsters and porters, peddlers and just plain poor folk. These were Jews who in their conversations or in the conduct of their business, be it in their homes or in the street, would fill the air with their noise. But in the study hall they observed silence, speaking quietly, out of respect for the place and its worshippers.

They had in the past set up a place of honor along the eastern wall of the old study hall for the honored and important ones among the city's residents: Reb Leizer Antipriner, son-in-law of the Hassidic Gaon Rabbi Ben-Zion, the teacher and head of the Hassidim in Ostroveh; Reb Nachman Goldberg, the respected son-in-law of Feige Zissel Bromberg, the richest of all the Jews in town, who served for many years as head of the community; Reb David Bandrymer, father-in-law of the Gaon Rabbi Menachem Mendel Albek, the famous prodigy who served as chief of the rabbinical court of Zyrardow; the wealthy Reb Dan Bromberg and Reb Hersh**Error! Bookmark not defined.** Yitzchak Wizenberg, Reb Yaakov Moshe Flatau, and others. Almost all of them were Mitnagdim who observed long-standing traditions of generations without deviation. For decades serving as cantor of the old study hall was Reb Cheikel, whose voice was most pleasant and whose wonderful prayers could be heard from a distance. A special role was carved out by the aged *shamash* [*shames* or beadle], Reb Tanchum, who became an integral part of the ambience of the study hall and who was always pleasant and happy.

The old study hall was located on the road to Komorowo. It stood for generations as a central place for Torah and prayer. It was always full of worshippers, and at all hours of the morning and evening there were *minyanim* [prayer quorums] of Jews praying there one after another. In the study hall there were places for the elderly and for young men, Jews reciting the Psalms and residents who gravitated there towards evening for various study groups. In the years before the Holocaust the students of the *Beit Yosef* [House of Joseph] *yeshiva*[65] studied there. The old study house was always warm from the crowds and the sound of Torah and prayer could be heard from afar.

---

[65] Part of a network of *yeshivot* by this name that had originally been established in Novhardok [Navahrudak, today in Belarus], which had been shut down by the new communist government and which, therefore, now opened schools in independent Poland. See Chapter 11 below.

Before World War I the gates of the old study house had never been locked. Day and night Jews would be sitting there and studying. Young single men and newlyweds studied there regularly at all hours of the day. Towards evening each table would revert to its regular designation. At one table there would be seated the members of the Mishnayot [pl. of Mishnah] study group to hear a regular talk from a lecturer. A second table would be taken by the study group on *Chayei Adam* [*The Lives of Man*], a third was the place of the study group for *Ein Yaakov* [*The Well of Jacob*]. Until the wee hours of the night the most devoted among the students would remain and articulated the sound of Torah. Before they would return to their homes the early risers could already be seen, who would take their places alongside the open volumes of the Talmud. The voice of Torah was not silent even for a moment.

Every Friday night, at two o'clock after midnight, Reb Leizer Loew, a simple, good-hearted Jew, innocent and loyal, would pass through the streets of the city crying, "Jews, awake to worship the Creator." Whether in the summer or winter, in the rain or in the frost, he always fulfilled his mission with devotion. Every Sabbath evening the fearful sound of those who recited the Psalms at the old study house could be heard as they poured out the bitterness of their hearts to the Creator of the world.

The New Study Hall

The site of the new study hall was on Brok Road. It did not succeed in competing with the old study hall. Its worshippers also included some of the respected people of the city, scholars and the wealthy alike, who were also overwhelmingly Mitnagdim and sharply opposed to Hassidim and Hassidism. It was a place of Torah and a place of prayer for the elite, but the masses were not to be found there. Before the Holocaust a number of its worshippers joined the Zionist movement, even though some of them were loyal to Agudat Yisrael. Along the eastern wall of this study hall prayed Reb Dov Ber Shapira, who was wealthy and learned, son of the Gaon Isaac *Charif*, the Rabbi of Slonim, Reb Gedalyahu David Morgenstern, Reb Avraham Yaakov Freidman the prodigy, the respected Reb Mordechai Drozdowski, Reb Motel Miller, the excellent and well known scholar, and others. During the brief period of service of the Gaon Rabbi Zalman Sorotzkin in Ostroveh, when he had been chosen chief of the rabbinical court of the city, he had established at the new study hall a group for the regular group study of the Talmud. Rabbi Sorotzkin soon left the city, moving on to serve as the rabbi of Lutzk, but the Talmud study group that he founded rapidly developed. There were days when it counted some one hundred members or more who would assemble every night to study a lesson of Talmud together. Serving as lecturers were the *gabbai* [officer of the congregation], Reb Yitzchak Yadover, Reb Avraham Yaakov Friedman, Reb Aryeh Margolis, Reb Motel Miller, Reb Avraham Tzvi Polkowitz the *shochet* [ritual slaughterer] and Reb Gershon Srebrnik, all of whom were killed in the Holocaust. Serving as the *shamash* of the study hall for many years was Reb Hersh Balbier, a Jew who was respected and honored by everyone, and who excelled in his flawless and beautiful handwriting. Among his responsibilities was to record all the births and the couples who got married with the municipal authorities, according to the law. He would frequent the city hall as the permanent representative of the Jews to the department of population registry and such.

The Hassidic Prayer Houses in the City

The Hassidic prayer houses held a special place in the city. The largest and most active among them was the Hassidic house of Ger [Gur or Gora Kalwaria]. Several hundred people worshipped there, where the balance of Torah and prayer never let up day or night. In the last years before the Holocaust increasing numbers of young men knowledgeable in Torah and Hassidism chose this Hassidic house as their permanent home for study. This organized and united group of young Ger Hassidim operated similarly to those in hundreds of other cities and towns in central Poland. Young men from other Hassidic movements joined them, and the group grew from year to year.

The group operated with a strong internal discipline and according to permanent procedures determined in advance. In the very early hours of the morning the young men were already to be found in the Hassidic house. They studied in pairs up until the fixed time of prayer of Ger Hassidim in recent generations, precisely 7:30 a.m. After a brief break for breakfast, all the members of the study group reconvened in the Hassidic house and studied in pairs until the afternoon. Then came a very brief break for lunch and then studies continued until evening prayers. The most devoted among them continued to study enthusiastically until the late hours of the night. Others turned to the study of Hassidism in the evening hours. They often ate their evening meals together.

The young members of the group were aware of every need for charity and good deeds. They never refused any assignment, no matter how difficult. When any worthy guest or a poor person came to town, the members of the group went out to collect funds for them, always out of joy and willingness. For every holiday and special occasion they would travel to Ger, to the court of the *rebbe*.

They would travel together and stay over in Ger together, praying and studying, with joy and dancing. They would eat and live together, sharing funds, making due with the very least, with two or three young men serving as managers of the common household, going out to the market and buying supplies and cooking and baking themselves, living in a room or a few rooms that they would rent for the time they stayed in Ger. They were one big, united family, full of enthusiasm, among hundreds of other groups of young bachelors and married men amidst the masses of Hassidim who filled the court of the *rebbe* of Ger. They basked in the glory of the great *rebbe*, from his Torah and his behavior.

To Fortify the Torah and Religion

The Hassidic house of Ger in Ostrow Mazowiecka not only served as a center of Torah and Hassidism but also as a center for every community activity that served to guard the Judaism of Torah and for the battle for everything holy, and against secular and anti-religious movements. Those who attended the Hassidic house of Ger were those who founded and built the Agudat Yisrael movement, who led it and were devoted to its affairs heart and soul.

With the sacred enthusiasm of true Hassidim the Hassidim of Ger were not deterred by any difficulties or impediments in their battle for pure Judaism, for Torah education and an orthodox environment.

It was they who established all of the Agudat Yisrael institutions in the city, the *Yesodei Hatorah* [Foundations of the Torah] schools [for boys], and the *Beit Yaakov* [House of Jacob] educational institutions [for girls], as well as the *B'not Agudat Yisrael* [Daughters of Agudat Yisrael] and *Batyah* [Daughter of God] organizations. With diligence and steadfastness the Hassidim of Ger worked hard to firmly establish the institutions of Agudat Yisrael and to guarantee a faithful future for the Judaism of Torah.

People of other Hassidic movements were also organized within Agudat Yisrael, as were those who were opposed to Hassidism. Nevertheless, the Hassidim of Ger served as the most motivating and activist force in Agudat Yisrael. In other Hassidic houses and in the study halls members of Agudat Yisrael and Mizrachi, or non-partisan people, sat side by side, supporters of Agudat Yisrael and those who opposed its way, those loyal to Torah education and those opposed to it. The Hassidim of Ger, under the leadership of the Hassidic *rebbe* Rabbi Avraham Mordechai, saw in their attachment to Agudat Yisrael and in their opposition to all non-orthodox movements an integral part of their being and their identity. In the Hassidic house of Ger or in its membership there was no place for indifference or non-partisanship. The mission of Hassidism and the mission of Agudat Yisrael had a common aspiration to fortify the ramparts of Judaism.

The Hassidim of Ger – The Pioneers of the Hassidim

A person who changed the customs of generations, who sent his children to be educated in an institution that was not fully orthodox, a person who allowed a non-religious newspaper or a secular book to enter into his house, a person who changed his dress from the traditional one that was accepted in Poland was not to be found in the Hassidic house of Ger. He was forced to move to another Hassidic house, to one of the other six Hassidic houses in the city that willingly accepted anyone who wished to pray there, without checking on the minutest details of his observance and without demanding absolute identification in all his actions and utterances and in all the activities of the members of his household with the principles of that Hassidic house.

The Hassidim of Ger in Ostroveh, as in hundreds of other cities and towns all across Poland, were considered therefore extremists in their behavior and zealots in their ideas and outlook, as extremely consistent and stubborn fighters vis-a-vis the secular movements, the Zionists and others.

Despite their loyalty to pure and avid Hassidism, the activists of the Ger Hassidim who were devoted to Agudat Yisrael also exerted much effort in organizing orthodox girls and in the education of girls in the city. After lively prayers and long study sessions, the activists of the Hassidic house of Ger went out, dressed in fine silks and wearing full beards and side locks, to deliver timely lectures or just regular talks to the members of *B'not Agudat Yisrael* gathered in their clubhouse. The unofficial leader of *B'not Agudat Yisrael* in Ostrow Mazowiecka was the Hassidic Gaon Rabbi David Mintzberg, who later served as the spiritual adviser at the *yeshiva* of *Chachmei Lublin* [The Sages of Lublin].[66] Heads of the Ostroveh community, such as Reb Aharon Yashinsky, the chairman of the council, and Reb Anshel Knorpel, were among the activists of the Hassidim of Ger.

---

[66] This grand *yeshiva*, established and headed by Rabbi Meir Shapiro under the auspices of the Agudat Yisrael movement in 1924, was housed in an impressive modern five-story building on a grassy campus that was completed in 1930. It housed a major Judaica library, a large synagogue, as well as a dormitory for its two hundred rabbinic students. Immediately closed down by the Nazis, after the war it was home to the medical school of the University of Lublin, but has more recently been returned to the ownership of the Jewish community, and its synagogue restored. See also footnote 117, p. 178.

There were seven Hassidic houses in Ostrow Mazowiecka. The largest of them in terms of the number of worshippers and that also served as a fortress for community activity, Torah and the education of the younger generation was, as mentioned, the Hassidic house of Ger. A large and diverse crowd also prayed at the Hassidic house of Alexander locally, and Warka-Amshinov guarded the Hassidic tradition of Warka. A special status adhered to the Hassidim of Amshinov, which grew and thrived since the *rebbe* of Amshinov, Rabbi Yosef, served as chief of the rabbinical court of the city, and many of the residents were counted among the friends and admirers of the *rebbe*. The Hassidic house of Sokolow in fact replaced that of the Hassidim of Kotsk, while the Hassidic house of Radzymin brought together modest Jews, peddlers and artisans.

The Two *Yeshivot* in Ostroveh

Two *yeshivot* [pl. of *yeshiva*] functioned in old Ostrow Mazowiecka. The city *yeshiva* was founded in the year 5610 [1849-1850]. Serving as heads of the *yeshiva* were the Gaon Rabbi Nisan Lewinsky, sharp and broadly knowledgeable and one of the outstanding Hassidim of Amshinov, and his son-in-law Rabbi Yehoshua Leib, Rabbi Wolf Ber, a well known scholar, and Rabbi Hershel Yaglowitz, who had an unparalleled ability to explicate. During all the years of its existence the *yeshiva* had great and noted scholars as faculty members and lecturers. There were times where there were as many as one hundred fifty students. Many of the graduates of the *yeshiva* later became well known as educators, and some served as rabbis and judges.

The wealthy Mrs. Feige Zissel Bromberg donated funds to construct the building of the *yeshiva*. When that building burned down, Feige Zissel Bromberg contributed again to re-build the structure. In the building of the *yeshiva* was also located a *Talmud Torah* [religious elementary school], in which some two hundred children studied, mainly children of the poor, whose budget was covered in part by allocaions from the community. For many years Rabbi Meir Itzi Augustower, a gifted pedagogue, was the head of the *Talmud Torah*, whose instruction was enjoyed by the children and gave them much pleasure. In the last years of the existence of the community, serving as heads of the institution were Rabbi Yaakov Kagan and Rabbi Zeev Shulman, assisted by and under the supervision of Rabbi Asher Rosenblum. Members of the Board included Rabbi Avraham**Error! Bookmark not defined.** Petziner [Pecyner], Rabbi David Mintzberg [Mincberg], Rabbi Yosef**Error! Bookmark not defined.** Mandelkorn and others.

In the year 5682 [1921-1922] there was established in Ostrow Mazowiecka the *Beit Yosef* [House of Joseph] *yeshiva* of Novhardok. The Gaon Rabbi Yoel Kleinerman, son-in-law of the founder of the movement of the *yeshivot* of Novhardok, the Gaon Rabbi Yosef Yozel Horowitz, headed the *yeshiva*. The principal of the *yeshiva* was Rabbi Aharon Ogolnik. The *yeshiva* developed rapidly, and on the eve of the Holocaust it numbered nearly three hundred students, most of whom were killed. The *yeshiva*'s influence on the life of the city and its residents was great. It contributed to the inculcation of the idea of devotion and sacrifice on behalf of the Torah and ethics among wide circles. (There is a separate chapter on the *yeshiva*, its heads and leaders, below.)

Chapter Nine
The Hassidic Gaon Rabbi Ben-Zion Rabinowitz

The Symbol of Pure Hassidism

He became a symbol, a legend in his life, but still trembled for fear of falling victim to pride. Hundreds of thousands of Hassidim in Poland spoke his name. For members of the more recent generation of Hassidim in Poland, the words "Rabbi Ben-Zion of Ostroveh" symbolized a bygone era of glory that has disappeared, an exalted generation among whom spiritual giants once walked, whose feet touched the ground but whose heads reached the heavens, scattered the clouds and brushed up against the stars, who served as a bridge that connected the high heavens with the world below.

In his early days, when Rabbi Ben-Zion first appeared in the study house of the old *Seraph* of Kotsk [Kock],[67] he was a young man of tender years, one among the many links in a long and thick chain. But in the evening of his life Rabbi Ben-Zion remained the sole and unique representative and symbol of an entire period, an entire world, the last of the Mohicans, who reminded the masses of the Hassidim of Poland of the fire from which they were forged, of the holy and pure, of the innocent and truthful foundations upon which the mighty and grand Polish Hassidic movement was built. It had encompassed entire worlds and had attained previously unknown dimensions both in its content and scope, placing its indelible imprint upon the entire Jewish people.

Generations came and went, one watch came on duty while another exited. But the wonderful period of Kotsk never ended in the eyes of hundreds of thousands of Hassidim in Poland. It still stood before their eyes even after the *Seraph* and his students had long disappeared in a whirlwind up into the skies. It remained standing in the singular image of the aged, but forever young, Rabbi Ben-Zion, who represented it in all its purity, holiness and exaltation. The period of Kotsk did not end in the eyes of the Hassidim of Poland as long as the great Rabbi Ben-Zion walked among them, the teacher and educator, the influencer, the true Hassid who was created without a blemish.

Rabbi Ben-Zion was born in Warsaw in the year 5600 [1839-1840] to his father, the Gaon Rabbi Binyamin David, a *dayan* and preacher in that great center of Jewish life. He was opposed to

---

[67] Rabbi Menachem Mendel of Kotsk (1787-1859), known as the Kotsker *rebbe*.

Hassidim and Hassidism, but was one of the great scholars and activists. Yet he was a loyal friend of the leader of the Hassidim in Warsaw and the outstanding genius of Polish Jewry, Rabbi Yitzchak Meir of Ger [Gur or Gora Kalwaria]. Rabbi Ben-Zion was a bright and talented child, who studied diligently and was fearful of sin. Before he was eight years old he had already come up with innovations in his studies and even offered some of his insights in writing to the renowned Gaon Rabbi Shlomo Kluger of Brody.[68] When Rabbi Binyamin David realized how special his young son was, he immediately sent him to the home of Rabbi Yitzchak Meir so that he might test him in his studies. The many Hassidim who always filled the house of Rabbi Yitzchak Meir played with the gifted child, who came by frequently. They became close to him and came to adore him. Ties of mutual love grew between the bright boy and the brilliant Hassidim and elderly men. They quickly brought the young Rabbi Ben-Zion into the world of the Hassidim. After a time the young lad became a Hassid with all his heart and soul, to the point where he joined the group of Hassidim that traveled from Warsaw to Kotsk.

Among the Hassidim of Kotsk

Joining the Hassidic community did not interfere with Rabbi Ben-Zion's studies, nor did it detract from his diligence. On the contrary, with true devotion he added areas of study to his regular program. He dedicated all his senses and desires to the Torah. When he first arrived in Kotsk the Hassidic *rebbe*, known as the *Seraph*, said to him: "Hassidism without Torah is merely an external trapping. We want a true internal Hassidism. To achieve that kind of Hassidism is only possible by means of Torah."

Rabbi Ben-Zion was immersed in his studies of the Torah. His entire objective and aspiration was to attain wholeness through his studies, a true Hassidism, and not to turn his Torah studies into some kind of practical instrument. He quickly ascended in the levels of the Torah. His breadth of knowledge amazed many. And his acuity went extremely deep. His father, the Gaon Rabbi Binyamin David, the Mitnaged, acquiesced in the adherence of his beloved son to the Hassidim. The fact that his Hassidism did not detract from his study of Torah, but rather the opposite, gladdened his father. But because of his extensive studies, his eyesight was being harmed. The doctors ordered that he abstain for a short time from his studies so as not to strain his eyes by poring over books. Rabbi Yitzchak Meir was told about the doctors' orders. The sainted *gaon* said to him: "So for a time you will study

---

[68] Rabbi Shlomo ben Yehuda Aharon Kluger (1783-1869).

by heart." But Rabbi Ben-Zion did not weaken in his resolve and claimed: "No subject is that well retained in my memory that I am able to study it by heart." But Rabbi Yitzchak Meir went on to say, "If someone cannot also learn by heart it is a sign that he does not truly harbor Torah within his heart."

He was saddened by this. So Rabbi Ben-Zion left for Kotsk, where he met with the Hassidic *rebbe* there and laid out his problems before him. The reply of the *Seraph* was entirely different. He said, "Those doctors object to your studies. Don't listen to them."

Rabbi Ben-Zion did not listen to them. He quickly got well. His vision no longer troubled him. But he began to fear pride or haughtiness or boastfulness. So he performed a self-evaluation. Here he was, a talented young man, fully formed, a scholar and a Hassid. But the gaping chasm of pride loomed before him. He could have easily fallen into this trap, and who would save him? If he did so, all his Torah and all his prayers, his labor and hard work would be of no value and no purpose. Feeling depressed, he appeared before Rabbi Yitzchak Meir and laid out his fears.

The holy *gaon* replied, "An empty vessel prefers the noise of pride more than a full vessel. One who lacks knowledge prides himself more in what he knows than one who has knowledge and does not brag. So what do we have to be boastful about and why should we be boastful?"

Rabbi Yitzchak Meir was not serving officially as the *rebbe* at this time, declining the mantle of office. He even paid homage to the *rebbe* of Kotsk by frequently visiting him as one of his most loyal Hassidim. Therefore he would respond, advise, guide and direct only those of his students who were closest to him. So when the Gaon Rabbi Binyamin David came with his son, the now groom Rabbi Ben-Zion, to the house of Rabbi Yitzchak Meir before they left for Ostroveh to seek his blessing for his wedding, Rabbi Yitzchak Meir took the groom into a special room and whispered to him secretly, "If it [sex] is refined, there is no greater refinement than it. But if it is vulgar there is nothing in the world more vulgar."

The father-in-law of Rabbi Ben-Zion, Rabbi Leizer,[69] much like his own father Rabbi Binyamin David, also objected to Hassidim and Hassidism. But this was not sufficient to discourage the enthusiastic fourteen year-old young man whose entire being burned with pure Hassidism. Even though he was young in age, he was among those in the court of the aged *rebbe* of Kotsk who

---

[69] Leizer (or Lajzor) Aronson (or Arenson). Rabbi Ben-Zion's marriage to Chana Gitla Aronson was recorded in the town records of Ostrow Mazowiecka in the summer of 1856. She was born in Suwalki in 1840 and died in Ostrow Mazowiecka in 1914.

were the very best, older people who had led distinguished lives and were giants in the Torah and in Halacha, in deeds and in Hassidism. Nevertheless, the young man from Ostroveh found an attentive ear and an open door wherever he went.

From Kotsk to Ger

The final hour was closing in on Kotsk, enmeshed as it was in a holy storm, where everyone was seeking the naked, pure, nameless truth that was hidden there. But it held off the masses knocking at its gate, which was tightly closed with a thousand locks and bolts. But the way for Rabbi Ben-Zion was open. People related to him with complete seriousness, with affection, despite the fact that he was just a beginner Hassid, taking his first steps in the garden of Hassidism. Yet he already carried the secret of the *Seraph rebbe*, who was hidden away, removed and separated from the world. In his final days Rabbi Ben-Zion said, "Once the *rebbe* of Kotsk revealed to me some miraculous things which I cannot reveal until the final hours before my death." But a brain clot struck him in the last days of his life and prevented him from revealing his secret.

Before Rabbi Ben-Zion reached nineteen years of age, the great *rebbe* of Kotsk was called to his maker. The glorious annals of Kotsk, written in blood and fire, stormy and turbulent, seemed to be coming to their end. More than 10,000 Hassidim assembled and came to Kotsk, in mourning and deeply distraught, to participate in the funeral of the *Seraph rebbe*. The young Rabbi Ben-Zion walked about in a daze. He could not believe what he had heard with his ears and what he had seen with his eyes. It was not possible that the *rebbe* had died just like any other person. Was he not like an angel from above, like a divine *seraph*?

The large congregation of Kotsk all but fell apart after the death of the aged *rebbe*. The large majority, including Rabbi Ben-Zion, affiliated with the Hassidic sect of the *rebbe* of Ger. From then on he was always counted among the students of that great Polish *gaon*. Henceforth he was considered one of his most devoted Hassidim, loyal to him with all his heart and soul. He took no step in his life without consulting his holy teacher. And while still young in years, he was thought of as one of the greatest and sharpest students in the circles of the *rebbe* of Ger. Although young in age, his deeds and actions were like those of a tried and true Hassid. Everything he did was weighed and measured. He was great in Torah and Hassidism, in ethics and actions, and very close to the *rebbe*, whom he went to visit often.

A number of years had passed since his marriage. All the while he was dependent upon his father-in-law, who took care of all his needs. But the time had come for him to provide for his household. And he did not want to enter the rabbinate. He did not want to accept the mantle of the office of rabbi. He decided that he would instead enter the world of business. He visited the *rebbe* and presented his thoughts. But the *rebbe* decided otherwise, saying, "There are many merchants. But I want to hold on to you."

Torah and Hassidism

So Rabbi Ben-Zion was no longer inquiring about or interested in business. In a single moment he adjusted his thoughts and aligned them with those of the *rebbe*. He continued to devote all his time to Torah and Hassidism. His modest income somehow made due. It did not worry or burden him. Many years had passed since his marriage, but he still had no child. From time to time he would mention this to the *rebbe*, who would reply, "If you trust in God, He will assuredly come to your aid."

But trust in God, true trust, is an exalted status in the eyes of a true Hassid, a level that is not easy to attain. Besides, who can guarantee that one will ever attain that level of wholeness? So Rabbi Ben-Zion did not relent with the *rebbe*, and reminded him at every opportunity that he was deprived of children. The *rebbe* would say, "If someone really wants to obtain something with all his heart and soul, he should confine himself to a particular place, where he should pour out his pleas before God with sincere tears, and intensify his prayers until God answers him."

That same night Rabbi Ben-Zion closed himself in the room where he lived, and poured out his prayers all that night with hot tears, praying that he would be granted living children. In the morning he left his room, his pleas and prayers complete. In a year his first child was born. At the same time his second rabbi, the *rebbe* of Ger, was called to heaven in a whirlwind on high, seven years after his [Rabbi Ben-Zion's] marriage [1866]. Once again the large sect of Hassidim was greatly bereft, shaken to its foundations.

The Hassidim of Kotsk-Ger stood before a difficult transition problem. In Augustow, *rebbe* Yechiel Meir opened up his house of study; in Strikov [Strykow], so did *rebbe* Zeev Wolf,[70] in Chizov [Czyzewo], *rebbe* Baruch,[71] in Lipno, *rebbe* Nahum Yisrael. And some of the Ger Hassidim returned to Kotsk, where they joined the

---

[70] Rabbi Zeev Wolf Landau of Strikov (1807-1891).

[71] Rabbi Baruch Shapiro (ca. 1787-1877), known as the Czyzeve *rebbe*.

congregation of *rebbe* Rabbi David,[72] the son of the late aged *rebbe*. For his part, Rabbi Ben-Zion, like the overwhelming majority of the Ger Hassidim, went to Alexander, to the *rebbe* Rabbi Chanoch Henich Hacohen, the lion among the various groups of Hassidim and students of the late *rebbe*.

In Alexander and Ger

Rabbi Ben-Zion was friends with the grandson of the *rebbe*, Rabbi Aryeh Leib of Ger,[73] who was seven years younger than him. He was considered his best friend and companion. Rabbi Aryeh Leib was beloved unto his great and esteemed grandfather like no other, and valued by the masses of the Hassidim. He was eighteen when his father's father, his teacher and the one who raised him, the Hassidic *rebbe* of Ger, passed away. He reluctantly agreed to accept the position of rabbi in the town of Ger, in place of his grandfather. But he adamantly refused to accede to the wishes of the masses of Hassidim to serve as the *rebbe* in lieu of his grandfather the *rebbe*, that prince of the Torah.

In Ger, Rabbi Aryeh Leib remained in that now orphaned house, as the eyes of the masses of Hassidim throughout Poland were lifted towards the outstanding young man, who was considered a supremely holy person. He did not go into town or any other place. Rabbi Ben-Zion maintained the faithful and strong friendship with the rabbi of Ger. Whenever he traveled to Alexander, to visit the great Hassidic *rebbe* Hacohen, the "High Priest," on the way back he would divert to Ger and met with Rabbi Aryeh Leib, who was completely isolated and shared confidences with him.

Once when he was returning from Alexander, Rabbi Ben-Zion came and told the young rabbi of Ger what he had heard from the Hassidic *rebbe* Rabbi Chanoch Henich Hacohen when he was expostulating before thousands of his Hassidim who were crammed into his court. He said, "It is written, 'They wandered aimlessly in the desert and were lost. They could not find a city to settle in. They were hungry and thirsty. Their souls were sad and silent. And they cried to God when they were in trouble to save them from their distress and to lead them on a straight path towards a habitable city.' They wandered aimlessly in the desert and wasteland' refers to those who erred and err in the teachings of the Torah. 'A place to settle they did not find' means that they

---

[72] Rabbi David Morgenstern of Kotsk (1809-1873), Hassidic leader who spent the last twenty years of his life in seclusion.

[73] Rabbi Yehuda Aryeh Leib Alter (1847-1905), also known by the name of his book, the *S'fat Emet* [*The Language of Truth*].

studied and studied, but for some reason were not able to achieve the desired purpose, and therefore, they were 'hungry and thirsty' for the teachings of the Torah. 'Their souls were sad and silent and they cried to God when they were in trouble,' then 'from their distress he saved them' means that God rescued them from the predicament which they were in and God led them on a straight path towards the desired goal."

When Rabbi Ben-Zion finished speaking, the young rabbi of Ger decided right then to join the Alexander Hassidic sect as just one of its Hassidim. He visited Alexander and from then on went there regularly at specific times determined in advance every year to see the *rebbe* Rabbi Chanoch Henich.

For four years the *rebbe* of Alexander led the largest Hassidic sect of those days. When he passed on to the high heavens [1870], a portion of the Hassidim gravitated to the Hassidic *rebbe* Rabbi Avraham of Sochachew and crowned him as *rebbe*. But the large majority of the Hassidim of the *rebbe* of Alexander once again flocked towards Ger, to the young rabbi. Once again they did not want to accept the determined declination of Rabbi Aryeh Leib to serve as *rebbe*.

During the period of service of the great *rebbe* of Alexander, Hacohen, the "High Priest," the *rebbe* Rabbi Aryeh Leib would study in the great house of study in Ger, which was now nearly empty and which had been built during the period of service of his grandfather, the *rebbe* Rabbi Yitzchak Meir. Since the passing of the *rebbe* of Alexander masses of Hassidim flocked to Ger. Hundreds of Hassidism surrounded the young *rebbe*, who still refused to accept the post, from all sides and wherever he went. When he entered the study hall as usual to give his regular lessons, he was immediately surrounded by many who crowded around his place of study. He was forced to return home and his room. When Rabbi Ben-Zion came he sighed and said, "Look at this, Ben-Zion, I have even been chased out of the study hall."

The Study of Hassidism

In those days Rabbi Ben-Zion was already considered one of the giants among the Hassidic sects, one of the central pillars in this great movement which, from its very founding, changed the image and substance of Polish Jewry. He was one of the closest people to the *rebbe* Rabbi Aryeh Leib of Ger, one of his confidantes and advisers. From a temporary business in the sale of lottery tickets, which were purchased by regular subscribers, he made a modest living. His business did not interfere with his rest nor did it rob him of his time. He was always available for Torah and Hassidism, for regular classes from early morning until late at night, and for very long trips to Ger, to the *rebbe*.

In Ostroveh young men gathered around him and became his finest and most devoted students. They learned from his Torah teachings and they listened to his words, to his talks and discussions. Whenever Rabbi Ben-Zion would come to Ger he would be surrounded by many Hassidim, young and old, who spared no effort to be in his presence, to listen to his stories and words. He created cadres of students who followed in his path, and educated many young men in pure Hassidim. They studied his words and analyzed his stories. They were prepared to go into great depth to learn and study the meaning of Hassidism. They examined his conduct and deeds in great detail in order to understand the true pathways of a Hassid.

Guide and Teacher

To dine in the presence of Rabbi Ben-Zion was an experience never to be forgotten by any Hassid, whether young or old. It was always possible to learn something from him, whether in Torah or Hassidism, in ethics or in human behavior, a veritable living guide to wisdom and knowledge. The Gaon Rabbi Avraham Leib,[74] the rabbi of Brok and one of the greatest rabbis of his generation, was much older than Rabbi Ben-Zion. He was among the Hassidim of Kotsk and considered by many as a holy man. Many turned to him with questions and asked for his blessing and prayers. As one of the Hassidic *rebbe*s, he received many personal notes of petition. People told of wonders emanating from the holy spirit in his house of study.

Once during a very snowy season, when it was freezing cold and strong winds were blowing, the Gaon Rabbi Avraham Leib suddenly appeared before the house of Rabbi Ben-Zion in Ostroveh. He was wrapped in a big fur coat and was breathing

---

[74] Rabbi Avraham Yehuda Leib Kozak (1814-1895), known as the Broker *rav*.

with difficulty. The rabbi of Brok was old and weak by this time, and walking the roads was difficult for him, especially in the winter. But no impediment or difficulty would prevent him from his strong desire to meet with Rabbi Ben-Zion and to have dinner with him. The next morning, after having met with Rabbi Ben-Zion and dined with him, he would return to his home, to his town and his *yeshiva*.

Once a number of great rabbis shared a Saturday evening meal. Included among them were a number of outstanding Hassidim, among them the Gaon Rabbi Avraham Leib of Brok, Rabbi Ben-Zion and Rabbi Yisrael Yitzchak of Ostrolenka, the well known Hassid, and other Hassidim.

Rabbi Ben-Zion opened with the following words: "We learn in the Midrash [rabbinical commentary] on the Book of Proverbs that when a scholar sits and propounds, God forgives the sins of the people of Israel. And why would that be?" Rabbi Ben-Zion asked. He continued, "Because a wise man recognizes the lowliness and worthlessness of man. But when he sits broken-hearted and studies, God is filled with mercy and forgives the sins of the people of Israel."

The rabbi of Brok then arose and said, "My fellow Jews. Rabbi Ben-Zion has never said anything nicer than this. It is the essence of the truth. Jews come to me with various written pleas of petition, but I am at a loss to answer them. I stand before them full of embarrassment and shame, my heart breaks. They go on their way to do everything they need to do. And so from broken-heartedness comes their salvation...."

With No Official Position

Rabbi Ben-Zion never accepted any such written special pleas and declined to accept any official position. Whatever the appointment, he fled from honors, even though honors pursued him. His standing grew steadily, despite his unwillingness. Many proposed various rabbinical positions in large and important communities to him, but Rabbi Ben-Zion fended off such proposals with both hands. He was not even prepared to entertain the thought of such a position. When they pressed him, he would tell the following story:

There were once two Hassidim of Kotsk who were loyal and devoted friends. They were excellent scholars, but were plagued by many serious problems. They suffered from such stresses that one of them finally could no longer stand the pressure and went out to look for and find a respectable position as a rabbi in one of the cities. The second was able to withstand the pressure and refused to take a rabbinical position, continuing along his path as a full-fledged Hassid.

After a time, when the pressures overcame the Hassid, who had continued to shoulder his burden, he went out on the road for a time to collect some money to meet his pressing needs. He arrived in the city where his old friend was serving as the rabbi. The rabbi recognized him and began to shudder as he approached. He made a fuss over him and immediately invited him to his house. They were both glad that they had met once again. The rabbi stood and told his friend about all his heavenly as well as this-worldly duties: in the morning he had to deliver a lecture to the young single men; and in the afternoon to the older, married ones who were preparing to be instructors. In the evening, after evening prayers, there were once again two classes that he had to give, one for the more learned local people and a second for the average person. Day and night people would come and asked him questions, simple ones as well as complex ones. And the affairs of the community at large also weighed upon him. Added to all this were his own needs to study as well as other matters, and the rabbi never had a free moment.

The poor Hassid let out a heavy sigh. The rabbi was alarmed, thinking to himself that he had sighed because of his wretched condition and his difficult situation, as he has nothing compared to my status, that is, my having the best of both worlds [Torah and material well being]. So he decided to console his old pal and friend. He turned to him and said, "One must accept everything with love. Not everyone gets to benefit from both tables. As it is said, one may have more and one may have less, as long as their heart is directed heavenward." The poor Hassid replied, "I did not sigh for myself or my situation, but rather for you and yours. You are busy day and night, summer and winter, and not a moment of free time do you have to evaluate your deeds or to reflect on the quality of your way of life. As such, you may end up departing from this world, heaven forbid, without having done penance."

Rabbi Ben-Zion did not serve as a rabbi or a Hassidic *rebbe*, nor as a *dayan* or a teacher, nor as a community leader or head of a *yeshiva*, repulsed by any official or exalted position. He did not occupy any role, but his personality was radiant. It spoke to the community and symbolized the highest, most complete, purest and holiest form of Hassidism, free from any blemish, the Hassidism of wholeness, a pure Hassidism that asks nothing in return for itself, a Hassidism that raises and elevates one to ever higher levels, a Hassidism that contains all the elements and characteristics that the sages enumerated.

He was an outstanding *gaon*, his knowledge equally broad-based and sharp in all subject matter of the Torah. He studied with diligence and enthusiasm all of his days, investing all of his great abilities in his studies. He made his study of the Torah an integral part of his life, but refused at any price to turn it into a means of making a living, or to use his innovations or teachings into a means of aggrandizing himself or others. He was fearful with all his being of the thought that people would call him a great person of Torah. Moreover, how could he give knowledge to others before acquiring it himself, how could he be concerned with the improvement of others, before he improved his own soul?

He Was a Legend

The Hassidim surrounded him without let up, always besieging his house, accompanying him wherever he went, hanging on his every word, his stories and words becoming a permanent part of the legacy of the masses of Hassidim, who uttered his name with trembling voices, saying "Rabbi Ben-Zion told," or, "Rabbi Ben-Zion said." In Ger he was educated in the court of the Hassidic *rebbe* Rabbi Aryeh Leib, author of the *S'fat Emet* [*The Language of Truth*], the eldest son--and one who was always destined for greatness--of the *rebbe* Rabbi Avraham Mordechai. The elder *rebbe* once turned to his son and said, "The sages have said, acquire a friend for yourself. Everyone should have a good friend. Even you should have such a friend. Take Rabbi Ben-Zion as your friend."

Time passed by and, in the prime of his life, Rabbi Aryeh Leib of Ger passed away [1905]. His oldest son, Rabbi Avraham Mordechai, filled his place. Once again, one watch departs, while another takes its place. Rabbi Ben-Zion continued to travel to Ger with enthusiasm. This was now his fifth teacher. He was now a Hassid who was reaching maturity. In the eyes of the masses he was "the great Rabbi Ben-Zion," but in his own eyes he was a simple Hassid in need of a teacher and a guide, a Hassid who thirsts for every word that emanates from the mouth of the *rebbe*.

Tens of thousands streamed into Ger, trailing in the dust of the *rebbe*'s footsteps, adhering to him heart and soul, receiving his teachings on the Torah as if they came directly from Sinai, crowding around his table with sacred trepidation. They turned their ears with enthusiasm to hear every word that the great *rebbe* articulated. Around his table were seated the greatest of his Hassidim, rabbis and laymen, crowded together and completely in his thrall. Among them was Rabbi Ben-Zion. Now the *rebbe* began to speak words of Torah. Thousands melded into a single bloc, holding their breath. The *rebbe* now recounted some of the thoughts of the greats of Hassidism of previous generations, like the Besht [acronym for ***Ba'al Shem Tov***, Master of the Good Name][75] and the Seer of Lublin,[76] the "Holy Jew" from Peshischa[77] and Rabbi Bunim,[78] as well as the aged rabbi of Kotsk[79] and the *rebbe* of Ger, Rabbi Yitzchak Meir.[80] These are the angels of the heavens who have, over the generations, gone to heaven and left behind their teachings to illuminate the eyes of those living on the earth below. Once he began, "And Rabbi Ben-Zion says...."

Rabbi Ben-Zion was sitting there at the table as just one Hassid among many Hassidim, but this did not affect him in any way. He remained what he was all his life, a true Hassid, who submits to the *rebbe* with all his heart and soul. Once on the holiday of Shavuot [the Feast of Weeks], when the *rebbe* had concluded his audience, he went out for a walk in the garden next to his home, which was adjacent to his large house of study. At the window overlooking the garden stood Rabbi Ben-Zion and some other Hassidim, looking towards the *rebbe*, who suddenly came over to the window and called for Rabbi Ben-Zion. The by-then elderly Hassid, who had already come to know illness and pain, did not move towards the somewhat distant door so that he could go out to the garden. Rather, he jumped right out the window like a boy, and stood before the *rebbe* like a servant before his master.

---

[75] Rabbi Yisrael ben Eliezer (d. 1760), an itinerant mystic from Podolia, Poland, considered the father of Hassidism.

[76] Rabbi Yaakov Yitzchak Horowitz (c. 1745-1815), early Polish Hassidic leader and "miracle worker."

[77] Rabbi Yaakov Yitzchak Rabinowitz (1766-1813) of Peshischa [Przysucha], another early Hassidic leader.

[78] Rabbi Simcha Bunim Bonhart (1765-1827), also of Peshischa, an early Polish Hassidic leader.

[79] Rabbi Menachem Mendel Morgenstern (1787-1859) of Kotsk, Hassidic leader who spent the last twenty years of his life in seclusion.

[80] Rabbi Yitzchak Meir**Error! Bookmark not defined.** Alter Rothenberg (1799-1866), founder and first *rebbe* of the Hassidic dynasty of Ger [Gur or Gora Kalwaria], one of the largest.

The One and Only

Throngs of people streamed to Ger. Nearly one thousand rabbis, *dayanim*, and heads of *yeshivot* were among the Hassidim of Ger, many of whom were exceptional scholars, giants of Torah. Many of them were considered outstanding Hassidim. But Rabbi Ben-Zion was alone among this huge congregation, for he had attained hitherto unknown levels in the history of Hassidism, so unique was he.

Rabbi Ben-Zion was loyal to his rabbi and was also devoted to him in every capillary of his soul. Every day Rabbi Avraham Mordechai taught a class to his sons and sons-in-law. Rabbi Ben-Zion participated in that class whenever he was staying in Ger. Once he was a few minutes late. He heard in the adjoining room that the *rebbe* had already begun his lecture, so he refused to enter. He did not want to disturb the *rebbe*, who was younger than him by many years, but who would rise from his chair to greet him.

Rabbi Ben-Zion had now reached his later years. He was about seventy years old, but he still made tracks to his teachers, the *rebbe*s, never desisting from his travels. His illness and weakness did not prevent him from doing so. It was correct, he said, as Rabbi Bunim of Peshischa had once said, that the adherence of Hassidim to their *rebbe*s was like a punishment for them from on high, because the children of Israel had not listened to their prophets, and had mocked their words, so now they were being punished by being covered in the dust of the feet of their *rebbe*s. But Rabbi Yitzchak Meir of Ger said that this was the correction of later generations to the flaws of the preceding generations. The Hassid travels to the *rebbe* to repair things that were damaged thousands of years earlier.

Up until his later years, until a very advanced age, Rabbi Ben-Zion never changed his way of life. He refused any official office. He did not serve as a teacher or educator, nor was he a leader or guide. He saw himself as just a Hassid among Hassidim, one among equals. But neither did he chase away the enthusiastic young men who were devoted to him, who learned Torah and Hassidism from him, and who viewed themselves as the students of Rabbi Ben-Zion. These students were different from others. They were more enthusiastic, deeper, stronger than others of their type. Their knowledge of Hassidism was broader and more comprehensive. They withstood every test and were purer of heart because of the strength of Rabbi Ben-Zion that devolved upon them.

The Propounder of Torah

He taught at pre-determined sessions every day. Young unmarried and married men were happy that he allowed them to study with him. Every morning he taught a class in Gemara [the later parts of the Talmud] and Tosafot [commentaries thereon], following the set order of the Talmud. The lesson included regular study of the earlier commentators, like the Rashba [acronym for Rabbi Shlomo ben Aderet],[81] the Ritva [acronym for Rabbi Yom Tov ben Avraham Asevilli],[82] the *Shita M'kubetztet* [*The Collected Interpretations*],[83] and others. After a recess he taught a second session following the order the *Shulchan Aruch* [*The Set Table*].[84] This was a more hands-on lesson in the application of the law, starting with the Gemara that deals with a particular Halacha and then the commentaries of the Rif [acronym for Rabbi Yitzchak Alfasi],[85] the Rosh [acronym for Rabbi Asher],[86] and then the *Tur* [*The Column*],[87] the *Shulchan Aruch* and other later decisors, until the law became clear. The same approach was applied to each paragraph of the *Shulchan Aruch*. His teaching was in-depth, endeavoring to fully understand both the particular issue as well as the law that was being studied.

His teaching was undertaken with the fear and awe [of God], with actual trembling. Once when he was about to begin the

---

[81] Eminent rabbi/Talmudist from Barcelona and leader of Spanish Jewry (1235-1310).

[82] Eminent rabbi/Talmudist from Seville, Spain (1250-1330).

[83] Principal work of Rabbi Betzalel Ashkenazi (ca. 1520-ca. 1592), a leading Talmudist of Ashkenazi origins, but who lived in the predominantly Sephardi Ottoman Empire, chiefly in Egypt and Palestine.

[84] A chief work of Rabbi Yosef Caro, born in Toledo in 1488 and, after the expulsion of the Jews from Spain in 1492 and from Portugal in 1497, lived in Ottoman Turkey, Salonika, Egypt and Safed, Palestine. The book, a condensation of his larger *Beit Yosef* [*House of Joseph*], is one of several--and the most widely accepted--medieval compilations of Jewish law. He was also leader of the famous mystic kabbalist group in Safed. He is the ancestor of the contemporary historian Robert Caro.

[85] North African-born Sephardi rabbi/Talmudist of Fez, Morocco (1013-1103), author of *Sefer Hahalachot* [*The Book of Laws*], one of the earliest codifications of Jewish law.

[86] Born ca. 1250 in Germany, from which he fled, he died in 1327 in Toledo, Spain, where he served as rabbi. He is the author of *Piskei Halachot* [*Decisions of Law*], a core legal commentary on the Talmud that is still widely consulted.

[87] Shortened title for *Arbaah Turim* [*The Four Columns*], a work of Jewish law written in four topical parts by Rabbi Yaakov ben Asher (ca. 1270-ca. 1340), son of Rabbi Asher (see above).

lesson, before he had even opened the Gemara, he said to his students with holy enthusiasm, "In earlier times, when Hassidim approached the opening of the Gemara, they gave a drop of blood from their hearts out of a feeling of subjugation and shame, as they realized how low their status was and how sad their condition, how disgusting their behavior was as compared to the scholars of the Gemara, who towered over these students to articulate their pronouncements." And his words, which as usual came forth from the depths of his big heart, penetrated the hearts of his students who heard his moral teachings. They were excited to hear all of his discussions, all of his stories. His students, who excelled in their knowledge of the Torah and in their exceptional Hassidism, learned much from him. He had hundreds, if not thousands of students who were dispersed all across Poland before the Holocaust. Many who passed them by would say in admiration, "There goes a student of Rabbi Ben-Zion."

Rabbi Ben-Zion expressed his approach to teaching in a few sentences, which he once wrote down on the title page of the *Sefer Hachinuch* [*The Book of Education*][88] he had in his home, which was only found after his death. The following sentences he apparently wrote for himself: "This book is called *Education...* because of the requirement to educate one's child and not to deviate from this obligation, for the commandments themselves teach a person to adhere to God. As it is said in the Gemara and Midrash, His [God's] fringes will strike man's face. And as it is written in the *Zohar* [*Radiance* or *Splendor*],[89] the 613 commandments of the Torah were given to us by God for our advantage, so that we might be together with Him, which is the very meaning of the word 'commandment.' Fortunate is the man who will always immerse himself in this holy book so that he might know the difference between 'thou shalt' and 'thou shalt not.' Because even though man is mired in the desires and worries of this world, if he but remembers that God has commanded that this is what you should do and this is what you should not do, he surely will not stray from the commandments of God. How much more so if he remembers that He who commanded him what to do and what not to do is the one who created and produced him, who supports and sustains him, and who can kill him and take his sustenance from him, and make him ill and also heal him, and take everything from him from his very breath to his body and

---

[88] An anonymous book written in 13th century Spain enumerating and elucidating the 613 commandments of Jewish law, one of several such compilations.

[89] A book of much debated origins that first appeared in 13th century Spain and is the foundational work of the Jewish mystical movement known as the *kabbalah*.

wealth and children and everything else that he possesses. Therefore, he surely will observe everything that He commands him to do."

The Students of Rabbi Ben-Zion

Occasionally Rabbi Ben-Zion would dine with his students, whether young Hassidim or elderly ones. And he sometimes would tell stories. And each of these stories was a treasure in itself, aimed at a particular target, uncovering new worlds and opening up new horizons. They were more influential than formal lessons of ethics and reproof. A story would take on flesh and bones of its own. It became a part of the reality of their past that was more influential than anything else on the young men and on the aged who pressed in to hear him and who absorbed every word. Some of his stories resulted in complete revolutionary changes in the hearts of his listeners. They served as food for thought or for in-depth analysis, and led to the understanding of entire aspects of life and to the leveling out of life's pathways. It is said that only Hassidim fully understood the value of his stories, and that at his feet were educated generations. Rabbi Ben-Zion told many stories, and they became the permanent legacy of the Hassidim of Poland.

The stories of Rabbi Ben-Zion were intertwined like chains, one story being connected with another like pearls on a necklace. He was likely to sit for over an hour with his Hassidim and tell stories. And he did not indulge in exaggerations. Everything was on point and on subject. So it happened in the days of the *rebbe* who was the author of the *Chiddushei Harim* [*The Novellae of the Rim*, Rabbi Yitzchak Meir of Ger], Rabbi Ben-Zion told, that there were very sharp young married men who worked diligently on their Hassidism. Once the *rebbe* said to one of these outstanding young men, "It is true and correct that you aspire to be a Hassid on the one hand, but on the other hand you do not wish to separate yourself from your baser side, from your young man's characteristics [Yiddish, *fun gruben yung deines*]. So what will be the outcome?"

"The main thing is to act and to completely fulfill, to carry out things by means of one's own actions. Something that is done by means of an agent is acceptable, as a person's agent is tantamount to himself. But in any event it is not like the real person himself, in actual fact." And Rabbi Ben-Zion went on:

"Once the Hassidic congregation of Kotsk in Warsaw split up. For some reason the wealthy separated themselves from the poor, who sat around all day and studied Torah. The former proceeded to create a new Hassidic house. The wealthy put forth a claim that since they had donated all the money to acquire the books in the old Hassidic house, they felt that the books belonged to them and that they therefore should be transferred to the new house. Furthermore, because they had not only donated all the money for the books, but had also purchased all the privileges of being called up to the Torah, and had also paid for the right to read the portion of *Atah Horeitah* [*You have taught*][90] out of their pockets, the books of the old Hassidic house rightfully belonged to them."

"But the poor learners who remained in the old Hassidic house claimed that the books belonged to them. This was because all the honors that were fully paid for in the Hassidic house were actually owned by those who study day and night. But because those who sit and delve into the Torah are so immersed in their studies, they have no time to go out into the streets and engage in business. And while the Hassidic house needs money to acquire books and for other expenses, the learners sell the honors that belong to them at full price in exchange for the purchase of books and other needs of the Hassidic house. The rich have therefore received full value for their money. They have no right to claim any further compensation, whereas the poor learners hold full rights to the books in the house of the Hassidim."

"The *rebbe* Rabbi Yitzchak Meir, to whom both sides brought their claims, decided in favor of the poor learners who remained in the old Hassidic house."

Revulsion from Honors and Wealth

Rabbi Ben-Zion was put off by money and by the wealthy. He spoke with awe about the fear of honors by great Hassidim who were desperately poor, and who were not ashamed of their poverty. As Rabbi Ben-Zion told:

"It was told about Rabbi Hersh Ber of Grabovitz [Grabowiec], a great Hassid, who was marrying off one of his sons. When it came time for the wedding he went with his son, the groom, to the town where the bride lived for the pre-wedding ceremonies. They arrived there and entered the inn. Rabbi Hersh Ber asked that the bride and her mother come over. The mother-in-law, the mother of the orphaned bride, arrived to clarify some matters. It was also necessary for the groom to see the bride, for it is forbidden for a man to marry a woman until he has seen her. After the widow had returned to her home, the bride appeared. Rabbi Hersh Ber inquired as to why the two had not appeared together, was there a lack of harmony between the mother and her daughter? He found out that they were so poor that they had only one coat between

---

[90] An honor on the holiday of Simchat Torah that is often auctioned off to the highest bidder.

them, so that when one went out, the other had to stay home. When Rabbi Hersh Ber heard this, he was overcome by emotion and turned to his son the groom and said: 'God has granted us a great favor in regard to the commandment of providing for a bride, my son. Come with me to the town square and we will collect money for the poor bride so that she will have her own clothing.' "

Seventy Years of Work

Rabbi Ben-Zion lived as a resident in Ostroveh for more than seventy years. He became a veritable bone of its skeleton, an integral part of its body, the head of the Hassidim and the glory of the community. Both the old and the young took pride in him. Even the local Mitnagdim felt honored because of him. He never accepted any official position in his life, but his influence was felt in everything. And if Ostrow Mazowiecka was transformed into a citadel of Hassidism and Hassidim, it was chiefly because of Rabbi Ben-Zion. Many of the opponents of Hassidism became Hassidim because of Rabbi Ben-Zion.

In the early years of Rabbi Ben-Zion's presence in Ostroveh the influence of the Hassidim on the residents of the city was still weak. The officers and congregants of the old house of study, almost all of whom were opponents of Hassidim and Hassidism, for all intents and purposes were the ones who determined the direction of the community. They were the ones who ultimately decided who would serve and who would not serve as rabbi of the city. Slowly but surely the strength of the Hassidim grew. The influence of Rabbi Ben-Zion steadily increased to the point where no rabbi or *dayan* was chosen without the assent of this famous Hassid.

When the candidacy of Rabbi Yehuda Leib Gordin was proposed as rabbi of Ostroveh, people went to interview him in the place of his previous position in Augustow. Among them was Rabbi Ben-Zion and Rabbi Berish Shapira, son of the Gaon Rabbi Isaac *Charif*, the rabbi of Slonim, and one of the heads of the Mitnagdim of the city. But only after the candidacy of Rabbi Gordin was deemed acceptable by Rabbi Ben-Zion was he chosen as rabbi and chief of the rabbinical court.

Before Rabbi Gordin, the Hassidic *rebbe* Rabbi Gershon Chanoch of Radzyn had served as chief of the rabbinical court. There was no love or understanding lost between the Hassidim of Ger and those of Radzyn. Rabbi Ben-Zion was not among the supporters or friends of the *rebbe* from Radzyn. But loyal to the truth, he praised the work of Rabbi Gershon Chanoch as rabbi and chief of the rabbinical court, and his strong stand concerning everything regarding religion and Torah. But more than once

Rabbi Ben-Zion told how the *rebbe* of Radzyn prevented anyone who derived learning from non-Jewish sources or who sent his son to a gymnasium [secular academic high school] from even entering into his house. Could not such a person just pray at another house of Hassidim or visit another *rebbe*?

Love of the Truth

Rabbi Ben-Zion loved the truth and was one of those who was not afraid of the truth. He was devoted to the pure approach of Kotsk that was committed to the pursuit of truth. He praised every revelation of truth and justice no matter its source. More than once the students of Rabbi Ben-Zion heard him praise Mitnagdim, simple people, no matter who. He lauded the Gaon Rabbi Ben-Zion, the chief of the rabbinical court of Bielsk,[91] a sharp opponent of Hassidim and Hassidism, because of the following true story: Once Rabbi Ben-Zion [of Bielsk] preached against dissolute women who went out without covering their hair, as required by Halacha.

When he finished his lecture one of the residents approached him and asked: "Was it not true that the rabbi's own daughter went out into the streets with her head uncovered? Is it appropriate for her father, the rabbi, to preach such piety to others?"

The rabbi replied: "So what? If my daughter would convert, God forbid, or would mount the pulpit and preach to the public that she had converted, would that make it permissible?"

Battling at the Gates

Rabbi Ben-Zion did not involve himself in the ongoing affairs of the community. He was always burdened and busy with his own matters, his study of Torah and his prayers. But neither did he restrain himself when it came to matters of the breach of the walls of religion. When the Germans captured Ostroveh, during World War I, members of the Zionist parties in town assembled in order to decide upon the establishment of a gymnasium in the city that would provide a co-educational education having a clearly secular and anti-religious curriculum. When Rabbi Ben-Zion was notified about the meeting, he immediately went there accompanied by his outstanding student, the Gaon Rabbi Moshe Goldblatt.

This sharp Rabbi "Moshaleh," who was then a young man, entered the place and raised his voice in pain against the flawed idea of transforming Ostroveh into a den of educational iniquity. The assembled crowd was prepared to consider the matter. Rabbi

---

[91] Rabbi Ben-Zion**Error! Bookmark not defined.** Sternfeld (1835-1914) of Bielsk Podlaski.

Ben-Zion sat next to him, defending his beloved student. He, too, raised his voice, demanding and insisting that the crowd disperse in order to prevent steps that would destroy this glorious community. No one dared to raise his voice against Rabbi Ben-Zion in reply. The attendees dispersed and returned to their homes without further discussion. The plan never materialized. A gymnasium was never established in the city up until its destruction.

As Rabbi Ben-Zion aged, his honored position in the community only rose. But the elderly Hassid continued to act as just a simple resident among the other residents. There was never a mourner in town to whom Rabbi Ben-Zion did not pay a visit of consolation. There was never a matter in which Rabbi Ben-Zion did not shoulder his share of responsibility. Every month he would visit the rabbi of the city at his home, as the sages of old had prescribed.

In the years following World War I, Rabbi Ben-Zion became weaker. He passed the age of eighty. His vision declined. Walking became difficult for him. But despite all this, he never changed his customs or his daily routine. It was difficult for him to go to the house of the Hassidim, so he agreed that a small *minyan* [prayer quorum] of young scholars who were his students would regularly assemble to pray at his home.

Despite his weakness deriving from his extreme advanced age, Rabbi Ben-Zion never changed his daily set routine, with its long teaching sessions that were scheduled in advance. But he did begin to speak of his departure from the world that was getting closer. He said to his only son, Rabbi Yitzchak Meir Rabinowitz, "I am in no hurry for you to recite *kaddish* [the memorial prayer] or for you to study Mishnayot [the early part of the Talmud often studied in memory of a deceased individual] after I depart. But remember that I did urge you to honor the Hassidim with the fear of God and with refreshments on the first anniversary of my death."

The Hour of Departure

In his book, *Vayelaket Yosef* [*Joseph's Collections*], the Gaon Rabbi Yosef Mandelkorn, one of the immigrants from Ostroveh in Jerusalem, writes: "On the eve of the last holiday of Hoshana Rabba [the seventh day of Sukkot] of his life, I was invited to his home. His eyes were failing from weakness, and as such he requested that I read for him from the biblical chapter of *V'zot Habracha* [*And this is the blessing*]. It was one part text and two parts interpretation, as usual. When I reached the verse, 'And Moses, the servant of God, died there,' he stopped my reading and did not permit me to continue to the end of the chapter. I said to him that it is appropriate to finish a worthy deed, especially on the eve of Hoshana Raba. But Rabbi Ben-Zion refused to listen, and ordered me to stop and that was it."

And for the holiday of Shavuot that year he once again made his way to Ger, to the court of the *rebbe*. He was weak and wracked with illness and pain. With great effort he was able to make this last journey, refusing to hear anything about canceling his trip to the *rebbe*. He had traveled seventy-one times on the High Holidays to five different *rebbe*s, and sixty-nine times for the holiday of Shavuot to mark the receiving of the Torah in the study house of the *rebbe*.

Because of his weakness he was not able to sit at the table of the *rebbe*, which was surrounded by thousands of Hassidim who devotedly crowded in to absorb something of the Torah and the conduct of the *rebbe*. Rather he sat in the room of the *rebbe* adjacent to the great study hall because of his weakness. And when the *rebbe* passed by, the great Hassid broke out in bitter tears. A chapter that spanned seventy years of effort and holy work was coming close to its end.

After the holiday Rabbi Ben-Zion took his leave from the *rebbe* and set off to return to Ostrow Mazowiecka. On his way he stopped at an inn in Warsaw, and was immediately stricken by a blood clot in the head. The time of his departure was closing in. Rabbi Ben-Zion had thought that he would find his eternal rest in Ostrow Mazowiecka, the city of his residence. He now asked that the boards of his study table be sawed up and re-configured into his coffin.

He ordered that his grave be dug alongside that of a simple water carrier, a man by the name of Salzberg, a Jew who had served for twenty-five years in the army of Tsar Nicholas I, but who remained observant of the Torah and its commandments, be it the most minor or the most serious. But it was in Warsaw, the city in which he was born, that his soul was returned to his maker. It was on the nineteenth day of Sivan, 5686 [June 1, 1926]. He was eighty-six years of age.

In their masses his students and admirers streamed into Warsaw, to 13 Twarda Street, the site of the inn where he died. On a wagon hitched to horses the deceased was taken to the cemetery in Warsaw. This time the Hassidim diverged from local custom, in honor of the greatest of Polish Hassidism. The wagon was pulled by the masses to the edge of the cemetery. But when the cortege reached Gensia Street, which is on the way to the cemetery, the mourners took out the stretcher upon which he lay and the students carried it to the grave site. A sea of humanity filled the gigantic cemetery of the community of Warsaw. Tens of thousands came to pay their respects to a glorious chapter in the Hassidism of Poland, which came to an end with the death of Rabbi Ben-Zion.

His only son, Rabbi Yitzchak Meir Rabinowitz, and his son-in-law, Rabbi Moshe Leib Wolman,[92] the son of the rabbi of Plonsk, were both killed in the Holocaust.

---

[92] Rabbi Moshe Leib [Moszek Lejb] Wolman, son of Victor [Wictor] Wolman, was married to Rabbi Ben-Zion's daughter Freida [Frejda] (b. 1877). They had at least three children: Leizer [Lejzor] (b. 1895), Liba (b. 1903), and Yisrael Yaakov (Srul Yankiel) (b. 1910).

Chapter Ten

Personalities of Ostroveh Who Had Passed On

The Gaon Rabbi Yissachar Berish Shapira

For decades the uncrowned head, spokesman and representative of those who were opposed to Hassidism, especially the learned and exceptional among them, was the Gaon Rabbi Yissachar Berish Shapira, a wise and learned man, of distinguished lineage and many talents. He continued the golden heritage of the *geonim* of Lithuania of previous generations faithfully and with true dedication.

The *Gaon* Rabbi Yissachar Berish Shapira was born in Kalwaria, Lithuania,[93] to the illustrious *gaon* who was its pride, Rabbi Isaac *Charif* ["the Sharp"], who later served as the rabbi of Tiktin [Tykocin], Kutno and Slonim. He became known in his and in later generations as Rabbi Isaac *Charif*.[94]

Rabbi Isaac was born in Globanka [Glubokie, today Hlybokaye, Belarus], a town near Minsk, in the year 5561 [1801], to his righteous father Rabbi Yechiel, son of the Hassidic Gaon Rabbi Mordechai. His father and grandfather were great scholars whose renown as righteous men came mostly from their deeds and ways of life. They were among the most respected Jews of their times.

From early in his youth it was already apparent that Rabbi Isaac was an extraordinary and exceptional genius, sharper than all others, wise and sharp-witted from childhood. He studied at Blumke's study hall in Minsk, under the supervision of the famed Gaon Rabbi Avraham Dworitzer. At a young age one of the important citizens of Minsk, Reb Yitzchak Fein, took him as a son-in-law. Since that time he was called Rabbi Isaac *Charif*, whether it was because of his sharpness or whether it was that the letters of *Charif* stood for the first letters of "**Ch**atan **R**eb **Yi**tzchak **F**ein" (son-in-law of Reb Yitzchak Fein).

When he was just seventeen he was considered the stand-in for the famed Rabbi Avraham Dworitzer as a lecturer in the study hall and even as a gifted preacher. His father-in-law, Reb Yitzchak Fein, supported him and refused to hear anything about his beloved son-in-law leaving Minsk. But when the residents of Kalwaria came and offered the job of rabbi in their town to the young Gaon Rabbi Isaac, whose name had spread far and wide,

---

[93] According to Ostrow Mazowiecka town records, Rabbi Berish was born in 1827.

[94] Rabbi Yehoshua Yitzchak (1801-1873), a/k/a Eizel *Charif* (or Little Isaac the Sharp), as described above in the text.

Rabbi Isaac quickly accepted the offer. He moved with the members of his family to that town, as he could not abide Minsk and its wealthy people.

From Kalwaria, the small Lithuanian town, he then went to Kutno, the well respected and well endowed Polish city, where he had been selected as chief of the rabbinical court. He remained there for a while before he moved his family there, but the Polish Hassidic atmosphere of Kutno did not please him. He left the city and never came back. He went on to serve as the chief of the rabbinical court of Tiktin, and from there went on to occupy the chair of the rabbinate in Slonim, where he remained until his final days.

This exceptional *gaon* was superior in the sharpness of his intellect and his greatness in the Torah to all others of his generation. His name was mentioned with praise in Jewish communities everywhere. His Torah teachings lasted for generations. His books included: *Emek Yehoshua* [*The Valley of Joshua*] and *Nachlat Yehoshua* [*The Legacy of Joshua*], *Noam Yerushalmi* [*The Delight of Jerusalem*] in four large volumes, as well as *Avi Hanachal* [*Source of the River*], *S'fat Hanachal* [*The Bank of the River*], *Marbeh Eitzah* [*Extending Advice*], and *Atzat Yehoshua* [*The Advice of Joshua*], and his last book, *Marbeh T'vunah* [*Promoting Understanding*], a book of lectures and ethical teachings.

Rabbi Isaac was particularly known for his wisdom and his great acuity. His sayings became a permanent asset of the legacy of his generation and of those that followed. A pithy, wise and sharp pronouncement was the greatest weapon of this great *gaon*, who behaved with extreme modesty and whose behavior was without blemish. In this spirit he educated his three sons, the Gaon Rabbi Yissachar Berish of Ostroveh; the Gaon Rabbi Moshe Shapira, one of the rabbis of Riga, and author of *P'nei Moshe* [*The Face of Moses*], *S'fat Haemek* [*The Edge of the Valley*] and other works; and Rabbi Mordechai, the youngest of his sons. The Gaon Rabbi Isaac took ill on Thursday, the third day of Tevet, 5633 [January 2, 1873], and the next day, on the eve of the Sabbath, the fourth of Tevet, he passed away. His son-in-law, husband of his only and wonderful daughter, Rabbi Yosef Schleifer,[95] the genius of Denenberg [Dinaburg-Dvinsk, today Daugavpils, Latvia], took the place of his father-in-law in Slonim for many years.

Rabbi Berish first married a woman from Nowy Dwor near Warsaw, and lived there for several years, supported by his wealthy father-in-law. But his first wife died young. The name of

---

[95] Rabbi Yosef Schleifer (d. 1905), who was married to Rabbi Isaac's daughter, Nechama.

Rabbi Yissachar Berish was circulated all over the country, and many respectable matches were proposed to him. Rabbis and *rebbe*s wanted to have him as a son-in-law. But Rabbi Berish preferred to marry a woman who was the daughter of a wealthy merchant family. He rejected the rabbinate or other public role. But on the other hand, he was not prepared to dedicate too much of his time either to business or to the maintenance of a household. The daughter of a merchant family would know how to run a household and would be able to help him run a business, which in turn would enable him learn Torah extensively.

Therefore Rabbi Berish married a woman of the wealthy Bromberg family of Ostrow Mazowiecka.[96] In the year 5610 [1849-1850] he came to that city and stayed there more than fifty years. He became the spokesman for the Torah-oriented community of Ostroveh, and an integral part thereof, the pride of the community in its glory days.

He had a textile store in the heart of town, which for all intents and purposes was managed by his wife, and to which Rabbi Berish devoted only a small part of his time, solely in regard to its accounts and its correspondence with its suppliers. He never set foot in the store itself, never even crossed its threshold. He belonged completely to another world, the world of the Torah.

His true place was to be found on the eastern wall of the new study house, the stronghold of the Mitnagdim, as he was counted among the strongest opponents to Hassidim and Hassidism, especially the Hassidism that was not distinguished by its Torah learning. Like his father he despised the ignoramus and the unlearned. He negated the Hassid who was not well versed in the Torah and did not devote at least some of his day to it.

Upon his arrival in Ostroveh he became the spokesman of the Mitnagdim, their leader and guide. His own lineage and that of his ancestors served him well. Great scholars and learned men of the city gathered around him, and since his coming they, like the Hassidim, became a united and permanent force. The power of the Hassidim always derived from their unity, by their appearance as a single body given to following a *rebbe* or other great Hassid as their representative vis-a-vis their rivals, the Mitnagdim. The weakness of the Mitnagdim in Ostroveh was in their divisiveness, in the absence of a single force of great influence and standing, to whom they would submit and whose authority they would willingly accept. Rabbi Berish fulfilled this function from the very moment he settled in the city. He was a learned man of Torah and good

---

[96] The second wife of Rabbi Berish was Sura Shendla Bromberg (1826-1900), daughter of Wolf and Bluma.

works, a servant of God who was meticulously observant of His commandments, yet also a wise man and a man of action, one who was wealthy enough not to be dependent on anyone.

Hassidim and Mitnagdim came into conflict in Ostroveh. The city, which lay in the approaches to Lithuania from Poland, and whose Jewish population had come from various different places, both from Lithuania and from central Poland, had become a battleground between fervent Hassidim and sworn Mitnagdim. Each movement endeavored to dominate the institutions of the community and to extend the lines of its influence. Hassidim and Mitnagdim fought over the selection of a rabbi. If the Hassidim succeeded in choosing a rabbi, the Mitnagdim would do battle with him up to the point where he had to leave his position. If a Mitnaged became the rabbi, the Hassidim would fight with him until he packed his bags and left the place. The Mitnagdim believed with all their hearts that in their battle for hegemony over the community they were fighting for the rule of the Torah and scholarship, for true unlimited and uncorrupted rule of the explicit Halacha as found in the *Shulchan Aruch*. The Hassidim believed with all their hearts that in their fight for hegemony over the community and its institutions that they were fighting for a life of holiness and purity, for a life of pure Hassidism that would guarantee a faithful character to the community and its institutions for generations to come.

At the head of the Mitnagdic camp stood the Gaon Rabbi Berish Shapira, while at the head of the Hassidic camp was the Gaon Rabbi Ben-Zion Rabinowitz. Both of them were exceptional people that few could hope to match. Thanks to them the conflict never exceeded reasonable, accepted bounds. It never reverted to means that were beyond proper community relations, but relations were nevertheless tense. However, false accusations, physical confrontations or the resort to the dominant non-Jewish authorities for them to determine an issue were unknown in Ostroveh.

Rabbi Berish was firm in his beliefs and outlook, but he was prepared to concede on minor details, on monetary matters, or on matters of personal honor. But he was as hard as flint stone on matters of *weltanschauung* [world view], on matters of Judaism. In his battles over these matters he did not accept compromise and did not accept things as they were. Without weakening he held to his position as he understood and recognized it. Honest efforts of the Hassidim to convince him were unsuccessful. On the contrary, they only strengthened his opposition.

Rabbi Berish faithfully and devotedly adhered to the ways and views of the Gaon Rabbi Isaac of Slonim. Rabbi Isaac successfully led his flock with great wisdom, preserving the ancient character of the institutions of the community and rabbinic traditions. The pathways and actions of his father served as an example and a model for him, the true path from which one should not veer right or left, a well paved road that was obligatory unto all.

Rabbi Isaac *Charif* of Slonim visited with his son Rabbi Berish several times. His visits to Ostrow Mazowiecka became impressive occasions. The learned people of the city prepared for such visits. They surrounded the great *gaon* all the time that he was in town, and hardly ever left Rabbi Berish's house. The famous and extraordinary rabbi of Slonim was like a flowing well that never ceased to supply life-giving water, whether they were innovative ideas in Halacha or in the Babylonian or Jerusalem Talmuds that evoked amazement and appreciation, or whether they were other sharp or wise thoughts that learned people mulled over much. Whenever the great *gaon* came, he expounded in the study house, to which masses of young men streamed just to hear him. Rabbi Isaac *Charif* would usually deliver words of Torah and ethics, expounded and innovated, interwoven with great depth and acuity. Even the best of the listeners had to try hard to plumb the full depths of the ideas of this prince of the Torah, but at times did not succeed in doing so. No one dared to approach this great *gaon* to seek a further explanation of his words out of awe and politeness, admiration and love. Rabbi Berish served as the address for the explanation of his great father's thoughts, as he was among the few who quickly grasped the depth of his thought and the amazing sharpness of this leading *gaon* of the generation.

The visits of the Gaon Rabbi Isaac to Ostroveh only strengthened the Mitnagdic camp and the position of Rabbi Berish, as its leader and spokesman. Despite all this, relations between Rabbi Berish the Mitnaged and Rabbi Ben-Zion the Hassid remained proper and friendly. Their differences remained in the realm of their respective outlooks, but never entered the personal sphere. Whenever they met they were genuinely glad to see one another.

When the question of the selection of the Gaon Rabbi Yehuda Leib Gordin as rabbi of the community arose, Rabbi Berish and Rabbi Ben-Zion traveled to Augustow, the place of residence of the rabbi, to evaluate his character and nature. These two exceptional people traveled together in a friendly manner, despite the fact that they represented two camps, two different worlds.

This took place after Rabbi Berish had worked hard to choose the Gaon Rabbi Shimon Dov Anolik as rabbi of the city. At that time he was the rabbi of Shaki, that small Lithuanian town. Rabbi Anolik was among the sharpest students of his father, Rabbi Isaac

Charif, and a soul mate of Rabbi Berish, who finally convinced the members of the community to select "the black genius" (as Rabbi Shimon Dov was called in Lithuania) as rabbi of the city. But things did not work out for Rabbi Berish. While the community did present a rabbinical contract to Rabbi Anolik, and while he did appear in Ostroveh, the people of Shaki opposed this with all their might. They put pressure on the rabbi's wife, who absolutely refused to move to Ostroveh in light of what its Hassidim had done to the previous rabbi because he was a Mitnaged. Rabbi Anolik returned to Shaki. (Later he served as chief of the rabbinical court of Tiktin and from there went on to become the rabbi of Siedlce.)

Rabbi Berish prayed at the new study hall, where he was a leader and member of a study group called Tot, a Mitnagdic group of exceptional men of action. They did not remove their prayer shawls or phylacteries after morning prayers, but rather sat down to study throughout the morning hours still wearing their prayer shawls and phylacteries without having yet eaten anything. During the twenties and thirties of the seventh century of the fifth millennium [5620-5640 on the Hebrew calendar, equating to 1859-1880], this group included tens of members, among them some extraordinary scholars, well accepted and exceptional people, whose entire lives were dedicated to serving God in extreme modesty and devotion, with unparalleled self-sacrifice.

Like his father the great *gaon*, Rabbi Berish was noted for his great sharpness that amazed many people. He was particularly known for his ability in mathematical Hebrew word games [*gimatriyot*]. In a split second he was able to calculate the mathematical values of any saying, from which he could reveal secrets of the Torah inherent therein, which impressed many people. After his death he left a large book of these computations. His sons intended to publish it, but for some reason they did not succeed in doing so and the manuscript was lost in the Holocaust. Some of the novellae of Rabbi Berish were published at the end of his father's book, *Emek Yehoshua* (in the second edition that was published by his brother the Gaon Rabbi Moshe Shapira, one of the rabbis of Riga). These are innovations in various subjects of the Talmud, according to the method of his father, the *gaon*.

After the death of his second wife,[97] Rabbi Berish immigrated to the Land of Israel. He remained for a time in Jerusalem. But because he was a Russian citizen, he was subject to the draft when war broke out between Russia and Turkey, which then ruled Palestine. So after half a year he returned to Ostroveh, and

---

[97] According to town records, Rabbi Berish's second wife died in 1900.

remained in the city until the day of his death, the tenth of Adar, 5662 [February 10, 1902].[98]

His son, Rabbi Yechiel Shapira, moved to Linshitz [Lenczyca]. The grandsons of Rabbi Berish, including the Gaon Rabbi Moshe Aaron Nathanson, chief of the rabbinical court of Zlochow [Zloczow or Zloczev], became Hassidim of Ger.

The Gaon Rabbi Yitzchak David Shulevitz

Among the outstanding *dayanim* [religious judges] of Ostroveh and the rabbis who graced the rabbinate there was the Gaon Rabbi Yitzchak David Shulevitz, who served as a *dayan* and teacher of Halacha [rabbi] for nearly fifty years, first in Komorowo and then in neighboring Ostroveh.

Rabbi Yitzchak David's origins were in an outstanding and completely Hassidic family. He was the grandson of Rabbi Yaakov of Zarnovitz [Zarnoviec], one of the important students of the *rebbe* Rabbi Simcha Bunim of Peshischa. Already at an early age he stood out as an excellent and diligent student whose whole world consisted of the universe of the Torah.

He studied at various *yeshivot* and was ordained by the leading *gaon* of the generation, Rabbi Chaim Soloveichik, the chief of the rabbinical court of Brisk [Brest-Litovsk] and one of the greatest of rabbis. At a young age he was appointed as rabbi in Komorowo near Ostroveh. After a few years he was selected as a *dayan* in Ostroveh. From then until the community's final destruction he never abandoned his high position.

He was a *gaon* of the Torah and an exceptional teacher of Halacha, whose name was widely known. He was especially diligent. Starting in 5670 [1909-910] he would complete the study of the entire Talmud every year. Thus he completed it thirty times until the outbreak of the Holocaust, his other responsibilities as a *dayan* and his other studies notwithstanding.

Rabbi Yitzchak David was close to the long line of *tzadikim* [*rebbe*s] of the house of Amshinov, especially the *rebbe* Rabbi Yosef. He was among his best friends. He never deviated from the bounds of Torah and Halacha. He loved people and brought them closer to the Torah. He was also non-partisan, and never got involved in any dispute or conflict between the various movements in town.

On a Friday, the first day of the last war, the day that the German hordes invaded Poland, Nazi airplanes bombed Ostrow

---

[98] According to town records, he died on February 14, 1904. According to the Russian calendar then in use in this part of Poland, this would coincide with the tenth of Adar.

Mazowiecka and caused deaths and serious injuries in the city. Rabbi Yitzchak David was among the wounded and never recovered. He was expelled from the city by the cruel murderers and went to Bialystok in the Soviet zone of occupation. Despite the efforts of the doctors, he still did not get well. On the sixteenth day of Shevat in the year 5700 [January 25-26, 1940], he passed away. Thousands from among the residents of Bialystok as well as from the masses of refugees from the Nazi zone of occupation attended his funeral.

The Gaon Rabbi Avraham Frenkel

The Gaon Rabbi Avraham Frenkel[99] was yet a young man when he arrived in Ostrow Mazowiecka to marry the daughter of Reb Tevel Kelewitz [Kieliwicz], a well known wine merchant of the city. He immediately distinguished himself with his greatness in Torah and his superior personal traits. A moderate and modest young man, he exhibited a refined manner that evoked admiration and affection from everyone.

He quickly joined the Ger Hassidic community in town. He was among the sharpest and best of its young men, one of the group of followers of the Hassidic Gaon Rabbi Ben-Zion Rabinowitz. He was also modest in everything that he did and welcomed everyone with a smiling face. Young in age but great in Torah, immediately upon his arrival he was deemed one of the greatest students in the city, which was full of outstanding Torah scholars.

At the young age of twenty-four Rabbi Avraham was named by the Gaon Rabbi Yehuda Leib Gordin, the chief rabbi of the city, to be a *dayan*. He quickly excelled in his public role and in his contacts and relationships with people with affection and dedication. He served with devotion as a *dayan* and teacher of Halacha, and despite his young age succeeded in earning the trust of all the residents of the community, both Hassidim and Mitnagdim. The scholars and wise men of Ostroveh heaped praise on Rabbi Avraham's rulings, with his decisions being considered like those of a veteran.

Rabbi Avraham was admired and respected by the large community Ger Hassidim. He was close to and beloved by Rabbi Avraham Mordechai of Ger. Many had high hopes for him, believing that he would eventually attain an exalted and central

---

[99] According to town records, Abram Frenkel, son of Leizer Ber and Tema, was born in Tomaszow in 1879 and was recorded as having registered in Ostrow Mazowiecka in 1909. He died in 1915. His wife was Ides, daughter of Tevel and Reila Kielewicz [Kelewitz].

position among the rabbis of his generation and the giants of Torah.

But in the year 5775 [1915], when Ostroveh was conquered by the imperial German army, illnesses and plagues broke out in the city. The Gaon Rabbi Avraham was struck with an infectious disease and died in the prime of his life--he was not quite thirty-six years old--to the great sorrow of the members of the community.

Lest the Jews of Ostrow Mazowiecka be defined strictly by their various movements, masses of people cried in the streets at the death of Rabbi Avraham at the prime of his years, at the very threshold of his life. No one remained in their home during the funeral of the young *dayan.* He was brought to his final resting place amidst deep mourning. His widow and children remained in Ostroveh, and were killed in the Holocaust.[100]

The Gaon Rabbi Yisrael NatanError! Bookmark not defined. Plotzky

He was the son of the Gaon Rabbi Meir Dan**Error! Bookmark not defined.** Plotzky, chief of the rabbinical court of Dvart and of Ostrow Mazowiecka. He was born in the year 5648 [1887-1888] in Dvart. He studied in the *yeshiva* of his father the *gaon.* He excelled in his great acuity and his strong desire to study, viewing his studies as the most important aspect, the essence, of his life.

After his marriage he continued in his studies with great enthusiasm and diligence. He studied out of a sense of need, with joy and dedication. Like his father the *gaon,* Rabbi Yisrael Natan was one of the sharpest and most devoted Hassidim of Ger. He frequently traveled to visit the *rebbe,* the author of the *S'fat Emet,* in Ger, and later his son, the *rebbe* Rabbi Avraham**Error! Bookmark not defined.** Mordechai.

In the year 5688 [1928] the Gaon Rabbi Meir Dan Plotzky died in Warsaw, after he had previously left his post in the rabbinate of Ostrow Mazowiecka and moved to Warsaw to serve as head of the *yeshiva* called *Metivta.* The family of the *gaon* then demanded the post of rabbi of the town for one of his sons, claiming that Rabbi Yisrael Natan was an appropriate replacement for his great father.

The people of the community of Ostroveh objected. They rejected any right of inheritance, arguing that Rabbi Meir Dan had left the seat of the rabbinate in Ostroveh voluntarily and therefore had renounced any claims to that position and willingly accepted

---

[100] According to town records he had two surviving sons: Noach Eliash (b. 1904) and Tevia (b. 1914). His daughter Dvora Leah died the same year as her father.

the idea of another rabbi being selected in his stead. In their view, then, there was no basis for the family's claim. Yet there were some in the community who supported the claim of the late *gaon*'s family, as many of the residents of Ostrow Mazowiecka were among his admirers.

After extended discussions, a rabbinic law suit was initiated. But with the agreement of both parties it was decided that Rabbi Yisrael Natan would serve as a *dayan* and teacher of Halacha in the city. But on the other hand the members of the family agreed to waive any rights to the community's chief rabbinate.

From that time until the outbreak of the Holocaust, Rabbi Yisrael**Error! Bookmark not defined.** Natan served among the rabbis of Ostroveh. He took an active part in rabbinical matters and matters of religion in the community, and worked diligently and with his characteristic passion to preserve Judaism. At the same time he did not desist from his diligent study day or night.

His father, the Gaon Rabbi Meir Dan, had mentioned his son Rabbi Yisrael Natan in many places in his book. And after the death of Rabbi Meir Dan, his son re-published his father's novellae along with his own additions. Rabbi Yisrael Natan wrote several different books, novellae on the Talmud and on Halacha. These manuscripts remained in Ostroveh until the outbreak of the Holocaust but then disappeared.

With the capture of the city by the brutal Nazi soldiers, Rabbi Yisrael Natan moved to Slonim in the Soviet zone of occupation. He was still there when the Nazis conquered it at the time of the outbreak of the war between Soviet Russia and Nazi Germany. Rabbi Yisrael Natan suffered greatly in the Slonim ghetto that was established by the Nazi murderers. But even in those difficult and bitter days he did not cease to study and teach. With the destruction of the ghetto, Rabbi Yisrael Natan, along with his wife and four daughters, became part of the overall sacrifice of those who were killed.[101]

The Gaon Rabbi Avraham Yosef Zinowitz

The Gaon Rabbi Avraham Yosef Zinowitz [Cynowicz] was born in the year 5625 [1864-1865] in Zambrow [Zambroveh],[102] the

---

[101] Among the many other Ostrowers (she actually had lived in the nearby town of Ostrolenka, where some of the Feinzeig clan resided) who fled to Slonim in 1939 and were killed there in the town's ghetto by the Nazis in 1942 were the editor's great-aunt, Dina Feinzeig Weinzimmer, her husband Meir, and their four children, Feige, Zalman, Avraham and Moshe.

[102] According to town records, he was born in Zambrow on March 1, 1858.

third of four sons born to the *gaon* and *tzadik* Rabbi Chaim Tzvi, one of the elite of his generation. It was said of Rabbi Chaim Tzvi that he fasted during the study breaks and only ate each day after afternoon prayers. His entire life was dedicated to Torah and good works, while his entrepreneurial wife ran a store for manufactured goods to support the household. Rabbi Chaim Tzvi was very righteous. He prayed for extended hours at a time, and secluded himself in his room every day, wearing shrouds that he had prepared for himself and placed pottery shards on his eyes to remind himself of the day of his death. On such days he would cry a lot and would do complete penance before his maker.

His son, Rabbi Avraham Yosef, was considered an excellent student from the earliest days of his youth, when he went to the Volozhin *yeshiva* to study Torah. He stood out as a very diligent pupil with an unusual memory. When he was just twenty years old he was selected as a *dayan* and a teacher of Halacha in Ostroveh, which was at the time full of superior scholars and students. He served as a *dayan* in the city for twenty years, at the time when brilliant rabbis and famous *geonim* served in the city's rabbinate.

In the year 5665 [1904-1905] Rabbi Avraham Yosef moved to Lomza, where he was appointed as a *dayan* and teacher of Halacha. He served for thirty-five years in that major provincial city, where he was much beloved unto its residents. Over the years Rabbi Avraham Yosef acquired an enormous library of Torah-related books that included thousands of valuable volumes. His name became famous beyond the city of his residence as a wonderful bibliographer, in addition to his greatness in Torah. Diligence characterized him all the days of his long life. Every free moment was dedicated to study.

His manner was pleasant. He received everyone with kindness, and worked in particular to attract the youth and bring them to Torah, in the study of which he envisioned the image of everything. In his conversations with people it was clear that he was a true lover of the Jewish people, a fortress in people's times of sorrow, one who penetrated to the depths of their troubles. When he sat in judgment he always sought to plumb the depths of the law. He preferred compromise and would be lenient wherever it was possible without deviating from the explicit Halacha.

Since the rise of the Mizrachi movement[103] within the Zionist organization, Rabbi Avraham Yosef was among its loyal followers.

---

[103] Mizrachi, an anagram for *Merkaz Ruchani* or Spiritual Center, was the first separate political party in the World Zionist Organization. Founded in 1902 in Vilna by Rabbi Yitzhak Yaakov Reines, it was the party of religious Zionism, later called the National

Already from his days in Ostroveh he was supportive of the organizers of the religious Zionist movement locally. He did this not out in the open, because he preferred not to get involved in controversy with the Hassidim in the city, who completely negated Zionism and the Mizrachi. Once he had moved to Lomza, however, Rabbi Avraham publicly joined the Mizrachi movement and supported it on every occasion. The rabbi aspired to immigrate to the Land of Israel. It was his dream, but he was never able to fulfill it. He was among forty rabbis who signed a petition on behalf of the Jewish National Fund[104] in Poland.

By nature he was modest, and generally tried not to stand out. The same applied to his son-in-law, Rabbi David Rosenbaum, who in his youth was famously referred to as the "Genius of Goworowo."[105] He, too, turned down the rabbinate out of modesty. At the same time Rabbi Avraham Yosef did stand out in terms of his comprehensive knowledge about medicine, which attracted him. He learned to understand the nature of medicines that the doctors in Lomza gave to the ill, and more than once debated with them, and occasionally they admitted that he was correct. For a time Rabbi Avraham Yosef was hospitalized at the hospital in Warsaw, under the care of Dr. Frishman. While there, he spent most of his time learning about the methods of medicine. He spoke extensively with the doctors, who explained to him the bases of modern medicine. When he realized that Dr. Frishman was overly interested in money, and cared for patients in accordance with how much money he received, he reproved him for this without reservation.

But the basis of his life and its substance was the Torah and its study. And until his last day he did not cease to learn and to teach. He wrote many novellae on the Talmud and on Halacha, but out of modesty declined to publish them. His grandson, Rabbi Shmuel Chaim Rosenbaum, may God avenge his death, finally published his book, *Salsalot Yosef* [*The Adornments of Joseph*].

Rabbi Avraham Yosef was seventy-five years old when the Holocaust broke out. He remained in the city and suffered much

---

Religious Party (or in Hebrew, *Miflagah Dadit Leumit* or *Mafdal*). For a history of its founding and development, see Gary S. Schiff, *Tradition and Politics: The Religious Parties of Israel*, Chap. 2.

[104] The Jewish National Fund (in Hebrew, *Keren Kayemet L'yisrael*), founded in 1901, is the land acquisition and development arm of the World Zionist Organization.

[105] According to town records, the daughter of Rabbi Avraham Yosef, Noima (Naomi), married David Rosenblum in 1906. Note that in the conclusion of this sub-chapter the author uses the name Rosenblum instead of Rosenbaum.

under Soviet rule. With the outbreak of the Soviet Russian-Nazi German war, Lomza was conquered violently by the German hordes. Rabbi Avraham Yosef was exiled. He suffered his pains with love, and remained diligent in his studies until the day he was taken to be killed and became a martyr. His oldest daughter, Naomi, was married to Rabbi David Rosenblum, the "Genius of Goworowo;" his second daughter, Bracha, was married to Rabbi Yehoshua Mondliak of Warsaw; and his youngest daughter was married to Rabbi Yechezkel Kaplan, chief of the rabbinical court of Podbriza [possibly Podbereze-Paberza near Vilna, Lithuania].[106]

Rabbi Wolf Ber

Rabbi Wolf Ber lived his life in Ostroveh with certainty of faith, enthusiasm and divine inspiration. He was a first year lecturer in the local *yeshiva*. He was a wise and sharp Jew, an outstanding scholar and true Hassid, who combined Torah and good works. He was a Jew who was full of the love of Torah and of God, who had great trust in God, and was truly devoted to his work all the days of his long life.

For most of his life he served as a lecturer in the first year of the *yeshiva*. His daily lectures were given with great enthusiasm and energy, with his voice reaching great distances. He regularly taught his students his material, day in and day out, year in and year out, but he always looked like he was just a beginner in his work. His enthusiasm increased as he got into the subject matter that was being studied, to the point where Rabbi Wolf Ber and the Gemara that was open before him became a single inseparable living creature.

His enthusiasm did not interfere with his actual study. It was not superficial at all, despite the fact that his students were very young lads who were just entering the *yeshiva*. In his lessons he did not introduce many innovative ideas. He refrained from that in order not to impose upon the boys. But he wove into his lecture profound distinctions, questions and answers, as if they were an inseparable part of the Gemara itself. He was happy when he found a student who could go into depth in his study, who could understand the implications of what he had learned. His joy then knew no bounds, his eyes lit up, as if he had won a big prize in the Russian lottery.

---

[106] According to town records, daughter Noima (Naomi) was born in 1884 in Zambrow, daughter Bracha Esther was born in 1889 in Ostrow Mazowiecka, daughter Sheina was born in 1890 also in Ostrow Mazowiecka, and daughter Pessia Beila was born in 1894 also in Ostrow Mazowiecka. There was also a son, Yedidya, who was born in 1877 and who lived with his family in Ostrow Mazowiecka.

Rabbi Wolf Ber was a very smart Jew. He understood people well, and one had to be cunning with him. While he witnessed everything that going on about him, and understood the changing times, he himself belonged to another world, a higher world, a world of Torah and pure Hassidism. His used his great understanding to preserve a secret, like spring in his heart. He never had any money in his life. He did not make a fortune from his job. Therefore he concealed his pain. He hid it behind a facade of true happiness.

Rabbi Wolf Ber was a true Hassid, one of those early Hassidim whose very essence was devotion and self-sacrifice, whose flame of Hassidism burst forth from the inner, extremely positive wellsprings of his heart. He was an Amshinover Hassid, coming from the house of study of the Warka [Vurka, Vorki] Hassidim. He worked on this pure Hassidism all the days of his life. It demanded everything that was in his heart and soul. Therefore Rabbi Wolf Ber invested the essence of his life, his vitality, in Hassidism.

He was poverty stricken all his life, managing to get by during the week by sheer improvisation. But on the Sabbath his table was a veritable holy altar. The nobility of his life was expressed on the Sabbath, in his prayers and in his songs, in his conversation. His family did not follow in his footsteps, but Rabbi Wolf Ber learned to live with this disappointment as well. His son-in-law, the well known writer Tz. Z. Weisberg, writes about him in his autobiographical book, *Drachim Aveilot* [*Mournful Pathways*], "... He was an old man, more than seventy, with a distinguished face, a teacher in the local *yeshiva*, wise and understanding, and an outstanding scholar. Most of his life was full of trouble and poverty. He was tested by many challenges, with many family tragedies. But he overcame them purified and cleansed. Now a widower, still carrying the burden in his old age of his sons and daughters, still full of strength and power. He knew how to assuage the pain of the members of his family and to expel sadness from his home."

It is told that once on the Sabbath Rabbi Wolf Ber was sitting at his meal, full of devotion and enthusiasm, when a rumor went around in the neighborhood where he lived--far from the center of town--that Poles in the suburbs had begun to attack Jews. They would soon reach the street where Rabbi Wolf Ber lived. The Jews in the house and on that street were gripped with panic. Both young and old knew what such attacks meant and what Poles were capable of doing once they went beyond their limits and attacked defenseless Jews. Rabbi Wolf Ber stopped his meal and went to find out the truth of what was going on. He put on his armor of trust and faith. And radiating joy and happiness, he calmed the people in his house. He then returned to his table and his singing, and ascended to a higher world.

Rabbi David Leib Eitzels

One of the early heads of the Hassidim of Kotsk in Ostroveh was Rabbi David Leib Eitzels, a true, distinguished and wonderful Hassid. His living, derived from a limited amount of elementary level teaching, was very modest. His actual and principal work was Hassidism.

He had no children, but he was always full of happiness and enthusiasm. Unlike other Kotsk Hassidim, he prayed in the early hours of the morning, which freed him up to teach his young students, except on those days when he would stay with his teacher in Kotsk or in Ger. Towards evening he would appear in the Hassidic hall, where he would drink a small glass of liquor. He never hid his happiness from others, and was always ready and willing to dance and to manifest other aspects of his devotion to God with gladness.

He was a true Hassid and a very modest person, given the nature of his work. He was convinced that if something was lacking in his life, he apparently was undeserving of it. Therefore he had to work hard to attain a higher form of happiness that lifts a depressed soul. He thus overcame his torment and ignored the woes of the times. Even in the evening of his life, when he endured illness and pain, he never abandoned his happiness. Whenever Rabbi David Leib would appear in the Hassidic house, he brought joy along with him, as if it accompanied him in all his ways and deeds. Its light penetrated the whole house and all its attendees as well.

He was one of Rabbi Ben-Zion of Ostroveh's adherents, one of his friends and loyal followers. He was full of Torah, a real scholar who endeavored to conceal his extensive knowledge from the eyes of others. Only his students knew that he was an expert in the Talmud, and never even needed a book to remind him of anything. An old man who lived a full life, he died before the outbreak of World War I. The Hassidim of Ostroveh mourned his passing greatly.

Rabbi Zundel Lichtenstein[107]

---

[107] According to town records, Rabbi Zundel (or Abram Zundel) was born in Brok in about 1804 and died in Ostrow Mazowiecka in 1887.

One of the earliest Hassidim in Ostroveh was Rabbi Zundel. He was learned, wealthy and a distinguished and great Hassid, who was one of a kind in his character, in his deeds and in his ways. Few were like him, even in the glory days of Hassidism.

From his earliest days Rabbi Zundel was among the sharpest and best of the Hassidim of Kotsk. He was an excellent scholar and a true Hassid. He was a successful merchant who had attained wealth. He was also a great philanthropist, and given to acts of charity that would amaze anyone who heard about them. For example, there was a poor widow who sold liquor for Passover. Once, the holiday came and the poor woman had not been able to sell her beverages, which had cost her a lot of money. She was unable to keep the liquor for Passover of the following year or to sell it during the year. As liquor for Passover is expensive, while liquor during the year was inexpensive, it was both an obvious and a great loss for her. The unfortunate widow was downtrodden and depressed and did not know what to do. Rabbi Zundel heard about the incident. He quickly went over to this widow and purchased all the liquor from her at Passover prices, saying that he needed Passover liquor in particular and he needed it immediately.

Another story is told about Rabbi Zundel. Once he was on his way to Kotsk. He left the city in a wagon hitched to horses. Some Hassidim, who were his friends and from his Hassidic house, accompanied him along the road. Those who accompanied him now parted, except for one who continued on the journey. He was full of sadness and his head hung low. Rabbi Zundel did not cease to try to help him to overcome his depression. He later revealed his problem. He had just concluded an agreement for the engagement of his daughter, for which he was required to promise a dowry. The time had come to pay it, but he had no money available. It would be an embarrassment for him and his family if the engagement were called off.

Rabbi Zundel wrote a note to his wife saying, "Please pay the bearer the sum of...", which was the amount of the dowry. He gave the note to the poor Hassid to take to his wife, who thought that her husband Rabbi Zundel owed this Hassid this large sum of money.

Rabbi Zundel owned a large store in Ostroveh, which provided his income and wealth. Once on a Sabbath a fire broke out in the store. Rabbi Zundel, as usual, was in his Hassidic house. They came and told him that your store is on fire. Rabbi Zundel turned away nonchalantly. He did not get up or move, saying, "The fire is not my concern, because on the Sabbath I have no store."

When the Hassidic *rebbe* Rabbi Menachem Mendel of Kotsk died, Rabbi Zundel joined with the community that crowned his son, Rabbi David, as *rebbe*. He continued going to Kotsk. He was chosen as one of the heads of those Hassidim and one of their leaders. He was honored and admired by all. He was one of those rare personalities who combined greatness in Torah and Hassidism with ethics and good deeds. He was one of the elite few who controlled their desires and became a symbol and model in their lifetimes.

Up until the destruction of Ostrow Mazowiecka the Hassidim of the city would still mention the name of Rabbi Zundel, speaking of his wonderful deeds and ways as a symbol for his generation and the generations that followed.

Rabbi Pinchas Breinsker[108]

He was one of the first Hassidim in Ostrow Mazowiecka and one of the outstanding ones. He would frequently travel to the Hassidic *rebbe* Rabbi Menachem Mendel of Kotsk. He was an excellent scholar, possessing exceedingly rare abilities. He was thought of as one of the greatest scholars of the city in the previous era, a time when Ostroveh was full of very learned men and great scholars, and when only a few of the respected residents were not immersed in the sea of the Talmud.

The acuity of Rabbi Pesach amazed many people, and exceeded any previously known dimensions in town. Rabbi Pesach was used to entering into the old study hall in the afternoon hours, which in those days was full of people studying, both young and old, bachelors and young married men. Each one of them would be studying by himself or with a partner. Others sat together at a table and studied, one the tractate of *Ketubot*, a second the tractate of *Baba Batra*, a third the tractate of *Shabbat*, a fourth *Shulchan Aruch*, a fifth would be looking into one of the books of the early [medieval] commentators, and so forth. Rabbi Pesach would go from one to the other, glance for a moment at the subject being studied, and would begin a sharp disquisition on it, linking it to the topic that the second person would be learning. He continued on to each of the students, weaving subject to subject, tractate to tractate, building a full structure with his acuity. The attendees of the study hall enjoyed this very much. But the group of Hassidim who were loyal to Kotsk objected to these Torah games. They claimed that this was not based on the study of Torah built on the foundations of truth, but rather on the

---

[108] In the title of this sub-chapter the author lists the first name as Pinchas, but in the subsequent text he uses the name Pesach.

coincidental and exceptional sharpness of Rabbi Pesach, and not on the truth that underlay those topics. Despite the objections of the Hassidim, Rabbi Pesach continued to give pleasure to himself and to the students with his games of acuity, which justifiably earned him the title as the sharpest of the scholars in Ostroveh.

Rabbi David Ostrower

One of the greatest of the Hassidim of Ger and one of the important people in our city was Rabbi David Ostrower, who was one of the veteran residents of Ostrow Mazowiecka. He was a great scholar, who knew the entire Talmud and the rabbinic decisors, both early and later, by heart. He was also the most diligent person in town. Day and night, summer and winter, he was seated and pursuing his studies diligently.

Much like his greatness in Torah was his devotion to Hassidism. He frequently visited Hassidic rebbes. In his youth it was to Rabbi Chanoch Henich of Alexander. And so told Rabbi David, "One time when I was in Alexander, there the rabbi and tzadik Rabbi Tzvi Hersh of Tomashov [Tomaszow] was also staying. He was the right hand man and confidante of the aged rebbe of Kotsk. When Rabbi Chanoch Henich entered the study hall, all the Hassidim (myself included) ran towards him. Rabbi Tzvi Hersh, who was standing alongside me, turned to me and said, 'Listen, previously Hassidim were afraid and embarrassed to show their faces before their rebbe, and now they run to greet him?'"

After the death of the rebbe of Alexander, Rabbi David joined the community of the Hassidim of the rebbe Rabbi Aryeh Leib of Ger, author of the S'fat Emet. Rabbi David told the following story: "When I first came to Ger after the death of the rebbe of Alexander the rebbe of Ger said to me, 'When someone opens a book on earth, they open a book for him in heaven as well.'"

Therefore Rabbi David always opened a Gemara with trepidation and fear of the Divine. It appeared on his face that he envisioned the opening of the gates of heaven before him. And thus in dread and fear, trembling and sweating, he sat down to learn day and night. He did not have much and was rather modest and weak-kneed. He was one of the first Hassidim who got by on very little. And even that he saw as an undeserved gift, as he was not worth very much at all.

For many years Rabbi David graced the house of the Hassidim of Ger. He was usually the last to leave the place. He always sat in his corner learning, without disturbing anyone, until he was called to the great yeshiva on high.

The Gaon Rabbi David Mintzberg

A Beautiful Branch

One of the grandest and most esteemed personages in the history of Hassidism was that of Rabbi David of Lelov[109] [Lelow, Lelovo], one of the founders of Hassidism in Poland and among its spiritual giants. There is no end to the legends and heartwarming stories that about this great figure, who made a decisive contribution to the establishment of the image of Hassidism in Poland in general, and to Polish Jewry in particular. He was a popular personality, much like Rabbi Levi Yitzchak of Berditchev[110] and Rabbi Moshe Leib of Sasov,[111] serving as a model for many generations.

Rabbi David was not a Hassidic *rebbe*. He did not create a dynasty as is usually understood in the Hassidic movement. But he was a *tzadik* who created long lists of wonderful organizations by means of his personality and his deeds. He was considered one of the leading students of the Seer of Lublin and of the Jew of Peshischa, the fathers of Hassidism in Poland and Galicia. But he was not just a usual student, but rather a pillar of fire that was elevated and stood out over his surroundings. Rabbi David of Lelov became a concept, a noun, an expression of the wholeness of a person and the wholeness of his characteristics.

Rabbi David's only son, Rabbi Moshe,[112] the son-in-law of the Holy Jew of Peshischa, did become a *rebbe* to the masses. But he left his exalted position and immigrated to the Land of Israel, along with his son and grandchildren. Of this esteemed family there remained in Poland only his son, Rabbi Avraham, the rabbi of Jozefow, and his grandson, Rabbi David. He, too, refused to become a *rebbe*, following in the footsteps of his illustrious grandfather. He was modest and shy. He sat and studied Torah and its good deeds. He was satisfied with his status as the rabbi of the small community of Jozefow, where he expounded on the Torah extensively.

---

[109] Rabbi David Biderman (1746-1814) of Lelov.

[110] Rabbi Levi Yitzchak of Berditchev (1740-1809), one of the early leaders of the Hassidic movement, known for his stories and parables, and as the advocate of the Jewish people before God.

[111] Rabbi Moshe Leib Erblich of Sasov (1745-1807), another early leader of Hassidism.

[112] Rabbi Moshe Biderman (1776-1851) of Lelov.

Rabbi Avraham had a brilliant son by the name of Yerachmiel Yeshayahu.[113] The super-human talents of the boy were apparent early in his youth. He was like a lime pit that never lost a single drop of water. It was sufficient for him to skim through a particular book quickly, and he immediately knew all the information in the book by heart, without having to dwell on a single word. His trenchant utterances became something of note. He was very sharp, and had a mind like a steel trap. As a boy he was able to plumb the depths of complex matters, and to review difficult and deep issues. Nothing was too difficult for this tiny genius from Jozefow, who progressed practically all on his own initiative, having received most of his knowledge from his father the *gaon*.

The name of the genius of Jozefow preceded him. His nobility and greatness of spirit he apparently inherited from his father and grandfather, and they integrated well with his abilities and his powerful thirst for knowledge. It was not long before Rabbi Yerachmiel Yeshayahu became a serious *gaon*. He was seen as a rising star in the firmament of the rabbinate in Poland. A bright future was seen for the young *gaon*, who captured the hearts of all the leading scholars of Torah with his brilliance, of the Hassidim with his conduct, and of the masses with his love for Jews and his superlative character traits.

When the young Rabbi Yerachmiel Yeshayahu decided soon after his marriage to accept a rabbinical position, which seemed to him to be an opportunity to devote himself to his studies and dedicate most of his time to Torah, there was no question that he would obtain a position in the rabbinate. Thus he was chosen at a very young age to be the rabbi of the community of Lukova and then the rabbi of Zdunska Wola.

Rabbi Yerachmiel Yeshayahu progressed in giant steps. His name preceded him throughout Poland as a model rabbi. Rabbis who were much older than he turned to him with very difficult questions. He was rightly thought of as a shining star in the skies of the Torah in Poland. His many admirers viewed him as becoming the outstanding *gaon* of the next generation, as the greatest rabbinic authority in this glorious Diaspora. Great hopes were pinned on him by the leading rabbis of the generation, who would take notice of him and seek his opinion. Authors would

---

[113] It appears that the author either omitted a generation or added one (or both). According to other information, Rabbi Yerachmiel Yeshayahu Mintzberg [Mincberg] was the son of Avraham Eliezer Mintzberg and Devorah Chana Biderman, and Devorah Chana was the daughter of Yitzchak David Biderman (1815-1886). Thus, it appears that Rabbi Yerachmiel Yeshayahu's father, Rabbi Avraham Eliezer Mintzberg (1834-1904) of Jozefow, was the son-in-law of Rabbi David of Jozefow (i.e., Yitzchak David Biderman) described in the paragraph above, rather than the son of Rabbi Moshe of Lelov. Other information also suggests that Rabbi David of Jozefow was the son, rather than the grandson, of Rabbi Moshe Biderman of Lelov, who went to Israel.

come to him with their books [to endorse], while young scholars would seek teachers' certificates from the famous rabbi of Lukova. His home became a meeting place for the wise men of the country, and he himself became a great locus of Torah. His legal rulings were accepted without question or challenge. He quickly became a classic decisor, who willingly and quickly replied to every inquirer with amazing clarity and breadth of knowledge. No question went unanswered. Even the most difficult questions were answered by him with amazing ease and simplicity. And it was all done without ambiguity or complexity, but briefly and logically.

But the great hopes of his many admirers did not come to pass. Divine will determined otherwise. Rabbi Yerachmiel Yeshayahu passed away at a very young age, even before he reached the age of attaining one's full stature.[114] Two little orphans, a boy and a girl, were left behind, along with a young widow. The rabbis of Poland mourned greatly for this cedar that was cut down at the beginning of its efflorescence, for this lion who had disappeared leaving behind an empty space, even before he committed his knowledge to book form, and who was only at the very beginning of his flowering and fame.

His Youth and Biography

There was no limit to the love and affection of the *gaon* for his only son, whom he named for his sainted grandfather, Rabbi David of Lelov.[115] As he sat on the seat as a *dayan*, in the very same room in which he taught and gave his lessons, Rabbi Yerachmiel Yeshayahu would hold his son on his knees, stroking his hair with tenderness and love. In his only son he saw his future, his spiritual heir, the one who would continue the golden thread.

---

[114] According to the entry for Zdunska Wola in *Pinkas Hakehilot: Encyclopedia of Jewish Communities* (published by Yad Vashem), Rabbi Yerachmiel Yeshayahu Mintzberg served as rabbi there from 1902 to 1905. He was a Hassid and a child prodigy who had been ordained at the age of sixteen by Rabbi Yehoshua Trunk of Kutno. Not long after his appointment to the Zdunska Wola rabbinate he fell ill and died on the eve of Rosh Hashanah in Warsaw, where he had gone to seek treatment. He is buried in the Okopowa Street cemetery in Warsaw, where his *matzevah* [gravestone] gives his Hebrew name as Yerachmiel Yeshaya son of Avraham Eliezer, and his date of death as September 29, 1905 (per the listing of his gravesite on the website of the Foundation for Documentation of Jewish Cemeteries in Poland). There is an extensive inscription on the *matzevah* describing his good character and accomplishments.

[115] According to other sources (including the *yizkor* book for the town of Lachwa, where Rabbi David perished), Rabbi David Mintzberg was born in either 1902 or 1903 in either Lukowa or Zdunska Wola, making him no more than three years old when his father died.

But he did not live to educate and raise his son. As a small boy who did not yet understand much, David walked behind the coffin, surrounded by the concern and compassion of his father's many admirers. Many pampered the charming and bright-eyed little orphan, who became the favored child of the greatest rabbis of Poland. Many were concerned about him and made sure to nurture his abilities, which he had inherited from his great father. He was of noble spirit from the day he could understand things, and he had an expansive soul. His superior characteristics were apparent from the earliest days of his childhood. But above all else were his memory and his quick grasp of things that reminded one of his father, that thirst for knowledge and deep understanding that characterized him throughout what was also to be a short life.

The boy did not remember his great father. He was too small when his father passed away, too small to know his great and devoted personality. He did not reach the point where he could have absorbed anything from the teachings of his father, Rabbi Yerachmiel Yeshayahu. He had not yet had the privilege of studying with him, to hear words of Torah from the *gaon* of Lukova, who had loved him so much and who was concerned with him from the moment he first saw the light of day. Nevertheless the son inherited many of the characteristics of his father, those which were recognized in the *gaon* of Lukova in his youth and were now perceptible in the young Rabbi David, as he was just like him.

The son was of noble spirit in everything, in his studies and in his ways, in his logical thought and in his understanding of Torah. It was an innate nobility, a superior quality that is not self-conscious and becomes an integral part of the personality in which it resides. It was a nobility that was expressed in everything, in daily activities, in day-to-day ways of life, and in contact with people. Thus, like his father, he merited admiration not only because of his knowledge or his status, but more so because of his personality, which few like him had, even in those shining glory days of Polish Jewry.

Rabbi David was educated in the home of his widowed mother, under the supervision of the giants of Torah in Poland. But this pampering did not negatively affect his thinking or his characteristics. The fact that he was an orphan also had its influence in him. He grew up quickly, seeming like a person much older than his actual age, serious, introverted. He plumbed the depths of every problem and issue and loathed superficiality. As a very young man Rabbi David was considered a person who was fully developed in his personal characteristics and his actions, without blemish, and a great person in his knowledge of Torah and his behavior.

He had inherited his phenomenal memory from his brilliant father. And like his father, too, he was a lime pit that never lost a drop [of water]. As for his diligence, there was no limit. He sat and studied eighteen hours per day, researching, digging deep, first mostly studying Talmud and the decisors. But during the course of years he did not leave any branch of Jewish learning unexplored. Every new book was precious to him. His thirst for knowledge only increased over time. He did not leave any book that came his way unread, whether studied in depth or merely leafed through. In a few years Rabbi David became a veritable well of knowledge, a living encyclopedia.

Rabbi David was eighteen years of age when he married the daughter of one of the wealthy Hassidim of Ostrow Mazowiecka, Rabbi Eliyahu Lau[116] (may God avenge his blood), one of the important people of the city. His wealthy father-in-law, a lover of Torah, promised him that he would support him and would provide for all of his needs for the rest of his life. This was a dream for Rabbi David, who desired to dedicate his entire life to Torah, without distraction, without financial worries and daily burdens. He was free of any need to be concerned with secular matters and the material world.

There was no limit to the good fortune that Rabbi David had without any worry, so that he could lead a life of Torah in Ostroveh. How fortunate was this man who was able to continue his studies, who was able to devote himself entirely to a life of Torah. In a small room reserved for him in the house of his rich father-in-law, that wealthy and great man, alongside walls lined with books, he sat and studied. He sat and thought about Torah day and night. He progressed day by day and became a wonderful *gaon* in the entire Torah.

Rabbi David did not aspire to the rabbinate, to authority, to any official position. On the contrary, he sought to escape and hide from the gaze of people. The four cubits of the Halacha provided him with all he needed, a higher reward. He aspired only for the Torah and to study it. And he attained this, and the more he studied the more his diligence increased, seeking to plumb the very depths of an issue, to clarify it and to clear it up, to swim forever in the great and gigantic sea of the Talmud.

A Public Figure and an Exceptional Educator

---

[116] According to the Ostrow Mazowiecka vital records, Icek Dawid Mincberg [Mintzberg] married Szeyna Gitla Lach [Lau?] in 1923.

Ostrow Mazowiecka had served as a Hassidic stronghold for many years. It was a very weighty center for the Hassidim of Ger. It was in this city that lived the Gaon Rabbi Ben-Zion Rabinowitz, one of the greatest Hassidim of Poland and one of the last of the Mohicans of the early and great Kotsk era of Hassidism. He created in this city a kernel of enthusiastic Hassidim, young people who were great in their knowledge of the Torah and who were also activists. Rabbi Ben-Zion led them, drew them close to the sources of Hassidism, and brought them into the precincts of holy work.

Since Rabbi David's arrival in Ostroveh, the Ger Hassidim in Ostroveh, headed by Rabbi Ben-Zion, had sought to attract the promising young genius. Slowly they succeeded in bringing Rabbi David into their circle, until he became one of the pillars of the group.

He began making his way to Ger, to the court of the great *rebbe*, there to perfect his Hassidism and his holy work. The *rebbe* Avraham Mordechai, the greatest of the *rebbe*s of his generation, tried to bring him close and to love him. Thus, he became an enthusiastic Hassid and one of the best of the young men at Ger. A whole new world was revealed to Rabbi David, a world of pure holiness and of total effort on behalf of God, a world of self-sacrifice and of true exaltation. Hassidim was well absorbed by Rabbi David, who was already full of Torah and ethics when he came to warm himself by its light. It was as if Hassidism attached its wings to the young *gaon*.

News of the brilliant young man, who was cordial and big-hearted, reached far and wide. This former favored child of the greatest rabbis of the Torah became widely known. His Hassidic friends and acquaintances spoke of him with awe and admiration. By their very nature and essence they tried to negate this-worldly things, and did not praise people very much either, but this time they went beyond their usual limits. They honored and admired Rabbi David. They elevated him and praised him, whether they were following in the footsteps of their rabbi, *rebbe* Avraham Mordechai, or whether it was because of the unique characteristics of Rabbi David himself. His great personal charm, his ways that were full of grace and light, that honored the Divine name in public, acquired for him a much respected position among the great Torah scholars of Poland, and a most visible place among the younger tier of greats in the country.

His extensive and universal knowledge in all aspects of Judaism; his profound understanding of all the problems that came across his path; his big eyes that radiated kindness, love and great understanding; his heartfelt and gracious approach, all created entire legends around this young man, who flew away from any honor or publicity, from any public position or official post, like an arrow from a bow. The longings of Rabbi David were not for a respected rabbinic post, for rabbinical honors, or for widespread fame. He sought to escape to the four cubits of the Halacha, to his small room in the house of his wealthy father-in-law where, amidst walls and shelves laden with many books, he found his soul, his true self.

Responsibility to the Public and to the Individual

And much like his thirst for Torah was powerful, so, too, was his feeling of responsibility both towards the individual and the public, responsibility to the Jewish people at large and to the younger generation of Jews. No one better than Rabbi David understood the soul of the young Jew in Poland, and the young Jewish soul altogether, despite the fact that he was totally enveloped within the four cubits of the Torah. The principle that says that you can understand better from outside than from within proved itself in Rabbi David, a man who was beyond the concerns of the lives of young and old alike, a man who never had any contact with daily life or with grim reality, yet who nevertheless understood that reality and that environment better than others, plumbing the depths of the soul of every young man and woman.

His concern for the future of the nation and its character brought him to the Agudat Yisrael movement, to which he was attracted heart and soul, becoming one of its most loyal soldiers and officers in Poland. Here as well, as in other areas, Rabbi David fled from any official or honorific position. He refused to accept any official post or honorary position within the movement's central body, or in its local branch. He vigorously pushed aside any attempt to be elected by it to any institution whatsoever. Nevertheless he stood firmly at its side when it came to practical work of the Agudat Yisrael movement. This man, for whom the study of Torah was precious above all else, did not hesitate to defer his study and to use his time to speak on behalf of Agudat Yisrael, to debate its opponents, to give a lecture to the girls' branch of Agudat Yisrael or to the youth arm of Agudat Yisrael.

He devoted much of his time to develop the ideology of Agudat Yisrael, to broadening the boundaries of its vision, and to strengthening its foundations. Thus he inadvertently became one of the ideologues of Agudat Yisrael. Like his teacher, the *rebbe* of Ger, he came to see in Agudat Yisrael the instrumentality of salvation for the Jewish people in the difficult days of its Diaspora.

He did not see in the movement a material crutch or a means of personal success or of financial gain, but rather a pure idea, holy and ennobled, that was likely to save the Jew and accompany him on his difficult path. This idea was that of an organized Torah life, whether in the life of the community or in the life of the individual.

Rabbi David was a gifted psychologist and a teacher of great skill by his very nature. By means of casual conversation he was able to bring about revolutionary change in the life of his interlocutor. His influence on youth and the young, who were attracted to him by his charm, was enormous. His lectures and speeches always engendered many echoes, for he knew how to give expression to the deepest and most original thoughts in a light and attractive manner, simple enough to be understood by a child. Because of his abilities, they never gave him a moment's rest. They pressured him often to give lectures to teachers and youth, or to community leaders and activists. He unwillingly had to devote some of his time to the supervision of orthodox educational institutions in his area, both as to the curriculum and the methods of teaching and pedagogy. Rabbi David became the favored choice of the Torah-oriented youth movements of Agudat Yisrael, both in his own immediate area as well as further afield.

The man became a symbol. He was never just one who spoke but did not act, but rather he was one who acted as well. He was a man of character without blemish, who never got angry and never engaged in frivolous talk. He always received people with kindness, with love and devotion, with a genuine concern for the good of all, with a hearty and charming smile always seen on his lips. He was always ready to help and to fulfill any request or wish that was possible to fulfill. For every question, even the most complex, he had a clear and correct answer at hand.

The Spiritual Guide of the Yeshiva of the Sages of Lublin

In Lublin Rabbi Meir Shapira had built the grand Yeshiva of the Sages of Lublin.[117] This *yeshiva* enrolled many exceptional

---

[117] In Hebrew, *Yeshivat Chachmei Lublin*, it was established under the leadership of Rabbi Meir Shapira (1887-1933), a leader of the Polish branch of Agudat Yisrael, under whose auspices it operated. It harked back to the great *yeshivot* that had once existed there. The foundation stone for the impressive spacious five-story building, surrounded by a large gated and landscaped campus, was laid in 1924. With contributions from Polish and world Jewry, it was opened in 1930, and remained functioning until 1939. The building housed classrooms, offices, and living facilities for over two hundred students, as well as a major Judaica library of over 22,000 volumes and a large synagogue/auditorium. Under Nazi rule it became regional headquarters for the military police, and after the war it housed the medical school of the University of Lublin. The facility was returned to the ownership of the Jewish community in 2003, and the

students of the Torah, diligent and brilliant, who came to study Torah at the famed Yeshiva of the Sages of Lublin. Among them were students from Galicia, the grandsons of famous *rebbe*s, giants of the Torah, as well as Polish-born students, some of whom were sons of industrialists and wealthy merchants.

There were young men from all the religious streams in the country. The best of all the Torah-oriented youth in Poland were brought together to study. This institution required an appropriate personality who was both well versed in the Torah and a gifted educator, who possessed both great personal charm and broad-based ideas in order to create in this large *yeshiva* a single, unified atmosphere of Torah as well as a harmonious relationship among the students.

The late Rabbi Meir Shapira of blessed memory passed away at a young age. His loyal assistants who had worked with dedication to set up the *yeshiva* were now faced with a critical problem. There was an urgent need for a spiritual director for the *yeshiva*, someone of unusual personality, someone who could crystallize the *yeshiva* into a unified body, at least within the *yeshiva* itself. Serving as heads of the *yeshiva*, as the instructors, were the Gaon Rabbi Tzvi Aryeh Frumer[118] from Koziglov [Kozieglowy] and the Gaon Rabbi Aryeh Leib Landau from Kolobel [Kolbiel]. Overseeing the spiritual side were some of the greatest *geonim* of Poland, the *rebbe* of Boyan, Rabbi Moshe,[119] the Gaon Rabbi Menachem Ziemba,[120] and others. But these men came to Lublin infrequently. There was need of a personality who would take up residence within the *yeshiva*, who would actually take part in the life of the *yeshiva*, and who would serve as father and teacher to hundreds of young men, among whom were those who excelled in their

---

synagogue and other facilities have been renovated for use by the Jewish community. The name of the institution and its founder are now emblazoned in large letters on its exterior in both Hebrew and Polish. Among Rabbi Shapira's other major innovations on behalf of Agudat Yisrael was the institution of the *daf yomi* [daily page] Talmud study program, under which all participants world-wide study the same page simultaneously, so that the entire cycle is completed in seven years. In 2005 participants returned to Lublin to celebrate the completion of the eleventh cycle of the study program at the very *yeshiva* where it began. See Gary S. Schiff, *In Search of Polin: Chasing Jewish Ghosts in Today's Poland*, pp. 81-82, and photograph on p. 87.

[118] Rabbi Aryeh Tzvi Frumer (1884-1943), who perished at Majdanek.

[119] Rabbi Moshe ("Moshenyu") Friedman (1881-1943), who perished at Auschwitz.

[120] Rabbi Menachem Ziemba (1883-1943), who perished in the Warsaw Ghetto uprising, of which he was a leader.

knowledge of Torah, extraordinary young men of understanding and substantial knowledge.

Meanwhile there had occurred a very serious change in the status of Rabbi David Mintzberg of Ostrow Mazowiecka. His father-in-law, who had hitherto supplied all his needs, had suffered catastrophic losses, and could no longer provide for his illustrious son-in-law, his wife and their seven young daughters.[121] The good times of plenty, the days in which Rabbi David could devote himself entirely to Torah and Hassidism, were over. He rejected all proposals of appointments to the rabbinate. Such an appointment was not acceptable to him. In his mind such a position would require him not to be at one with himself. The life of business and work were also foreign to him. He hardly had ever gone out into the marketplace, and had no idea what business was all about.

And even though earning a living with one's hands now seemed to be the most acceptable option, on the other hand he now also understood how fortunate he had personally been in the past insofar as any anxiety he may have had of getting involved in anything but the most pure undertakings were then unnecessary. But now his aversion to anything to do with money would not make it easy for him to support his large family.

So when the heads of the Yeshiva of the Sages of Lublin decided to "recruit" Rabbi David, he responded positively to their request willingly. This position was close to his heart and to his inclinations. To educate young men for a life of Torah, Hassidism and ethics, for true wholeness and good morals, this was his life's work. For their part the great scholars of Poland who headed the Yeshiva of the Sages of Lublin saw in him the right man for the job. His extraordinary scholarship, his amazing knowledge would likely enhance his standing in the eyes of the students and guarantee his success. His abilities as a gifted educator, and the fact that he was a pure Hassid, and that he had a blemish-free personality, all assured his complete success.

The Gaon Rabbi David Mintzberg carried out this difficult task wholeheartedly. From the first day when his feet first stepped into the enormous *yeshiva* building in Lublin up until the Nazis locked the gates of the building and devastated it, the spiritual director had held complete sway over the hearts of its hundreds of students. He never used any coercion. He never raised his voice or

---

[121] Ostrow Mazowiecka vital records and other sources show that Rabbi David had nine children, seven daughters and two sons. They were: Rachmil Shaya (Yerachmiel Yeshayahu in Hebrew), Mariam, Sara Devoyra, Fayga Rochel, Chana Brayna, Leya, Chava, Perla and Moshe Meir.

threatened a student. He never relied on the administration of the *yeshiva* or utilized any official methods. All these were foreign to his nature. He viewed all these as non-educational means.

He never flaunted his superiority over the students. He worked to remove all barriers between him and even the youngest of the students. He walked among them as if he were just another one of the guys, a somewhat older one perhaps, but devoted to them with all his heart. One could open up one's heart to him and confide in him any secret. Students would say, "If you tell Rabbi David things, it is like you buried them in the ground. He would never divulge their content. Rabbi David would never mention them, he would not use them. And it did not matter whether they were important things, provocative things or just plain things."

The Gaon Rabbi David Mintzberg left his family in his house in Ostroveh. He sent his entire salary every month to his wife, while he lived the life of the *yeshiva*, living among the students, sharing their concerns, their joys and their sorrows, as if they were not his students but his own sons. Only on holidays did he return to his home or to his rabbi, the *rebbe* of Ger.

With rare wisdom and with great love and ability he penetrated into the hearts of hundreds of students and implanted in them the aspiration for wholeness and ascension, the strong desire to study Torah and to meticulously observe the commandments. He always knew how to find the exact right moment, so as not to impose on the students. He did not give public lectures on ethics, nor did he preside over the table on the Sabbath and holidays. He dealt with the students on an individual basis, with each one privately, and without official sanctions, and not at pre-set times.

The decided majority of the students came from Hassidic families. They belonged to all of the sects of Hassidism. Only about half came from the Hassidim of the *rebbe* of Ger, while others were adherents of dozens of other *rebbe*s. On this basis there occasionally developed controversies among the students of the *yeshiva*. More than once the relations among them became strained. Rabbi David, with great understanding and symbolism, succeeded in overcoming these problems, which occasionally harmed the day-to-day life of the *yeshiva*. Rabbi David himself was counted among the enthusiastic adherents of the *rebbe* of Ger, but in the *yeshiva* he knew how to elevate himself and the students above the differences of the various sects of Hassidism. Slowly but surely he managed to put the way of life of the *yeshiva* on a different track, one of tolerance and respect for one another, of respecting the customs and traditions of others and of mutual love and an attitude of acceptance towards all. All his work was undertaken with great patience, every step was thought out in advance, planned to the last detail. And all was done quietly, with amazing patience and great devotion.

His work did not go unrewarded. For their part the students repaid his love with their love and his devotion with theirs. They were prepared to do anything for him. Their loyalty to their teacher and guide had no limits. One always felt fortunate when Rabbi David turned to him and asked him to do something.

For the Sanctification of God's Name

When the skies over Poland began to cloud over, and the Nazis began their final preparations for conquering the country, a great fear hovered over Polish Jewry. One's heart could feel the bitterness in one's soul, and the masses felt that difficult and bitter days were coming whose exact nature was difficult to predict. The administration of the Yeshiva of the Sages of Lublin decided to send the students home "until the fury passes." Only a handful of students, who had no homes to go back to, remained at the *yeshiva*.

Rabbi David did not abandon the great ship of Torah during this stormy time. He did not return home, but rather worked to help find safe havens for those orphan students who had no homes to go back to. The great building of the *yeshiva* was immediately closed by the Nazi invaders. Rabbi David worked for months to enable the small group of students who had remained in Lublin to continue their studies in secret and in a regular manner.

The Jews of Ostroveh were expelled from their homes. The city became a border town between Russia and Germany. After the eastern parts of Poland were absorbed into Soviet Russia, most of the residents crossed the border and turned to Russia. Rabbi David also crossed into Russia, where he joined his family.

After a short time the masses of Jews in these areas were expelled to the distant tundra of Siberia. Among those who were expelled were the wife and the seven daughters of Rabbi David. He remained in the Lithuanian city of Lachva [Lakhva, Lachwa, part of Poland before the war, today in Belarus], still immersed in Torah and good works, sending packages of food and clothing to his family, who were starving in that great wasteland.[122]

---

[122] Rabbi David's wife and daughters survived the war. According to the 2013 obituary of his daughter, Chana Friedman, Rebbetzin Shaina Gittel Mintzberg immigrated to Crown Heights, in Brooklyn, with her daughters. Passenger records show that she arrived in New York in 1952 with her four younger daughters (Leya, Chana, Chaya and Perla), and that a fifth daughter also came to New York later that year (Sara, who had married her cousin, Rachmiel Shaya Kempinski).

The letters of Rabbi David from this period, in which he was wandering alone and lonely among Jews who hardly recognized him, far from his family and his students, and in which his fellow Jews were being rounded up in their communities and being killed, are full of hope and faith and elevation of the soul. It was clear that the man was going higher and higher in those days of pain and suffering.

In these difficult days, when Rabbi David was wandering around alone and lonely in an environment he hardly recognized any more, when his heart was full and pain and yearning, fear and sadness, the greatness of his spirit and the powerful resources hidden in his soul came to their fullest expression. There are those who question him for not having done everything he could to join his family in their exile in Siberia. But he was not able to do this. He apologized for having stayed in a settled area, among people, where he could obtain food to send to his family and to his acquaintances to save them from death by starvation.

Indescribable spiritual bravery is manifest in his letters from this bitter and difficult period of his life. He overcame in these days of anger and rage even more than in the good days. He became a veritable torch of holiness and purity. "To learn from pain, to worship God when you are drowning in sorrows, there is nothing loftier than that," [he wrote]. Or, "Your soul cannot attain in the good years what it can achieve in a short time in bitter days."

In other letters to his students this giant of the spirit called upon them to invest themselves with every fiber of their being in their studies of Torah and in good works. "After all, these days were created for the purpose of having us worship God. In these days there is no opportunity for us to make our fortunes, to build houses, to assure our material future, or to provide a pleasant life. If we examine matters it will become clear that thunder was created in order to straighten out the crookedness of the heart, that these difficult days were created so that we may overcome and rise above them, that we would forget about all the vanities of this world and purify and sanctify ourselves in anticipation of better days."

And so the difficult and oppressive days under Russian occupation passed for him. He saw to it that his loved ones would not perish of starvation at a time when absolute evil hovered over the earth. Yet, he learned much in this period. He plumbed and observed some of the secrets of the Torah, thereby escaping to a world that was all good. "Even in hell one can also taste the tastes of the Garden of Eden...."

The times of pain and suffering were nearing their end. The Nazi monsters launched a war against Soviet Russia. They quickly conquered vast territories. They captured little Lachva, where they swept up the local Jews and many refugees. From the first day of their arrival they sowed death and destruction on this land rife with pain. Somehow Rabbi David still managed to send a number of letters from this terrible captivity to some of his students and admirers. He told how it was impossible for a Jew to go out of his house for weeks at a time. He found a small refuge, with a narrow roof. There was once again no possibility of his aiding his family members, to prevent their starvation and pain. Rabbi David prepared himself for what was to come. He had no illusions about the future.

One of the survivors of Lachva, which was destroyed, who was himself saved from the flames, writes in *First Ghetto to Revolt: Lachva* that from the day of his arrival the Gaon Rabbi David Mintzberg, may God avenge his blood, assumed the role as the spiritual leader of the Jewish population of the town. He was especially concerned with help and succor for the families of the Jewish refugees from central Poland. As a great Torah scholar and a wise man he became a guide and adviser to the Jewish council. The council considered every decree and tribulation that befell them. The Gaon Rabbi David would provide guidance to the head of the council. The local rabbis, Rabbi Eliezer Lichtenstein and Rabbi Chaim Zalman Osherovitz, would meet with him as well and would come up with ideas on how to deal with the problems and mitigate the brunt of the evil decrees. With his ideas and advice he served as a source of great encouragement and help to Mr. Dov Lopatin, head of the council and the official representative of the Jewish community, more than once saving the Jewish community that was confined to a ghetto.

On the night of the twenty-first of Elul 5702 [September 2, 1942], the ghetto was surrounded by cadres of armed murderers, consisting of companies of the SS and their murderous assistants. In reply to the question of Mr. Dov Lopatin, head of the Jewish council, as to why there were so many soldiers, the officers of murder at the police station said that they were there to eliminate the prisoners of the Lachva ghetto. He added, "out of the goodness of his heart," that thirty selected Jews, headed by Mr. Dov Lopatin, head of the council of trustees, would be left alive. Mr. Dov Lopatin, may God avenge his blood, replied, "You will not kill us piecemeal. Either we all remain alive, or we will all be killed."

Lopatin and some of the other council members went back into the ghetto. The murderers rested a bit before carrying out the *aktion*. They had just returned from eliminating the Jews of the

Kozhan-Horodok [Kozhan-Gorodok] and Luniniec [Luninyets, today in Belarus]. And they had not eaten for six hours.

The murderers prepared for the action, while the heads of the Jews went about implementing their own plan, which had been devised in advance, as soon as it had become clear that there was no escape from total destruction. The adults and youth gathered in the section of the ghetto alongside the house of Zeev Rochczyn. At the orders of the committee, at the head of whose planners and advisers stood the Gaon Rabbi David Mintzberg, the Jews began to set the houses of the ghetto on fire and to consign to the flames the little of their property they still had, so that the murderers would not both kill the Jews and inherit their assets. Dov Lopatin was the first, and entered the house of Zalman Cheifetz and set it ablaze, according to plan. Dense clouds of smoke covered the ghetto. House after house was set on fire. The German murderers, with the aid of the local Polish police, went into action. They entered the ghetto and ordered the Jews, who had gathered according to their plan, to disperse and to return to their homes, some of which had in the meantime become plumes of fire.

At that moment Yisrael Darevsky, may God avenge his blood, one of the members of the Jewish council, ran into the house of Zelig Dolgopiti and set it afire from within. He exited and flames shot out from it. A German policeman, who happened to be standing there and saw what was happening, drew his pistol and shot him dead on the spot. Chaos erupted in the community. Yitzchak Rochczyn jumped on the German and split his head open with an axe, killing him. A single bullet hit Yitzchak Rochczyn and killed him. Then Asher Cheifetz attacked a second German policeman that was quickly moving towards the group of Jews, and he, too, split his head open with an axe. A bullet struck Asher Cheifetz, may God avenge his blood, who fell on the spot. Asher's brother, Moshe Leib, removed a pistol from another bloody German dog, and began to direct fire towards the murderers who had gathered near the ghetto's fence. Young Chaim Cheifetz ran towards the gate, instantly overcoming the surprised German policeman and killed him, then opened the gates. The Nazi "heroes" fell back in confusion. The Jews pulled themselves together. They began to attack the nearby fence and gate. They broke out into the marketplace and ran for their lives. The murderers quickly began to run up to balconies and to the roofs and rained withering fire down on the escapees. Many Jews ran to the forests and marshes in the area, but most were killed. Hundreds of corpses of the fallen were piled up in the marketplace and nearby alleys.

At the head of the group of people who stood by the gate of the ghetto, the Gaon Rabbi David Mintzberg, the Gaon Rabbi Eliezer

Lichtenstein, and the Gaon Rabbi Chaim Zalman Osherovitz, wrapped in their prayer shawls, cried out in anguish and blood, *Sh'ma Yisrael* [*Hear, O Israel*]. Many people then began to whisper the final prayers of confession.

The holy Gaon Rabbi David Mintzberg had come there in the shrouds that he had prepared for himself, over which he wore a white *kittel* [prayer robe]. He came with head held high. He face shone and his eyes burned. He was prepared to sanctify God's name in public. Within an hour he had fallen dead from a murderer's bullet.[123]

The Gaon Rabbi Yerucham Fishel Dan

The Gaon Rabbi Yerucham Fishel Dan was one of the closest students of the Gaon Rabbi Meir Dan Plotzky during the years of his residence in Ostrow Mazowiecka. He was sharp and possessed rare abilities that enabled him to grasp things quickly and with great diligence. Rabbi Yerucham Fishel Dan was considered a prodigy, and was ordained by the greatest rabbis when he was only sixteen.

Rabbi Yerucham Fishel was among those younger fellows in Ostroveh who first set up the group of young men among the Hassidim of Ger that sat night and day in the house of Ger and studied. He frequently traveled to Ger, to the *rebbe*, and worked on pure Hassidism with other young men his age.

From the house of Ger he found his way to the Agudat Yisrael movement, and from a young age began to work on behalf of that party, imbued as he was with the Agudist ideology. He quickly became one of the most outstanding and devoted leaders of Agudat Yisrael, prepared to do whatever was needed on behalf of his movement. He was soon elected to the central committee of Agudat Yisrael in Poland and traveled frequently on missions on behalf of his movement. No assignment was too difficult for him if it had the potential to advance the cause of Agudat Yisrael on some level.

At quite a young age he was selected as the Rabbi of Kosov [Kosow Lacki], and remained in his post up until the last day of the existence of that veteran community. He left Ostrow Mazowiecka with the members of his family. Even while serving as the rabbi of Kosov he did not abandon his loyalty to Agudat Yisrael or his adherence to the Hassidism of Ger.

With the outbreak of the Holocaust he was exiled with his family from Kosov and landed up in Slonim. He refused to save his

---

[123] According to an article on the website of the U.S. Holocaust Memorial Museum, approximately 1,500 Jews were killed in the Lachva ghetto uprising, and of the 600 who managed to escape to the forests, another 420 soon perished. At the end of the war only 90 of those who escaped from the Lachva ghetto remained alive.

own life but rather remained in the valley of death with many of his flock. He was killed by the Germans when they liquidated the Slonim ghetto.

The Gaon Rabbi Moshe Goldblatt

Among the outstanding members of the Hassidim of Ger was the Gaon Rabbi Moshe Goldblatt, one of the great scholars in Ostroveh. A native of Wyszkow, he came there after his marriage to the daughter of Aaron Bengelsdorf, a prominent citizen of Ostrow Mazowiecka. At a young age he stood out thanks to his acuity and his greatness in Torah. Since the time he was of age, he never began morning prayers until he had studied three pages of Talmud in depth along with commentaries. As a young man he wrote a high quality interpretation of *Baal Henefesh* [*Master of the Soul*] of the Rabad [acronym for Rabbi Abraham ben David, ca. 1125-1198], which remained in manuscript form and was never published.

From the time of his arrival in Ostroveh Rabbi "Mosheleh" was counted among the students of Rabbi Ben-Zion, who very much drew him in and liked him. Rabbi Ben-Zion saw him as one of the best of his students, outstanding and distinguished in everything. When secularist circles in Ostroveh proposed to establish a Jewish gymnasium [secular high school] in the town, and organized a gathering to that end, Rabbi Ben-Zion negated the idea, and went to the meeting place accompanied by his beloved and great student, Rabbi Mosheleh, to speak harshly against the organizers and their aspirations. The attendees of the meeting were about to pounce on him angrily. Rabbi Ben-Zion, who was already old and frail but respected by all, stood before them, and reprimanded those who would insult Rabbi Mosheleh. "Do you know who my student is?" He raised his voice and praised his student heartily. For lack of alternative, the organizers had to forego their proposal.

When it was suggested to Rabbi Mosheleh that he serve as *dayan* and *motz* [*moreh tzedek*, literally instructor in justice], he refused for reasons known only to him. But he did agree to move to Warsaw and to serve for a time as an instructor in the *yeshiva*, *Metivta*. He taught Torah to many until the outbreak of the Holocaust. Rabbi Mosheleh was killed in Trawniki along with his wife and their six children, to which he was sent by the Nazi murderers from the Warsaw ghetto as part of their destruction of Polish Jewry.

Rabbi Avraham Yaakov Friedman

One of the great scholars of Ostroveh in the last generation before the Holocaust, the pride of the last of the Mitnagdim in the city, was Rabbi Avraham Yaakov Friedman, one of the important congregants of the new *beit midrash* and one the town's leaders. He was both a great scholar and a community activist, a wealthy man and a propagator of Torah, a throwback to the period when there were in Jewish communities in the Diaspora superlative scholars that were also successful businessmen who combined Torah and prominence.

Rabbi Avraham Yaakov was born in the town of Nowogrod near Lomza into a respected family of excellent lineage. His father was considered a sharp person and the leading scholar in and around his town. At a young age Rabbi Avraham Yaakov was enrolled in the Volozhin *yeshiva*, where he was one of the students of the Gaon Rabbi Chaim Soloveichik, the rabbi of Brest-Litovsk, who was serving at the time as the dean of the Volozhin *yeshiva*. He stood out particularly for his acuity, but he did not neglect knowledge of the substance either, nor the learning necessary to acquire such substance.

After his marriage to a young woman from Ostrow Mazowiecka, the daughter of Nachman Goldberg,[124] he settled there and became one of the leading scholars of the town. He refused to use his knowledge of Torah for material purposes. He turned down rabbinical positions and any other sacred occupations. He preferred to try his hand at business, while still devoting most of his time to Torah. For decades Rabbi Avraham Yaakov sat and studied Torah with great dedication, while taking off a few hours every day to engage in business and communal affairs.

Rabbi Avraham Yaakov was the scion of a long line of Mitnagdim, who did not adopt Hassidism. But on the other hand he got along with the Hassidim and never got involved in the conflict between Hassidim and Mitnagdim. Rabbi Avraham Yaakov was a practical man, who liked to delve deeply into an issue and examine its roots and its raison d'etre. He thus saw the conflict between Hassidim and Mitnagdim as a legacy of the past that had already disappeared. In its place there now stood new movements, secular and anti-religious ones, which arose in the Jewish community in the last generation before the Holocaust. He joined Agudat Yisrael and did much on its behalf.

Since Nachman Goldberg had left his position as head of the community during World War I, Rabbi Avraham Yaakov was chosen in his place, and he served until 5684 [1923-1924] as head of the community. With his encouragement and active support, the community chose the Gaon Rabbi Meir Dan [Plotzky] as chief

---

[124] According to the Ostrow Mazowiecka records, Abram Jankel Fridman [Friedman] married Bluma Judes Goldberg in 1895.

of the rabbinical court. On behalf of the community he went to Dvart, the previous place of service of the rabbi before Ostrow Mazowiecka. Once he saw the unique qualities of Rabbi Plotzky, he did all he could to get him to be chosen.

But Rabbi Avraham Yaakov stood out most in relation to his acuity and his superlative learning. There was no lack of high level scholars, of outstanding knowledgeable people in Ostroveh in the last generation before the Holocaust. And whereas in the previous generation some of them were concentrated in the Mitnagdic camp and some in the Hassidic camp, in the immediate generation before the Holocaust the number of great Torah scholars in the Mitnagdic community declined. Rabbi Avraham Yaakov, who served as their spokesman and advocate for their cause, elevated the status of that community as a *gaon* of the Torah and perpetuated the glorious tradition of the renowned Volozhin *yeshiva*.

He continued to propagate Torah and to give his lectures in the new synagogue, and it was a pleasure to hear him. He explained even the most difficult and complex subject with simplicity and great ability, as he led the listeners via his teachings into the depth of the issues with the hand of an artist.

With the outbreak of the Holocaust, Rabbi Avraham Yaakov Friedman escaped to the Soviet zone of occupation. Weak and ill, he reached Slonim with the masses of the refugees from his city. But a serious illness struck him and on the twenty-ninth day of Cheshvan, 5700 [November 11, 1939], on the very day that the last Jews of Ostroveh were killed, just two months after the outbreak of the Holocaust, he returned his soul to its maker, as a war refugee in Slonim.

Rabbi Avraham Yitzchak Bromberg

One of the important congregants of the old *beit midrash* in Ostroveh was Rabbi Avraham Yitzhak Bromberg. He was a learned man who frequented many regular lectures, but also was involved in business with the help of his wife, Mrs. Feige Zissel [Bromberg].

Rabbi Avraham Yitzhak died when he was still quite young, leaving behind his widow and eight young children, six sons and two daughters.[125] After the period of mourning, the young widow

---

[125] According to the Ostrow Mazowiecka records, he died in April 1895 at the age of 62. Avraham Yitzchak Bromberg (1832-1895) and his wife Feige Zissel Bromberg nee Wainberg (1835-1923) had the following children:
- Leyb Don [Dan Aryeh] Bromberg (1856-1920), buried in Warsaw, married Mala Mariem, daughter of Yaakov Mendelson;
- Esther Perl (1857-1917), wife of Nachman Goldberg;

gathered up her strength and began once again to run her large household and to educate her offspring in the ways of Torah. It was soon apparent that Feige Zissel was an astute and successful businesswoman. In a few years she had amassed a considerable fortune. Her enterprises branched out all across Poland. She became the wealthiest woman in all of Ostroveh and its nearby and outlying areas. She dealt with the owners of some of the largest enterprises, while her holdings in Poland and her overall wealth was estimated to be in vast sums.

Feige Zissel married off all of her sons and daughters into other very wealthy and extremely respected families in Poland. Her oldest son, Rabbi Dan, an outstanding scholar and public persona, was the son-in-law of Hershel Mendelson, one of the richest and most respected men in Warsaw. For many years he served as the cantor on the High Holy Days in the old *beit midrash* in Ostroveh. During World War I he moved with his extensive family to Warsaw, where he died.

Her second son, Rabbi Chaim Mordechai, was considered a well rounded person. He was a Judaic scholar who also knew German, Russian and Polish perfectly. A successful, wealthy merchant, he was the son-in-law of Rabbi Ziskind Shachor of Biala. Her third son, Rabbi Yaakov, was the son-in-law of the richest Jew in Kutno, the Hassidic Rabbi Yehuda Meir Lipsker, a Hassid and a scholar, who was well known for his great wisdom. For decades he ran a bank. In his later years he immigrated to Jerusalem, where he died in the year 5695 [1935].

Her fourth son, Rabbi Zeev Wolf Bromberg, was very successful in business and was one of the wealthiest Hassidim. The fifth son, Rabbi Tzvi Hersh**Error! Bookmark not defined.**, was the son-in-law of Rabbi Leib Schechter, a wealthy manufacturer from Lodz. He was a scholar and ardent Hassid, who was known as an honest and reliable man. The youngest of the brothers, Rabbi Natan Bromberg, was the son-in-law of Rabbi Chaim Shidlovsky, a wealthy Hassid from Piotrkow. Rabbi Natan resided for many years with his large family in Ostroveh, but later moved to Warsaw. He was a Hassid and a publicly-oriented person as well. He was among the most devoted and active members of the Agudat Yisrael

---

- Chaim Mordechai Bromberg (1861-1921), buried in Warsaw, married Esther Leah, daughter of Yaakov Alexander Ziskind Bialer;
- Tsveytl Gittel (b. 1862), wife of Shlomo Hershel Reichman;
- Wolf Bromberg (b. 1863);
- Yankel/Jakob Bromberg (1865-1935), married the daughter of Yehuda Meir Lipski;
- Hershel Bromberg (b. 1866), married Yudes, daughter of Shaya Shreyter; and
- Nosek Bromberg (1869-1941), married Royza, daughter of Chaim Shydlovski.

movement in Poland. He represented his movement as an officer of the Warsaw Jewish community.

Feige Zissel married off her daughters to the sons of highly respected families as well. Her first son-in-law was Rabbi Nachman Goldberg, one of the most important and respected residents of Ostrow Mazowiezka. Up until World War I he had served as head of the community. Her second son-in-law was Rabbi Shlomo Reichman of Czestochowa, one of the most important and richest Hassidim of that city.

Rabbi Avraham**Error! Bookmark not defined.** Yitzchak Bromberg and his wife Feige Zissel were among the opponents of Hassidism, but all their children became loyal Ger Hassidim thanks to the influence of the Hassidic Gaon Rabbi Ben-Zion [Rabinowitz], head of the Ger Hassidim in Ostroveh.

Feige Zissel was widowed as a young woman. She invested her energy and talents in the education of her children, in the running of her large and diverse businesses, and in her household, which she famously ran in a model fashion. Her great wealth was matched by her lavish charitable giving. When a *yeshiva* was established in Ostroveh, Feige Zissel built a beautiful building in which to house it from her own funds. When a fire broke out and consumed that building, this noble and generous woman did not hesitate but a moment and immediately donated the entire amount necessary to rebuild it. And it stood on that very spot until the horrific Holocaust. Hundreds of students of Torah had studied there.

Her home was totally open to any poor person or wandering visitor. Every Monday and Thursday the entire student body of the *yeshiva* ate in her home. Tens of Jewish soldiers and needy guests graced the table in her large home every Sabbath and holiday. Large numbers of paupers streamed to her house and received food to satisfy their needs. The devoted widow established and ran a renowned home all by herself for decades, with her sons and daughters and sons-in-law and daughters-in-law around her. And from these children there grew many extensive families in Poland. She was full of initiative and energy, and was never deterred from undertaking any project or work.

Feige Zissel was the granddaughter of Rabbi Dan Landau of Plotzk [Plock], the famous *shtadlan*[126] in his day, and father-in-law

---

[126] In European Jewish history, a *shtadlan* was an influential Jew who, because of his wealth or connections at court (in German *hof*, hence the Germanic term *Hofjude* or court Jew) or otherwise, was in a position to influence the government on behalf of the Jewish community and its interests. In Poland, the position developed into a more formalized one during the period of the autonomous Council of the Four Lands (1580-1764), when

of the Hassidic rebbe Rabbi Avraham of Ciechanow,[127] and father-in-law and step-father of the Gaon Rabbi Zeev Wolf Lipschitz, the rabbi of Ozorkow. Rabbi Dan was a man of outstanding attributes and characteristics. He knew many languages, including French. When Napoleon Bonaparte, the French emperor, passed through Poland on his march to conquer Russia, he camped for a number of days in Plotzk. There was not a single person in that city, except for Rabbi Dan, who knew French. Rabbi Dan secretly met with the ruler, who borrowed ten thousand gold thalers from him, and received a signed note attesting to the receipt of that sum from Rabbi Dan.

Napoleon failed in his mission, and was forced to retreat back to France with the remnants of his army. It was not long before he was removed from his throne by the very nations that fought him, Britain and Russia, Prussia and Austria, and who replaced him with a king of the Bourbon line. The new French government did not recognize the borrowings of Napoleon. Thus, Rabbi Dan became impoverished. He lost his wealth and was forced to earn his living from the community coffers as a *shtadlan*.

Feige Zissel had inherited the loan document signed by the emperor. The Bourbons once again were no longer the rulers of France, while the name of Napoleon was once again on the lips of the French people. Feige Zissel decided to try to collect the debt from the government of France. She engaged a lawyer, who made his way to Paris. He presented a formal claim on her behalf to a French court, which rejected the plea and which accepted the position of the French government that had specifically decided not to honor the debts of Napoleon.

During World War I, when the Russians conspired against the Jews in general and the rich Jews in particular, Feige Zissel moved from Ostroveh to Warsaw, where most of her children now lived. She was eighty-seven when she arrived in Warsaw, but her mind was as lucid and bright as ever, and she was still full of energy and action. She remained in Warsaw even after World War I with her children, grandchildren and great-grandchildren. She lived to the incredible ripe old age of ninety-six, when she died in the year 5683 [1923] in Warsaw.

---

the *shtadlan* became a professional, paid lobbyist, with all the accoutrements of the modern lobbyist: a salary, budgets for "walking around money" and actual bribes, for staff, etc. There were often similar paid communal officials on the provincial level as well.

[127] Rabbi Avraham Landau (ca. 1789-1875) was known as the "Tzadik of Ciechanow" or the Ciechanower *rebbe*. His wife Itta was the daughter of Reb Dan Landau.

The Hassidic Rebbe Rabbi Yaakov David of Amshinov

He was born in Ostrow Mazowiecka to his father, the Hassidic *rebbe* Rabbi Yosef of Amshinov, during the period when Rabbi Yosef was the chief rabbi of the city. He was raised and educated in Ostroveh. Even when he was young, his characteristics of fear of God and fear of sin stood out, while a streak of charm adorned his noble face, as a son of such an outstanding family. It was said that he resembled his great-grandfather, the first *rebbe* of the house of Amshinov, Rabbi Yaakov David, who was the first son of the old *rebbe*, the famous Rabbi Yitzhak of Warka [Vurka, Vorki]. His hair was as black as coal; his side locks were curled and added the beauty of the ages to his image; his large velvety eyes glowed. Wherever he went he aroused attention. Everyone who passed him, Jew or non-Jew, was interested in knowing who this beautiful, elegant young boy was.

The dynasty of *rebbe*s of the house of Amshinov maintained its long tradition of a passionate love for the people of Israel, while at the same time being careful not to cause any harm or pain to anyone. The young Rabbi Yaakov David adhered to this tradition with all his being, full of positive characteristics like a pomegranate, educated and brought up to continue this tradition of generations. Already at a young age he memorized the *Orech Chaim* volume of the *Shulchan Aruch*. He studied diligently and enthusiastically, and also worked hard on his Hassidism as soon as he was mature enough.

When his father, Rabbi Yosef, left the seat of the rabbinate in Ostrow Mazowiecka in order to succeed his father Rabbi Yosef [sic Menachem] of Amshinov, Rabbi Yaakov David left Ostroveh with him. But until his last day Rabbi Yaakov David considered himself as being a native of the city.

He was seventeen when he married the daughter of Rabbi Shlomo Yoskovitz, the son-in-law of the Hassidic *rebbe* Rabbi Avraham Mordechai of Ger. For some years he lived with his father-in-law in Warsaw and in Ger, and was later chosen as chief of the rabbinical court of Zhiradov [Zyrardow].

In the year 5696 [1936][128] Rabbi Yosef died. The Hassidim of Amshinov chose Rabbi Yaakov David to succeed him as rabbi and *rebbe*. But as per the request of the residents of Zhiradov, Rabbi Yaakov David did not give up his rabbinical position there. So from that point forward he served both as the *rebbe* and chief of the

---

[128] According to information on Warsaw cemetery burials, Rabbi Yosef Kalisz [Kalish] died on January 27, 1936 (other sources indicate an unspecified date in 1935). His father, Rabbi MenachemError! Bookmark not defined. Kalisz, died on January 12, 1917 (other sources indicate an unspecified date in 1918).

rabbinical court of Amshinov, as well as chief of the rabbinical court of Zhiradov, where he spent two days a week.

Every year on the memorial day for his father, the *rebbe* Rabbi Yosef, who was buried with honors in the great Jewish cemetery in Warsaw, the *rebbe* Rabbi Yaakov David would arrive in that city, where he would provide tables of food for all of the Amshinov Hassidim who gathered there, coming from all the places in which they lived. He surveyed his loyal community of Hassidim, many of whom would frequently visit him in Amshinov. They were enthusiastically and loyally devoted to him, seeing in him the great heir of the glorious tradition of the house of Amshinov.

With the outbreak of the Holocaust, Amshinov was burned. The *rebbe* Rabbi Yaakov David fled to Warsaw with his family and devotees. He remained in the capital of Poland, suffering the torture and pain of the Polish Diaspora at its worst, days when it was writhing in its terrible and bitter death spasms.

It was then that the full splendor and glory of the *rebbe* Rabbi Yaakov David as a lover of the people of Israel was revealed. His heart was open to all. The pain of his brothers was his pain, the suffering of Jews was his suffering. He trembled like a leaf in a storm to hear the pain. In those mad times many people had learned how to harden their hearts, to become inured to suffering, to listen to terrifying tales of horrors that were perpetrated by the bloody dogs of Nazism with indifference. But the young Rabbi Yaakov David was able to tap the wellsprings of love for the people of Israel that were hidden deep within his great soul. As the tortures and suffering grew, so did his great love for every Jew. He not only participated in the sorrow of every person, but also felt the pain of all who came within his sphere.

Rabbi Yaakov David was imprisoned behind the walls of the Warsaw Ghetto along with the masses of his brethren and hundreds of his Hassidim. He continued to lead his followers from a garret. In the year 5702 [1942] he contracted typhus and died in the ghetto.[129] He was buried in the mausoleum of his grandfather, the *rebbe* Rabbi Menachem, alongside his father, the *rebbe* Rabbi Yosef. His wife and four children were also killed in the Holocaust.

Rabbi Shmuel Grudke[130]

---

[129] According to information on Warsaw cemetery burials, Rabbi Yaakov David Kalisz (Kalish) died in March 23, 1942.

[130] Probably Szmul Grudke [Grudka] (1836-1891), son of Litman and husband of Sura Leah.

This is the story of Reb Shmuel Grudke [Grudka], one of the leading citizens of Ostroveh in the beginning of the seventh century:[131] I was released from service in the Russian army after twelve years. I returned to my home and my wife without so much as a penny in hand. Upon the advice of my wife, I traveled to Ciechanow to see the *tzadik* Rabbi Avraham to seek his blessing. The rabbi blessed me with success when I would go out to do business. "But what will I go out with?" I asked. "With my blessing," he replied. So I went forth with the blessing of the *tzadik* of Ciechanow to the market place in Ostroveh, but with nothing else in hand. I walked around among the peasants and peddlers with a heavy heart. Then I saw a peasant alongside a wagon loaded down with grain. "Do you want to buy it, sir?" he asked. "But I have no money," I replied. "So I will lend it to you, and you will sell it for a profit and pay me back." I did not refuse. I put the grain into my courtyard, sold it for a good price, and made a decent profit, all in two or three days. A week later market day was again held in Ostroveh and I went there. I saw a group of peasants and in the middle one of them was one who was yelling and tearing his hair out. I approached them out of curiosity and alas it was the very same peasant who had sold me his grain. He was bitter and blamed himself for acting like a real fool. He had come to the market a week before with his grain and had sold it trustingly to a Jew whom he did not know, and now the grain was gone, the money was gone, and the Jew was gone.

I went over to him and took him aside and said, "I am the one who bought your grain. I came to look for you and to pay you what is owed to you. I have the money in my rucksack, and I will count it out for you down to the penny."

I gave the peasant his money and his eyes lit up. In a second he completely changed and became very happy. He hugged me and slapped me on the shoulder repeatedly. "There is no more trustworthy a Jew like you in all the world," he muttered without hesitation, "and from now on I will do business only with you" permanently.

And from that day forward, Reb Shmuel related, I became agent for that farmer and all the others from his village and from nearby villages. They faithfully brought me all their produce, and I sold it and served them faithfully as well. This is how Reb Shmuel became wealthy. He fully believed that it was due to the merit of the *tzadik* that he had obtained his livelihood and wealth. And the peasants remained loyal to him until his last day. And after his

---

[131] Meaning the 7th century of the fifth millennium on the Jewish calendar, or the 5600's, the equivalent of 1839-1939 on the general calendar.

death they remained loyal to his children and heirs, who continued doing business with them up until the outbreak of the Holocaust. And at every occasion they would tell people that it was all due to the blessing of the *tzadik* of Ciechanow, which continued in force.

Rabbi David Lichtenstein

Among the honored and respected residents of Ostroveh of the last generation before the Holocaust was Rabbi David Lichtenstein. He was chairman of the community council, chairman of the *Linat Hatzedek* society, one of the officials of Agudat Yisrael, and one of the most active Jews locally.

Rabbi David Lichtenstein was a gentle soul and possessor of excellent personal characteristics, an observant Jew, as well as one who recognized the need for, and was willing to undertake, action. His comings and goings and his actions were always thought out and evaluated in advance. He fought for pure Judaism. He identified with all his being with the fundamentals of Agudat Yisrael, but he also conducted himself with refinement and caution.

He was a figure who inspired respect. There was never a spot on his clothing. His home was open to all, and he willingly welcomed guests. He was prepared to help others with all his heart, to support the person who was ill and those who needed help and succor. And he did all this quietly and carefully. He was an honored Jew who in his actions represented the rare paragon of an activist who undertakes responsibilities without any expectation of reward. He was a businessman engrossed in his enterprises, but who always found time for communal affairs.

In the year 5684 [1923-1924], after the first democratic community elections in Ostrow Mazowiecka, he was chosen to represent his party, Agudat Yisrael, on the community council.

After the elections Rabbi David was chosen as chairman of the community council, a truly representative role, and a position of honor. With great ability and sensitivity he fulfilled this role to the satisfaction of all.

Rabbi David was a party man, a man of Agudat Yisrael. Nevertheless, many in Ostrow Mazowiecka correctly saw in him a man of the entire community.

At the outbreak of the Holocaust, Rabbi David escaped from Ostrow Mazowiecka with his family to the Russian zone of occupation. He was among the masses of refugees from Ostroveh in Slonim, and was incarcerated in the ghetto there when the city was conquered by the Nazis. He was killed when the Jews of the city were destroyed.

Rabbi Anshel Knorpel

A native of Plotzk, Rabbi Anshel Knorpel was one of the most important citizens and leaders of Jewry in Ostrow Mazowiecka, having served as chairman of the executive body of the community until the outbreak of the Holocaust and the destruction of the city. At a young age he married the daughter of Rabbi Dan (known locally as "Pious Dan"), and from then on was a resident of the town.

He was one of the Hassidim of Ger, and as such he traveled to visit the *rebbe* Rabbi Aryeh Leib, and after his death, to see his son, the *rebbe* Rabbi Avraham Mordechai of Ger. He conducted his home according to the best traditions of pure Hassidism, that of Ger Hassidism, which brooked no compromises.

Rabbi Anshel was an accomplished scholar. He both loved Torah and persevered in his study of it. He studied in depth, with profundity and great effort. He did not subscribe to superficial study that did not endeavor to penetrate to the depths of the matter or to discuss a theory or issue. Rabbi Anshel especially studied Halacha and stood out for his knowledge of the opinions of both the early and later decisors.

In addition to being an outstanding Judaic scholar, Rabbi Anshel also knew Russian and Polish, as well as accounting. He inherited a vinegar factory, and was so successful in his business that he came to be known as one of the richest men in the city. He always contributed to all worthy causes.

Rabbi Anshel was thought of being something of a zealot, a man who stood by his ideas and who refused to depart from his path. He loathed compromises and the very idea of compromise, opportunistic approaches and weak positions. In public affairs as in private ones, he always knew what he wanted and where he was headed, stubbornly and determinedly taking steps in that direction.

He was an activist in communal affairs. And since the establishment of the Agudat Yisrael movement in Ostrow Mazowiecka, he was considered one of its most loyal participants. He represented Agudat Yisrael on the city council and was chosen as chairman of the executive body of the Jewish community in the last elections of the community in Ostroveh. He served as the last chairman of this bustling and outstanding community.

As a man of public affairs and as the representative of the Jews of the city, Rabbi Anshel excelled in his own unique and characteristic way. He did not subscribe to the theory that the end justifies the means. This idea was absolutely unacceptable to him, as it was to every conscious observant Jew. But at the same time he never forgot the goal, and that attaining that goal was obligatory. Deviations only lengthen the path to that goal and detract from the mission.

In the last years of the existence of the community in Ostrow Mazowiecka, Rabbi Anshel Knorpel was head of the community and its representative on the city council, a task that was not an easy one in the difficult period that led up to the Holocaust. Anti-Semitism in Poland increased materially from day to day. The Jews suffered greatly from the economic boycott, from deprivation of their rights and from discrimination. The Jewish community council became the central address for all the problems of the Jews of the locale and its environs. The head of the community knew no respite day or night. Rabbi Anshel persevered in his difficult position with honor, and until the last day of the existence of the community he never relinquished his post.

The city council was comprised mainly of Poles, despite the large proportion of Jews among the residents of Ostroveh. Under the cover of officially democratic elections, the authorities worked hard to minimize Jewish representation, while inflating the Polish representation out of all proportion. The representatives of the Jews on the council, headed by Rabbi Anshel Knorpel, had the difficult task of combating both blatant and subtle anti-Semitic aims of the Polish leaders of the city. Rabbi Anshel also stood this test with honor and ability.

In the horrific Holocaust he and his family were killed. With the destruction of the community, so too was destroyed its last head and representative.

Rabbi Nachman Goldberg

Rabbi Nachman Goldberg was born in Trestina [Trzcianne], a small town near Bialystok, in the year 5618 [1857-1858] into a prominent family of merchants, scholars and honorable men. He studied in the *yeshivot* of Lithuania, and at a young age married the daughter of the wealthy Feige Zissel Bromberg of Ostroveh, and became one of the important residents of the town. He was considered a scholar, a businessman, and a trustworthy individual who was acceptable to all. A Jew with a pleasing appearance that evoked great honor and admiration among all groups, he reveled in fulfilling the commandments and observed all of them meticulously. He loved the Torah and was loyal to pure Judaism without deviating left or right. He conducted himself with calm, and his conversation was well considered. He rejected rashness in general and rashness in thought in particular. He respected every human being, and did not embrace new theories and approaches. His appearance was always well put together, pleasant and spotless, as was his manner, well laid out and organized. He was not taken in by precipitous actions or rash efforts. He was serious and practical by nature, shunning light headedness in thought and deed.

He was a devoted and respected merchant, who successfully conducted his diverse businesses for decades in Ostroveh. In the synagogue he sat along the eastern wall among the other merchants and businessmen of the city. He rejected quick profits that came from trickery or subtle actions or that did not conform to the respectable and accepted conduct of honorable merchants. In general he would not touch any transaction that even bordered on fraud of any kind.

He thus developed a reputation as trustworthy and honorable, a man whose word could be relied upon, whose word was his bond. His word was more important to him than any profit or loss. He knew how to stand up for his rights, but at the same time respected the rights of others as well. He never coveted what others had and never demanded anything that was not his due. He was a gentleman merchant of the old school.

For many years Rabbi Nachman Goldberg served as the head of the community in Ostrow Mazowiecka, up until the time of World War I. He had an excellent command of the Russian language, and represented the Jewish community to the authorities with honor and brilliance. At the same time, he succeeded in conducting the affairs of the community with great skill, including its relationship with its rabbis. He was the archetype of a head of a community in those days, who knew how to bring glory to his post and to elevate it.

Rabbi Nachman was an opponent of Hassidism, the scion of a Mitnagdic family of many generations. He worked in Mitnagdic circles for decades, even as all of his brothers-in-law of the Bromberg family had become devoted Hassidim of Ger. During the years when the *rebbe* Rabbi Yosef of Amshinov served as rabbi of Ostroveh, Rabbi Nachman drew close to him and became a loyal friend and his greatest admirer. Under the influence of the *rebbe*, Rabbi Nachman became a Hassid, and during the latter years of his life was to be counted among those Hassidim of Amshinov who were attached to their rabbi.

After World War I Rabbi Nachman moved to Warsaw, where he lived up until his death. In the year 5686 [1926][132] Rabbi Nachman passed away in Warsaw with an admirable reputation. He was sixty-nine years old at his death, which evoked great sorrow among his many acquaintances and admirers.

Rabbi Aaron Yashinsky

Rabbi Aaron Yashinsky arrived in Ostroveh as a young man in order to marry the daughter of Rabbi Moshe Schwartz.[133] He settled in the city and assimilated like a fitting link into the multifaceted chain of the respected people of the town, who took pride in the lively community and transformed it into a outstanding shining pearl of the great paradise that was the Diaspora of Poland, Lithuania and Galicia. With his deeds and actions, his characteristics and his very being, Rabbi Aaron added yet another element to the beautiful edifice that was the Jewry of Ostrow Mazowiecka.

Being that he was a "nice young man," Rabbi Moshe Schwartz took him into his home as a son-in-law. He was well learned in Torah, although he never thought to transform his knowledge of Torah into a means of earning a living. He lived in the house of his father-in-law for some years, after which time he turned to business, and eventually became a successful merchant, who walked the straight and narrow path. What was on his lips was also what was in his heart. He was among the handful of merchants who brought honor to Jewish commerce, and who acquired the trust of both Jews and non-Jews.

---

[132] According to Warsaw cemetery information, Nachman son of Yehuda Goldberg died on May 7, 1926. According to a parallel article in the other, larger *Yizkor Book of the Jewish Commmunity of Ostrow Mazowiecka,* edited by A. Gordin and M. Gelbart, written by many contributors partially in Yiddish and partially in Hebrew and published originally in Israel in 1960, and later translated by multiple people and published in English translation by JewishGen in 2013, his wife Esther Perl died on the ninth of Iyar 5677 [April 30-May 1, 1917].

[133] According to the Ostrow Mazowiecka records, Aron Jasinski [Yashinsky] (b. 1869) married Ruchla Leja Szwarc [Schwartz] (b. 1875) in 1892.

Rabbi Aaron Yashinsky was charming and possessed outstanding personal characteristics from his earliest days. And as he got older his traits, his measured ways and his pleasant mien came to symbolize his fine and distinguished personality. He always saw the good that was about him and sought out the good. He always knew what he was faced with, but approached it without conflict or contention. He steered clear of gossip and disputes. He was beloved by all who came into contact with him, whether in his business or in the great house of the Hassidim of Ger.

Thus Rabbi Aaron he was a true Hassid and scholar who adhered to his teacher, the *rebbe* of Ger. By nature he was not assertive, and was not among those Hassidim who were aggressive and sharp. He was rather devoted heart and soul to pure Hassidism, without ever deviating from it. At the house of the Hassidim of Ger he would regularly deliver a lecture on the Gemara,[134] and many would listen to his disquisitions and explanations. His lectures resembled his manner, that is, quiet and restrained. He was devoted to the truth of the Halacha, and rejected tortuous logic, but did so with his characteristic gentility and charm.

In addition to all this he was also active on behalf of the good and welfare of the community, but on a completely voluntary, non-remunerative basis, and without seeking any honors or position for his work on behalf of his fellow man. He was always ready to undertake any task or deed, but always with quiet and restraint, and with careful forethought. He had great energy, which always translated into positive outlooks. He did not like the noise and tumult that often surrounds general and communal affairs. He would walk along in a quiet and modest manner towards any goal. He was devoted to the mission and not to the noisy behavior that so often accompanies public affairs.

When the economic condition of deprivation worsened in the final period before the Holocaust, Rabbi Aaron established a charitable fund, which he ably directed and into which he invested great effort.

As a devoted Hassid of Ger, he was an Agudat Yisrael man. In the last elections for the Jewish community that were conducted in Poland, he was nominated against his will to head the Agudat Yisrael slate, which received a majority of votes in that election. Rabbi Aaron Yashinsky was chosen as chairman of the community council alongside Rabbi Anshel Knorpel, who was chosen as the

---

[134] The later, larger section of the Talmud, compiled between 350-500 of the Common Era.

chairman of the executive of the community council. He served in this capacity up until the destruction of Ostrow Mazowiecka.

In the community as well he conducted himself in his usual calm and pleasant manner. It is said that Rabbi Aaron had virtually no enemies in Ostroveh, as he never had offended anyone and never caused pain to any person. On the contrary, he did everything to help others, to assist Jews who were left without sustenance, as anti-Semitism in Poland began to rear its ugly head in Poland with the rise of the Nazis.

When the Holocaust broke out, Rabbi Aaron Yashinsky escaped with his family to Slonim, which was in the Soviet zone of occupation, where he died a martyr's death along with his family.

The Gaon Rabbi Avraham Petziner

Who has not heard the stories of wonder about great scholars and exceptional righteous men, great Hassidim and activists, whom we had in the cities of Poland, and in its towns and villages? They worked hard and sacrificed and devoted all their days to becoming holy and pure, to arise and motivate themselves to attain a higher level without seeking any *quid pro quo*, without seeking any tangible benefit, without enjoying any pleasure whatsoever from their knowledge of the Torah or their Hassidism, from their hard work and their efforts, which they devoted entirely, along with themselves, to the objective to which they aspired, to the goal that stood before their eyes.

Who has not heard of these exceptional people who were not concerned with themselves, those few extraordinary people whose hearts are open like a great hall to everyone who seeks or needs it, but who themselves need nothing? They were wonderful people who were prepared to undergo all manner of suffering and sacrifice, every task and action without asking anything for themselves. They were towering figures, who never thought of themselves and never worried about themselves, but rather who were pure and free of that motivation of selfishness that causes such destruction in the world, that renders mountains into valleys and valleys into mountains, that distorts the straightforward and confuses all thought and conversation, that same personal interest that blinds the eye and darkens even the brightest of lights.

There were not many of these even during the days of glory and greatness of the grand Diaspora of Poland, even fewer during its decline and fall. One of few who in their very being and in their deeds resembled that exalted tradition was the *gaon* and Hassid, the activist and devotee, Rabbi Avraham Petziner [Pecyner].

There are those who stand out as a Hassid, and those who stand out as a scholar. There are those who are distinguished by their activism, and those who are distinguished by their wisdom. There were those who rose above personal considerations, but never made any effort to stand out, to ascend to the pinnacle of society. They remained indifferent to honor or status. There were very few like these who refused honors or status symbols, who worked hard and struggled without hesitation but without trying to stand out. One of these few was the Gaon Rabbi Avraham Petziner, may God avenge his blood.

This Rabbi Avraham appeared to be a simple and regular Jew, one of the hundreds of thousands who lived in Poland before the days of the Holocaust. He wore a traditional Jewish hat, and was wrapped in a long, simple coat. He was a leather merchant in town, who dealt with tanners and shoemakers, a merchant of the second or third tier or below. His limited, even shriveled up business, yielded less than those of his competitors in this field, who far exceeded him in their enterprises. With his limited income, he was far from wealthy, but was rather a Jew under [financial] pressure.

Rabbi Avraham was born in Sokolka[135] to his father, Rabbi Menachem Mendel Petziner, a learned Hassid. He was a merchant and a smart man, the son of Rabbi Zalman Zelig Petziner.

Rabbi Zalman Zelig was from Ostroveh. He was one of the first --and one of the leaders--of the Hassidim of Kotsk, and one of its

---

[135] According to the Ostrow Mazowiecka records, Rabbi Avraham was born in Sokoly.

pathfinders in a city with many opponents to Hassidim and Hassidism. His Torah, his faith and his Hassidism seemed inherent in his very blood, profound, enthusiastic and evoking respect. He was one of the outstanding people of his generation, and a central pillar of Hassidism in his city of residence. He refused any official position, honor or status. He was always full of happiness and enthusiasm. When asked what his role was in Ostroveh, he would reply without hesitancy, "a fool on the holidays," as he served as service leader in the house of the Hassidim, where he would take to the podium to lead the additional service on holidays.

The local residents remember Rabbi Zalman Zelig with awe and respect. They looked back on his past in sacred awe. He was a giant of the spirit hiding behind the cloak of regular Hassid. All of his days and years were devoted to good works on behalf of God. He had no time for everyday secular problems. His daily studies became an integral part of his persona, the essence of his being. He would begin them in the early hours of the evening and finish them in the hours before noon. The measure of Torah is far from the land, from the seas and the oceans [he believed]. Thus, a short sail just to satisfy the minimal requirements, meaning one who begrudged the long hours of study, was not even considered true study, according to Rabbi Zalman Zelig.

Such people would finish the lesson and go right to prayer, to worship. A Hassid of Kotsk is not accustomed to running like that from study to prayer, like a peddler who moves from counter to counter. Preparation is important. In the winter it would be necessary to cut it short, as the day is short. In the summer it was possible to extend it. But it never ended until shortly before the afternoon prayer which followed it. And so did Rabbi Zalman Zelig pray, morning, afternoon and evening prayers almost in a single breath.

After evening prayer they reminded themselves that they in effect were in a state of fasting for most of the day before even they tasted any food, except for a glass of whiskey that they would drink at the time of being called up to the Torah, or between lessons. But who is it that cannot feed his soul, if only slowly, with restraint, with forethought? Being hungry, craving for food, is not a characteristic for Hassidim. Then they would grab one more lesson, learning something. Only in the hours of the night would they go home, to their only real meal in the day, meager and limited though it was, just enough to revive the soul. By the time they finished their meal the hour was late. There were still a few small lessons waiting to be had, looking something up in a book.

And then it was necessary to rest a bit in order to have the strength to rise again to worship God.

As for support of the household, raising the children and caring for them was the responsibility of the loyal spouse. The expenses were not all that great, so they could be loaded upon the shoulders of the woman as well. And so long years of a life of Torah and good works passed. They rose further and further and reached extraordinary peaks of exceptional learning and devoted Hassidism. In the refinement of their personal characteristics and the purification of their deeds the worked hard and repeated and worked hard again until they became elevated people, men of exaltation.

The Gaon Rabbi Avraham Petziner

Thus did Rabbi Zalman Zelig conduct his life. But his son, Rabbi Menachem Mendel Petziner, differed. At an early age he married a woman from Sokolka in Lithuania, in the heart of Polish Lithuania. Nevertheless, even here there was a Hassidic house of Kotsk. They had been set up by some young lions of the Torah who lived there, whether it was by Rabbi Eliahu, who was considered to have the divine spirit, or Rabbi David, who fasted for decades as he lacked time to eat and for thirty years did not experience a bed. He slept on a bench in the house of the

Hassidim in order not to spoil his vulgar body, which was nothing but a bony skeleton, as pockmarked with wounds and pains as a the skin of a pomegranate.

But these giants passed on. They left behind them a great desire to transcend, a yearning and an oppressive empty space, and a treasure of stories and experiences. The next generation invested these experiences and desires, these yearnings and longings in Torah, in study and research. Rabbi Menachem Mendel Petziner was among this generation. Like his father-in-law, he was also a leather merchant. He devoted a number of hours each day to business. He conducted his business with energy and diligence, but was always in a hurry, trying to compress his entire business into a few hours, which he viewed as being superfluous, as too much. Rabbi Menachem Mendel did not believe in light learning, just grabbing a book in off-times during business hours, which has no real impact. If one is going to study it should be study worthy of its name, study with full use of knowledge and time. A person who is limited or preoccupied will never succeed in plumbing the depths of the Talmud.

Rabbi Menahem Mendel, the Hassid and scholar, the merchant and diligent person, did not abandon the traditions of his fathers of unlimited loyalty to Hassidism, of the Kotsk-Ger variety. From Sokolka in Lithuania he would often travel to Ger to the court of the *rebbe*. He trained his oldest son, Rabbi Avraham, in this tradition as well.

Rabbi Avraham was born in Sokolka in the year 5639 [1878-1879].[136] As with all the boys of the town, he learned in the *cheder*s [one-room elementary schools] of the local teachers. An outstanding boy, he was different from the other boys, more alert, sharper, standing out by virtue of his intelligence and his deeper understanding. He was a skinny, short boy. He advanced from *cheder* to *cheder*, and attached himself to older boys and soon outdistanced them. His teachers said that he was a genius.

From time to time he would travel with his father to Ger, to the court of the *rebbe*, author of the *S'fat Emet*, who captured his heart and soul. As a small boy he already became an enthusiastic Hassid. He would occasionally come to Ostroveh, to the house of his grandfather, Rabbi Zalman Zelig, the noted and devoted Hassid, who loved his gifted grandson and towards whom he exhibited deep feelings of affection. This influence of the elderly

---

[136] According to the Ostrow Mazowiecka records, Avraham Pecyner [Petziner] was born in Sokoly on December 24, 1887; his father, Mendel Pecyner, was born in Ostrow Mazowiecka in 1866; and his grandfather, Zelman Zelek Pecyner, was born in Ostrow Mazowiecka in January 1846.

grandfather on the boy was great. His image never left him until his last day.

But Rabbi Avraham was still too young to invest his time in Hassidism. Young in age but possessed of rare talents that few others have, he had first to learn a great deal. The teachers in Sokolka were still not of the caliber needed for his studies. He went to Sochachow, to the *yeshiva* of Rabbi Avraham, author of *Avnei Neizer* [*Jewels in the Crown*].[137] The genius of Sokolka became close to the *rebbe/gaon*, and became the star pupil of this elderly prince of the Torah. Rabbi Avraham admired his teacher, and the rabbi of Sochachow adored his young student who came from afar and praised him highly.

Even at the *yeshiva* of Sochachow, where the few students there were the best of the best, Rabbi Avraham Petziner stood out. Many were knocking at the door of this *yeshiva*, aspiring to a title that evoked honor, "student of the *gaon* of Sochachow." Many streamed to this *yeshiva*, but only a few were accepted. These few were only accepted after extensive selection and testing. The students had to pass many tests before they were accepted at the *yeshiva*. Only a small number of sharp young men, great in their knowledge of the Torah, true geniuses, sat and learned in the *yeshiva* of the author of *Avnei Neizer*.

The lectures of the *rebbe/gaon* excelled in their great acuity and in their amazing depth. Even the best students had to work very hard to keep up with their teacher and to absorb the knowledge of Torah of the *gaon* of Sochachow. Rabbi Avraham withstood this test and stood out among the others. He was already considered a genius in Sokolka when he was a boy. And he was also thought of as a genius in Sochachow as a young man. It was clear that he was destined for greatness. After his marriage he would likely obtain a position as a communal rabbi or as an instructor in a *yeshiva*, as a majority of the students of the great *yeshiva* of Sochachow became rabbis or instructors, if not decisors and leaders of the people, who filled official positions.

But Rabbi Avraham Petziner's path was different. He refused to enter the rabbinate or any other official position, however distinguished it might be. This sharp and mature young man, who knew the entire Talmud by heart, who was learned and expert in both the early and later commentators, refused to contemplate any offer that involved removing him from his simple way of life as a young man studying with other young men, a new Hassid among the throngs of Hassidim, who was living among the people as one of them.

---

[137] Rabbi Avraham Bornsztain [Borenstein] (1838-1910).

In Ostrow Mazowiecka, where his Hassidic grandfather lived, he established his place as well. The house of the Hassidim of Ger became his principal residence. There he sat and learned in every available moment. On holidays he would make his way to Ger, to his teacher and rabbi, the *rebbe*. For a number of years he lived at the home of his father-in-law. But he then left his board there and Rabbi Avraham turned to a business in hides.

He did not have much time to devote to his business, as he had a set learning schedule each day and would never deviate from it. Rabbi Avraham would never proceed to prayer before he had reviewed several pages of Gemara in depth, as he would suggest innovative interpretations of them. And in addition to lessons in Talmud and Halacha he did not neglect looking into books with a research orientation and those of a homiletic nature, as well as books on Hassidism and *kabbalah*. Studies require time, especially when they demand further depth and analysis of issues even after study.

In Ostroveh there was to be found Rabbi Ben-Zion, the greatest of Hassidim, and it was worthwhile to spend time--a lot of time--in his presence, to learn from him what exactly Hassidism was in effect. And who better than Rabbi Avraham to absorb the words and teachings of Rabbi Ben-Zion? Rabbi Avraham became the star pupil of Rabbi Ben-Zion, who brought him near and loved him and showered his affection upon him.

The young Hassid, Rabbi Avraham, while becoming even more fully developed, still rejected any official service. But he quickly rose in the levels of pure Hassidism. His great modesty dominated him and his inherent natural characteristics. He became one of exalted and extraordinary values. Even the most critical Hassidim, who negated just about everything, looked sympathetically and acceptingly upon Rabbi Avraham Petziner as the complete man.

Rabbi "Avramaleh," as he was widely called, was a smart man, a wise man who would always think and penetrate to the depths of matters. He knew how to distinguish between what was important and what was not, between the wheat and the chaff. He operated on the basis of what was essential in Hassidism, on the fundamentals of this approach, much as he worked hard on the bases of the Halacha and on the roots of each issue therein. They said that Rabbi Avraham was a scholar who understood the nature and meaning of study, a Hassid who knew the nature and essence of Hassidism, a man of great understanding in Hassidism.

He was full of profound and far reaching ideas in all aspects of the Torah, full of acuity and wisdom. Rabbi Avramaleh soon stood out among the masses of Hassidim all over Poland in general, and in the halls of Ostrow Mazowiecka in particular, as an exceptionally modest man who fled from honor and distinctions and who rejected titles and positions. He was unwillingly elevated into the front row of orthodox, Torah-oriented personalities in Poland.

The Hassid who worked hard at all his Hassidism, the scholar who never neglected his studies even for a day, the merchant who worked hard to earn a living, also found time for communal affairs, for efforts on behalf of others. This was true whether in was in the social welfare realm of providing aid and succor to a Jew who had lost his income, or to a suffering family, for a needy bride, or the redemption of captives, or whether it was on the municipal level, in the local context.

Rabbi Avraham joined the Agudat Yisrael movement from the day it was founded. With every fiber of his being he took upon himself the obligation and concern of building this Torah movement which, according to his best understanding, was potentially able to save an endangered people. Rabbi Avraham viewed the ideological conflict that was raging in the Jewish community as a matter of life and death for the nation, as one that cut the nation off from its true purpose, from the mother lode of its quarry, which would lead to the elimination of the nation, to its destruction. There is no survival for the Jewish people but for its Torah, or without its religious mission. Why would a non-religious Jew even identify with Judaism? Would he not convert, would he not assimilate into the other nations? Would he not cut all his ties to his past, to his national identity? And if not in the first generation, the second or third generation would abandon its eternal sources, resulting in the elimination of the nation. And to what end were these worthless prescriptions of socialism, of Zionism, which would only lead to the spiritual scaffold, to substantive suicide?

His great and stormy soul, which researched deeply and aspired to reach great heights, knew neither rest nor peace. Enemies arose that sought to undermine the house of Israel, to bring about its physical demise. Friends, brothers arose who shared our troubles and suffering, but who proposed false and harmful solutions that are dangerous and threatening and that instead of deliverance were likely to bring about destruction, God forbid. In the eyes of Rabbi Avraham the people of Israel were enmeshed in woes and captivity both from within and from without. He felt that he was drafted to seek to save them and to help them with devotion and sacrifice.

But Rabbi Avraham was drafted into this work as a simple soldier. He preferred to remain a plain soldier, just one of the gang who does the dirty and difficult work. But there really was no hard work on this front. Because work is measured according to the value and significance of its goal, not according to the labor invested in it. He became known as an orator and author. He did not sign his articles with his real name, not because he did not identify with what was said in them, but rather because of a sincere desire not to stand out.

Both his articles and his speeches were full of enthusiasm. He was a deep thinker in his conversations with individuals, and it was sometimes difficult to fully comprehend his thoughts. But in his public appearances, as he toured cities and towns on missions on behalf of his party, Agudat Yisrael, he appealed to the everyday person, to the masses. He delivered his message while quaking with emotion, expressing things that came straight from the heart and that penetrated the hearts of his listeners. With devotion and sacrifice he made his rounds, for he required nothing for himself, and everything was for others.

The party had been founded on behalf of the people, of the simple Jew. It had to get involved in all areas and spheres of life, economic, political, educational and spiritual. It was necessary to draw in the masses of members and adherents or potential adherents to explain things, to direct them. But it was from the activists of the movement, that thin layer of representatives of Agudat Yisrael, that one could demand exceptionalism, an exemplary life as a model for the masses, something greater than normal.

And Rabbi Avraham demanded this with his customary enthusiasm and feeling. After all, was not the final goal to achieve that high level, to lift oneself up from the raw earth somewhat, from the vulgar material world? The activist should always hold the goal up before his eyes, without any other, secondary factors, without any deviations whatsoever, without any personal ties that would directly or indirectly lead to imperfections in thought or deed.

Rabbi Leibel Petziner

Rabbi Avraham saw the period in which he was living and working as a period of crisis that necessitated total commitment, as a dangerous period that required every effort, as a period which forbade every son of Torah, even the greatest, to lock himself up in his home and to hide from the battle. He proposed establishing a *B'nei Torah* [Sons of Torah] organization. He worked to draft all such ennobled young men for the battle on behalf of the rule of Torah and the life of Torah amidst an endangered people, some of whom were converting, as other dangers also threatened its spiritual existence and its future.

His income continued to decline, and he knew much suffering, hardship and pain. But it was as if he drowned his sorrow in his studies and his holy work. His friends and admirers proposed a rabbinical position, as appropriate for a *gaon* like him. But Rabbi Avraham turned down every such offer, and absolutely refused to accept a rabbinical position. He managed to support his family with great difficulty. He preferred to invest his unusual talents on behalf of the community, for others, for the movement that had become an inseparable part of his being and which he served without blemish.

Despite the fact that he was a party man, despite his unending battles with other movements and his unconditional identification with Agudat Yisrael, Rabbi Avramaleh remained beloved by the masses, from near and far, from among those who were his supporters and those who were his opponents. For they knew the purity of his deeds and his character, his big, beautiful soul, pure and lacking any flaw. People knew that what he did he did in truth and sincerity, with full knowledge and without personal thoughts or private agendas.

When the Holocaust broke out, Rabbi Avraham and his family fled to Bialystok, and from there to Slonim, where he remained until he met his death, a sacrifice to the glory of God. They said that in the last days Rabbi Avraham became an extraordinary man, who rose to unanticipated heights. In the dark ghetto he took almost no food or drink, but was completely devoted to holy work. Pure and holy, he returned his sacred soul to its creator, as he fell at the hands of lowly murderers.

His son, Rabbi Leibel, an outstanding young man who in many ways resembled his father, who was a great Torah scholar and Hassid, and who for many years served as a leader of the Ger Hassidim in Ostrow Mazowiecka and as head of the Agudat Yisrael youth movement, died with his father in the destruction of the ghetto in Slonim.[138]

Rabbi Gershon and Rabbi Yisrael David Podgorowitz

Among the earliest Hassidim in Ostroveh and its pathfinders was the old Rabbi Gershon. In his youth he was among the sharpest and most devoted young men of the Hassidim of Kotsk. Thereafter he was one of the leaders of the Hassidim of Ger.

His profession was as a teacher of young children. The *rebbe* of Ger, author of the *S'fat Emet*, invited him to teach his oldest son, Rabbi Avraham Mordechai, who eventually succeeded him as the *rebbe* of Ger. For a number of years Rabbi Gershon lived in Ger, studying with the exceptional son of the *rebbe*, until he reached the age of thirteen.

Once the teacher and student were dealing with a particular question. After many years, after Rabbi Avraham Mordechai had ascended to the chair of his father, Rabbi Gershon came to visit him as one of his many Hassidim. The great *rebbe* kept him in his room for a moment and quickly took a book off the shelf and showed him a comment on that very question that the *rebbe* had once studied with him.

---

[138] According to the records of Ostrow Mazowiecka and the Yad Vashem Pages of Testimony, Rabbi Avraham's wife was Mariam, daughter of David Migdal of Zaremby Koscielne, who died in 1922. Their children who perished with their father in Slonim in 1942 were: Leyb (b. 1912) and his wife Hudes (b. 1915); Zalman Zelig (b. 1913); David (b. 1916); and Chana Malka (b. 1921). Other children who are not on the list of Slonim victims were Freyda Leya (b. 1911); and Basha.

Rabbi Gershon was an excellent and exceptional scholar. He was deeply invested in the study of Torah and Hassidism. He gave many daily lectures. He regularly held forth on Mondays and Thursdays of *Tat Shovavim*.[139] And after his fasting he would remain in the house of the Hassidim, finalizing his many lectures. Only after ten at night would he finish his daily routine of study and have his meager meal.

He was a poor man all his life, making due with very little, but he did not lack for anything that was within his grasp. His entire world was Torah and Hassidism. When he reached an advanced age he stopped teaching young children. He survived on a little bread and water. He was satisfied with his lot, studying Torah and Hassidism day and night, the content and essence of his life.

In the year 5672 [1911-1912] Rabbi Gershon died at the age of eighty.[140] His son, Rabbi Yisrael David Podgorowitz was, like his father, considered an outstanding scholar and a true Hassid. He would frequently visit the *rebbe*, author of the *S'fat Emet*, and his son, the *rebbe* Rabbi Avraham Mordechai of Ger.

For many years he lived in Tiktin [Tykocin], where he got married. He was immersed in Torah and good works. He was a diligent person, and worked hard at his studies. He had a very beautiful voice, and was an exceptional prayer leader, who charmed his listeners. People suggested that he give up living in poverty and become a cantor and thereby earn an ample and honorable living from leading prayers. But Rabbi Yisrael David refused, saying "I would rather lug my sack of flour around and earn my living from the sweat of my brow than make a living on the payroll of the community." He remained committed to this refusal until the outbreak of the Holocaust, in which he was killed in the destruction of Polish Jewry.

The Gaon Rabbi Chaim Yosef Ozarov[141]

Up until the outbreak of World War I, the Gaon Rabbi Chaim Yosef Ozarov, son of the Gaon Rabbi Yerucham, served an instructor at the *yeshiva* of Ger and as a *dayan* and *moreh tezedek*

---

[139] A special penitential period in the winter when each of the first eight chapters of the Book of Exodus is read weekly to avert illnesses.

[140] Rabbi Gershon's death is not recorded in the records of Ostrow Mazowiecka. The records indicate that he was born in Grajewo in 1828. His son, Srul Dawid Podgorowicz, is listed as having been born in Ostrow Mazowiecka in December 1885.

[141] According to the Ostrow Mazowiecka records, Rabbi Chaim Josek Ozarov was born in Pultusk in 1877, and was registered as having moved to Ostrow Mazowiecka in 1922.

in Rozan. He was a gifted and excellent teacher, as well as a very diligent person who studied day and night. His job as the *dayan* in a small town like Rozan did not impose upon him too much and did not impinge on his free time. He was free to devote most of his time to Torah to his heart's desire.

After the war Rabbi Chaim Yosef decided for some reason to leave the rabbinate. He moved to Ostrow Mazowiecka and began to engage in business for several hours a day. He removed his rabbinical garb, preferring the dress of the masses of Hassidim in Poland. It was not apparent that he had once served in the rabbinate.

As before, he dedicated most of his time to his studies. Every year he would complete the study of the Babylonian Talmud, over and above any other lectures and studies. He always viewed the few hours per day that he devoted to the business he ran as being excessive, a long break between his morning lesson and his afternoon one, but he soon finished up his secular work and returned to his studies.

And this was his daily routine: at three o'clock in the morning he would appear in the house of the Hassidim of Ger to pray and study. First he would regularly study the Bible, which he knew by heart, and from the Bible he would go to the Mishnah, and from the Mishnah to a close study of the Gemara. When Rabbi Chaim Yosef was engrossed in his studies, he forgot about everything else. Nothing in the world was of concern to him other than the Gemara and the topic that was there before his eyes.

In the house of the Hassidim he would give a regular daily lecture, and would study with tens of Hassidim the *daf yomi* [daily page].[142] He studied with awe and reverence, as he was a devoted and excellent Hassid, and few were like him. His prayers awed many people, as he stood in his corner and prayed at great length with fear and trembling, his body quaking. He would be very enthusiastic in his prayers and his other holy tasks.

Rabbi Chaim Yosef was an extremely devoted Hassid. He would frequently travel to the *rebbe* of Ger. And even among the masses of Hassidim in Ger he would be thought of as an exceptional scholar and an ardent Hassid, a true servant of God. Some years before the Holocaust, because of the lack of opportunities for

---

[142] A program of the simultaneous daily study of a particular page of the Talmud by orthodox Jews around the world, with the cycle being completed every seven and a half years. It was initiated by the Agudat Yisrael movement at its world convention in Vienna in 1923, under the aegis of Rabbi Meir Shapiro, who later became the dean of the *Yeshivat Chachmei Lublin* in Lublin. The program continues to this day. See also footnote 117 on p. 178 above.

earning a living in Ostroveh, he moved to Warsaw. He was imprisoned in the Warsaw ghetto along with hundreds of thousands of others of his brethren. When the ghetto was destroyed, he was transported to a death camp, where he died to the glory of God's name.

Rabbi Tuviah Eisenkramer

Among the first groups of Hassidim in Ostroveh was Rabbi Tuviah Eisenkramer (a merchant dealing in iron products). He was born in Bialystok. In his youth he studied in the *yeshivot* of Lithuania and settled in our city. At a young age he joined the Hassidim of Kotsk, and was thought of as one of the sharpest among them, respected by all, as a scholar and a wealthy man. He was both a Hassid and a man of compassion, a merchant who performed many good deeds and who helped others, but a merchant who devoted precious little of his time to business.

He was a scholar who studied in depth and with great effort. He approached his studies only after extensive preparation. Every lesson was carefully constructed and an entity unto itself. He did not leave the Gemara as long as he was innovating ideas, as long as he was uncovering new horizons and hidden pathways through the topic being studied. He was invested heart and soul in his studies. As he sat quietly, his pipe in his mouth, the entire world around him during these hours did not even exist. No shouts or yelling, no disturbances or controversies were able to prevent him from spinning the thread of his thoughts concerning the issue he was studying.

His style of prayer style matched his method of study. There were not many signs of passion, no outward movements. He approached worship in peace and quiet. Only his wandering big eyes indicated that Rabbi Tuviah was floating in higher realms, and that he was totally immersed in thought relating to his prayers.

He would regularly travel first to Kotsk and later to Ger, to the courts of the *rebbe*s whose authority he accepted. The style of his Hassidism resembled that of his studies, organized and well planned in advance, never deviating from the framework that the Hassid Rabbi Tuviah established. The first among those who traveled to Kotsk and then Ger was Rabbi Ben-Zion Rabinowitz. And when he traveled to Ger, or on other longer trips, frequently Rabbi Tuviah would take his place. And for holidays, all the Hassidim of Ger would come to his house and happily spend time in his company.

His wife and family actually ran his place of business. Rabbi Tuviah did not have sufficient time to dedicate to iron products, to conduct business with farmers and contractors. He really belonged to another world, a higher one. Was he born and created to supply chains and rakes, bars and hammers to non-Jews in the environs of Ostroveh? Whenever the volume in the store increased and the problems multiplied, it would vex Rabbi Tuviah, because all worldly things are, after all, nothing but annoyances that disturb and prevent one from fulfilling one's great goal in life.

Rabbi Tuviah merited living to a ripe old age, and never ceased his studies or his work until his final day, when he returned his soul to his creator in holiness and purity.

The Gaon Rabbi Avraham Mendel Galant

Rabbi Avraham Mendel Galant was a native of Goworowo. In his youth he excelled in his great diligence and in his fear of heaven and of sin. His father, Rabbi Yitzchak Yaakov, was a committed and devoted Hassid of Warka and a scholar who dedicated his soul to Torah and Hassidism.

Rabbi Avraham Mendel was diligent from a young age, and loved Torah and its study. They said that he studied Torah eighteen hours a day. He was among the first to arrive at the study hall and the last to leave his bench there. Whether in the summer or the winter, on weekdays or on the Sabbath or holidays, he was always to be found sitting and learning, completely immersed in his studies.

He was eighteen when he married the daughter of Rabbi Yeshayahu, a maker of *talitot* [prayer shawls] in Ostroveh, and thus settled in the town.[143] He came to Ostroveh as a young man knowledgeable in the Talmud and the decisors, and he continued his studies diligently, particularly in the old *beit midrash*, which was full of scholars in those days, and from which the sound of Torah study emanated day and night.

His father-in-law Rabbi Yeshayahu had provided a substantial dowry. He was a Jew who worked very hard for a living, but who saved enough from his earnings to provide such a dowry that would in turn merit a bridegroom who was well learned in the Torah. Rabbi Yeshayahu said that he would acquire a rabbinical position for his son-in-law that he would subsidize, but Rabbi Avraham Mendel refused. In the house of his devoted Hassidic father he had learned to dislike the rabbinate and such honors. He

---

[143] According to the Ostrow Mazowiecka records, Abram Mendel Galant married Slawa, daughter of Szaja Kaczor, in 1902.

refused to turn his learning into an instrument by which he would earn a living for his family.

So he invested the dowry in a business, and succeeded in earning a respectable living. For a few hours a day he freed himself up from the yoke of earning a living, from business affairs, in order to make time for Torah study. During World War I, Rabbi Avraham Mendel became impoverished and lost his means of making a living. Under pressure from the *rebbe* Rabbi Yaakov David of Otvotsk [Otwock], son of the *rebbe* Rabbi Simcha Bunim of Warka, he agreed, for lack of an alternative, to an offer of a rabbinical position. He was then chosen to be chief of the rabbinical court of Zaremba [Zaremby Koscielne], that small city near Ostrow Mazowiecka. He served in the rabbinate from that time until the outbreak of the Holocaust.

With the outbreak of the Holocaust he was forced to escape to the Russian zone of occupation, from which he was exiled to Siberia. For many years he suffered hunger and want, and was very hard on himself. He was lenient in his rulings concerning others, because of the circumstances and the danger of plague and illness, but was strict with himself. Even in the difficult and bitter conditions of a labor camp he somehow managed to find a *shofar* [ram's horn] to blow on Rosh Hashanah as the law required, despite the danger inherent in doing so. On the holiday of Sukkot he built a *sukkah* [booth] despite the peril. And for Passover he faithfully baked *matzot* [unleavened bread].

After the war he was able to immigrate to Israel and died in Jerusalem on the twenty-fifth day of Tevet 5715 [January18-19, 1955], when he had just reached the age of eighty.

Rabbi Akiva Stavisker

Rabbi Akiva was a native of Stavisk [Staviski] when he arrived in Ostroveh in the twenties of the seventh century of the present millennium [equivalent to the 1860's on the general calendar]. He quickly joined the Hassidim of Ger locally, and was considered a devotee of the first *rebbe* of Ger, author of *Chidushei Harim*. He frequently traveled to that *rebbe*, but upon his death he would often visit his successor, the *rebbe* Chanoch Henich Hacohen of Alexander, and the *rebbe* of Ger who was the author of the *S'fat Emet*.

It was said of him that he was a great scholar, one who easily sailed through the Talmud, the early commentators as well as the later ones, and that he knew entire issues by heart. But he never showed off his prominence in Torah study, determinedly concealing his deep and broad knowledge. In general he did not enter into disputes and extended discussions among the many learners, who were very numerous in the house of the Hassidim of Ger in Ostroveh. He stuck to his own studies and pretended as if he did not understand the conversation among the exceptional students who loudly debated their views and enthusiastically defended their particular approach and understanding of their studies. He only rarely got involved in these debates.

He was a true Hassid, extremely sharp, who dedicated all his days and years, all his strength and ability to pure Hassidism. He worked on his Hassidism day and night. He merited living to a very old age. And until his very last year he worked like a soldier on guard duty to defend Hassidism. He overcame all the obstacles in his way. Even as a very elderly Hassid it appeared as if there were combined within him two or three young, enthusiastic men, as he was always happy, merry and gay. He sometimes lacked for bread, sometimes suffered tribulations and pain, but they did not affect Rabbi Akiva, were never reflected on his shining face, never impinged upon his happiness, which infected everyone who came into contact with him.

Already in the wee hours of the night he appeared in the house of the Hassidim, as he rose early. And immediately upon his appearance, the house of the Hassidim was full of joy and gladness. This is how it was when he was young and continued to be in his very old age. He did not shrink from a funny joke, a dance, even a mildly sharp remark in order to bring happiness into the hearts of others as well as his own. He disliked sourpusses, those who assumed angry poses, or those who were pedantic. He could never reconcile himself to them. He pursued those with negative attitudes aggressively and stubbornly, and thus joy prevailed in the house of the Hassidim.

Rabbi Akiva died at an advanced age. They said that with his death, joy departed from within the walls of the house of Hassidim of Ger in Ostroveh. Bit by bit gloomy clouds covered the skies of Polish Jewry. Years of suffering and hardship came and caused the old days, the golden days of the merrymakers, to be forgotten.

Rabbi Nisan Romm[144]

Rabbi Nisan the Lithuanian was a regular instructor in the second grade of the local Talmud Torah and in the town's *yeshiva*. He was an exceptional scholar who excelled in his personal characteristics and behavior. He was a skinny man, a bag of bones. As a product of the Lithuanian *yeshivot*, he was an opponent of Hassidism who strictly followed the approach of the

---

[144] The name Romm is actually an acronym for ***rosh metivta***, or senior lecturer in a *yeshiva*, an especially common appellation among Jews in Lithuania, the epicenter of *yeshivot*. There was also a famous family of printers/publishers of religious books by that name in Vilna.

GRA[145] of Vilna. He was meticulous in his observance of the commandments and particular in all matters, an opponent of easy ways out and of permissive approaches.

He slept very little and was one of the early risers in Ostroveh. His asceticism and lack of sleep left their mark on the man, who walked around like a skeleton and persisted in his difficult way of life. Every night he would hold a midnight study session, and during the day he would walk about wrapped in his phylacteries and prayer shawl. The fear of heaven always engulfed him. He was fearful of God, and spoke very little lest he fall into some forbidden act. Thus, he sought out new stringencies in the law to pile onto his already stooped back and his difficult way of life.

Much as he was strict in observing the word of heaven, in his dealing with people he was blatantly lenient. He taught his students to be endlessly forgiving. He explained to the children who studied with him that, "Every day is in effect Yom Kippur. A person must seek forgiveness daily for his sins, and should apologize to his compatriots, for the sins between man and man are not forgiven by repentance [to God], but rather only by reconciliation with his fellow man." In order to avoid this difficult task, Rabbi Nisan was careful not to harm anyone. He eschewed any conflict or dispute; he refused to reprove others; and he scrupulously avoided any interpersonal sins.

His entire life he got by on the bare minimum, in the manner of learned scholars in those days, who used to immerse themselves in the Torah. His income was very limited, as his salary as a teacher was very low. But Rabbi Nisan did not even require that much money. His needs were infinitesimal, and even they appeared excessive to him. He ate meager and shriveled meals, just enough to keep himself alive. His clothing was wretched and his home was very modest and austere. His iron bed served him his entire life.

Yet despite his adherence to the commandments and his caution about violating any of them, he wholeheartedly joined the Zionist movement. He acquired the annual *shekel* that was distributed among members of the Zionist movement. In doing so he was almost the exception among the teachers of the *Talmud Torah* or the old *beit midrash*. But Rabbi Nisan was not intimidated by anyone. Many insulted him, reproved him, and even persecuted him for having joined the Zionists, but as usual

---

[145] Acronym for *Gaon Rabbi Eliyahu*, Rabbi Eliyahu ben Shlomo Zalman (1720-1797), a/k/a the Vilna Gaon, a leading rabbinical figure and scholar of the period and vigorous opponent of Hassidism, hence the spiritual founding father of the Mitnagdim [opponents], the prevailing stream of orthodox Judaism in Lithuania.

Rabbi Nisan did not reply, did not respond to anyone. He preferred to be among those who are insulted, rather than among those who insult, and acted as if he did not even understand those who demeaned him. And he continued on this path until his last day, when he returned his soul to his creator.

The Rebbe Rabbi Naftali Tzvi Shpiegel

After World War I the *rebbe* Rabbi Naftali Tzvi Shpiegel arrived in Ostroveh at the request and as a result of the efforts of his Hassidim, headed by Rabbi Chaim Berel, a simple Jew full of happiness and energy, who was dubbed "the shoemaker from Kosovo" in Ostroveh.

Meir Yechiel from Ostroveh had settled in Kaluszyn, where his father-in-law, Rabbi Yaakov**Error! Bookmark not defined.** Yitzchak, served as *rebbe*. For eighteen years he lived with his father-in-law and studied Torah and Hassidism. For some years he served as chief of the rabbinical court of Czekhin [possibly Cycow], which is near Lublin, and afterwards as chief of the rabbinical court of Monkavid [Mokodoby], which is near Siedlce. After the death of his father-in-law he acceded to the wishes of his Hassidim to lead the community, and then came to Ostrow Mazowiecka and settled there.

He opened his house of study in the city, and many of its residents and others from the surrounding area streamed to him, were attracted by his light, and studied Torah with him. The rabbi from Kaluszyn succeeded in attracting simple people to Torah and Hassidism, who in turn were devoted to him and admired him greatly.

He suffered greatly during World War I. So when he was asked by his Hassidim who had immigrated to the United States to come there, he acceded to their wishes.

The *rebbe* Rabbi Naftali Tzvi was born in Lublin in the year 5629 [1869] to his father, the *rebbe* Rabbi Moshe (son of the *gaon* who was chief of the rabbinical court in Ludomir), who was the son of the Gaon Rabbi Moshe Rokeach, chief of the rabbinical court of Skolye [Skole], a kinsman of the *rebbe* Rabbi Shalom of Belz.

He was ordained at a young age by the *rebbe*. In the year 5686 [1925-1926] he left Ostroveh and settled in New York, where he opened a *beit midrash*, to which many people were attracted and where they received advice and assistance.

His contacts with people in America were always gentle and refined, as it had been in Poland. His unusual and superior traits, which he had inherited from many generations of his ancestors, great scholars and *rebbes*, were evident. His Hassidim and admirers and all those who came into contact with him liked him very much, and news of him spread far and wide. In New York he became known as the rabbi from Ostroveh, because it was from this city that he came to the United States.

For twenty-three years the *rebbe* Rabbi Naftali Aryeh[146] ran his house of study in New York. On the twentieth day of Tishrei 5709 [October 23, 1948], he died in his eightieth year. His sons, Rabbi Elchanan Yochanan Shpiegel, Rabbi Moshe Menachem Shpiegel and Rabbi Pinchas Eliyahu Shpiegel, continued in his footsteps, serving as rabbis in New York.

Rabbi Yosef Wolf Rekant[147]

One of the leaders of Ostroveh was Rabbi Yosef**Error! Bookmark not defined.** Wolf Rekant, a Hassid and communal leader, one who observed the commandments and performed them. He was full of love for the people of Israel, and his heart was full of compassion for every person created in the image of God. He was a Jewish *shtadlan* [intercessor] in the best of that old tradition. He was imbued with a sense of bringing people close and with a devotion to others.

Rabbi Yosef was among the Hassidim of Ger. An observant Jew who was careful to fulfill the most minor as well as the major commandments, he was opposed to every deviation from the holy way of life that was sanctified over the generations. He willingly accepted various responsibilities. In the house of the Hassidim he insisted on the sanctity of the place, making sure that no one spoke during prayers, even at those points where it was permissible. He stood by this rule for decades.

He had no children, but was successful in his business, a flour mill, which brought in significant income, but which did not overly

---

[146] While generally referred to in this volume as Rabbi Naftali Tzvi, his gravestone in Beth Israel Cemetery in Woodbridge, New Jersey, gives his name as Rebbe Rabbi Naftali Aryeh son of Moshe Shpiegel, the Ostrower and Kalushiner rabbi. The Ostrow Mazowiecka records give his name as Naftula-Lejb Szpigel son of Moszek, a rabbi, born in Wengrow in 1869; his U.S. naturalization papers give his name as Naftal Leib Spigel and his birthplace as Wienawa, presumably Wieniawa, near Lublin. They list his wife as Sura, daughter of Jacob Lejb Unger, born in Lublin in 1872. He and his wife are recorded as having arrived in the United States through Buffalo on July 22, 1926 under the names Naftal and Sura Spigel, traveling to the Ershte Wengrower Congregation in New York City.

[147] According to the Ostrow Mazowiecka records, Juszek Wolf Rekant was born in Zambrow in 1868; his death is not recorded. Rywka was his second wife; their marriage was recorded in 1908.

impinge upon him. He spent most of his time helping others. He was the Jewish *shtadlan* to whom the Russian authorities and police would turn. He was receptive to all requests to help Jews, and to arrange things with the authorities. He was always prepared to undertake such holy work, day and night, in the heat of summer or the storms of winter. He intervened in serious as well as minor matters. He was always ready to undertake a mission on behalf of a Jew with devotion and an open heart, and with dedication to his goal.

If a Jew were arrested, Rabbi Yosef would immediately go to the police station in an effort to have him released and to provide bail for him. In every instance of trouble or distress he was called in, and he came, ready to do whatever was necessary, even in the most difficult situation. He was an orphan who was left without parents, so in the case of a foundling, Rabbi Yosef would immediately deal with the matter, working hard and energetically and not resting until everything was arranged.

His wife, the righteous Rivka, always stood by his side in these matters of charity and mercy. For every Sabbath and holiday she would prepare a bounty of food. Rabbi Yosef Wolf**Error! Bookmark not defined.** and his wife would not sit down to their meal unless there were at least ten guests at their table. The couple worked hard to satisfy their hungry guests with smiles, to the point where it appeared that the guests were actually the ones providing generosity to Rabbi Yosef Wolf and his wife.

For many years Rabbi Yosef Wolf served as *parnas* [trustee] of the community. From World War I until the year 5684 [1923-1924] he served as one of the four officers of the community. In that year general elections were held for the communal institutions. Once again Rabbi Yosef Wolf was elected to the community council on the Agudat Yisrael ticket. On the council he was, as usual, interested in matters of providing assistance and succor to the poor and the ill. Until his final day he did not cease to work on behalf of others. When he died, the community of Ostroveh accompanied the coffin of this man of righteousness and mercy with pain and sorrow.

His widow, Rivka, remained in Ostroveh alone and solitary, as the couple had never had any children. She continued with all her strength to perform the acts of charity and compassion of her husband. She, too, like Rabbi Yosef Wolf, was always ready to help others, to do everything for the needy, the suffering, the ill and the depressed.

With the outbreak of the horrific Holocaust, when independent Poland was conquered by the Nazi hordes and parts of Poland were temporarily divided between Germany and Soviet Russia,

Ostroveh, which was half destroyed and flowing with blood, became the closest point to the Soviet border. Jews from all the surrounding cities streamed into Ostroveh, hid there for a while until they could cross the nearby border to the Soviet zone of occupation.

Her relatives and family members begged her to cross over into the Soviet zone of occupation as well and thereby save her life. But she refused. She opened her residence to the many refugees who were passing through Ostroveh. With great devotion she fed these poor people who were fleeing the murderers, who were tired and without means. On the twenty-fifth [*sic* twenty-ninth] day of Cheshvan, 5700 [November 11, 1939], the murderers assembled the remaining Jews in Ostroveh, the righteous widow among them, and took them out to be killed.[148]

Rabbi Meir Milner[149]

One of the first of the Warka Hassidim in Ostroveh, and one of the pioneers of Hassidism in the city and its environs, was Rabbi Meir Milner, a well known Hassid in town and its surrounding areas. He was one of the important Hassidim of the *rebbe* Rabbi Yitzchak of Warka and his son, the *rebbe* Rabbi Menachem Mendel of Warka, and his grandson, the *rebbe* Rabbi Simcha Bunim of Otvotsk. He was considered important, both welcome in the houses of the *rebbe*s and beloved among the masses of Hassidim, a man of charity and righteousness, and a servant of God.

Rabbi Meir had a flour mill near Ostroveh, from which he derived a munificent income to the point of attaining real wealth. He did not keep his money just for himself and his family, but made much available to his fellow Hassidim and to the courts of the *rebbe*s with great generosity. Rabbi Meir visited his mill just for a short time each day. Most of his time was spent in the house

---

[148] On November 11, 1939, some five hundred (some sources indicate five hundred sixty) remaining Jews in Ostrow Mazowiecka--those who were not among the approximately 7,000 who had previously crossed the footbridge over the main railroad line between Warsaw and Bialystok to the Soviet zone of occupation at the instigation of the Nazis, who relieved them of all their valuables, or who had otherwise escaped--were marched out of the town to a small forest, where they were made to dig large pits and were then shot. Among them were some relatives of the editor. A series of photographs, taken by a German military photographer of the event, which are on file at the United States Holocaust Memorial Museum in Washington, appear in the Addendum to this translation. A monument in Hebrew and Polish now stands at that spot, a photograph of which also appears in the Addendum.

[149] The family is recorded in the Ostrow Mazowiecka records as Milert, Milner or possibly Mlynarzewicz. Majer Milert's death is recorded in 1884. There is a Mordko-Lejb Goldwasser in the records who was born in Lomza in 1851 and died in Ostrow Mazowiecka in 1924, who was Rabbi Meir Milner's son-in-law.

of the Warka Hassidim in town, among whose founders he was. As one of the original Hassidim, Hassidism was for him primary, and his other affairs secondary. He would frequently travel to the court of the *rebbe*s in Warka. He would remain there for several weeks, and would return full of enthusiasm about continuing on his path in Hassidism.

Rabbi Meir was replete with exceptionally fine personal traits. He was a true Hassid who never thought or worried about himself. He negated himself on behalf of Hassidim, and did everything with sacred enthusiasm. He was always prepared to do anything that would sanctify the name of God. Many of those who attended the house of Hassidim benefited from his largesse. But a stranger would never have known who was the donor and who the recipient. Rabbi Meir was sharp, full of sacred energy, but also modesty and simplicity, like one of the first Hassidim who had enlightened Poland in past generations.

The son-in-law of Rabbi Meir was Rabbi Mordechai Leib Goldwasser, a native of Lomza, son of Rabbi Hersh, a Hassid who settled in Ostroveh. Like his father-in-law, Rabbi Mordechai Leib was also a scholar and a Hassid. He inherited the flour business from Rabbi Meir, and made a living from it all of his life. Rabbi Mordechai possessed great talents. His brother, the Gaon Rabbi

Yehoshua Mendel, served as one of the rabbis of Tiktin, and was well known as a great scholar. Like him, Rabbi Mordechai Leib was considered a wonderful man.

Like his father-in-law and his father, Rabbi Mordechai Leib devoted only part of his time to his business. The majority of his time he dedicated to Torah, to good works and to caring for the sick. He considered himself a real physician, after he learned the basics of medicine on his own, from various books, and from his involvement with various doctors in the city. He learned Latin and knew how to read about and to prescribe various medicines. The owners of the pharmacies in Ostrow Mazowiecka recognized Rabbi Mordechai Leib [as a doctor] and dispensed medicines on the basis of his prescriptions, even if legally he was, understandably, not entitled to prescribe medicine to the sick or to care for them at all.

Eventually Rabbi Mordechai Leib became proficient in medical matters. He studied some with Dr. Landinsky of Lomza, the most famous doctor in the entire region. After that the physicians in Ostroveh also took account of him. Dr. Klietschka [possibly Dr. Reuven Klaczko], the leading Jewish doctor in town, consulted with Rabbi Mordechai Leib more than once when treating a seriously ill patient and finding him in the sick person's home.

Rabbi Yitzchak Pragier

Rabbi Yitzchak Pragier was a man of especially distinguished appearance, whose large, gleaming eyes evoked the attention of all who met him. He was born in Yadov [Jadow],[150] and settled in Ostrow Mazowiecka. In his younger days Rabbi Yitzchak served as both a *shochet* [ritual slaughterer] and a *mohel* [ritual circumciser]. As he grew older he retired from slaughtering, but continued to serve as an expert *mohel* gratis. He was still eager to perform commandments, and as such viewed his work as a *mohel* as a religious calling that one should not ever relinquish one's entire life.

Rabbi Yitzchak was also an outstanding prayer leader, with an extremely pleasant and strong voice. He was one of the Hassidim of the *rebbe* Rabbi Tzvi of Lomaz [Lomazy].[151] Every year he would travel there to be in the court of his teacher the *rebbe*, where he also served as prayer leader. After the death of the *rebbe* of Lomaz, Rabbi Yitzchak joined the community of the Hassidim of the *rebbe*

---

[150] According to the Ostrow Mazowiecka records, Icek Mejer Pragier was born in January 1872.

[151] Rebbe Tzvi Hersh Morgenstern of Lomazy (1852-1926), brother-in-law of Rabbi Aharon Menachem Mendel Gutterman of Radzymin (see next footnote).

Rabbi Aharon Mendel of Radzymin,[152] where he also served as prayer leader on the High Holy Days from the time he arrived there. In the last years before the Holocaust, after the death of the *rebbe* of Radzymin, Rabbi Yitzchak affiliated with the community of Hassidim of the *rebbe* of Wyszkow.[153]

His children had immigrated to the United States, from where they sent him sufficient money for his needs, so that he could devote himself entirely to charitable work, to study and to prayer. He was involved in Hassidism for hours every day. The other hours were earmarked for acts of charity and compassion. There was not anything connected to the commandments or to charity in which Rabbi Yitzchak did not play an active role. He would not volunteer without being truly active.

He was a lover of Torah and a seeker of the study of Torah. As an avid Hassid, Rabbi Yitzchak prayed among the Hassidim of Ger. But he joined the Talmud study group at the new *beit midrash* in town, the stronghold of the Mitnagdim who prayed in the Ashkenazi manner.[154] For a few years he served as the officer [*gabbai*] of the Talmud study group, working hard for it, seeking to expand the number of regular participants in its classes and securing lecturers for its sessions. As a result, the group had as many as one hundred fifty regular members who took part in its classes.

Everything that involved strengthening the life of Torah in Ostrow Mazowiecka was of interest to Rabbi Yitzchak Pragier. He always was working to raise money for the general *Talmud Torah* in town, and never tired of performing this core task. There had been established in Ostroveh a branch of the *Yeshivat Beit Yosef* [House of Joseph] of Novhardok.[155] Rabbi Yitzchak was appointed as one of its overseers, working diligently to raise money for it and to strengthen it. This was so even though he was far removed from

---

[152] Rabbi Aharon Menachem Mendel Gutterman of Radzymin (d. 1934).

[153] Possibly Rabbi David Shlomo Morgenshtern of Wyszkow, or Rabbi David Shlomo's father, Rabbi Yaakov Aryeh Morgenstern, who moved to Radzymin in 1934 to take the place of his uncle, Rabbi Aharon Menachem Mendel Gutterman.

[154] One of the religious changes brought about by Hassidism was a reversion to the Sephardic form of liturgy (though not its pronunciation or music), considered by them to be more authentic, whereas Mitnagdim retained the Ashkenazi format brought earlier from Germany.

[155] Established in 1922, this was a branch of a network of *yeshivot* that originated in Novhardok [Navahurdak, now in Belarus], which had been shut done by the new communist government. See Gary S. Schiff, *In Search of Polin: Chasing Jewish Ghosts in Today's Poland,* p. 97. See also Chapter 11 below.

its essence or program as a Lithuanian-style *yeshiva* whose style was incompatible with pure Hassidism, the Hassidism of Kotsk and the movement which grew out of it, like that of Lomza or Wyszkow and so forth, to which Rabbi Yitzchak had adhered since the days of his youth.

Rabbi Yitzchak was aware of every charitable need, whether communal or individual. He frequently visited the sick, especially those who were poor. He sometimes even gave them medicine, convinced as he was that he knew all about medicine. He took an interest in every woe that befell one of the residents of the city. If an abandoned child would appear in Ostroveh, Rabbi Yitzchak would first take him to his own home and make all the necessary arrangements.

With the outbreak of the Holocaust, Rabbi Yitzchak, along with the majority of the town's [Jewish] residents, fled to the Russian zone of occupation. He settled with some other refugees in Stolin. When its Jews were liquidated, Rabbi Yitzchak (may God avenge his blood) was also killed by the Nazi murderers.

Rabbi Yosef Bendit Kelewitz

Before World War I, Rabbi Yosef Bendit Kelewitz [Kelewicz or Kielewicz] was among the wealthy residents of Ostroveh, one of the most successful merchants in town. He was an enthusiastic Hassid of Ger, a philanthropist whose hand was always open. He was involved in the public affairs of the town and in its life and activities. During World War I he was expelled from Ostrow Mazowiecka. After the war he never succeeded in reestablishing himself economically. His business affairs were no longer successful. He was viewed by many as one whose economic status had declined as compared to his secure situation in days gone by.

But the changes that befell him business-wise over the course of time did not affect his public service or his initiatives to strengthen Judaism in Ostroveh. He particularly stood out in terms of his work in rescuing the next generation for pure Judaism. He gathered up children, and if necessary removed them from their environment that was full of depression and suffering. At his own expense he built an organization of young activists and established a special prayer group for them. And from his own funds, he hired a lecturer who would study with these young people every Sabbath. Remarking on this project, the *rebbe* Rabbi Avraham Mordechai of Ger observed that he was able to extract the wheat from the chaff.

He was an avid Hassid who suffered much in his life, who knew pain, but he accepted it all with love. He was reconciled to his pain and suffering, and found encouragement and inspiration in the pure Hassidism of the house of Ger, to which he was connected heart and soul. People from near and far related to him with affection and respect, as people in town knew of his former standing and about his honest work on behalf of others. The people of Ostroveh remembered him for his generosity of heart from the days when he was one of the wealthiest merchants in town, and for his public service.

Once, when he was walking in the street in the city of Warsaw, he found a large, heavy leather briefcase. Rabbi Yosef Bendit took it into a courtyard and examined the briefcase. In it he found a fortune, a large amount of money, and various documents which indicated that the briefcase belonged to Professor Koscialkowski,[156] then a member of the Polish parliament as a member of the ruling party, who later served as Finance Minister and Prime Minister. Rabbi Yosef Bendit went to Ger with the briefcase to ask the advice of the *rebbe* Rabbi Avraham Mordechai as to what to do with it and the large amount of money found therein.

The *rebbe* advised him to return the briefcase to its owner. Rabbi Yosef Bendit returned to Warsaw, went to Professor Koscialkowski, and returned the briefcase with all its contents to him. Professor Koscialkowski was amazed to see an orthodox Jew who was returning a great sum of money, serving as a paragon of honesty. The incident became the subject of great discussion among the ruling circles of Poland at the time, and served to elevate the view of the Jews among many. "Whatever you want, you just have to just ask," Professor Koscialkowski said to Rabbi Yosef Bendit, who did not ask for or demand anything.

Rabbi Yosef Bendit's son, Rabbi Levi Kelewitz, was also an avid Hassid of Ger. He lived in Zaremba, which is near Ostroveh. He was a successful businessman and was both generous and communally involved. He established and supported a *Beit Yaakov* [House of Jacob] school[157] there, and was considered one of that town's outstanding residents. During the great Holocaust, the Nazi murderers liquidated all the members of this family.

---

[156] Maryan-Zyndram Koscialkowski (1892-1946), who also served in the Polish government as Interior Minister (1934-1935) and as Prime Minister (1935-1936). He served in the Sejm (Polish parliament) from 1922-1939.

[157] A network of orthodox Jewish day schools, the first for girls, the first of which was established by Sarah Schenirer in Cracow in 1917, and later taken over and expanded worldwide by the Agudat Yisrael movement.

Rabbi Yaakov Schwartz

Rabbi Yaakov Schwartz exhibited wonderful personal traits and deeds, and was a man of truth. He was one of the great Hassidim of Ger in Ostroveh. He was punctilious as to the commandments, and observed them with devotion and great sacrifice. He was a successful merchant as well as a very honest man like few others. It was said that Rabbi Yaakov never uttered a falsehood in his entire life. His heart and his mouth were always in harmony. He never tricked anyone nor put on any false pretenses. Nevertheless, he ran his business successfully and experienced good fortune.

Once after a day of clearing out the inventory in his store, when he had a great deal of money in hand, he went out to perform acts of kindness to people who had appealed to him for help. He looked for other merchants who were in great trouble in order to lend them a hand. Sometimes he approached others. He would go great distances to provide funds for a person who was in need of them.

And all this he did with simplicity, without asking for anything in return. He saw himself as just a simple Jew without any worthy characteristics or deeds. He traveled frequently to Ger, to the *rebbe*s, both the author of the *S'fat Emet* and Rabbi Avraham Mordechai, of blessed memories.

At the outbreak of World War I, Rabbi Yaakov was thought of as one of the great merchants of the city. The Russian authorities viewed him as one of the wealthiest people of the place, and therefore decided to appoint him to the list of prominent Jews who were "trustees" over the Jews of Ostroveh to see that the Jews of the city would not deviate from the orders of the authorities and would fulfill all of the demands of the harsh Russian rulers.

The governor of the district, Pentilov, a well known anti-Semite, decided to exile Rabbi Yaakov Schwartz, along with Dr. Klietschka, a highly regarded Jewish doctor, to Russia, in order to hold them as hostages until the end of the war. All efforts and interventions were of no avail. Rabbi Yaakov and Dr. Klietschka were transported via Bialystok to Russia under very difficult circumstances. Pain and great suffering were thenceforth the lot of Rabbi Yaakov. He was kept under very difficult and tortuous conditions for an extended period in Russia.

When he returned to Ostroveh after World War I he was a broken man and never managed to reestablish himself. His income kept shrinking and he was no longer considered to be among the wealthy people of the city. Nevertheless, this did not prevent him from doing acts of charity if he were in a position to do so. Jewish Ostroveh remembered his illustrious past and his good deeds in his days of prosperity, when he continued the tradition of his great father, the wealthy Rabbi Yosef Hersh Schwartz, who had funded the building of the house of the Hassidim of Ger.

Rabbi Yaakov was elected to the council of the Jewish community on the Agudat Yisrael ticket, and for many years served as an officer of the community. It is told that once, during a debate, he heard one of the disputants stating something that did not comport with the facts. He sprang to his feet, shouting, "How can a person utter something that is not true?"

At the outbreak of the Holocaust, Rabbi Yaakov fled the city. On the road, in Zaremba, he collapsed when his strength gave out and died there, returning his pure soul to its creator.

Rabbi Gedaliah David Morgenstern

One of the most respected men, and leader of the Mitnagdic camp in Ostroveh, was Rabbi Gedaliah David Morgenstern. He was respected and valued by all, a scholar, an activist and a meticulous observer of the commandments. Perfect in terms of his characteristics and deeds, he was one of the heads and leaders of those who prayed in the new *beit midrash* in Ostroveh.

Born in the city of Nowogrod near Lomza, Rabbi Gedaliah David arrived in Ostroveh at a young age, when he married the daughter of Rabbi Levi Kelewitz,[158] one of the important people in town. From then on he was considered one of its respected residents, who excelled in many areas.

He had studied in various *yeshivot* in Lithuania, and as a youth completed his training in Torah and teaching. In addition to this he found the time to learn Hebrew perfectly, excelling in his profound knowledge of Hebrew grammar. He also learned and mastered German, Russian and Polish. Everything that he studied he knew down to its basic core. He was diligent and did not like partial or superficial learning. Everything that he undertook he saw through to completion, never stinting on hard work.

From the time he settled in Ostrow Mazowiecka he diligently pursued his studies. He sat and studied Torah for days at a time, and until his last day he never let a single day pass without studying Torah. He made sure to attend all of his regular classes. He was so meticulous in his observance of the commandments that people who were close to him considered him a living *Shulchan Aruch* [*Set Table*, the most widely accepted digest of Jewish law]. He constantly evaluated and checked whether his

---

[158] This made Rabbi Morgenstern a brother-in-law to Rabbi Yosef Bendit Kelewitz. According to the Ostrow Mazowiecka records, Rabbi Morgenstern's wife Kejla, born in 1852, was the daughter of Lewin and Ruchla Kelewicz [Kelewitz].

deeds and actions were in conformity with the Halacha, with the explicit law, according to his understanding and outlook.

He was a sworn opponent of Hassidim and Hassidism. His place at the new *beit midrash* in the city, the citadel of the Mitnagdim, was along its eastern wall [the place of honor]. He was exacting in his deeds and actions. He was thought of in town as a man of truth. He refused to sign letters to people whom he did not know. He refused to attribute titles to people to whom he wrote unless he was convinced that they actually merited those titles. He viewed it as dishonest to attribute honorific titles to people just for the sake of it, for their pleasure, or because they had gotten used to it.

Rabbi Gedaliah David Morgenstern was thought of as a man of erudition, and the scope of his knowledge was great. He knew the entire Bible by heart, and loathed those who, because of their lack of precise knowledge, mangled passages from the Bible.

The handwriting of Rabbi Gedaliah David was astonishingly beautiful. Therefore he wrote requests on behalf of Jews to the courts and to the authorities. His writing in various languages was well laid out and elegant, and his style was polished. From very founding of the Zionist movement Rabbi Gedaliah David was a member. He was among the first and among the leaders of the Zionists in the city, and was elected as a representative of Ostroveh to the Zionist Congress. He died in the year 5682 [1922] at the age of seventy.

Rabbi Mordechai Mendel Markusfeld

Rabbi Mordechai Mendel Markusfeld was not among the sharpest scholars in Ostroveh and did not hold an important position in the Jewish community. He was a humble man, a simple man, modest by nature and in his very being. He loved Torah and pursued *mitzvot* [commandments]. He was one of the central pillars of the congregants of the old *beit midrash*. He did not stand out in particular and did not join any of the modern movements. A gentle spirit and a gentle soul, he was a noble and rare personage in Poland even during its glory days.

He was a *shochet* [ritual slaughterer] and a *bodek* [ritual examiner of slaughtered animals], an artisan in his profession, an expert in the laws of slaughtering and examining slaughtered animals. His work only occupied him for several hours a day. The rest of the hours he dedicated to the performance of the commandments and good deeds. His righteous wife, Mrs. Bracha, who excelled in her own good works and in her efforts on behalf of every charitable cause, was his helpmate. Both of them worked among the simple people, *amcha*, the masses. They loved the simple Jew and the simple Jew in Ostroveh reciprocated with love, affection and admiration.

Rabbi Mordechai Mendel would give a daily class in either *Ein Yaakov*[159] [*The Well of Jacob*] or in Halacha to a fairly large group of working men. They viewed themselves as students of Rabbi Mordechai Mendel, and he viewed himself as their elderly friend and guide. He was not only concerned with their studies, but also took interest in every issue that weighed upon these working men. Over time Rabbi Mordecai Mendel became the uncrowned teacher and rabbi of the working men, most of whom worshipped in the old *beit midrash*.

---

[159] A popular compilation of all the Aggadic (i.e., non-legal, but rather ethical and homiletical) material in the Babylonian Talmud by Rabbi Yaakov ben Shlomo ibn Habib (c. 1420-1516). He was born in Zamora, Spain, but after the expulsion of the Jews from that country in 1492, immigrated to Salonika.

He was a lover and pursuer of peace. He dedicated his energy and time in bringing peace to married couples, to suggest compromises and to guide them towards a happy home. His own home was always open to any guest, as Rabbi Mordechai**Error! Bookmark not defined.** Mendel and his wife, Mrs. Bracha, were glad for the opportunity to host guests in their home. Their home was never too small for strangers, who ate to their hearts' content at their table. He not only gave of his food, but also of his heart, which was open to all.

Rabbi Mordechai Mendel always sought to perform commandments. He worked hard for the individual, for his fellow man, seeing in each person a world unto himself, an entire world. He did not see himself as one involved in public affairs, a man of the community. But for decades he worked hard for people, for the poor and the sick, for the homeless and the needy. But he never asked for any reward for his many good deeds, never demanded any position for his many efforts. He was a Jew of the old school, performing commandments and good deeds, without any benefit for himself.

He was an impressive looking man, his white beard descending proportionately to his stature. His charm and his noble presence added much to the city. He would give encouragement to people when dark clouds covered the skies of Jewish Poland, when the whirlwind of the Holocaust approached and affected the daily lives of the Jews of Poland in general, and those of Ostroveh among them.

Rabbi Moshe Pokshiva [Pokrzywa]

Rabbi Moshe**Error! Bookmark not defined.** was born in Ostroveh, and grew up and was educated near the outskirts of the city, which had a beautiful tradition of Torah and Hassidism and righteous deeds. His origins lay in a family of Hassidim of Warka-Otvotsk. His father was a Hassid of the *rebbe* Rabbi Menachem Mendel of Warka, and then a Hassid of the *rebbe* Rabbi Simcha Bunim of Otvotsk. As a matter of course Rabbi Moshe would frequently travel to *rebbe* Rabbi Simcha Bunim of Otvotsk, and after his death to his son, the *rebbe* Rabbi Yaakov David.

Rabbi Moshe was a merchant all his life. He was in the lumber business. He was always under pressure and his income was not a munificent one. Nevertheless, he was always satisfied with what he had, a Hassid in every fiber of his being, loyal to the Warka tradition. His many financial troubles notwithstanding, he found time to engage in the needs of the community faithfully and devotedly. He undertook his projects with enthusiasm and with a full heart, and was therefore beloved unto a great many. The residents loved Rabbi Moshe, the man of the willing heart and soul.

With the rise of the Agudat Yisrael movement, Rabbi Moshe enthusiastically joined its ranks. He was one of its best leaders, and for many years represented Agudat Yisrael on the community council. In the community he particularly stood out for his work on behalf the *Maot Chitim* project [which provided funds for wheat to give to the needy in order to bake *matzot*] in honor of the Passover holiday. Every year he worked hard to collect significant sums to dispense to the many poor so that they could celebrate the Passover holiday with ample food. There was no end to his joy when he would succeed in this mission by collecting large sums of money that enabled a respectable distribution of funds in honor of the Passover holiday. In the days that preceded Passover, Rabbi Moshe hardly paid any attention to his own business. He put aside his own source of income and was involved day and night in the *Maot Chitim* project.

Another area in which Rabbi Moshe involved himself was the collection of funds for firewood for the poor as winter approached. There were always devoted and loyal activists to be found in every Jewish community in Poland who were committed to undertaking this project beginning after the High Holy Days. They accepted the responsibility to provide firewood that would prevent cold and frost in the homes of the many poor. These activists were particularly concerned for the poor who had many small children or the elderly or the sick, for whom the prevention of frost was a matter of life and death.

Rabbi Moshe labored on behalf of this project. No sooner had he finished, when he was again speaking about making sure that one had to remain on guard at any cost to provide heat in the homes of the poor of Ostroveh during the winter. He was fortunate in that he not only felt the need but was also in a position to supply wood needed for this purpose, to assure that there would be a winter without suffering for the masses of poor who lived in Ostroveh.

With the conquest of the city by the Nazis, Rabbi Moshe fled along with most of the [Jewish] residents towards Soviet Russia. For a short time he suffered along with other refugees in the Russian zone of occupation in Poland. Afterwards he was exiled with many other refugees to the steppes of Siberia. There, in exile on foreign soil, he took ill and died in Siberia at the age of seventy-five, in the year 5703 [1942-1943].

Rabbi Yechiel Slutsky

The image of Rabbi Yechiel Slutsky evoked honor and admiration. He was one of the most important and outstanding residents of Ostrow Mazowiecka. He was both an activist and man of exceptional personal traits, of great spirit and soul, a personage replete with the splendor of old, of rare personal appearance that few Jews could match in a town that was a place full of personalities of stature.

Rabbi Yechiel was considered a very righteous man by many of the Jews of the city. He dedicated only a small portion of his time to earning his modest living. His righteous wife assisted him in supporting their household. The bulk of his day was dedicated to Torah and good deeds, for which efforts he never asked any reward or thanks. He engaged in these efforts for many years, far exceeding his own strength.

He possessed exceptional personal characteristics. He never got upset and was never angry at anyone. He never overstepped his own personal serenity and the refinement of his ways. In virtual secrecy, he quietly went about his efforts aimed at a heavenly purpose. He despised tumult and publicity. Honors were alien to his gentle spirit and soul, which could not tolerate the loud manners of officialdom that were foreign to the beautiful tradition of pure volunteerism.

He set up a *minyan* [prayer group] called *Tiferet Bachurim* [The Glory of Young Men] in his home. And he would study with his congregants daily in regular fixed sessions. He worked hard with all his heart to instill Torah and the fear of God, fine personal attributes, and an adherence to pure Judaism into the hearts of these young men. And he did all this quietly, softly, with love and mercy, without any benefit to himself or his family whatsoever.

Rabbi Yechiel loved to perform good deeds for Jews, to do things for others with all his heart and soul. He never tired of raising money for the poor and suffering. He enthusiastically undertook various tasks, and was always careful to maintain the privacy of his actions. He preferred performing charitable deeds in secret. He believed that any such deed that was not publicly exposed was doubly or triply blessed.

As he aged he increased his good and noble deeds for others, in his work in spreading Torah and on behalf of the poor. He was an activist of the old school, who performed his tasks solely for their own sake and for the sake of the commandments, with no other intentions. He fled from honors and any official position. He worked hard on not being visible. In all the years of his work in Ostroveh, he never held any public position whatsoever.

As for himself, he studied intently. He studied in his home day and night. The lights went out very late in his room. And in the very early hours of the morning he was already studying with enthusiasm and diligence. He lived to an advanced age, but was killed in God's name in the horrific Holocaust, along with his wife.

Rabbi Yosef Pravda

Among the most outstanding personages of Jewish Ostroveh in the final years preceding the last world war and the destruction of its Jewish community was Rabbi Yosef Pravda. Born in Warsaw, he was married to the daughter of Rabbi Yitzchak Gershon Warshauer[160] [Warszawer], one of the honored citizens of this city, and thus established his residence in Ostrow Mazowiecka and became one of its residents. A relatively short time thereafter, Rabbi Yosef became known far and wide. His personality added another hue to the multi-hued rainbow of Ostroveh Jewry.

From the time he was a young man he joined the first group of young men who got together in an organized fashion and became enthusiastic Hassidim under the supervision and direction of the *rebbe* Rabbi Avraham Mordechai of Ger. While still young in age, Rabbi Yosef**Error! Bookmark not defined.** Pravda stood out in these circles for his devotion and sacrifice on behalf of pure Hassidism. With all his heart and soul, and with the passion of

---

[160] According to the Ostrow Mazowiecka records, Josel Prawda [Pravda] married Rachela Warszawer [Warshauer]. She was born in 1899, the daughter of Icek Gerszon Warszawer.

youth, he worked hard on Torah and Hassidism. In those days it was a rare sight to see a young man, full of life and energy, become an avid Hassid, a servant of God.

In the closing days of World War I and immediately prior to that, the great changes that had befallen Polish Jewry were affecting the courts of the *rebbe*s and their many study houses. The changing of the guard and the stormy times of the war precipitated profound unrest in Polish Jewry, which for generations had followed its established traditional path. The great shocks that affected the entire Europe were reflected in the younger generation as well as the middle-aged one. Many abandoned the tradition of the ages, seeking new paths and turning to new horizons that now appeared before the masses of Polish Jewry.

The benches of the study houses were increasingly emptied out with frightening speed. Glorious Poland, which had meticulously maintained the traditions of generations past, whereby hundreds of thousands of young men filled the study houses in every city and town, studying diligently day and night, suddenly changed its character and image. It seemed as if the younger generation of Polish Jews had turned their backs on Jewish tradition. Masses of them joined the Zionist movement. Even greater numbers joined revolutionary socialist movements. The benches of the study houses were just about empty.

There was the communist revolution in Russia, which followed in the wake of World War I. And the issuance of the Balfour Declaration, which promised the establishment of a Jewish national home, on the one hand, and the intensification of anti-Semitism in Poland, on the other, further strengthened the [Zionist] movement. It seemed as if the future generation of Polish Jewry had wrapped itself in a new mantle, socialist or nationalist, cutting all ties to everything in its glorious past. The sound of the Torah, which had echoed for hundreds of years all across Poland, which once emanated from the dwellings of the Jews day and night, was virtually silenced.

Even before these movements had crystallized, before this temporary change had taken hold, the *rebbe* Rabbi Avraham Mordechai of Ger had undertaken a comprehensive effort whose aim was to stem this abandonment of Torah and Judaism by the younger generation. This great *rebbe*, who had a decisive influence over hundreds of thousands of Hassidim, whose position was above and beyond that of any other traditional framework of Hassidim or Hassidism, began to organize unified groups of young men who would be brought into the great paradise of Hassidism.

This was a virtual revolution that was accepted by veteran Hassidim only with great difficulty.

Since the time when Hassidism was formed, young unmarried men had held no position or standing among Hassidim or in Hassidism. The great *rebbe*s had devoted almost no time or attention to those who came to their courts with their parents. The proper place for a young man was in the study hall, alongside an open Gemara, concentrating on its content, being diligent in learning Torah. The young man who immersed himself totally in study of the Talmud and the decisors was considered a good fellow.

The Hassidim of Poland [as opposed to orthodox Jews in Lithuania] did not accept the method of education that involved studying in [distant] higher *yeshivot* and the wandering of young men to study Torah outside their home communities. The Jews of Poland viewed learning in one's own home and in the [local] study house as complementary activities that were not separate from the study of the Torah or from the values that the youth received from one's parents at home in the context of the family. Removing a youth from his home, from his family circle, even for the sake of the study of Torah, was likely, according to this approach, to harm his character and his proper education and to cause harm to his spirit.

Out of all this came the negation of studying in higher *yeshivot* on the part of Hassidim in general. This was because the *yeshivot* that were far from home precluded education by the parents and the home. According to this widely accepted theory in Poland, it was incumbent upon the young man to study in the [local] study house even if it lacked the ongoing and individualized oversight of supervisors and teachers. This was based on the assumption that the diligent student would always study, even when he was not subject to official supervision, whereas the student who was not deeply committed to learning would not study even when confined within the walls of an organized *yeshiva* and when under the supervision of designated supervisors. The only exception was in the case of young prodigies who went to study Torah with the greatest rabbis of the times or in other exceptional circumstances.

Young men, even those from extremely ardent Hassidic families, did not study and were not introduced to the mysteries of Hassidism until they were married and were on their own. Only rarely did young men travel with their parents to *rebbe*s for specific holidays, but even then they did not remain in the courts of the *rebbe*s for more than a few days. Whereas veteran Hassidim would remain in the courts of *rebbe*s for long periods, the young men would be returned to their homes immediately after the particular Sabbath or holiday. The proper place for a young man even from the most ardent Hassidic families was in front of the Gemara and not in the court of the *rebbe*.

Both older and younger Hassidim studied and prayed the houses of the Hassidim, which became in effect their second homes. They would frequently take meals there as well, whether connected with religious celebrations or on other occasions. They spent entire days and nights within the walls of these houses of Hassidim. This was not true of the younger men, the sons of the older Hassidim. They studied and spent their entire time in the city's study hall, the place where the young men of the city or neighborhood would gather to study. Only rarely, for the Sabbath or holidays, did they come to the houses of the Hassidim to pray with their parents.

Shortly before fundamental changes took place in Polish Jewry, the *rebbe* Rabbi Avraham Mordechai of Ger saw in advance what was likely to happen. He changed the accepted methods of Hassidim, to the shock of the masses of older Hassidim who flocked to him. He began to bring the youth closer, to introduce them to the mysteries of pure Hassidism, to encourage them to organize and unite in fixed groups. Young men would now remain in the court of the *rebbe* of Ger for weeks and months at a time, studying Hassidism, working on the improvement of their personal traits, and engaging in the service of God with real enthusiasm, much like older and elderly Hassidim.

They were given preference by the *rebbe* over veteran Hassidim, who initially did not look upon these changes favorably and nor understand the need for them. It took a few years before these people came to agree with their rabbi, the great *rebbe*. Thousands of young people were thus saved for Judaism, for Torah. They became a loyal legion for pure Hassidism. One of the first and most outstanding of these was Rabbi Yosef Pravda, even before he moved to Ostroveh. Rabbi Yosef came to the city as a man young in years, but also as a veteran Hassid with a deep understanding of and an articulated position on all the problems that were on the agenda.

The bright young men of Ger were trained to study a great deal, to dig deep into Hassidism and the fundamental problems of Judaism and of ethics. Most of all they were educated for devotion and real self-sacrifice on behalf of holy and eternal goals. They were taught to negate the material. And first and foremost among material things was themselves. No sacrifice was too great for them in order to attain the goal that they established for themselves in their lives, that is to ascend higher and higher in pure Hassidism and holiness, to become true servants of God, to overcome indecent impulses and selfish motivations.

They did not know the difference between day and night. They always, at any hour of the day, worked hard on their Hassidism, while not neglecting their study of the Torah. The great *rebbe* disparaged illiteracy and ignorance. They adhered to their teacher with every fiber of their being. They were always prepared to traverse fire and water at the slightest intimation from the lips of the *rebbe*. In a very brief time the *rebbe* of Ger established an iron legion that served as a support for Torah Judaism in all of Poland up until the outbreak of the Holocaust. And in his footsteps other *rebbe*s followed suit.

Rabbi Yosef Pravda was a symbol and an iconic example of a young man of Ger, who became a leader among his people in Ostroveh, the town where he lived. He loved Torah and studied diligently with the enthusiasm of holiness, but was also aware of everything. He loved books and delved into them, especially books on thoughts that crystallized the basic ideas of Hassidism in Poland, be they books on Hassidism or books by the Maharal of Prague,[161] etc. From his great teacher, the *rebbe* of Ger, he learned to love books. He acquired a large library, and never passed up a valuable one without looking into it and reviewing its contents.

But he also remained at his core an ardent Hassid. He traveled to Ger frequently, where he received further inspiration to learn from the *rebbe* of Ger. His prayers were said with enthusiasm and without self-interest. He aspired to greatness, all the while convinced that he had yet to achieve anything, that he was an empty vessel that still needed much work. He was a person with superior personal traits, which he used to evaluate himself and his deeds. And he always came to the same conclusions, those of a true Hassid, that his actions were still flawed. Thus, his greatest and most fundamental concern was that he not turn into a "nice Jew," that is, that he not succumb to pride, as pride was likely to bring him down.

The true Hassid never belongs to himself, is not his own personal possession. He always is subservient to his teacher, the *rebbe*, and to the congregation of Hassidim. As a practical matter, he learns the meaning of self-abnegation in the court of the *rebbe*, where the group of Hassidim that surround him constantly keep a sharp eye on the Hassid, lest he become a reality in and of

---

[161] Acronym for *Moreinu Harav Loew* [Our Teacher Rabbi Leib], Rabbi Yehuda Leib [Loew] ben Betzalel, preeminent rabbinical scholar, philosopher and mystic (c. 1520-1609). He was born in Poznan, Poland, but lived mostly in Prague, and was closely associated with the legend of the Golem.

himself. For only in the absence of such a self-centered reality does the hope of correcting the flaws of a person and the repair of his characteristics and deeds, as well as the hope of his ascension and true service to God, still reside. Rabbi Yosef Pravda was a genuine product of this holy undertaking, a true Hassid.

For a short time he resided at the home of his father-in-law. Once he became independent he opened an iron products store and was successful, being thought of as a prosperous man who had a substantial income. He did not keep his money all to himself. He was a generous benefactor who contributed generously to every charity, and who donated, as a true Polish Hassid, as if his money was not really his and his donations were not merely the gifts of his own heart. It was as if he received funds for the purpose of giving them away, to share them with others. He was one of those who was not only called upon to give, but who also felt that it was incumbent upon him to do so, whether in the house of the Hassidim or in the community. They were commanded, as it were, to give, and accepted this demand as an order which could not be challenged or doubted.

Rabbi Yosef became a successful merchant. But this did not free him from giving charity. He donated and worked hard to raise funds from others, too. He performed good deeds and caused others to do so as well. He frequently left his place of business to circulate among the homes of residents in order to perform charitable acts. More than once he was sent by an organization to nearby towns and cities to collect for various urgent needs, such as to provide funds for the marriage of the daughter of a poor Hassid or for the needs of someone who was ill. It was not only money that he provided. He was also was available for any good deed that actually needed to be done. It was something that was taken as a given by Rabbi Yosef as a true Hassid who aspired to perfection.

His home was open to all, Hassidim and non-Hassidim alike, people he knew and those whom he did not know. They considered his home as their place of refuge, as something quite natural. After all Rabbi Yosef Pravda belonged to the community, to all Hassidim. And he was delighted to welcome guests, receiving them with joy and enthusiasm. For why does a person have a home if not to have guests? And why does a person have doors in his house if not to open them freely to all who seek entry? Rabbi Yosef did not view himself as one who welcomed guests as part of the commandment to do so. Fulfilling that obligation was still a long way off. He was still at the stage of aspiring to attain it. He was a servant of God.

Rabbi Yosef was sensible and wise. He succeeded in developing ties with the officials of the government, so that he might be able to help others, to take advantage of these contacts in times of need. So Rabbi Yosef became an unofficial *shtadlan*. He would often appear in government offices when he was asked by a Jew to do so. Willingly and joyously, without viewing himself as a *shtadlan*, without even making people aware that he was doing anything. After all, everything in life is a matter of being a representative, in a variety of many different and varied capacities. Helping another person is serving as a representative, and nothing more, a representation in order to perform one of the 613 commandments in the Torah.

As were many of the Hassidim of Ger, Rabbi Yosef was a member of Agudat Yisrael, a very loyal and devoted one. He saw in Agudat Yisrael the demand of the hour, and it was necessary to do everything to strengthen its foundations and increase its power. It was a holy obligation from which no Jew was exempt. Rabbi Yosef served as a loyal soldier at the service of Agudat Yisrael. He went out on every mission that was asked of him and did whatever he was asked to do. He never dodged his duty. Often, during decisive election periods, he went around making enthusiastic speeches, and proved to be a popular speaker who knew how to attract his listeners. He did everything in his power on behalf of Agudat Yisrael, but never saw himself as a leader, but rather as just a regular person who did his part.

At the outbreak of the last world war the Germans bombed Ostrow Mazowiecka ferociously. The first bomb that hit the city fell on the house of Rabbi Yosef Pravda. His son, Yitzchak Gershon, was killed on the spot, as was another young man whom he had taken into his home, as well as a guest he had been hosting, Reb Leib Yarmus. These were the first losses that Jewish Ostroveh suffered at the outbreak of the horrific Holocaust. Rabbi Yosef was wounded badly, and was not able to recover and get out of bed.

In those mad and difficult times, when Rabbi Yosef was already confined to bed, this ardent Hassid revealed the greatness of his soul and the breadth of his heart. Despite the extreme pain that never left him, he continued to serve God enthusiastically and out of love and with true loyalty to his creator. On the twenty-ninth day of Cheshvan, in the year 5700 [November 11, 1939], when the Nazi monsters killed the remaining Jews of Ostroveh, Rabbi Yosef Pravda (may God avenge his blood) was killed in the name of God, along with his distinguished, pious and elderly wife, with whom he had shared his life.

Rabbi Mendel Lichtenstein

Thought to be one of the richest Jews in Ostrow Mazowiecka and its environs both near and far in the years before World War I was Rabbi Mendel Lichtenstein, son of Rabbi Zundel Lichtenstein, one of the first Hassidim and one of the greatest of the Kotsk Hassidim in Ostroveh. Rabbi Mendel had inherited from his father an iron and construction materials business. He developed his business to the point where it attained very substantial dimensions that exceeded the usual ones in the city and region. He was a successful and honest businessman, a man of many principles and ideas.

Rabbi Menachem**Error! Bookmark not defined.** Mendel was a Hassid, who prayed and studied in the Hassidic house of Ger in town and who traveled to see the *rebbe* of Ger, author of the *S'fat Emet*. In that large Hassidic house he built an ark of wrought iron that he paid for, and did not stint in his efforts to beautify that house of worship. He was deeply involved in charity and always responded to requests. He was interested in participating in every charitable endeavor, in responding to everyone who asked, so much so that fundraisers never skipped his house nor forgot his address, which was well known throughout the province of Lomza and beyond.

He was by nature a good man. He was always ready to assist others, whether it was a businessman just starting out to help him get his enterprise established or someone who truly needed a helping hand. He had a special ledger for his charitable work. Over time he came to administer in effect a permanent [interest free] charitable loan fund out of his own money. Borrower after borrower, he never tired of helping others. Despite his great wealth, his charitable endeavors became the centerpiece of his activities. Wealth did not change the mentality of the rich Jews of Ostroveh in those days, who knew who their true master was, nor did it change their way of life, which resembled in every respect those of the rest of the Jews who resided there, most of whom were hard up to make a living. The rich and the poor alike rejected luxury, and did not speak in a boastful or bragging manner. They maintained their Jewish way of life, one that was profoundly modest.

Rabbi Mendel Lichtenstein had an open door for guests and the poor, who visited his residence frequently. The wife of Rabbi Mendel was known for her willingness to provide food to all who needed it. She was good hearted and spared no effort to provide ample nourishment to the hungry and to guests, both the unimportant people as well as the important ones.

Some years after World War I Rabbi Mendel Lichtenstein passed way.[162] His heir and the one who continued in his ways was his son, Rabbi Bendit Lichtenstein, also a Ger Hassid, who inherited from his father a portion of his wealth and his business. It was said that at the outbreak of World War I Rabbi Mendel Lichtenstein had transferred one hundred fifty thousand rubles in gold to the government bank in St. Petersburg for safe keeping. According to this story, these funds were lost to him and Rabbi Mendel never succeeded in recouping them. Nevertheless, the family still had a substantial fortune.

Rabbi Bendit continued in the footsteps of his father. He gave to charity and did right by many. When he married off one of his daughters, he arranged meals for the poor and needy during the entire week of the wedding celebrations, and fed them well. In the Holocaust Rabbi Bendit and most of his family were killed.

Rabbi Pinchas Leib

For many decades before the outbreak of World War I a short, elderly man, Rabbi Pinchas Leib, regularly sat in the old house of study in Ostroveh. He had come to town from one of the villages in the area and studied day and night. It was said of him that he knew the entire Talmud, as well as the earlier and later commentaries, by heart. He was a great and extraordinary scholar. He ate very little, did not engage in conversation with others very much, viewing his entire world as contained in his studies. His main aim in life was to help the young men in the *beit midrash* with their studies. As long as there were still young men sitting in the study hall, he did not leave. He sat and studied and waited until one of them would come over and ask him something about his studies.

He replied to all who asked him for help with great joy. It did not matter what the question was, whether a sharp query about something in the Talmud, or a question of Jewish law, or just a clarification of no particular significance. In moments such as these his eyes lit up with a glow, as if he had received some great unanticipated prize, as if he had attained the ultimate goal of his life. He answered willingly, with a giving heart, and did not tire of repeating his answer. Despite his advanced age, despite the weakness that was taking its toll on Rabbi Pichas Leib in the latter years of his life, he maintained his great patience and his

---

[162] According to the Ostrow Mazowiecka records, Mendel Lichtensztejn [Lichtenstein] was born in Ostrow Mazowiecka in 1866 and died there in 1928. His wife Basia, daughter of Aron Zeifman, was born in Bransk in Grodno *gubernia* around 1866.

generosity of spirit towards the young men who imposed upon him occasionally with meaningless questions.

The Torah and the study of Torah were the purpose and substance of the life of Rabbi Pinchas Leib and of others in that period. For Rabbi Pinchas Leib there was nothing other than confines of the Torah that was important. His joy and his pain, his suffering and his happiness he invested in his Torah. The idea that he was contributing something to the increased learning of the Torah, to the understanding of the Torah on the part of young men, the recognition that he was doing a *mitzvah* with his own knowledge of the Torah, filled his heart with great happiness and satisfaction. Even if young men were to stand beside him and ask their questions day and night, Rabbi Pinchas Leib would never tire, never need sleep or food. He was capable of standing twenty-four hours a day to provide others with his knowledge of the Torah with joy.

Up until the very last day of his long life Rabbi Pinchas Leib fulfilled this mission of his. His weakness and perhaps even his illness did not prevent him from doing so. He became an integral part of the life of the old study house, which was filled with Torah and studiers of the Torah day and night. And one night, he left the old study house for his home and returned to his soul to its maker.

Rabbi Eliyahu Lach

The image of Rabbi Eliyahu Lach was one that evoked respect and affection. He was one of the outstanding residents of Ostrow Mazowiecka, a scholar and a Hassid, a community leader and businessman, a man of righteousness and exemplary character. He was a Jew with a precious spirit and a precious soul, beloved by all and accepted by all. He was one of those who engendered feelings of honor and affection towards Hassidim in general, and towards himself in particular.

Rabbi Eliyahu Lach was a man of rare distinguished appearance. His black beard descended proportionately, while his broad forehead attested to the broad thinking of the man. His large, wise eyes indicated a good heart, while his appearance inspired respect and symbolized his beautiful and aristocratic inner self, which few had like him, even in those days when there still were hundreds of Hassidim and doers of good works around, good and dear Jews in the cities and towns of the great Polish Disapora. In those days there were still many who functioned on the basis of fine and exceptional character traits.

Rabbi Eliyahu was a Hassid of Amshinov, one of the heads of this respected community in Ostroveh. He was one of the trusted supporters of the *rebbe* Rabbi Menachem and afterwards of the *rebbe* Rabbi Yosef. During the time when the *rebbe* Rabbi Yosef served as chief of the rabbinical court in Ostroveh, Rabbi Eliyahu became tied to him with deep bonds of love and affection. Rabbi Eliyahu served as the central address for the Amshinov Hassidim in the city. The source of the actual expression of the Amshinov way derived in large part from the Hassidism of Warka, i.e., good and noble personal character traits and a devotion to the good of both the community and individuals; a good and empathetic heart; true modesty, combined with assertiveness and exuberance in whatever one does. It was a Hassidism that purified every aspect of the Hassid.

Rabbi Eliyahu Lach was a Hassid but also a man of action. He was the address for anyone who needed help among the Amshinov Hassidim in the city and its nearby and extended environs. There were many poor and needy in the community of Amshinov Hassidim in the area of Ostroveh. Many of them were grateful to Rabbi Eliyahu for his great help with everything he turned to. He was both the doer and the deed. He never turned anyone down. He would help one person marry off his son, a second to escape from poverty and distress, and a third to establish himself and earn a living. And all this he did with humility and modesty, without any publicity. Rabbi Eliyahu liked the idea of giving anonymously, of doing things without revealing to anyone what he was doing. He kept these secrets until his dying day.

He was full of confidence [in God] and faith, and exhibited an inner joy and true happiness. He believed deeply that all troubles and suffering were merely tests that ultimately would be swiftly reversed. He always had a smile and a radiant face for everyone. He would infect anyone who came into contact with him with his surety and faith. His words were usually interwoven with the words of the sages, with witticisms from the great minds of Israel. He would cite relevant scripture and infuse them into every conversation. He saw everything through the lens of a Torah-oriented outlook. When gloomy clouds loomed over the skies over Polish Jewry, such as when the state authorities openly encouraged an economic boycott against [Jewish] merchants and their situation worsened from day to day, Rabbi Eliyahu continued to exude confidence and faith and insisted that people wait for good days to return soon. The bad days would soon pass like shadows; they would disappear and never return.

Rabbi Eliyahu Lach was a successful merchant, who attained wealth and a generous income. His only daughter he married off to the Gaon Rabbi David Mintzberg, of excellent stock. He supported his son-in-law for many years, so that he might devote all his time to the study of Torah and the performance of good deeds without having any worries or concerns. Seven daughters were born to Rabbi David and his wife, the daughter of Rabbi Eliyahu, who took care of all their needs generously and willingly. He worked devotedly on behalf of his son-in-law and the members of his family.

He was a lover of Torah and a supporter of those who studied it. Not a day passed when Rabbi Eliyahu did not devote some of his time to Torah, to a regular class, while he also found time for communal work, whether for the benefit of an individual or the public. From the time of the establishment of the Agudat Yisrael movement, Rabbi Eliyahu joined it enthusiastically. For many years he represented Agudat Yisrael and the orthodox community on the community council, to which he had been elected. Despite the fact that he was a party man, he rejected conflict and divisiveness, and avoided any wrangling. He did not hate even those who did not agree with his philosophy and outlook, as he was unable to hate anyone, any person, even the worst among them. The love of the people of Israel that reverberated in his heart left no room for personal hatreds or enmity. Nevertheless, his gentle heart and natural flexibility did not prevent him from adhering to fundamental opposition to all the secular political movements that had arisen in the Jewish community.

It was in his work for the orthodox community, for Agudat Yisrael, that Rabbi Eliyahu fulfilled his main interests in pure orthodox Jewish education and his concern for its strengthening. Much of his time and treasure he dedicated to the establishment of the *Beit Yaakov* school for girls, an orthodox institution that educated hundreds of girls in Torah and a strict orthodox outlook. There were times when Rabbi Eliyahu just about maintained that institution out of his own pocket. He worked devotedly in this sacred task up until the horrific Holocaust that destroyed Polish Jewry in its entirety as well as all the institutions and programs that had been built, maintained and tended with so much effort and sweat, devotedly and with much self-sacrifice by trusted and dedicated leaders.

When the horrific Holocaust was approaching and struck, and many people fled out of desperation, Rabbi Eliyahu maintained his smile, his burning faith and his great confidence. Because of the Nazi barbarians he was forced to leave the city of his residence, escaping to the Soviet zone of occupation in Poland, where he died when the Germans conquered that area from the Russians.

Rabbi Motel Lichtenstein

Among the community of Kotsk Hassidim, one of the outstanding people was Rabbi Leibel Lichtenstein, a scholar and true Hassid, whose entire life was dedicated to Torah and pure Hassidism. Throughout his entire life he never strayed from the bounds of Torah. He was of those exceptional few who excelled both in his wisdom and great personal characteristics, a man full of self-sacrifice and devotion. He was a Hassid who left the worry and burden of supporting his family to his righteous wife, while he devoted his entire life to spiritual growth. He abstained from honors and position, from wealth and money, from all comfort and pleasure in life whatsoever. He was a Jew for whom no sacrifice or effort was too great to attain perfection, complete control over his behavior and character, and full oversight over his very existence and his desires.

In the year 5635 [1874-1875] a son was born to Rabbi Leibel the Hassid, Mordechai or "Motel," as he was called from that point on. Rabbi Motel was a wonderful and outstanding boy from his earliest days. He was fearful of heaven and of committing any sin, wise but inherently reticent, with exceptional abilities. He was only nine years old when he already knew the entire tractate of *Berachot* by heart, along with the commentary of Rabbi Jonah. He acquired extensive knowledge of the Torah, whether it was through his abilities or his great diligence. The excellent student always sat and studied. He completed his studies with his teachers at the *cheder* and quickly proceeded to the Hassidic house. He sat and learned without any supervision, solely motivated by his own will. The Gaon and Hassid Rabbi Ben-Zion, head of the Hassidim in Ostroveh, recognized something in this excellent boy, and began to draw him in and supervise him. When he was nine his father took him to see the *rebbe*, the author of the *S'fat Emet*, in Ger, and this wonderful boy became a Hassid. In the year 5650 [1889-1890] he married the daughter of Rabbi David Aharon Grudka [Grudke], one of the important residents of Goworowo and one of the leaders of the Alexander Hassidim there.

After his marriage Rabbi Motel intensified his diligence and perseverance, not desisting from his studies day or night. In the first years after his marriage he was supported by his father-in-law. After that his righteous wife undertook the burden of supporting the family. She ran a store and engaged in various businesses, while Rabbi Motel devoted all his time to Torah and good works. His name as an excellent scholar spread far and wide, to the point where a position as a rabbi and teacher of Halacha was offered to him in Praga, adjacent to Warsaw. Rabbi Motel turned it down, as did his wife, who wholeheartedly wished her husband to continue to concentrate on his studies, as she had no thoughts whatsoever of divesting herself of the burden of earning a living.

Rabbi Motel continued his studies in Goworowo for more than twenty years. Every day he virtually fasted, and did not take time to eat anything until the break between afternoon prayers and evening prayers. Throughout the morning hours he sat and learned with young men, as well as studying by himself. Not a second was wasted. All the days of his life were filled with Torah. He frequently traveled to visit the *rebbe* of Ger, author of the *S'fat Emet*, or his son, the *rebbe* Rabbi Avraham**Error! Bookmark not defined.** Mordechai. He would leave on his trip in the early days of the month of Elul [ca. September-October] and remain in Ger until Chanukah [ca. December-January]. Between Chanukah and the month of Elul he would travel there several times a year, for Purim or for the latter days of Passover, for the holiday of Shavuot or for no particular event, or for a Sabbath, or just for a few weeks.

He was always devoted to his studies and his intense efforts. On Friday evening, during the years when he was still in Goworowo, he would study until midnight, even in the short days of winter, and only then did he recite the Sabbath *kiddush* [sanctification] and eat a meal. He spoke very little with other people. He was reticent and his words were few and measured. He spoke with wisdom and understanding, but he always kept his own counsel, and fully observed the basic principle of Hassidism: "Do not look outwards, and do not look into the affairs of others." He was interested in what was happening in the world. He listened, but was then silent. He was always rushing to return to his work, i.e., his studies.

In the year 5674 [1914], with the outbreak of World War I, he left Goworowo and returned to his city of origin, Ostroveh. In his new place of residence, as before, he sat and learned day and night, mostly in the Hassidic house of Ger. He studied in regular sessions with the Gaon Rabbi Avraham**Error! Bookmark not defined.** Petziner and with the Gaon Rabbi David Mintzberg, while his wife continued to engage in business and to manage the affairs of the household. His noble wife had a courageous spirit. During this period they experienced hard times, and they often did not have sufficient food. His wife fasted for entire days and did not reveal her secret of the lack of means to Rabbi Motel, who continued learning enthusiastically. A few years later in 5682 [1921-1922], after his wife had succeeded in stabilizing their financial situation, her new store burned down. She wanted to open another business, and asked her husband to seek the advice of his teacher and rabbi, the *rebbe* Rabbi Avraham Mordechai of

Ger. The *rebbe* listened to his question and answered him saying, "Why do you need this business? It would be better if you went to the Land of Israel." As a trusting and loyal Hassid, Rabbi Motel did not hesitate much, nor did his righteous wife hesitate or object, even though this was not to her liking. They decided to sell everything they owned and to immigrate to the Land of Israel with their savings and their two sons, Leibel and Chaim Dov.

The Gaon and Hassid Rabbi Ben-Zion, Rabbi Motel's guide and teacher, traveled twice to Ger to try to change the decision of the *rebbe*, but he did not succeed. The *rebbe* Rabbi Avraham Mordechai said to him, "I cannot prevent Rabbi Motel from doing such a good thing." In the year 5682 [1921-1922] Rabbi Motel arrived in Tel Aviv, acquired a house and established his residence in that city. Only once did he travel back to Poland for a visit, and quickly returned to the Land of Israel.

The house of Rabbi Motel in Tel Aviv became a center for all the Hassidim who had immigrated to the Land of Israel in those days. For twelve years the house served as a meeting place for Ger Hassidim in the city. Rabbi Motel lived on rents and from the money he brought from Ostroveh, and his wife managed the household successfully. There were always guests staying there, and there were those who were supported in that way for years. Rabbi Motel and his family gave all those who sought his shelter a warm welcome. Sometimes Hassidim would hold their meals for special occasions there. A day did not go by in all the years that Rabbi Motel resided in Tel Aviv that there were not guests visiting his home or eating at his table.

As in Goworowo and in Ostroveh, in Tel Aviv Rabbi Motel sat and studied. All those around him knew that he was an excellent and distinguished scholar, who knew the Talmud and the decisors by heart, a veritable treasure chest filled with all the subject matter of the Torah, and that he was a true Hassid with exceptional values. But Rabbi Motel continued in his way, in his silence, listening to all but mostly staying quiet. He liked silence, and despised chatter and wasting time. In the year 5694 [1933-1934] he relocated to Jerusalem. He sold his house in Tel Aviv and bought one in Jerusalem, from which he made a living until his final day.

Before the outbreak of the last world war his righteous wife died in Jerusalem. Rabbi Motel lived long and reached an exceptionally old age. Amid admiration and honor, he died on the ninth day of Av in the year 5721 [July 21-22, 1961] in Jerusalem as one of the leaders and giants of the community of Ger Hassidim in the Land of Israel.

Rabbi Menachem Mendel Semiatitzky

Rabbi Menachem Mendel**Error! Bookmark not defined.** Semiatitzky [Siemiatycki] was a wise man and a Hassid, a lover his fellow Jews and of the Torah. He was one of the leading citizens of the city and one of the special personalities in Ostrow Mazowiecka. He arrived there when he was still young, when he married the daughter of Reb Binyamin Freyman [Frejman], a painting contractor and respected resident.[163] For many years Rabbi Menachem Mendel studied ardently while being supported by his father-in-law. When Reb Binyamin died [per the records, in 1906] his sons, the brothers-in-law of Rabbi Mendel, took over the contracting business. As Rabbi Mendel's share of the inheritance he received an interest in a house near a wall that Rabbi Binyamin had left which had several apartments, from which he eked out a living.

He was an outstanding scholar, one of the devoted Hassidim of Ger, and well versed in speaking, at which he excelled. Rabbi Mendel traveled to the United States,[164] where he lived for several years and where he appeared as a guest speaker in synagogues. After a while he returned to Ostroveh and published a book of his lectures entitled, *Divrei Menachem [The Words of Menachem]*. His book was full of pearls of his oratory and witticisms that attested to the greatness of Rabbi Menachem in Torah.

There were always novellae and witticisms coming out of his mouth. He was always innovative in terms of his lectures. People listened to him with interest and enjoyed his scholarship. When asked about a marriage match, for example, he proceeded to say, " 'For this should every righteous person pray to you, and when he finds it, no flood of water shall reach him' (Psalms 32).' We learn in the Gemara that Rabbi Hanina says that the words 'when he finds it' refers to a wife. But the meaning is not clear. How does the concept of prayer relate to a marriage? And how does a wife relate to a flood of water? We know that Sennacherib[165] took four

---

[163] According to the Ostrow Mazowiecka records, Mendel Siemiatycki [Semiatitzsky] married Estera Gitla Frejman [Freyman] in 1902. However, Rabbi Mendel's passenger list record gives his wife's name as Fejga. Estera Gitla may have died in Ostrow Mazowiecka in 1904, so that Fejga would have been Rabbi Mendel's second wife. She may have also been a younger daughter of Reb Binyamin Frejman, hence a younger sister of Estera Gitla.

[164] A passenger list record shows the arrival of Mendel Siemiatycki, age 46, rabbi, in New York City on January 28, 1926. It showed him going to stay with Mendel Kronenberg of 214 Henry Street. According to the record, Rabbi Mendel was born in Drohiczyn.

[165] King of Assyria, 705-681 B.C.E, who put down a Jewish rebellion and laid siege to Jerusalem, thought did not destroy it.

hundred young men and women captive. When they realized what would become of them, the girls committed suicide by jumping into water, into the depths of the sea, where there are floods of water. And it is said that their reward, when they would be returned to the world, it would be as women who rule over their husbands. And for this we pray, for a worthy and moral wife, and not for a flood of water, for those who sacrificed their lives for God and would rule over their husbands."

Rabbi Menachem Mendel was a true servant of God. For a long while before he began his prayers he worked devotedly to prepare his heart and his soul for prayer. Tears flowed from his eyes, and he trembled out of fear and awe. He was a man full of devotion, but also full of joy.

When he returned from America he opened a store in Ostroveh with the money he had earned. But he soon embarked on another long journey. When he returned he felt weak and ill. Not long after, Rabbi Mendel passed away in the prime of his years, to the regret of the many who admired and respected him.[166]

Rabbi Leib Zukrovitz

Rabbi Leibel**Error! Bookmark not defined.** Zukrovitz [Cukrowicz], like his brothers Rabbis Anshel and Moshe Hersh, were among the first Ger Hassidim in the city, and among the most respected of the residents of Ostroveh. In his youth Rabbi Leibel married one of the girls from the village of Zalisz [Zalesie], which is in the Ostrow Mazowiecka area. He remained in the village for twenty years being supported by his Torah-loving father-in-law, without any worries about making a living. In this period he reached greater heights in Torah and in pure Hassidism. He would frequently travel to the courts of the *tzadikim* of Ger, the *rebbe* who was the author of *Chidushei Harim*, the *rebbe* Rabbi Chanoch Henich Hacohen of Alexander, and the *rebbe* of Ger who was the author of the *S'fat Emet*, as well as his son the *rebbe*.

Rabbi Leibel was thought of as one of the greatest Hassidim, an exalted person with a sharp and profound mind, wise and insightful, who understood that which was before him but also delved deeper. He was respected by the *rebbe*s of Ger and by the masses of Hassidim, who spoke his name with admiration and affection. After the period when he was supported by his father-in-law, Rabbi Leibel moved to Ostroveh, but he did not turn to business or to a rabbinical position, even though he was a great and distinguished scholar. He dedicated all his time up until his

---

[166] According to Ostrow Mazowiecka records, Mendel died in 1937.

last day to Torah and Hassidism, and never left the confines of Torah and good deeds.

He served as prayer leader in the great house of the Ger Hassidim in Ostroveh. He officiated at the *mussaf* services on holidays and on the High Holy Days. His voice was very pleasant and moved the hearts of all who heard him. Up until a very advanced age he maintained this ability. In the last year of his life, when he had already was in the throes of his final illness and was no longer able to get out of bed, he was brought to the house of the Hassidim in his bed, which was set down next to the pulpit, where he began his last prayer as cantor. Rabbi Leibel died in the year 5685 [1924-1925] at a very old age.[167]

His brother, Rabbi Anshel Zukrovitz, lived for some years in the town of Ciechanowiec. He, too, was among the veteran and senior Hassidim in Ostroveh. In his youth he visited the *rebbe* who was the author of *Chidushei Harim*, and after his death to his successors as *rebbe*. He was a precious Jew who had a good heart. He sold *matzot shmurah* [specially supervised *matzot* for Passover], eking out a bare living. His brother, Rabbi Hersh, was also among the senior Hassidim in Ostrow Mazowiecka. He was a beloved Jew with fine personal traits and praiseworthy behavior.

Rabbi Yeshayahu Augustover

Among the first group of Kotsk Hassidim in Ostroveh the image of Rabbi Yeshayahu Augustover [Augustor] stood out. Born in Augustow in Lithuania, he joined the community of Hassidim and became one of its best known and most outstanding members, one of the sharpest in this community of sharp Hassidim.

Behind the sharp and assertive exterior of Rabbi Yeshayahu there lay a big heart, a good and merciful one, one with exceptional personal traits that were hidden behind a cloak of an austere visage. It was said of the Kotsk Hassidim that while they were meticulous about resisting any inclination towards sin, it was nevertheless easier to find sins among them than the performance of the commandments, even though they were performing the commandments all the time, day and night. But they worked with great determination, consistency and diligence to conceal their [performance of] the commandments and good deeds from the gaze of others.

They said of Rabbi Yeshayahu that he was a great scholar, an expert in all the fields of knowledge of the Torah, but also one who

---

[167] According to the Ostrow Mazowiecka records, Lejba Wigdor Cukrowicz [Zukrowitz] was born in the town of Ciechanowiec in 1847, and died in Ostrow Mazowiecka on March 4, 1923. His wife was Sura Ryfka Markowska.

delved deeply into matters as few others. Nevertheless he did not show off his greatness in Torah to others, even to the Hassidim who were close to him. Only on extremely rare occasions, in special lighter moments, would he reveal his greatness in Torah indirectly, to the amazement of others.

Rabbi Yeshayahu served as prayer leader in the Kotsk Hassidic

house in Ostroveh. He died at a ripe old age.[168]

Reb Eliyahu Feivel Petrushka

One of the first of the Warka Hassidim in Ostroveh was Reb Eliyahu Feivel Petrushka [Petruszka or Pietruszka], a typical Hassid of the older generation. He was a dear Jew who walked a straight line, not straying a whit from the path of pure Hassidism. He was tied to that pure Hassidism with every fiber of his heart and soul. He was meticulous in his observance of the commandments and sought them out. He worked hard throughout his long life on the purity of his actions and works.

Reb Eliyahu Feivel was born in the year 5580 [1819-1820],[169] and already in his youth joined the sect of Hassidim of the *rebbe* Rabbi Yitzchak of Warka. When he was young he learned the skill as a concrete worker in construction, and all the days of his life he worked faithfully as a simple workman with his hands. His difficult and tiring work did not interfere with his Torah and pure Hassidism. In the early morning and in the evening, after a hard day at work, he made his way to the house of the Hassidim. He remained there for many hours engaging in Torah and Hassidism. The essence of his life was pure Hassidism in the style of Warka.

He did his work faithfully. He worked for himself, as an independent contractor. This enabled him to stop his work whenever he heard an inspiring Hassidic story or a saying of Torah from one of the *rebbe*s. He would then put aside his work tools, and would abandon for a few moments the lower world, the world of work, hardship and bitterness, for the upper worlds of holiness and purity, of Hassidism and Torah.

---

[168] There was a Szaja Augustower in the Ostrow Mazowiecka records who was born in 1854 and died in 1913, but he was originally from Ostrow Mazowiecka, so it is not clear if he is the same one.

[169] According to the Ostrow Mazowiecka records, Eliasz Fajba Petruszka [Petrushka] was born in Zambrow in 1842.

Reb Eliyahu Feivel attained an incredibly advanced age. He died in Warsaw in the year 5675 [1914-1915] having lived ninety-five years.[170] Up until his last day he maintained his set ways of life. For some eighty years he would enthusiastically visit the house of the Warka *rebbe*. He adhered to his teachers with all his heart and his pure soul, with his innate modesty, and full of grace and glory he covered himself in the dust of the feet of the *tzadikim*. His was an image of purity that was devoted entirely to the great mission, one that did not seek anything for himself nor think of himself whatsoever. He believed with all his heart that there was no one in the world more flawed in his character and deeds than he, and that he was far from even a whiff of Torah and Hassidism. So he had to work hard, to repent sincerely each day in order to purify his flawed body and soul.

Rabbi Avraham Pinchas and Rabbi Yitzchak Meir Landau

Reb Simcha Bunim**Error! Bookmark not defined.** Landau had seven sons, all God-fearing and very accomplished men. He was one of the loyal and devoted Hassidim of Ger, who made his living as a notary in the towns of the Ostroveh region. From time to time Reb Simcha Bunim would come into nearby Ostroveh, where he was among those near to the Gaon and Hassid Rabbi Ben-Zion Rabinowitz, one of the greatest Hassidim of recent generations.

Reb Simcha Bunim sent some of his gifted sons to Ostroveh so that they might study regularly with Rabbi Ben-Zion, while during the remaining hours they would study with other young men in the Ger house of Hassidim. One of his sons, Rabbi Avraham Pinchas, was among the best students of Rabbi Ben-Zion in terms of Torah and Hassidism, and was ultimately considered one of the most outstanding Hassidim. For economic reasons and for the lack of opportunities to make a living in Poland, he immigrated-- with the permission of the *rebbe* of Ger--to London, where he set up house. Rabbi Avraham Pinchas did credit to his faith by virtue of his deeds, his manner, his interactions, and in everything he did in England at that time. He was full of devotion and self-sacrifice for Torah and Hassidism, for the fear of God and the fear of sin. Despite his long hours in business, not a day went by when he did not work on his Torah for many hours, in an exhausting way, with intensity and devotion. When his business imposed on him unduly, he would quickly go off to some quiet place and invest himself with all his senses in the study of Torah for an entire day or more in a closed place, where no one could bother him. He fully

---

[170] A database of Warsaw Jewish cemetery burials shows an entry for Eliahu Shraga Feivel Petruszka [Petrushka], son of Avraham David, with a death date of the seventeenth of Tevet 5685 (or 5688), corresponding to 1925 or 1928, rather than 1914 or 1915.

believed that after he isolated himself in the Torah, that complex business matters would become clear. Even in London he did not abandon pure Hassidism. From time to time he visited Ger, to the court of his teacher, the *rebbe* who had brought him near and who loved him so much, and who saw in him a loyal Hassid, a true Hassid. Rabbi Avraham Pinchas founded the Agudat Yisrael movement in England and worked on behalf of Torah and Judaism in London. He died during the last world war and left behind his sons, Rabbi Yitzchak Meir of blessed memory, Rabbi Simcha Bunim, and Rabbi Noach, who continue their father's legacy.

The brother of Rabbi Avraham Pinchas, Rabbi Yitzchak Meir, settled in Ostrow Mazowiecka during World War I. He was an outstanding and wonderful Hassid. He was a scholar like few others, who was considered knowledgeable in Torah and Hassidism, wise and insightful, with exceptional personal traits. He was a merchant who worked for a living. He was very close to the Gaon and Hassid Rabbi Ben-Zion, and moved his residence to Ostroveh to be near to him.

He was extremely diligent, learning entire days and nights, working hard with all his might on Torah and Hassidism. He was considered important and honored by his teacher, the *rebbe* of Ger who authored the *S'fat Emet*, and after the latter's demise was counted among the most loyal and devoted Hassidim of the *rebbe* Rabbi Avraham Mordechai of Ger. There were times when Rabbi Yitzchak Meir would sit and learn for eighteen hours a day. He would barely sleep or eat. He was a man of devotion and self-sacrifice, as if he were prepared and ready to sacrifice his soul for his maker, for Torah and pure Judaism, without straying from it one iota.

After World War I he fell ill with a terminal disease. He was confined to bed for nearly five years, to the despair of his loyal friends and companions and his many acquaintances and admirers among the Ger Hassidim. Even when lying in his sick bed he did not cease to learn, working hard on the Torah even when he was afflicted with suffering, like a good student of the *rebbe* Rabbi Baruch of Chizov [Czyzewo], with whom he studied as a child. Rabbi Yitzchak Meir died with a fine reputation on the sixteenth day of Tevet 5688 [January 8-9, 1928] in Ostroveh. He was fifty-nine years old at his death. He left a daughter, who was later married to Reb Simcha Bunim Shafranowitz [Szafranowicz], one of best of Ostroveh, who after the Holocaust immigrated to Israel.[171]

---

[171] The Ostrow Mazowiecka records show the marriage of Chana Landa to Symcha Binym Szafranowicz [Shafranowitz] in 1937.

A third brother among the sons of Rabbi Simcha Bunim Landau, Rabbi Pesach, was also a resident of Ostroveh. And he, too, was one of the students of Rabbi Ben-Zion. He was a precious Jew, a Hassid of Ger, who also died in the prime of his life at the age of forty-seven in Ostroveh.

Rabbi Tzvi Hersh Fabianitzer

Among the group of Hassidim of Sokolow in Ostrow Mazowiecka, the persona of Rabbi Tzvi Hersh Fabianitzer stood out. He established his home in Ostroveh after he married the daughter of Rabbi Mendel Meizlish [Majzlic], one of the distinguished citizens in town. Rabbi Hersh was one of the most ardent Hassidim of the *rebbe* Rabbi Yisrael of Pilov,[172] and after his passing he joined the community of the Hassidim of the *rebbe* Rabbi Yitzchak Zelig of Sokolow. In that community he was thought of as a true servant of God, as a Hassid who aspired to attain great height in Hassidism, and as a wise man who loved Torah.

In his younger days Rabbi Hersh worked as a ritual slaughterer and made his living from that sacred occupation. He later decided to leave his post, which was not to his liking. When asked about this step he said, "There is a story told about Rabbi Zelig of Shrantzk [Szrensk], one of the great students of the Seer of Lublin, of the rabbi of Peshischa, and of the rabbi of Kotsk, who once, at the behest of the Seer of Lublin, began to study the laws of slaughtering. He opened the *Shulchan Aruch* and read the first paragraph, which said that a slaughterer must be fearful of God. He immediately closed the *Shulchan Aruch* and decided to abandon these studies. He went in to see his rabbi, the Seer, and said, 'This not a job for me. A slaughterer must be fearful of God, but I am not fearful of God, so how can I be a slaughterer?' "

Once he left his job as a slaughterer, he devoted himself entirely to Torah and good works. He was a dear Jew, a true scholar for whom the Torah was from then on the decisive factor. His diligence only increased. He stopped studying only for his prayers. And his prayers were not just incidental. He was thought by many to be a mindful type of Jew. He devoted long hours every day in preparation for prayer. He would pace back and forth in the house of the Hassidim totally wrapped up in true devotion, like a man ascending to a higher realm. And only after extensive preparation would he commence his actual prayers.

---

[172] Rabbi Chaim Yisrael Morgenstern of Pilov [Pulawy] (1804-1905), a descendant of Rabbi Menachem Mendel of Kotsk.

On the Sabbath and holidays Rabbi Hersh was completely holy. He was like a burning torch full of sacred zeal. And so he lived his entire life in Ostroveh, adding an element of holiness and Hassidism to the city up until his departure from this world, a few years before the Holocaust.

Reb Eliezer Tzvi Shafranowitz

Rabbi Eliezer Tzvi Shafranowitz [Szafranowicz] was an endearing Jew, who possessed a warm and merciful heart. He was one of the beloved citizens of Ostroveh, and one of the outstanding Ger Hassidim in town. He was a native of Ostrolenka who settled in Ostroveh and became a successful merchant. He did not keep his money for himself, but rather dispersed it for various charitable and righteous needs. He was involved in community affairs, and was a fervent Jew, always ready for any sacrifice or effort to strengthen pure Judaism and to help others. He was one of the Hassidim of the *rebbe* of Ger, the author of the *S'fat Emet*, as well as of his son, the *rebbe* Rabbi Avraham Mordechai of Ger, who undertook while in the court of his teachers a responsibility for the entire Jewish people and everything concerning it.

As a successful merchant he devoted some of his time to the repair and improvement of the *mikvaot* [ritual baths] in Ostroveh, in which he invested much money and hard work. In addition he never refused anything having to do with loving kindness and the commandments. He was always aware of what was occurring around him and ready to help. He did not pursue honors or admiration, position or status, but like a simple soldier on duty was always prepared for action.

During World War I his financial condition declined as a result of the changing governmental authorities. For a short time he left for the United States. Upon his return to his city of Ostroveh he established an institution called *Lechem Laaniyim* [Bread for the Poor], whose purpose was to distribute free bread to the needy and hungry. In this period there was no lack of wretched poor people in Poland who simply were starving for bread, families who were simply not able to give their children a piece of bread to assuage their [pangs of] hunger. He frequently saw their swollen eyes. Reb Eliezer Tzvi Shafranowitz worked on behalf of this institution and invested his energy and time in it. He raised money for it and saw to it that loaves of bread would be distributed daily to the poor with no limits. Every day lines of poor people formed to receive the bread. In Ostroveh the loaves were distributed at the office of Young Agudat Yisrael.

Reb Eliezer Tzvi died in the prime of his life. His son, Reb Simcha Bunim Shafranowitz, continued in the father's footsteps.

As the son-in-law of Rabbi Simcha Bunim Landau, he established his home locally and became one of the enthusiastic younger people in Ostrow Mazowiecka. He served as *gabbai* [officer] of the great house of the Ger Hassidim, which had more than two hundred regular worshippers, and was one of the leaders of Young Agudat Yisrael and one of the organizers of groups of young Hassidim of Ger. Reb Simcha Bunim survived the Holocaust and went to Israel, settling in Jerusalem, where he continued his work of community service on behalf of the Hassidim of Ger and was among the leaders of Agudat Yisrael.

Rabbi Avraham Yitzchak Perkal

Among the respected residents of Ostroveh was Rabbi Avraham Yitzchak Perkal, an important Ger Hassid and a great scholar who had a logical and deep mind. A professional teacher, he was the son-in-law of Rabbi Mendel Ziegelbaum [Zygielbaum or Zygielboim],[173] a respected resident of Ostroveh. Rabbi Avraham Yitzchak spent some years as a teacher in Riga, the capital of Latvia, where he worked diligently on behalf of the education of children in Torah and genuine respect for godliness.

He returned to Ostroveh, and with the establishment of the *Yesodei Hatorah* [Foundations of the Torah] institution of religious education by Agudat Yisrael, he was named head teacher of that institution. He worked hard to strengthen orthodox education in his city.

Rabbi Avraham Yitzchak succeeded in escaping to Soviet Russia at the outbreak of the Holocaust. After the war he was privileged to immigrate to Israel, settling in Jerusalem, where he died in the year 5715 [1954-1955]. His son, Rabbi Moshe Reuven Perkal, continues in his father tradition in Jerusalem. He, too, is a Hassid and scholar who engages in Torah study day and night.

Reb Michael Teitel

An outstanding figure in Ostroveh Jewry was Reb Michael Teitel [Tejtel], one of the leading men of action in the city and its immediate vicinity. He was the model of a Jewish philanthropist and man of righteousness, who possessed extremely fine personal characteristics.

Reb Michael was very wealthy. He was also a gentle soul with an aristocratic bearing, and an educated man who knew many

---

[173] The Ostrow Mazowiecka records show the marriage of Abram Icek Perkal to Ela Bejla Zygielbaum [Ziegelbaum] in 1897. The records also show a daughter of Mendel Zygielbaum named Enja Bejla, born in 1879, presumably the same Ela Bejla from the marriage record.

languages, yet was loyal to the Torah and its commandments. Every day he would go to the new *beit midrash*. He was an observer of the Torah and its commandments as he understood them. He was a man of erudition and wisdom, well respected and liked.

From his youth he joined the Zionists, and did much on behalf of Zionism in his home town. He served as chairman and patron of that movement, although he did not engage in its battles with other movements, and in fact avoided disputes and conflict altogether. He was an opponent of Hassidim and Hassidism, but at the same time was prepared to help Hassidim and any other Jews who turned to him. He gave charity generously and willingly, with love and courtesy.

During World War I, after the conquest of Ostrow Mazowiezka by the Germans, Reb Michael served as deputy mayor of the city, and did much to prevent suffering on the part of its inhabitants. His wife was also generous and did much for the poor of the city and the area. She was always ready to offer aid and succor to the suffering, and never turned down performing an act of charity.

Reb Michael eventually established a charity [free loan] fund in the city, of which he served as chairman until his death. He also served as chairman of other institutions and projects in the area. Despite the fact that he was an enthusiastic Zionist, the people of the city did not view him as a party person, but rather as a man of the people who from his high position gave with his heart and with his best efforts for the good of both the community and the individual. He was a lover of Torah who made time to study Torah, but he was also knowledgeable in world literature and world affairs. When the Gaon Rabbi Shmuel Mohilever[174] established the Group of One Thousand for the purpose of seeing that one thousand families would immigrate to the Land of Israel, Reb Michael joined that organization, and throughout his life he aspired to go to Israel. But his many prosperous business enterprises in Ostroveh prevented him from realizing his dream.

His excellence in matters of charity and righteous deeds conferred upon him an unforgettable status among the Jews of Ostroveh. Local people told many stories about the deeds and generosity of Reb Michael, who had poor tenants living in his

---

[174] Rabbi Shmuel Mohilever (1824-1898), rabbi in Bialystok, one of the pioneers of the religious Zionist movement and of the broader *Chovevei Tziyon* (Lovers of Zion) movement, a precursor to the World Zionist Organization.

properties from whom he did not even ask rent. Reb Michael died in the year 5691 [1930].[175]

Rabbi Yisrael Yosef Mioduser

Rabbi Yisrael Yosef Mioduser [Mioduszer] was born in Brok to his father, Rabbi Shmuel Nachman Mioduser, who was the rabbi of the town and one of the important rabbis in the area. He was educated from childhood in pure Torah and Hassidism. He was among the stalwarts of the Hassidim of Ger. At a young age he was married to the daughter of Rabbi Yehuda Orszitzer [Orzycer] of Rozan, one of the veteran Alexander Hassidim. For some years he was supported by his wealthy father-in-law.

During World War I Rabbi Yisrael Yosef and his family moved to Ostroveh. He opened a store which was managed by his wife, while he devoted all his time to studying diligently. Rabbi Yisrael Yosef was beloved to the Ger Hassidim and to the *rebbe* of Ger, Rabbi Avraham Mordechai. In the awful Holocaust Rabbi Yisrael Yosef and most of his family were killed.[176] Only two of his daughters survived, as they immigrated to Israel before the war, where they lived with their grandfather, the Gaon Rabbi Shmuel Nachman Mioduser,[177] who served towards the end of his life as chief of the rabbinical court of B'nei Brak. One of the daughters of Rabbi Yisrael Yosef was married to Rabbi Yitzchak Meir, one of the leaders of orthodox Jewry in Israel.

Reb Moshe Yosef Suravich

One of the richest Jews in Ostrow Mazowiecka in the years before the outbreak of the Holocaust was Reb Moshe Yosef

---

[175] According to the Ostrow Mazowiecka records, Michel Tejtel [Teitel] died in 1930. He was born in 1862.

[176] According to the aforementioned other Ostrow Mazowiecka *yizkor* book (published in Israel in 1960) and Yad Vashem Pages of Testimony, Israel Josef Mioduser [Mioduszer] (b. 1895), his wife Sheva (nee Wygodzki), and their children Mendel (b. 1921), Chaim (b. 1924?), Sura Rivka (b. 1924) and Dvoyra perished in the Holocaust in 1943 in Bialystok. The Pages of Testimony were submitted by Israel Josef's daughter, Chana Ram of Petach Tikvah, and sister, Yocheved Birati. The other surviving daughter may have been Gittel.

[177] According to various sources, Rabbi Nachman Shmuel Yaakov Mioduser (spellings vary) was born in Warsaw in 1872 and died in B'nei Brak in 1948. He was rabbi and head of the *yeshiva* in Brok and published a book of commentaries, *Amudei Yonatan* [*The Pillars of Jonathan*], named after his ancestor, Rabbi Yonatan Eybeshutz, in 1910. Passenger list records show him visiting New York City in 1923 (when he was still living in Brok), and in 1927 (by which time he was living in Palestine). He was the second head of the rabbinical court in B'nei Brak.

Suravich [Surawicz]. He was a Hassid of Ger and an educated man, who was very successful in business as the owner of the largest wholesale market in the entire area.

Reb Moshe Yosef was a loyal Hassid, one of the honored men among the Hassidim of Ger who sat at the table of the *rebbe* of Ger. He gave to charity and served as the recognized address for serious major gifts. He was open to spending great sums for important undertakings. It is said that Reb Moshe Yosef gave significant sums anonymously, without unnecessary publicity.

With the outbreak of the Holocaust Reb Moshe Yosef and his wife fled to Soviet Russia, where he spent the war years. He never had any children. After the war he immigrated to Israel, where after a few years he passed away.[178]

Rabbi Eliezer Stelung

Polish Jewry was very diverse. Various different types of people inhabited its cities and towns. Each city and town had its own special characters and types. Every community had different and sometimes unusual people, both as to their personality and character, and in the ways they related to people. Among them were rare individuals who were larger than life and who were exceptional. Among them were a handful of extraordinary people, but who nevertheless did not live outside the bounds of the grim day-to-day existence of the masses. There were among them those who had great and pure souls that were hard to find in later generations. One such unique personality was a person who was referred to in Ostroveh as Rabbi "Leizer Yedshiver," who was in fact Rabbi Eliezer Stelung [Sztelung], may God avenge his blood.

Rabbi Eliezer was orphaned as a young child. He was then raised by his widowed mother, who worked to the very limits of her strength to stave off the shame of hunger from her children. As young Leizer grew up, he wandered from *yeshiva* to *yeshiva*, from city to city to learn Torah. In order not to be a burden on his poor widowed mother, he suffered greatly during his many years of wandering, but also excelled in his studies. It was as if he invested all his pain and suffering, the orphanhood that hovered over him from his earliest years, in his studies.

As a young man who excelled in his Torah studies he had reached the stage where marriage proposals began to come his way. A shoemaker from the small village of Yedshiveh [probably Andrzejewo] near near Chizov, which had some fifty Jewish

---

[178] According to the Ostrow Mazowiecka records, Moszek Josel Surawicz [Surawitz], son of Lejb and Szejna Gitla (nee Orlinski), was born in Czyzewo in 1874. In 1894 he married Chawa Markus in Ostrow Mazowiecka.

families, managed to "snag" him. In those days in Poland, before
World War I, it was the life's dream of every shoemaker or tailor
who worked hard for a living by the sweat of his brow to secure a
good son-in-law for his family, like a bright young student who
would eventually become a rabbi or a teacher in a *yeshiva* or at
least a scholar, a man of standing among his people. From early
morning to late evening these Jewish artisans would sit bent over
their small benches, engaging in their wearisome work. The never
took time off and never saw the light of day all year long. They
never left the confines of their home towns. Their place in the
house of study [and prayer] was along the western wall, near the
entrance, among the poor people. They understood Hebrew with
difficulty. They were embarrassed by their ignorance of the fine
print. They were jealous of the learned ones and the sharp
Hassidim who occupied the eastern wall and who looked down on
working people.

"Snagging" a learned son-in-law, a man of stature in society,
was seen by them as compensation for their years of hard work, as
a badge of honor, as an entry card to a more honorable status.
Such a father-in-law would boast about such a son-in-law, would
praise him frequently and would hold him up as a role model at
every opportunity. A poor shoemaker would make due all his life
with very little, only eating a modest main meal late at night, after
finishing an exhausting day of work, which at times lasted up to
fifteen hours. He would live in a small and wretched home. He
hardly ever changed his clothes all his life, keeping one suit for the
Sabbath and holidays and one beat up old garment for work. Over
the years he would save a penny at a time, ruble by ruble, from
his meager income. And from this money that he saved he would
provide a dowry to his son-in-law, would provide him with a nice
home, and would even provide for his needs for a few years. He
invested his entire life's work in his son-in-law who was a student
of Torah, a scholar who sat and learned in the study hall, who
gave pride to his father-in-law who worked with his hands.

It was a poor shoemaker like this who "snagged" Rabbi Eliezer.
He supported him for a number of years and saw to all his needs.
For many years Rabbi Eliezer sat and learned day and night in the
study hall in Yedshiveh without any worries about making a living.
He frequently would travel to his teacher and rabbi, the *rebbe* of
Ger, with whom he was connected by every fiber of his heart and
soul. He was prepared to do anything on behalf of his rabbi. Rabbi
Eliezer Yedshiver was thought of as one of the most ardent and
loyal Hassidim.

During World War I the small village was burnt to the ground
and all its inhabitants scattered. Rabbi Leizer moved to Ostroveh,

where he lived up until the horrific Holocaust. Problems and suffering marked all the days of his residence there. Sickness and pain afflicted the members of his family. But these troubles did not shatter his spirit, did not affect his pure Hassidism, his holy work or his studies. On the contrary, with his sweet voice--he was an unusually fine cantor and a gifted musician--was able to uplift himself and others with his melodies.

He was a great scholar as well, and he pursued his studies diligently up until his final day. At three in the morning he was to be found in the study hall, summer and winter, despite the difficult times he was experiencing, always awake and full of enthusiasm as he approached his daily lessons. He was an ardent Ger Hassid and remained so until he died. And he was a loyal and enthusiastic Agudat Yisrael person, as if this were a holy task. Following in this path of his, he was not afraid of anyone nor was he servile to anyone. If he saw something that in his opinion was counter to logic, justice and the public good, he would immediately raise his voice and express his strong opposition, whether it was in the Ger house of Hassidim, which was always full of worshippers and learners, or in meetings held by Agudat Yisrael. At the outbreak of the Holocaust Rabbi Eliezer escaped to Russia, where he died.

Reb David Rechtman

A unique and special person was Reb David Rechtman, one of the Hassidim of Ger in Ostrow Mazowiecka. He was a Hassid and a scholar who loved Torah, who was particularly scrupulous and stringent in his observance of the commandments. He was a merchant whose wife managed his store, leaving him free to engage in communal affairs, especially within the framework of Agudat Yisrael. He was a member of the central committee of Agudat Yisrael in Poland and its representative in Ostroveh. He frequently traveled to other cities in Poland to speak and to do work on behalf of Agudat Yisrael. He was an excellent speaker, much in demand, and he performed all this work gratis out of complete loyalty to the ideology and world view of Agudat Yisrael.

Reb David was full of inner energy and initiative. Not a moment in his life was wasted. He was always conscious and full of faith in the future. At the same time he never tolerated any wrongdoing or unjust act that might occur in Agudat Yisrael. He would immediately raise his voice and would not be silenced under any circumstances. He would never be reconciled to any corruption in public affairs, and was prepared to combat it even against those forces larger and more powerful than he. He was not intimidated by the fall-out from such a battle. He was not afraid of anyone nor did he cower before anyone. "When it is a matter of violation of public morals, one is not obliged to bow to the majority," he contended. Every act that violated the fundamentals of justice and pure morality, the finest sentiments of pure Hassidism, he saw as a public embarrassment. Such manifestations must be fought with all one's heart and with every means at one's disposal. In the horrendous Holocaust, Reb David died for the sanctification of God's name.[179]

Reb Leibel Segal

Among the outstanding Hassidim who filled the house of Hassidim of Ger in Ostroveh was Rabbi Leib Segal, son of the great and renowned Hassid Rabbi Yisrael Segal of Makow. He married the daughter of Rabbi Yitzchak Gershon Warshauer, one of the important residents of Ostroveh, and from then on lived in the city. Like his brother-in-law, Rabbi Yosef Pravda, he ran a store selling iron products in Ostroveh. At the same time he engaged in the study of Torah in all his spare time. He had a refined soul and spirit, replete with a fine character, a noble personality whom many adored and admired. He was a one who inspired respect for his honesty, his deeds and his contacts with other people, whether in his business or in any of his activities. He worked hard to continue the legacy of his father, the Hassid and well rounded man, Rabbi Yisrael.

Reb Leib passed away in Russia. His wife and children survived the war and immigrated to the United States, where they continue their father's great tradition. The son of Reb Leib, Rabbi Yitzchak Gershon, is a scholar and a man of high morals. Reb Leib's son-in-law, by the name of Tzivyak, is one of the top lay leaders of orthodox Jewry in the United States.

Others Who Passed On

There was no lack of outstanding people in Jewish Ostroveh, great scholars and dedicated Hassidim, people who performed good works and who were righteous. It was a city full of beloved Jews who stood out in every realm in which they were involved. Each group had its excellent people, every movement its people of great abilities. There were those who perished in the Holocaust along with the members of their families, who disappeared in that great sacrifice without leaving a trace or memory. Among them

---

[179] According to the Ostrow Mazowiecka records, Dawid Rechtman, son of Aron and Chawa Dwojra (nee Margulis), was born about 1882 and was married to Ruchla Leja (nee Seres). They had a son, Mnochim.

were those who did not succeed to have their names written in the pages of a book to be preserved for future generations.

Today Jewish Ostroveh is eerily silent, where it once bustled with activity in every realm. There is not even a trace of the old *beit midrash*, a place of Torah study and prayer for generations of Jews of the city. The voice of Torah and of prayer has been silenced in this holy site. The worshippers of this prayer house and its many wonderful people whose lives had become an integral part of the *beit midrash* have gone on to the heavens above.

In the silent streets of Ostroveh the voice of Reb Moshe Grudka, a poor man who devoted his life to the sick and weak, is no longer heard. A dear and beloved Jew and a Ger Hassid, he made his way on foot to the *rebbe* even in the last years before the Holocaust with just a little bread in his bag. He was an exceptional man who organized a late midnight study session every night. A poor and impoverished man, he was viewed by many as one of the *lamed vav*[180] in his generation. He was a Jew who worked hard to perform the commandments devotedly, in an effort to do everything whole heartedly. His son, Reb Leibel, a wealthy man, partially supported him so that Reb Moshe he could fulfill his heart's and his soul's aspirations. In the mines of Archangel, Siberia, where tortured captives exerted had labor and sweat, he returned his pure soul to its maker.[181]

Gone from the old study hall forever is Reb Yaakov Velvel the porter, a Jew who labored for his living, but who every evening sat in the old study hall, studying a chapter of the Mishnah with a large group. Reb Yaakov Velvel was a true son of Torah. Also gone were the *shamashim* [beadles] of the old study hall, the sweet elderly Rabbi Tanchum, a man of acuity and wisdom who, even when he was on his death bed nearing the end, never lost his sharpness, saying to his wife, "Don't cry, don't be afraid. As long as I am alive they won't take me from here."

Similar to him was Rabbi Natan Zelig, who was an even greater scholar than Rabbi Tanchum. In his youth Rabbi Natan Zelig studied at the famed *yeshiva* of Slobodka. As he was a giant in his knowledge of Torah as well as in his character, so much so that

---

[180] *Lamed vav*, the Hebrew letters corresponding to the number thirty-six which, according to an ancient Jewish legend, corresponds with the minimum number of unknown truly righteous people in every generation who exist in the world at any given time.

[181] Possibly the same as Mosze Grodke [Grudka], for whom a Page of Testimony was submitted to Yad Vashem by his daughter Sheyna, indicating that he was born in Ostrow Mazowiecka in 1892 to Avraham and Chaya, was married to Chana Vishka Levkovich (likely Olowkowicz), and died in Russia, as did his wife.

rabbis did not wish to accept his services, out of respect for the Torah. But Rabbi Natan Zelig was not deterred. Similar to him was Reb Aharkeh the beadle, a scholar and servant of God.

Silent, too, is the wonderful voice of Reb Chaikel the cantor, who had a beautiful tenor voice. The sweetness of his prayers was enjoyed by all the residents of the city, many of whom crowded into the old study hall just to hear his services. He was a smart man, a scholar and a sharp person. He, too, regularly taught the Pentateuch with commentaries to the congregation, adding his own innovative thoughts to his teaching.

Dear Jews with exceptional character traits were not lacking at the old *beit midrash* in Ostroveh. For example, there was Reb Moshe Chaim Wilenski,[182] a wine merchant whose home was always generously open to all comers. He suffered greatly beyond all measure, but this did not in any way diminish his charity and good works. Reb Moshe Chaim was not among the richest men in the city, but this did not prevent him from running a charitable [free loan] fund with his own money. And there was no one who was in need of such aid who was not helped by Reb Moshe Chaim. He was a true Hassid, a scholar, and was beloved by all. He was once asked to sign a guarantee in the sum of seven hundred zlotys. He responded positively, but added, "I will go home and check if my assets total that much." He went home and returned and signed the guarantee. In the horrendous Holocaust Reb Moshe, his wife and his five children were all killed.

Those who stood out for their acts of charity and righteousness, their devotion and self-sacrifice, were not rare. Reb Isaac Shtepper [Shteffer], an artisan who barely eked out a living, never tired of helping people. His home was like a real assembly hall for guests. Reb Mendel Feinzeig,[183] known in town as Mendel

---

[182] A Page of Testimony at Yad Vashem for Moshe Vilenski [Wilenski] of Ostrow Mazowiecka, submitted by a relative, indicates that he was born in Stok in 1880, owned a liquor store, and perished in 1943-1944. There are also Pages of Testimony for his daughters Sima (b. 1907) and Frida (b. 1910) and his son Yakov (b. 1913). According to the records of Ostrow Mazowiecka, his wife's name was Bejla (nee Kac or Katz). Their marriage was recorded in 1896.

[183] A relative of this editor. As the name Mendel (like the name Yaakov) was so common in the large extended Feinzeig family, sometimes holders of that name were given "nicknames," in this case that of his mother-in-law, Elke, to distinguish them from others of the same name. The story of Reb Mendel and his coat is still frequently told in the family. This editor heard it again from his cousin, H. E. Dr. Jaime Feinzaig [the Spanish spelling of the name], Ambassador of Costa Rica to Italy, when visiting him in the embassy in Rome in 2013. With the severe restrictions on immigration to the U.S. from Eastern Europe (largely Jews) imposed by the Johnson-Reed Act of 1924 (with exceptions made for immediate family of those already here, as in the case of this editor's direct ancestors), many other

"Elke's," excelled with his warm and big heart in an incomparable manner. It was told that Reb Mendel once ran into a poor man who did not even have a coat on his body. Reb Mendel took him aside to a quiet corner and made him put on his own coat. Reb Mendel went home without a coat.

There was no lack of such people in the new *beit midrash* either. Reb Nachum Levartowitz [Lewartowicz], who was thought of as a wealthy man, was a worshipper at the new study hall. Above and beyond his wealth he was known as a charitable man. Poor people stood in line outside his store, where he willingly and lovingly provided them with everything. This Reb Nachum was the son of Rabbi Fishel David, one of the distinguished citizens of Ostroveh, who was one of the leaders in education in the city. Similar to him was Rabbi Meir Leshtsh [Leszcz], an educated man who heart was open to all.

Feinzeigs who sought to leave Poland for the U.S. afterwards wound up in various Central and South American countries, including Costa Rica, Mexico, Argentina, Uruguay and Brazil. Others, especially the more Zionistically-inclined among them, went to Mandatory Palestine/Israel. Many of their descendants continue to live in those countries today.

*Rabbi Aharon Bengelsdorf, one of the
distinguished and honored citizens of Ostroveh,
father-in-law of the Gaon Rabbi Moshe Goldblatt
and the Gaon Rabbi Moshe Yosef Mandelkorn*

There were also Jews who were very knowledgeable in the Torah at the Hassidic house of Amshinov in Ostroveh. There was Rabbi Motel Kashimacher, a beloved Jew who sat and learned day and night, an excellent and renowned scholar who completed the entire Talmud every year, and Rabbi Godel, a distinguished citizen of the town, in whose home the Hassidim of Amshinov were wont to gather on every holiday. Rabbi Itche Itkis was a devoted Amshinov Hassid with whom few could compare.

Among the worshippers at the Amshinov house of Hassidim was Reb Mendel Bilgoray, known in town as Reb Mendel *chessler* [Polish for carpenter], a contractor who made his living with the labor of his hands, but who was knowledgeable in Jewish learning and was always content with his lot. Once Reb Mendel met another Jew who was smoking a cigarette on the the Sabbath. He chased him and hollered at him because he was violating the Sabbath. The Sabbath violator grabbed an iron bar and broke Reb Mendel's skull. Despite the fact that he was bleeding Reb Mendel continued to shout at this apostate. He immigrated to the land of Israel before the last world war and lived a long life. He died in Jerusalem on the eleventh of Adar 5714 [March 16, 1954] at the age of ninety-six. His grandson, Rabbi Leib Bilgoray, is one of the leading Hassidim of Ger in New York.[184]

Hassidim and outstanding people were not lacking in the house of Hassidim of Alexander in Ostroveh either. Take for example Rabbi Yissachar Srebrnik, who served for many years as a teacher, and afterwards as a supervisor in the *Talmud Torah* in the city. In the evening of his life he maintained the *Talmud Torah* through his own efforts. In the sweltering days of summer and in the difficult days of winter he beat a path to the doorsteps of the residents, working non-stop on behalf of the *Talmud Torah*. Despite his advanced age he did not cease his sacred work. He was a scholar and an enthusiastic Hassid, who did what he did for the sake of the divine. He attained an advanced age and died in Ostroveh a few years before the Holocaust.

Another example was Reb Moshe Rosenzweig, one of the important Hassidim of Alexander in town, a scholar and Hassid,

[184] Abram Mendel Bilgoraj was born in the town of Jablonka in 1861. He immigrated to Israel in 1936. His grandson Isaac Leib Bilgoraj (1921-1988) spent the war years in Shanghai and immigrated to the United States in 1947, taking up residence in Brooklyn.

as well as a community leader and activist like few in his time. He was a man of dedication and self-sacrifice. He was also among the founders and trustees of the house of Agudat Yisrael and one of the heads of the *Chevrah Kadisha* [burial society], who worked gratis for a higher purpose. He was a merchant who dedicated much of his time to Torah and Hassidism. Or take Rabbi Meir Leshtsh [Leszcz], son-in-law of Rabbi Chaim Vshebor [Wszebor], one of the distinguished citizens of Ostroveh. He was a devotee and scholar of Torah, but also an ardent and exceptional Hassid. He was one of the intimates of the rebbe who was the author of *Yismach Yisrael* [*Israel Will Rejoice*], and his stand-in in Alexander. For a few years he served as the representative of Agudat Yisrael and the Alexander Hassidim on the community council, as one of the officers of the burial society, and one of the leaders of the *Maot Chitim* project [literally "funds for wheat," which raised money for *matza* for the needy on Passover], as a founder of the municipal savings and loan society, and later as one of the heads of the Bank Spoldzielczy. He had a fine appearance and exceptional personal traits. Reb Meir died in Ostroveh at the age of seventy in the year 5695 [1935].

The Hassidic house of Ger served as a center of fine and beloved Jews, exceptional people, scholars and Hassidim, including those who were mentioned in this chapter and those who were not mentioned at all. Among them were very distinguished residents such as Reb Zalman Yosef Nutkewitz [Nutkiewicz], representative of Agudat Yisrael on the town council, a wealthy and charitable man, or Reb Hersh Yaakov Feinsilber [Fajnzilber], a charitable man of high personal traits, a devoted and outstanding son of the Torah, who gave charity with all his heart and soul, with both hands and with his heart in an manner beyond compare. There was also Rabbi Shalom Dorembus, a scholar and true Hassid, a poor man but one of the few truly exceptional men. There was also Rabbi Tzvi Hersh Rosen, a well known Hassid, one of the outstanding members of the Sokolow Hassidim, and Rabbi Yitzchak Yaakov Podbilewitz [Podbielewicz], one of the loyal Hassidim of Strikov, who was educated in the *yeshivot* of Lithuania, a scholar and a man of knowledge, who always set aside time to study Torah. He was a leader in the Mizrachi movement, who represented that movement in the community for many years. Rabbi Meir Yaakov Bergstein was one of the leaders of the Warka Hassidim in Ostroveh and father-in-law of Rabbi Avraham Eliyahu Munz, who pursued Torah and good works in Ostroveh for many years. Every seven years he would complete the study of the Talmud. He also performed many charitable deeds. He arranged a midnight study session and served as an officer of the *Talmud Torah* for nine years. He was one of the leaders of the burial society and of the *Maot Chitim* project. Rabbi Meir Yaakov immigrated to the Land of Israel in the year 5685 [1924-1925], and died in Jerusalem on the third of Elul, 5695 [August 31-September 1, 1935]. His sons are Rabbi Avraham Abba and Rabbi Naftali Hertz Livezer. Rabbi Meir Yaakov barely eked out a living while he lived in Jerusalem. Despite that he was always happy to serve God with youthful enthusiasm.

Chapter Eleven
The Yeshiva of Novhardok
in Ostrow Mazowiecka

The Gaon Rabbi Yosef Yozel

In about the year 5608 [1847-1848] the Gaon Rabbi Yosef Yozel Horowitz was born in the town of Plungian [Plunge] in Lithuania. He was the son of Rabbi Shlomo Zalman Ziv, who served as *dayan* [religious judge] in that town. From Plungian Rabbi Shlomo Zalman moved to Kurtuvian [Kurtuvenai], which is near Shavli [Siauliai], to serve as chief of the rabbinical court. And it was there that the man who would grow up eventually to be a founder of the *mussar* [ethics] movement[185] and of the Novhardok *yeshivot* was educated.

Rabbi Shlomo Zalman, his father, became known locally and beyond as a righteous man who was completely removed from worldly matters, a diligent person who studied Torah day and night. He never left the confines of his town. He lived and studied Torah in poverty. He generally studied by candle light. But if he lacked sufficient money to buy a candle, he would go out into the streets of the town and stand and study by the light of the moon. He was meticulous in his observance of the commandments like no one else. For example, he never wore anything other than clothing made of linen, lest he were to inadvertently violate the prohibition against *shatnez* [the wearing of a garment of linen and wool]. Therefore the locals called him the "Rabbi of the Linens."

Rabbi Shlomo Zalman did not even know what a coin looked like, except for the three kopeks [pennies] that he would pay the bath attendant every week. He once received a half ruble coin, which in size resembled that of a kopek. He gave it to the bath attendant, who was dumfounded, asking why he was being given such a coin? Rabbi Shlomo Zalman could not understand his surprise, explaining that it was the same coin he would give him every week, just a different color!

His wife, like him, excelled in her righteousness and in her acts of kindness. The two of them provide a very strict education to their children marked by extreme care in their performance of

---

[185] The *mussar* movement was an educational and social movement within Eastern European orthodox Judaism, especially in the non-Hassidic (Mitnagdic) *yeshivot* of Lithuania, beginning in the mid-late nineteenth century, which emphasized greater attention be paid both to individual as well as communal ethics in the context of Halacha. Its founder was Rabbi Yisrael Salanter (1810-1883).

commandments and in all their actions. But it was not easy to restrain Rabbi Yosef Yozel as a small child. He was a wild child like no other in town. He had a strong spirit, but also exceptional abilities. When he was barely sixteen he was already giving a regular lecture in the house of study in Kurtuvian to the young men who studied there under his father's aegis.

When he was still quite young he married a woman who was the daughter of Yaakov Stein, a shopkeeper in the city of Shvekshna [Sveksna] in Lithuania near the German [East Prussian] border. Between the time of the engagement and the wedding the father of the bride died, leaving a widow and eight small now orphaned children, as well as the eldest, the bride, still at home. Some members of his family now advised to call off the match, lest the entire burden of supporting the family would devolve upon the groom. But Rabbi Shlomo Zalman would not permit this harm to fall upon the fatherless bride. So after a brief period the wedding took place. Rabbi Yosef Yozel began to run the store and was very successful, while still devoting time to the study of the Torah and to delivering a regular lecture to the local residents. As a result of his business Rabbi Yosef Yozel frequently visited the city of Memel, where Rabbi Yisrael Salanter, the father of the *mussar* movement, then resided. Rabbi Yosef Yozel met Rabbi Yisrael Salanter and was profoundly influenced by him. He became an adherent of the *mussar* movement, abandoning his store and his business. From that day forward until the end of his life he was dedicated to Torah and *mussar*.

He moved to Kovno [Kaunas], and with incomparable energy threw himself entirely into Torah and good works. He studied eighteen hours a day, most of it standing so that he would not nod off. Under the supervision of the leaders of the *mussar* movement, students of the Gaon Rabbi Yisrael**Error! Bookmark not defined.** Salanter, he worked on the improvement of his own personal traits. He aspired to achieve perfection. It was not long before the name of Rabbi Yosef Yozel became known as a *gaon* of Torah as well as one of the giants of *mussar*. In this period his wife bore a daughter, her third and last child, after which she passed away. This tragic event greatly affected Rabbi Yosef Yozel, who gave his baby daughter over to a nursemaid and his two sons to members of his family, while he closeted himself in a room in the home of Reb Shlomo Hoffhach in Slobodka and did not leave it for a year and a half. Reb Shlomo and his wife, lovers of Torah, passed him small amounts of food through a passage in order to sustain him. During this period he did not speak to or see anyone. He was totally alone with his maker and his Torah, seeking perfection. This did not sit well with the rabbis. The secular people made fun of the isolate. Rabbi Yosef Yozel steeled his spirit and soul for what was to come. He paid no attention to those who mocked him, saying, "One has to achieve right thinking, clear thought." Secular "enlightenment" Jews could not accept Rabbi Yosef Yozel's actions, which had attracted widespread attention. They preferred to characterize the rabbis and the giants of Torah as leeches who sucked the blood of the poor. And now one of these giants of the Torah was thumbing his nose at the world. These critics hid a package of counterfeit bills near the room, and proceeded to inform the Russian police that a secret counterfeiting workshop was located in the hideout of this infamous loner. The purpose was clear: to portray Rabbi Yosef Yozef as a counterfeiter and not as a man of higher purposes, and along with him to denigrate the other Torah and *mussar* scholars as well. The daughter of Reb Shlomo Hoffhach happened to find the counterfeit money, and threw the package away. Soon thereafter the police appeared. They conducted a thorough investigation and did not find anything. Nevertheless they forcibly opened the door of the room of the self-secluded Rabbi Yosef Yozel and ordered him to leave it.

There was a property owner who had built Rabbi Yosef Yozel a small house in the middle of a thick forest near Novhardok, to which Rabbi Yozel moved. He continued to distance himself from all worldly matters and to abstain from all physical and material pleasures. He continued working on his Torah and character, and developed a new approach to the subject of ethics. Rabbi Yosef Yozel proposed to separate himself entirely from worldly matters, and to live out his days in that lonely house in the woods. But his great teacher, the Gaon Rabbi Simcha Zussel Broida,[186] one of the leaders of the *mussar* movement, influenced him to change his mind. For it is incumbent upon man to work to benefit the community, and not just himself. Rabbi Yosef Yozel accepted his advice and decided to do something about it.

The Novhardok Movement

Rabbi Yosef Yozel now became active on behalf of the Torah, seeking to strengthen it, and exhibiting an incomparable level of energy. He established a *kolel* [advanced study institute] for outstanding young married men in the town of Lubitz, which is near Novhardok. Once this *kolel* was up and running, and such young men were studying there, he turned to setting up a second *kolel* and a third. Soon a network of *kolel*s was operating in Shavli and Dvinsk, in Minsk and in Warsaw, in Berditchev and in

---

[186] Rabbi Simcha Zussel Ziv Broida (or Braude) (1824-1898), known as the *Alter* [Old Man] of Kelm.

Novhardok, in Odessa and in Zhetil (Dziyatlava, now in Belarus], and in Lida. Rabbi Yosef Yozel appointed the Gaon Rabbi Yitzchak Blazer as head of the network. He served as the central pillar and principal support for the existence and development of these *kolel*s. The young men of these institutes became the admirers of the Gaon Rabbi Yosef Yozel, who influenced them to spread the study of the Torah and to prefer the position of an instructor in one of these institutes over that of a rabbi. These young married students, among them many great Torah scholars, responded to his words enthusiastically. They were quickly attracted to the energy, enthusiasm and devotion of the founder of the *kolel*s.

The network of *kolel*s soon became a lively movement under the direction of Rabbi Yosef Yozel. From institutes for young married men he moved on to establishing *yeshivot* for younger, unmarried men. The first such *yeshiva* he set up was alongside the *kolel* in Berditchev, where he appointed his brother-in-law, the Gaon Rabbi Zelig Tarshish, who had succeeded his own father in the rabbinate in Kurtuvian, as head. He established a second *yeshiva* near his home in Novhardok, where there were soon some three hundred young students. The influence of Rabbi Yosef Yozel on his many students exceeded all previously known dimensions in the world of *yeshivot*. His devotion, his willingness to sacrifice, his energy that amazed so many, the incomparable strength of his endurance, his remarkable confidence, his manner and style that was like a guidebook for purifying one's character, all engendered enthusiasm and admiration in the hearts of his students, who adhered to his philosophy heart and soul and who were prepared to go to any lengths for their teacher.

Rabbi Yosef Yozel established specific procedures for the *yeshivot* under his influence. One basic foundation was the study of *mussar* and practical work to improve one's good behavior via active efforts to control one's ethics and good traits. As he had great rhetorical abilities, the students abandoned all else and followed his method with great enthusiasm. Around him there arose a circle of senior students who, in a few years, became lecturers of great status, giants in terms of *mussar* and personal character. They led groups that actively worked to eliminate undesirable traits while disregarding the critics. All this was done with attention to living modestly, in poverty, with loyalty to the fundamentals of the philosophy and methods of Rabbi Yosef Yozel.

When World War I broke out and the battle lines moved closer to Novhardok, the Gaon Rabbi Yosef**Error! Bookmark not defined.** Yozel and his *yeshiva* moved to Homel in Russia. Most of the *yeshivot* that then operated in Lithuania closed their doors and sent their students home until the crisis would pass. Rabbi Yosef

Yozel determined otherwise. He held on to his *yeshivot* with intensified energy precisely because of the emergency situation out of devotion and self-sacrifice. In this period, in addition to the yeshiva in Homel, he established eight other *yeshivot* that followed his methods and direction, calling them "Novhardok *yeshivot*," in all the major cities of Russia, in Kiev and Kharkov, in Nizhniy-Novgorod, in Rostov, Tsaritsyn, Saratov, Pavlograd and Chernigov. He even set up a *yeshiva* in Moscow near the Kremlin, under the very windows of the rulers of Russia. As heads of the *yeshivot* he appointed the most outstanding of his students, excellent unmarried or married young men who worked under this tutelage. The sacrifice and devotion that Rabbi Yosef Yozel and his students made and invested in the establishment of the *yeshivot* and their upkeep under extremely difficult circumstances and dedication were indescribable.

A revolution now broke out in Russia. Bloody domestic battles disrupted normal ways of life. The condition of the Jews deteriorated from day to day. But Rabbi Yosef Yozel and his students were not deterred. They intensified their efforts with greater energy, and their enthusiasm only grew. The Red Army strengthened its rule and was about to destroy the existing *yeshivot*. Rabbi Yosef Yozel ordered that they continue, ready to make any sacrifice. The *yeshivot* of Novhardok continued to function out of devotion and glorification of God's name. More than once they endangered their lives, standing up to drawn guns, but they were not intimidated. As the situation worsened and matters reached an intolerable point, Rabbi Yosef Yozel and his students continued, but for lack of choice the *yeshivot* began to move from White Russia [Belarus] towards Ukraine. But the cruel arm of the communist regime reached the *yeshivot* of Novhardok everywhere. The heads of the *yeshivot* and their students were brought before people's courts. Without fear or timidity the students of Rabbi Yosef Yozel stood up at their trials. They mocked their tormentors and continued in their own ways.

Rabbi Yosef Yozel moved from Homel to Kiev, where he set up the center of the Novhadrok *yeshivot*. Gangs of murderers of the anti-Bolshevist Russian White Army now launched pogroms on the Jews of Ukraine and Kiev. The students of the Novhardok *yeshivot* had all moved to the Kiev area to be within the sphere of operation of the Gaon Rabbi Yosef Yozel. At times entire groups of young men were taken out and killed by these murderers. Sometimes students and their teachers were arrested and incarcerated under difficult conditions. But the *yeshivot* of Novhardok continued to function despite all the difficulties. Some studied in dark basements, while others hid in cemeteries. They persevered under all conditions.

The situation only got worse. When the forces of the murderous Ukrainians triumphed and slaughtered thousands of Jews wherever they found them, Rabbi Yosef Yozel ordered his students to gather in Kiev into the five *yeshivot* that he had established there in five different districts in the city. He continued in his work with full confidence and with incomparable strength of will. He would frequently cite the scriptural passage, "I have hidden my face from you in anger, I have quickly turned away from you, but with mercy will I gather you up." On Yom Kippur, the last of his life, all of the students of his *yeshivot* who were Kiev gathered around him. Rabbi Yosef Yozel outdid himself on that holy day. He had demanded of himself and of his students to withstand the madness of the times at all costs, not to retreat, to demand of themselves to fight for the greater truth until their last breath, to hold on despite the very difficult and bitter challenges.

The war left its impact. A plague of infectious typhus broke out in Kiev, especially among the many refugees living in the synagogues and among the students of the *yeshivot* who lacked the most basic conditions of a normal life. Nearly all the students of Rabbi Yosef**Error! Bookmark not defined.** Yozel were sick in bed. Sixteen of them died of the disease. Only three students and Rabbi Yosef Yozel himself were not infected. Under his supervision they began to devotedly tend to the ill. The *gaon*, who was over seventy, greatly weakened himself and seriously endangered his own life. People said that he should be restrained from undertaking such efforts, from dangerously tending to the sick, but Rabbi Yozef Yozel paid them no heed. He tended to the sick day and night until he himself was infected with the disease. Having used up his strength, he fell sick into his bed, from which he never would emerge. On the seventeenth day of Kislev in the year 5680 [December 9, 1919] he returned his pure and holy soul to its maker.

In grief and pain his many students, along with thousands of the residents of city, transported Rabbi Yosef**Error! Bookmark not defined.** Yozel to his grave. At his grave they took upon themselves the obligation to continue in his path and not to abandon his teachings. For two years his students had fought the tough battle in Bolshevik Russia. They worked underground and they even organized *yeshivot* in prisons. In the year 5682 [1921-1922] the Gaon Rabbi Yisrael Meir Hacohen, author of the *Chafetz Chaim* [*Lover of Life*], ruled that they should give up this hopeless battle, and should move to Poland by any means possible, even by sneaking across the border. They fulfilled this instruction with great dedication. Thus opened a new chapter in the history of the *yeshivot* of Novhardok, but this time in [newly] independent Poland.

The Yeshiva of Novhardok in Ostroveh

By whatever means possible the students of Rabbi Yosef Yozel arrived in Poland, fanning out across its cities. Schooled in suffering and self-sacrifice, prepared to work even under the worst and most terrible conditions, they confronted the task of rebuilding the movement of the Novhardok *yeshivot*. They crossed the border illegally into Poland. By way of forest paths the loyalists of the Novhardok *yeshivot* eluded the men of the Yevseksia [the Jewish division of the Soviet secret police]. They established more than sixty *yeshivot* across the length and breadth of Poland, succeeding in their mission far more than could be expected. Even in Ostroveh two students of the Gaon Rabbi Yosef Yozel arrived, the Gaon Rabbi Yoel Kleinerman and the Gaon Rabbi Aharon Anolik (or as he was called by those from Novhardok, Rabbi Aharon Kamaier), as well as the Gaon Rabbi Meir Segal (today in Haifa).

All this was in the year 5682 [1921-1922]. Life in Poland had not yet resumed its normal course after the war and its terrible shocks. The secular movements in the Jewish community made every effort to recruit Jewish youth into their ranks, to cut them off from their roots, to remove them from the houses of study. The students of the Gaon Rabbi Yosef Yozel contributed their great efforts to strengthen the ramparts of pure Judaism, to rebuild the fortresses of Torah in the country, albeit in the style of the Lithuanian *yeshivot* and according to the methodology and path of the Gaon Rabbi Yosef Yozel Horowitz.

The first group of young men who arrived in Ostroveh met with a mixed reception on the part of the residents of the city. The local Hassidim were not used to the Lithuanian style of learning and prayer, and to this type of yeshiva altogether. Opponents among the town's residents included those who had been educated in other, regular Lithuanian *yeshivot*, who did not subscribe to the Novhardok method in theory or practice, nor to their manner of dress or their behavior. The heads of the [new] *yeshiva* in town paid no attention to the views of the residents or their reactions. They had been trained by their esteemed rabbi to function under any circumstances, and even escaped from Russia, where conditions were difficult and terrifying. So their situation in Ostroveh seemed like a veritable Garden of Eden.

The *yeshiva* was located in the old *beit midrash*. The students who enrolled, whether from the town or nearby areas, somehow managed to find lodging among the residents of the city. With the help of a very minimal budget it all started to function. Bit by bit the new *yeshiva* struck very deep roots in the city. Many residents began to relate with growing affection to the *yeshiva*, which became a fortress of Torah and *mussar*, and which at its height enrolled up to two hundred young men. Serving as head of the *yeshiva* was the Gaon Rabbi Yoel Kleinerman, a relative of the Gaon Rabbi Yosef Yozel Horowitz, the father of the movement and in whose honor the *yeshiva* was called *Beit Yosef* [The House of Joseph]. His assistant director was the Gaon Rabbi Meir Segal, his brother-in-law. The Gaon Rabbi Aharon Anolik served as spiritual supervisor[187] of the *yeshiva*. The new *yeshiva* became a powerful force in the community, an integral part of its existence. It made a decisive contribution to the strengthening of religious life in the city and to the education of many of the younger generation in Torah and *mussar*.

Loyal to the approach of their great rabbi, the heads of the *yeshiva* in Ostroveh continued his methodology and philosophy. In the outskirts of the city they created a place where students of the *yeshiva* could go to be alone with their maker, to examine themselves and the clarity of their thought. Reb Ben-Zionwski, a shoemaker by trade who had no children, managed during his life to save a considerable sum of money, and acquired two houses in town. In his later years he decided to bequeath the houses for the benefit of the *Beit Yosef yeshiva*. One of the houses was on Pultusk Road, and the other on Kazhia Road. By this means the *yeshiva* became viable economically and thus became a permanent and stable force in town.

With the outbreak of the last war the Gaon Rabbi Yoel Kleinerman and the Gaon Rabbi Aharon Anolik tried to continue their work, but the hand of the murderous beasts caught up with them. They glorified the name of God with their deaths, as did the majority of the students of their sacred *yeshiva*.

---

[187] Given its emphasis on personal ethics and behavior, the *yeshivot* of this movement and some other Lithuanian *yeshivot* created this unique position, called *menahel* or *mashgiach ruchani*.

Chapter Twelve
Destruction and Annihilation

Ominous Clouds in the Skies over Poland

Terror that cannot be described in words, fear that could be felt with one's hands, darkness that strained one's eyes and oppressed one's heart, all hung over the entire Polish Jewish community from the moment that the Polish broadcast service announced the German invasion. Panicked and afraid, trembling at the thought of what might happen, engulfed in a flame that seemed to rise up from the depths of hell, the Jews of Poland walked out of their homes on that bitter Friday. It was a day that marked the end of a thousand years of effort and work, a symbol that also represented some hesitation, sadness as well as joy, that had occurred in the land of Poland, a day that foretold the coming of a thousand days of loss of loved ones and ruin, destruction and annihilation.

It was as if the hearts of Polish Jews just stopped beating for an hour. The heart understands the bitterness of the soul. And the Jews of Poland felt and sensed in those difficult and bitter hours what was coming. Without hesitation the Jews of Poland left their homes that day, abandoning everything they owned, their assets and property, produced by the hard work of their hands with blood and sweat, with just their shirts on their backs. They fled wherever their eyes would direct them in order to avoid the claws of the terrifying Nazi snake that had viciously assaulted an undefended Poland which was exposed to destructive bombing, which was virtually without defenses, and which was abandoned to the mercies of bloody dogs devoid of restraint.

The Jews wanted to flee, but to where? The German serpent had surrounded Poland on three sides, now that it ruled over Czechoslovakia, which became a subservient state to the Teutonic nation, a "superior race." On the fourth side of surrounded Poland stood the guards of Stalin, who smiled in a way that struck terror and fear. They had also contributed to the outbreak of this terrible conflagration, but they now stood and watched with glee as plumes of smoke arose from the cities and settlements of Poland. They stood their ground and intended to prevent the many refugees from finding even a temporary haven in the vast wide open spaces of the socialist power, Soviet Russia.

At the outbreak of the last war, the Jews of Poland felt like prisoners who were locked in their cells as vicious wild animals were approaching. The Jews had no illusions about what was coming. It was clear that the German troops were bringing ruination and murder, destruction and a holocaust with them. Very few believed in Poland's power to withstand the German attack or in its ability to repel the bloody dogs armed from head to toe. And the illusions of those few were quickly proven false, dashed on the hard, tough wall of reality. Poland fell like prey to the murderous hordes, wild animals dressed as human beings.

It soon became known that the German air force had amazing, precise maps of the locations of the Polish aircraft. And they operated with typical *yekke* [derogatory Yiddish word for German, implying extreme, if not obsessive meticulousness] precision. They secured a decisive advantage of mastery over the skies of Poland for themselves by means of this not all that difficult method without much risk. It also became clear that Poland was crawling with spies and saboteurs, local Germans [Volksdeutsch], sworn anti-Semites who regularly infiltrated into the country. The Jews avoided every security position set up by the anti-Semitic Polish authorities, who were replaced by Nazis saboteurs and agents, who made a decisive contribution to the destruction of Poland.

From the minute the war broke out confusion and chaos reigned at all levels of the Polish administration. They were not at all prepared for the difficult and complex task of governing during a time of emergency and under the conditions of war. If the Polish army was not in fact prepared for battle with the German army, the Polish civilian authorities were certainly not ready to face the emergency conditions in a time of war and confusion. The central administration quickly lost all contact with and influence over the local authorities who, out of their own panic, added yet another major element to the general chaos and confusion that directly aided the German invaders.

The targets were largely areas where many Jews resided. Jews were the first sacrifices lost to Nazi bombing. Flames leapt from the houses of Jews, which were filled with Jews. Polish Jewry was now forced into a period of holocaust and destruction. Thousands of Jews were struck by the murderous German bombing. The cries of bereaved families, of orphans left without parents, of parents whose children were cruelly slain, pierced the fraught, oppressive atmosphere that prevailed in Poland during this period.

The Destruction of Ostrow Mazowiecka

From East Prussia a column of Germans burst forth into the strategic areas of the Bialystok district and the northeastern approaches of the Warsaw district. The aim was clear: to divide Poland lengthwise and to hook up with the German column that had invaded Poland from the south. Ostrow Mazowiecka and its surrounding area quickly became a dangerous battlefront. The battle line moved closer with terrifying speed.

The first bomb that struck in Ostroveh hit the house of Rabbi Yosef Pravda, shearing off the legs of this wonderful Hassid and killing his son and two of his guests. Thus, the city underwent its first trial by fire and blood. All the surrounding towns and villages were turned into torches of flame that leapt skyward. The entire area, which became an arena of bitter and cruel battles, went up in flames. But the flames did not illuminate the dark recesses of the hearts of the Jews of Ostroveh and the area. They only foretold that the great Nazi columns were closing in. A week after the war had broken out, the first German troops were seen in the streets of Ostrow Mazowiecka.

It was on a Friday, just a week after the world war had broken out. The sounds of shots and shouts of triumph announced the arrival of the murderers. The Jews generally hid themselves in their homes, afraid or refusing to witness the arrival of the hangmen. The few who happened to cross paths with the conquerors paid for this awful pleasure with their lives. Fifteen Jews were killed in the streets when Ostroveh became an occupied city.

With great devotion and sacrifice, the bereaved, distressed and terrified Jews collected the corpses for burial. Exhibiting great spiritual courage, the Gaon Rabbi Yaakov Shraga Singer, with the help of Reb Moshe Rosenzweig, Rabbi Shimon Hersh Goldwasser and Reb Yaakov Farbiarz, arranged the funerals of the victims. Nazi troops appeared at the very edge of the graves and, firing shots, ordered the rabbi and his helpers to desist, against the sound of the terrified voices of the families of the murdered and of the small orphaned boys and girls. Perhaps the horrific screams had some effect on these bloodthirsty enemies, who sufficed with murderous beatings and abuse of the defenseless mourning Jews.

The first Sabbath of the Jews of Ostroveh under the terrifying rule of the Nazi murderers passed relatively peacefully. The blood thirsty dogs made due with "only" three victims, only three Jews were murdered just like that, for no particular reason. Then came the first real bloody day. All the men of the Jewish community were ordered to appear in the market square on pain of death for anyone who did not obey. From morning until four in the afternoon the Jews were forced to stand in the market with their hands raised, as the Germans conducted extensive searches in the city. When the searches were over the time for abuse began. The unfortunate Jews were required to run the gauntlet of murderous beatings and to lie on the ground as the Nazi beasts of prey trampled upon them. This terrible scene concluded at six thirty in the evening. Then the Jews were ordered to return to their homes quickly, as it was announced that after six o'clock in the evening it was forbidden for a Jew to be found outside his house. Those who violated that order would be killed on the spot with no excuses or explanations accepted. As the Jews hurriedly ran to their homes a hail of bullets followed them, and thirty Jews fell victim.

The next day Ostroveh was enveloped in fear. Many had succeeded in escaping. Only a few remained in the city that was now in the clutches of the cruel enemy that lacked all restraint. German soldiers who were patrolling the city out of curiosity entered the house of Rabbi Mordechai Ber Tornovsky, a scholar and merchant, one of the important Warka Hassidim. They found him sitting and learning the tractate *Sukkah* with his young son, Menachem Yosef. They immediately took them outside and shot them dead in front of the other members of their family. The bereaved family tried to gather up their loved ones to be buried together. But they were chased back under a rain of murderous beatings by the monsters.

The reign of terror was now upon them: deadly beatings, abuse, plundering and scorn, round-ups for forced labor accompanied by severe suffering were from now on the lot of the distressed Jewish community. The rabbi of the community and its secretary, the head of the community and its leaders became the objects of abuse by the bloodthirsty Nazis. The situation of the Jews got worse from day to day. It was impossible to continue under these horrific and difficult conditions. The final escape towards the Soviet zone of occupation began.

In accordance with the secret treaty between Nazi Germany and Soviet Russia, Poland was divided into two zones of occupation. The eastern districts of Poland were attached to the Soviet sphere of influence. The Red Army entered these areas and occupied them almost without a shot being fired. The western and central districts of Poland remained in the hands of the German occupiers. Ostrow Mazowiecka became the closest point to the new border between the zones of occupation of Russia and Germany. As the border posts had yet to be finalized and the soldiers in place had not yet become familiar with the area, sneaking across the border in the depths of night was not especially difficult.

Masses of Jews passed through Ostroveh and nearby towns, fleeing for their lives to the Soviet zone of occupation. The large majority of the Jews of Ostroveh slipped across to the Soviet Russian side at night. They escaped with just the shirts on their backs, because of the oppressor. Only a few hundred Jews remained in the city, including some of the elderly and the sick. For about two months those last Jews lived under the Nazi nightmare. On the twenty-ninth day of Cheshvan in the year 5700 [November 11, 1939], the last Jews were cruelly taken to be killed. Only a very few succeeded in escaping alive. The Jewish community of Ostrow Mazowiecka ceased to exist.

This was the result of a fire that broke out in the city that had been caused by a Pole named Antek Bezhestak. This same Bezhestak was thought of before the war as a "good goy," a progressive with certain leftist ideas. He was a Pole who spent much time with the members of left-wing secular Jewish youth movements. Now the same Antek Bezhestak also took part in looting Jewish property. He took over a Jewish residence and moved in to live there. It was apparently uncomfortable for this "progressive" Pole to live there, as it reminded everyone of the Jews who had preceded him. He went to Mr. Berel Teitel at his house on the market square and demanded wallpaper with which to cover the walls of his residence, in order to remove any reminder of the previous Jewish residents. While Antek demanded it, Berel Teitel, who sold wallpaper, had nothing to give him, as his stock had been looted some time ago. The Pole got angry, gritted his teeth, and lit a bottle of gasoline, throwing it at Teitel. The house was set aflame.

Antek Bezhestak rushed to inform the Germans that Berel Teitel had set his house on fire. The troops arrived, looking for Teitel and shouting, "Where is that filthy Jew who is setting fire to houses?" Without thinking too long, Berel went into a corner and hung himself on a rope. The monsters decided to take revenge on all the Jews of the city. The next day, the twenty-ninth of (Mar)Cheshvan, the last five hundred sixty Jews of Ostroveh were taken out of their homes. They were imprisoned in the basement of the local beer hall in horrendous conditions. From their place of imprisonment they were taken to the place of execution. Most of them were killed by the shots fired by the bloody dogs. A few were buried alive. The community of Ostrow Mazowiecka was destroyed once and for all. The last remnant of this holy community that had functioned for so many generations was eradicated.

Addendum
The Destruction of the Jewish Community of Ostrow Mazowiecka
(not included in the original *yizkor* book)

As described in the *yizkor* book, those members of the Jewish community of Ostrow Mazowiecka who had not managed to flee the town were murdered by the Nazis on November 11, 1939, the anniversary of the armistice that ended World War I and of the creation of the modern Polish state. Below are photographs taken by the Nazis of the massacre. These photographs come from the archival collection of the State Museum Auschwitz-Birkenau in Oswiecim, and are reproduced with the permission of the State Museum. Scans of the photographs were provided by the United States Holocaust Memorial Museum Photo Archives.

The information accompanying the photographs describes the event as follows:

> Early in November 1939, a part of the city of Ostrow Mazowiecka was destroyed by fire. On orders from the HSSPF in Krakow, SS-Obergrueppenfuehrer Krueger, Colonel Brenner, the commander of the 4th Police Regiment, conducted an investigation and was told by Polish witnesses that the fire was supposedly set by local Jews. On 11 November, after it was determined that the Jews were 'guilty', an undetermined number of Jewish men, women, and children, were rounded-up by Wehrmacht patrols and SD personnel. The prisoners were then marched to pits outside of the city that had been dug by men of the East Prussian Police unit. Once there, Police Major Kurt Kirschner and Senior Police Commissioner Hans Hoffmann received orders from Krueger that the Jews were to be shot. The shootings were then carried out by the policemen present, many of whom reportedly were upset by their orders. Regarding the number of Jews shot, it ranges from 162 to 500.

The captions below are from the archival copies of the photographs (which are file numbers 50073, 50076, 50394, 50397, and 50400 in the Photo Archives of the United States Holocaust Memorial Museum).

In addition, preceding the photographs is a copy of the Nazi execution order that was posted in the town on November 11, 1939. It is in German and Polish. This copy, along with an English translation, is courtesy of Stanley M. Diamond and reproduced with his permission.

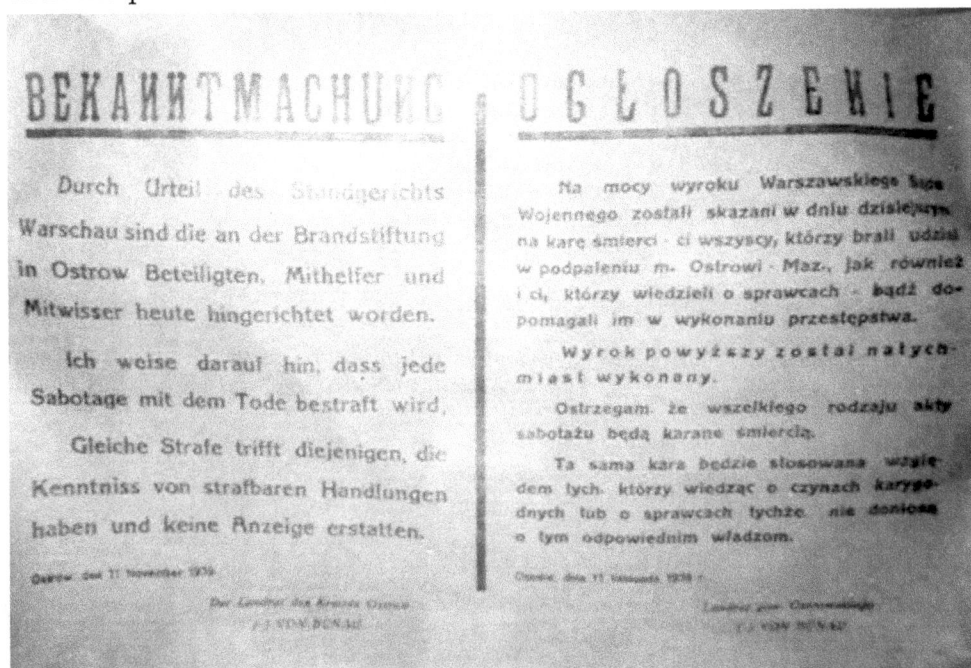

BEKANNTMACHUNG

Durch Urteil des Standgerichts Warschau sind die an der Brandstiftung in Ostrow Beteiligten, Mithelfer und Mitwisser heute hingerichtet worden.

Ich weise darauf hin, dass jede Sabotage mit dem Tode bestraft wird.

Gleiche Strafe trifft diejenigen, die Kenntniss von strafbaren Handlungen haben und keine Anzeige erstatten.

Ostrow den 11 November 1939.

Der Landrat des Kreises Ostrow

OGŁOSZENIE

Na mocy wyroku Warszawskiego Sądu Wojennego zostali skazani w dniu dzisiejszym na karę śmierci - ci wszyscy, którzy brali udział w podpaleniu m. Ostrowi - Maz., jak również i ci, którzy wiedzieli o sprawcach - bądź dopomagali im w wykonaniu przestępstwa.

Wyrok powyższy został natychmiast wykonany.

Ostrzegam że wszelkiego rodzaju akty sabotażu będą karane śmiercią.

Ta sama kara będzie stosowana względem tych którzy wiedząc o czynach karygodnych lub o sprawcach tychże nie doniosą o tym odpowiednim władzom.

Ostrów, dnia 11 listopada 1939 r.

Landrat powiatu Ostrowskiego

ANNOUNCEMENT

Based on the verdict of the Warsaw Court Martial, all those who participated in arson in Ostrów Mazowiecka, as well all those who knew about them, or helped them to commit the crime, have been sentenced to death.

The sentence has been executed immediately.

I warn that all kinds of acts of sabotage will be punished by the death sentence.

The same sentence applies to those who know of any criminal offences or any perpetrators committing them but do not denounce them to the authorities.

Ostrów, November 11, 1939

Landrat of Ostrów District
(-) VON BUNAU

*Order Police lead a column of Jews from Ostrow Mazowiecka
to the execution site*

Police prepare Jews from Ostrow Mazowiecka for execution

The last Jew to be executed is ordered to the edge of the pit

Police execute a group of Jews from Ostrow Mazowiecka.
at the edge of a mass grave

The bodies of executed Jews from Ostrow Mazowiecka in a mass grave

Today, there is a monument at the location just south of the town where the executions took place. Above is a photograph of Dr. Gary S. Schiff, the translator/editor of this yizkor book, with the monument

INDEX

Please note that the Appendix that follows was not included in the index.

PICTURES OF THE PEOPLE OF THE JEWISH COMMUNITY OF OSTRÓW MAZOWIECKA

(Not in the original book)

The pictures on the following pages were provided by people with ancestors who lived in Ostrów Mazowiecka during the late 19th-early 20th century.

Family Group Pictures from the Ostrów Area

The following family group pictures illustrate the changes over time in the Ostrów and nearby Jewish communities:

- The first, from around 1902, shows a Chasidic family, all dressed in the manner of Chasidic Jews at the time.

- The second, from the mid-1920s of translator Gary Schiff's Goldstein family living in Makow, a town about 30 miles west of Ostrów, shows a mix of traditional and modern dress. It includes a visitor from the United States – Gary's great-great-uncle Alex Goldstein, who had left Poland for New York City in 1913. He returned to New York City in October 1927, so the picture was likely taken that year.

  Absent in this picture is Gary's great-grandmother, Leah Gittel (Goldstein) Feinzeig, an older sister of Alex, who had left Poland with her younger children in 1923 to join her husband, Chezke, in New York City. Chezke Feinzeig, who had left Poland for New York City in 1911, was the scion of one of the oldest and largest Jewish families in Ostrów. Leah Gittel had a wholesale business supplying the Polish army base in nearby Komorowo.

- The third, from September 1938, shows the family of Zelek Widelec, a great-uncle of Stanley Diamond. Like the second picture, it shows a mix of traditional and modern dress and includes a visitor from the United States.

- Two additional pictures show the Widelec family of Poremba, a small village south of Ostrów.

All reproduced with permission.

Rycher Family

Left to right: Feyga Leia (1857-1929), Anna (Enia Ryfka) (standing) (1894-ca. 1941), Rose (Reychla) (seated, in front) (1898-1964), Morris (Meyshe Aron) (1892-1976), Neach Leyb (1858-ca. 1919)

They were Chasidim, probably Gerer.

This studio picture was probably taken around 1902, judging from the age of Rose. Note that she and her mother are holding matching baskets, and the father, who was a *melamed* (teacher), is holding a book.

The photograph was taken at the studio of G. (or J.) Rudy (Josef Zelmanovich Ruda) of Glowna Street in Ostrów. Surviving pictures from this studio also include ones of soldiers stationed at nearby Komorowo.

Goldstein Family

Family of the paternal great-great-grandparents of Gary Schiff, the translator, from the mid-1920s:
Seated center: Chaim Dovid and Chana Rochel Goldstein, the great-great-grandparents
Standing, second from left: Alex Goldstein (visiting from the United States, explaining his clothing)
Standing, second from right: Ziskind Goldstein, son of Chaim Dovid & Chana Rochel
Standing, first on right: Chaya Goldstein, daughter of Ziskind, who later married her uncle Alex. They (and later Ziskind) went to the United States.

WIDELEC FAMILY OF OSTRÓW

Family of Zelek (or Zelig) Widelec, taken in Ostrów in September 1938. Zelek (born 1873) is the older man, middle row, second from left. Behind him, second and third from the left in the back row, are his son Jankiel, born 1910, and Jankiel's wife Sarah Markowitz, born 1913. Next to Sarah (fourth from the left in the back row) is Zwelka Widelec, nephew of Zelek, born 1892, and the boy next to Zwelka is his son Jankiel Mejer, born 1920.

Of all the people in this picture, only Jankiel and his wife Sarah survived the Holocaust. Jankiel had a U.S. visa as a result of his marriage to Sarah, who was born in New York and had come to Poland to marry Jankiel. Sarah returned to the United States in October 1938, following their wedding in Poland. After the war started in September 1939, Jankiel was able to escape to the Soviet side of Poland, traveling first to Lithuania, then to Sweden, then to Japan, and then to Vancouver and Seattle. He wrote a chronology of the last four weeks of the Jewish community of Ostrów for the 1960 *yizkor* book.

WIDELEC FAMILY OF POREMBA

Zelek Widelec of Ostrów had a twin brother Icek Ajzik (Itzik Isaac) Widelec (1873-1925) who lived in Poręba-Kocęby, a small village south of Ostrów. Icek Ajzik appears in the center of this picture, which presumably was taken in the early 1920s and includes his wife Chana Sura Mindla, most if not all of their seven children and several grandchildren.

The next photograph, from 1934, shows Icek Ajzik's son Moszek Jankiel Widelec, who was a blacksmith in Poremba; his wife Chawa; Moszek Jankiel's niece Chana and her husband Nachman Moszek Paluch, a brother of Chawa; Chawa's sister Sara and her husband Moszek Malowany; and Chawa's brother Aron Lejb Paluch, who later married a sister of Moszek Jankiel. Moszek Jankiel, Chawa, Chana and Nachman Moszek perished in the Holocaust.

Photograph key, Left to right:

Back Row:

Moszek Jankiel WIDELEC (14 May 1908 – ca 1941),
Moszek MALOWANY (23 March 1909 – February 1991),
Nachman Moszek PALUCH (1908 – ca 1942)

Front Row:

Chawa PALUCH WIDELEC (1909 – ca 1942),
Sara PALUCH MALOWANY (20 August 1914 – 2 January 1972),
Aron Lejb PALUCH (1 September 1919 – 13 May 1990),
Chana WIDELEC (ca 1908 – ca 1904)

Photographed ca 1934 in Poręba Kocęby
(Ostrów Mazowiecka District, Białystok Region)

Photograph provided by Stanley Diamond, Montreal, Canada
Source of Photograph: Meir Gover, Gaurey Yehuda, Israel

SCHOOL CLASS PICTURES

There are many surviving school class pictures from Ostrów. The following pages include class pictures from the Bait Yaakov (Bais Yaakov) school, part of a network of Orthodox schools for girls that was started in Poland in 1917, and the Tarbut school, part of a network of Zionist, Hebrew-language schools started in Poland in 1922. In most instances, the only individuals we are able to identify are from the family of the person who donated the picture.

Ostrów Mazowiecka Girls School. (Postcard dated 19 Sept. 1922

It is unclear whether this picture is of the Bait Yaakov school or a Polish secular studies school.

The photograph was provided courtesy of Dorothy Becker, the daughter of Elka Sora Augustower (born 1910) (later Ellen Friedman), who appears in the middle of the second row from the front (with the long ponytails).

Bait Yaakov Girls School, around 1928

On the floor, bottom left, is Touba (Tobey) Wondolowicz. Seated behind her is Necha (Nettie) Wondolowicz, and on far right seated is Elka (Alice) Wondolowicz.

The Wondolowicz family immigrated to the United States in April 1929, taking up residence in Chicago, Illinois. The family name changed from Wondolowicz to Greenberg.

Photo and information courtesy of Jerry and Madeleine Isenberg.

TARBUT SCHOOL

The Tarbut School in Ostrów Mazowiecka was part of a network of coeducational Jewish schools in Eastern Europe that emphasized study in Hebrew. According to an article in the 1960 *yizkor* book, the Tarbut School in Ostrów was founded in 1922. After starting in a house, the school rented a vacant two-story building on the lane opposite the Russian Orthodox church—the location next to the Tejtel sawmill shown in an earlier section of this appendix. In addition to Hebrew and Jewish subjects, the school also taught the official Polish government curriculum. It had seven grades, and there was a kindergarten in a separate location. Some students went on to the Hebrew High School in Bialystok.

In April 1925, the school celebrated the opening of Hebrew University in Jerusalem with a procession of school children holding little blue and white flags. This event is described in the 1960 *yizkor* book article, including a picture.

On the following pages are group pictures of students and teachers from the school, taken between 1922 and 1939.

Tarbut School, 2nd class—5682-5688 (1922-1928)

Note the picture of the school building on the lower right, showing the house next to the Tejtel property.

Pictured (as best can be determined from the Hebrew spellings):

Top row, left to right across the photo: Sh. Niedzwichowicz, L. Niedzwichowicz, J. Perec [Jakob Perec, one of the founders], J. Zipman [or Zajfman], Dubrowski, L. Finkelsztejn, A. Aharonit, Ch. Izralit, Y. Rozental [possibly Yitzchak Rozental, who authored the article on the Tarbut School in the 1960 *yizkor* book and went on to Bialystok Hebrew High School]

Middle row, left to right: R. Berenzon, M. Frider, M. Holcman, N. Polakiewicz, R. Donszczyk, D. Weber, C. Jeruchim

Bottom row, left to right: Z. Lipsker, A. Mularzewicz, Sh. Fejgin [possibly Szmul Fejgin, who went on to Bialystok Hebrew High School], M. Wszebor [possibly Meier Wszebor, who went on to Bialystok Hebrew High School], J. Tejtel

Photo by Zalman Goldsztejn (name in lower right corner), who had a photography business in Ostrów

Tarbut School Pictures, late 1930s

The pictures on the following four pages were donated to the United States Holocaust Memorial Museum by Aaron Rubinstein, and are reprinted with permission from the Museum.

Aaron Rubinstein was the son of Benjamin and Chaja Rubinstein. He was born in Sokolow Podlaski, Poland on February 28, 1928. Aaron had four siblings: Rivka, Lea, Shlomo and Joseph. In 1935 his family moved to Ostrów Mazowiecka, where they lived until the outbreak of World War II. About one month later, the Rubinstein family fled to the Soviet-occupied sector of Poland. In 1941 they were all deported to Siberia. A year later the Rubinsteins succeeded in placing Aaron with a group of one thousand Jewish children, who were being taken from the Soviet Union to Teheran in the company of a unit of Polish soldiers and other refugees. After they reached Iran, the British government granted the children immigration permits for Palestine. The "Teheran Children," as they came to be known, traveled via Karachi and Suez, finally arriving in Palestine on February 18, 1943. Aaron's parents survived the war in the Soviet interior and returned to Poland.

After living for a time in Lodz and Ostrów Mazowiecka, they immigrated to Israel in 1949.

The descriptions of the pictures are from the information in the United States Holocaust Museum files.

Second graders in the Tarbut school, between 1935 and 1939

The caption reads: The school Tarbut in Ostrów Maz., 2nd grade at the time of *shacharit* [morning prayer—all the boys are clad in small *tallitot*]

United States Holocaust Memorial Museum, courtesy of Aaron Rubinstein

Group portrait of the first grade at the Tarbut School – 1936

Among those pictured are: Shmuel Podwilewicz (top row, fourth child from right); H. Podwilewicz (middle row, third from left); Ruth Zlatkowska (front row, second from left); Shimon Epstein (front row, center); Aaron Rubinstein (middle row, first on right)

United States Holocaust Memorial Museum, courtesy of Aaron Rubinstein

Students pose in front of the Tarbut School – 1938

The caption reads: Students of the school "Tarbut" in Ostrow-Maz., in the year 5698
United States Holocaust Memorial Museum, courtesy of Aaron Rubinstein

Tarbut School students on an outing in the woods—May 19, 1938.

Among those pictured are the teacher Mrs. Siedlecka (top row, second from the left); her son, Aaron Rubinstein (front row, center); Chana Schwartz (front row, second from the right); Shimon Epstein (front row, first on the right); Lea Rubinstein (middle row, first on the left); Moniek Lichtenstein (middle row, third from the left); Miryam Galant (top row, third from the right); Moshe Friedman (middle row, center); and Tema Sosnowska (middle row, fourth from the right)
United States Holocaust Memorial Museum, courtesy of Aaron Rubinstein

Kohn/Berenholc Family and Friends

The pictures on the following pages were provided by Alan Droz. Most of them originally belonged to his cousins Bella Berenholc (1917-2002) and Helene Faytelowicz / Chana Berenholc (1918-1999), who appear in many of the pictures. Bella and Helene carried these photographs with them in their flight from the Nazis that took them from Ostrów first to Bialystok, then to a forced labor camp in the Soviet Union (Camp Jumpasz in the Vologda region), and later (after they were freed) to a work camp in Kazakhstan, where they remained until the end of the war. The photographs show them and many of their friends in and around Ostrów during the 1930s, and also include several class pictures. Reprinted with permission from Alan Droz.

Alan's great-grandfather, Avrumche Kohn (Abram Kon in the Polish records), was born in Ostrów in 1856. Alan's grandfather Meyer Moszek and Perla, the mother of Bella and Helene, were the children of Avrumche's first wife, Bejla.

The next page shows a family tree of selected descendants of Avrumche's parents, courtesy of Alan Droz, covering the family members who appear in the pictures.

Selected Descendants of Judah Lejb KOHN & Rivka HUSS

Judah Lejb KOHN (1817 - 1887)
& Rivka HUSS (1822 - 1874)

Menachem Mendel KOHN (1850 - 1931)
& Elka Bejla WAJNBRUM (~1853 - ?)

Alta Nechama (Emma) KOHN (1884 - >1947)
& Mordka (Max) GOLDSTEIN(1888 - ~1950)

Lejb KOHN (Leo J. COHEN) (1894 - 1986)
& Ryfka (Rita) JELLEN (1891 - 1971)

Avram "Avrumche" KOHN (1856 - 1941)
& Bejla BRONZOWY (1855 - 1908)

Sura Rivka KOHN (1879 - 1944)
& Gerszon MROCZKOWSKI
(George Moskowitz) (1875 - 1946)

Alta Basia MROCZKOWSKI
(Alice Moskowitz Zarember) (1904 - 1987)

Chaja Bejla MROCZKOWSKI
(Belle Moskowitz Schwartzenfeld) (1909 - 2005)

Mala MROCZKOWSKI (Molly Moskowtiz) (1911 - 2001)

Pearla MROCZKOWSKI
(Pearl Moskowitz Brown) (~1915 - ~2007)

Meyer Moszek KOHN (Cohen) (1884 - 1974)
& Golda Dyna ZYLBERSZTEYN (1885 - 1947)

Fejga KOHN (Faye Rodner) (1906 - 1937)

Bejla KOHN (Belle Levine) (1909 - 1996)

Basia KOHN (Beatrice Banks Belfer) (1912 - 2002)

Feyga KOHN (Fannie Danzig) (1890 - 1966)
& Abram Izrael DOMBCZYK (1876 - >1930)

Bejla DOMBCZYK (Barbara Danzig) (1910 - 1971)

Mala DOMBCZYK (Mildred Danzig Romanoff) (1911 - 1975)

Pinchas DOMBCZYK (Phillip Danzig) (1913 - 1994)

Pearl KOHN (~1896 - 1956)
& Froim Mendel BERENHOLC (1886 - 1944)

Bella BERENHOLC (1917 - 2002)

Chana BERENHOLC (Helene Faytelowicz) (1918 - 1999)

Basia KOHN (HOLOCAUST) (~1900 - 1941/42)
& Moshe BURSZTYN (HOLOCAUST) (~1892 - 1941/42)

Yidel Lejb BURSZTYN (HOLOCAUST) (-1926 - 1941/42)

Beyla BURSZTYN (HOLOCAUST) (~1931 - 1941/42)

Peshka BURSZTYN (HOLOCAUST) (~1934 - 1941/42)

Baruch BURSZTYN (HOLOCAUST) (~1937 - 1941/42)

Alan's mother's family:

Goldie (Zylberszteyn) Kohn (born 1886, originally from Ostrolenka), wife of Meyer Moszek Kohn, with her daughters (from left) Bejla (born 1909), Fejga (born 1906), and Basia (born 1911)

Taken in Ostrów around 1918, after Meyer had left for the United States

Alan's great-grandmother Goldie Kohn (left), reading a letter from her husband
Meyer Moszk, who by this time had emigrated to the United States

Looking on his her husband's sister Basia (who later married Moszek Bursztyn)

Taken in Ostrów around 1915

Grandchildren of Avrumche, taken in Ostrów around 1920

Front: Chana (Helene) Berenholc

Back, left to right: Mala Dombczyk (Mildred Danzig), Perla
    Mrockowski (Moskowitz), Bejla Dombczyk (Barbara Danzig),
    Mala Mrockowski (Molly Moskowitz), Bejla Mrockowski
    (Belle Moskowitz), Pinchas Dombczyk (Phil Danzig), and Bella
    Berenholc

Bella and Helene as children

Left to right: Nechama Goldsztejn (wife of Max Goldsztejn and daughter of Menachem Mendel Kohn and Elka Bejla Wajnbrum); Chana (Helene) Berenholc (child, seated); Chana's mother, Perla Berenholc (wife of Froim Mendel Berenholc and daughter of Avrumche Kohn and Beyla Bronzowy); Perla's other daughter, Bella Berenholc (child with blond hair, standing); Rita Kohn (nee Ryfka Jellen and wife of Leo (Lejb) Kohn); and Alta Basia Mroczkowski, daughter of Sura Rivka Kohn (an older daughter of Avrumche and Beyla) and Gerszon Mroczkowski

Ostrów, early 1920s

Alan Droz's great-grandfather Avrumche Kohn, standing outside his home at 29 Warszawska Street with his third wife, Szeyna; his granddaughter Bella Berenholc is in the background. Mid-1930s.

Above is a 1995 photograph of a house on Warszawska Street, which a relative recognized as resembling the house in which Avrumche lived.

Family of Basia Bursztyn, Alan's great-aunt

Basia (born ca. 1900), a younger daughter of Avrumche and Beyla, was married to Moszek Bursztyn. They had four children – Yidel Leyb, Beyla, Peshka, and Baruch. The entire family was murdered in Slonim, Belarus during the Holocaust.

Left: At Pesach, April 11, 1936

     Back, left to right: Bella Berenholc; her mother, Perla; unknown; Basia (probably)

     Front, left to right: Basia's children – Beyla, Yidel Leyb, Peshka

Right: Mid-1930s – Moszek with children Yidel Leyb (left), Beyla (behind Peshka), Peshka (front)

Class photos, early 1920s. In both, Bella Berenholc is to the left of the teacher.

Class photos, early 1920s. In the top picture, Chana Berenholc is seated on the far right of the 2nd row. In the picture below, she is seated in the 2nd row, far right.

Class photos with Bella Berenholc. In the top picture, from the mid-1920s, she is in the 2nd row, 4th from the left, next to the teacher. In the lower picture, from the late 1920s, she is kneeling on the far right between the 1st and 2nd rows.

Class photo, May 15, 1932. Chana Berenholc is in the 3rd row, 6th from the left.

Possibly a class photo, dated July 25, 1934, by the photographer Ciechanowiecki. Masha Albester and Chana Berenholc are third and fourth from the left in the back.

Hashomer Hatzair, 1935

Hashomer Hatzair, or "young guard," was a socialist-Zionist secular Jewish youth movement.

Above: A group outing. Masha Albester and Chana Berenholc are in the front row.

Below: Lag BaOmer outing, 5695 (May 1935); on the back of the photo is written: "This I give for a memory to my friend … Bella [Berenholc]. From Avraham Wengrowski"

Above: Probably a Hashomer Hatzair group photo, late 1930s—including Bella (upper left)
Photo by Ciechanowiecki, a local photographer—there are other surviving photos credited to him
Below: Probably a Hashomer Hatzair group outing, dated May 29, 1935
Bella is in the photo, just left of center in the second row from the bottom

Above: Hashomer Hatzair group photo, dated June 20, 1935, with Chana Berenholc and Masha Albester

Below: same, dated February 16, 1935

Above: Hashomer Hatzair group photo, mid-1930s, with Bella Berenholc (second row from bottom, right of center)

Below: Hashomer Hatzair group photo, dated April 22, 1934, with Chana Berenholc and Masha Albester (second row from top, flanking the two boys in the center)

Above: Hashomer Hatzair group photo, mid-1930s, with Bella Berenholc (back row, fourth from left)

Second row from front, on the right, with hand on hip—Pejsak Cynamon

The caption reads: "Festive meal, August 24, by comrade Zelik Yagodnik to honor the wedding of his sister on August 29th", probably mid-1930s; Masha Albester appears upper right

In 1936, Alice Moskowitz Zarember, a cousin of Bella and Chana who had immigrated to the United States in 1926 (see the family photo from the early 1920s on page App-23, where she appears as Alta Basia Mroczkowski), came back for a visit to Ostrów.

Left: Alice is the woman in the center front. In the background is the Ratusz, or City Hall. Dated August 15, 1936.

Right: Alice, center, with Chana (left) and Bella (right)

Mid-1930s

Left: Bella Berenholc (left) and Enia on a street in Ostrów

Right: Chana (left) and Bella Berenholc on a street in Ostrów

Two pictures taken at the Sadzawka (city pond), with the Tejtel Brothers Brewery in the background.

Left: On the top step is Bella Berenholc; on the lower step is Masha Albester. Late 1930's.

Right: At the top is Chana Berenholc; on the lower step is her friend Masha Albester. Dated April 5, 1939.

Above - On an Ostrów street, June 14, 1936
Middle left—Masha Albester
Middle right—Chana Berenholc

Below - September 15, 1937:
Second from left—Chana Berenholc
Right—Masha Albester

January 2, 1939, before the departure of Bella Berenholc to live on a kibbutz (in Poland)

Top picture—second and third from left—Masha Albester & Chana Berenholc

Above: Bella Berenholc is second from the right in this photo from the late 1930's

קן „הנוער - הציוני" באוסטרוב - מזוב .
לפני צאתו של האח זאב גולודזר לצבא -
23 - III. 1938

"Hanoar Hatzioni" in Ostrów Mazowiecka
Before the departure of Comrade Zev Golodzierz for the army – 23 March 1938

Hanoar Hatzioni group

Jewish Cemeteries of Ostrów

There were two Jewish cemeteries in Ostrów—the old cemetery and the new cemetery. By the early 20th century, most if not all burials were in the new cemetery.

Both cemeteries were largely destroyed during the German occupation. Some *matzevot* from the old cemetery were discovered a few years ago when a nearby house was torn down, but little was readable. The new cemetery is a forest with few remaining fragments of *matzevot*. As a result, the only clear remnants we have of the cemeteries are photographs that may have been taken to send to relatives abroad.

Matzevah of Beyla Kohn

Perla Berenholc (nee Kohn) at the grave of her mother, Beyla Kohn (nee Bronzowy)

Not clear if this was taken in the old cemetery or the new cemetery

Courtesy of Alan Droz (grand-nephew of Perla)

Matzevah of Moszek Mejer Gabinet

Moszek Mejer Gabinet (Moshe Meir son of Yechezkel) was born in Brok in 1870 and died in Ostrów on August 22, 1934.(11 Elul 5694). The people surrounding the *matzevah* are presumably Moszek Mejer's children and grandchildren, and possibly his widow as well. The woman sitting on the right side is Sara, or Sorche, one of his daughters, who later immigrated to Uruguay.

The back of the photograph indicates that it was taken by Ch. Ciechanowiecki's Photography and Portrait Studio of Rynek 11 in Ostrów.

The *matzevah* in the background on the right is for Kalonimos son of Yisrael Arye, age 71, who died in 5692 (1932). He is likely Kelman Grossman (1861-1932), son of Srul.

The *matzevah* in the background on the left is for two brothers (it says as much just below the pediment), one who died in 5632 (1932-33) and the other who died in 5633 (1933-34). The names are not readable.

Courtesy of Mario Gabinet, a grandson of Moszek Mejer

Matzevah of Hersz / Hershel Tejtel

Hershel Tejtel was born in 1867 and died in Ostrów on November 26, 1919. He owned the sawmill and grain mill on Rozanska Road, pictured earlier. Standing next to the *matzevah* is his son Joseph (Juszek Nosek, born 1901).

The *matzevah* contains an epitaph using as the first letter of each word the letters of Hershel's Hebrew name—Tzvi Hersh son of Yisrael Isser. It gives his date of death as the 4th day of Kislev, 5680.

SUPPLEMENT

MAPS AND PICTURES OF OSTRÓW MAZOWIECKA

Not in the original book

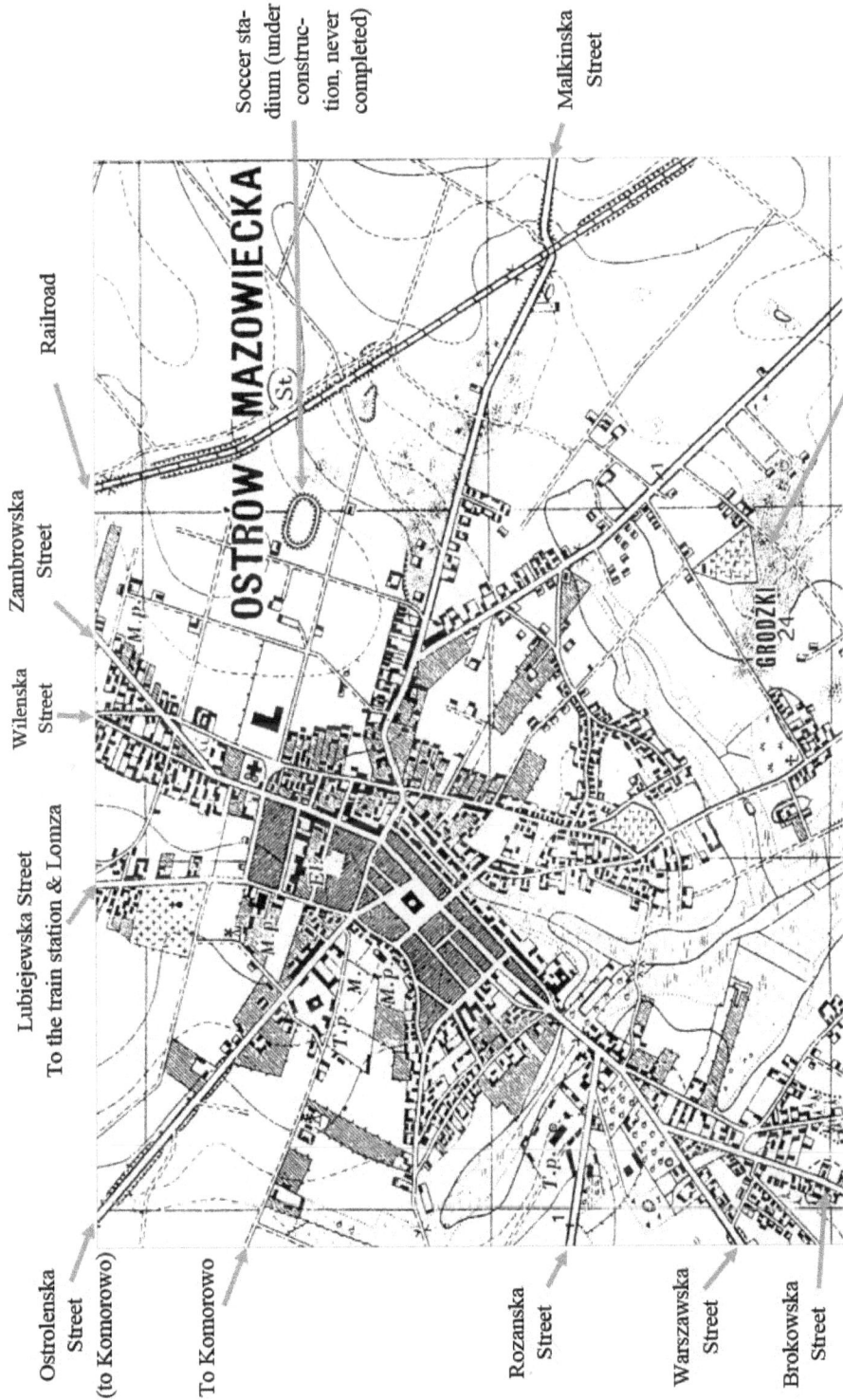

Soccer stadium (under construction, never completed)

Malkinska Street

Railroad

Zambrowska Street

Wilenska Street

New Jewish cemetery

Lubiejewska Street
To the train station & Lomza

Ostrolenska Street (to Komorowo)

To Komorowo

Rozanska Street

Warszawska Street

Brokowska Street

OSTRÓW MAZOWIECKA

Map of Ostrow Mazowiecka—from a 1933 series of detailed maps of Poland in the files of the U.S. Library of Congress map division. For more detail of the center of town, see next page; for an aerial photograph from around 1941, see the following page (the photograph is from the U.S. National Archives' collection of German reconnaissance photos; annotations are based on observations by Mr. Andrzej Penzinski). Locations were confirmed with Ryszard Ejchelkraut, a local historian.

Tejtel house at 6 Sikorskiego Street

Catholic church

Gymnasium (high school)

Jewish school (now 16 Dubois St.)

Yeshiva Beis Yosef on Batorego Street

Grammar school— Algemeine Shule

Neuer Beis Medrish (New Study House)

Catholic cemetery

Kagan flour mill "Automat"

Old Jewish cemetery

Tejtel Brothers Brewey

City Pond / Sadzawka

Governor's house and gardens

Ostrolenska Street

Alter Beis Medrish (Old Study House)

Town hall / Rynek

Jewish girls school (48 Prusa St.)

Swierczewski Street (now 3rd May Street)

Tejtel lumber yard & Tarbut school (see later page for detail)

Rozanska Street

Park Napoleon (Promenade Garden) (formerly the Russian Orthodox church)

Warszawska Street

Brokowska Street

Soccer field under construction

Grammar School for the Jewish poor - its manager was a Ukrainian who during WW II collaborated with the Germans

Yeshiva on Batorego Street

The fire of November 9, 1939 started from a house owned by Blumberg on the corner of Warszawska and Mieczkowski street; this shows where Mieczkowski street reaches the market square

Grammar School with its playground in Kościuszki Street

Gymnasium with a playground behind the premises on which there are military vehicles

Catholic church

Catholic cemetery in Lubiejewska Street; the road appears to show an assembly of military vehicles

Grammar School for girls (started 1937); earlier everybody attended school in Kościuszki Street

An observation tower to control the town built by Germans on area of property owned by Mr. Kazimierz Matusiewicz

Town Hall

Old Jewish Cemetery

This shows the green area in front of the town hall. Originally it stretched between the town hall and 3rd May Street; later the area was expanded to the other side of 3rd May Street after the fire of Nov. 9, 1939, when wooden houses were destroyed. The area released by the burnt buildings was also used for installing high posts like lanterns on which Germans hung loudspeakers to promulgate news and propaganda. Poles ignored them. The first gathering of civilians around the posts was after the Russian invasion, when the Germans advised about findings in Katyń and their investigation of the Russian murder of the Polish prisoners of war committed there.

PICTURES OF THE TOWN

There are many photographs of the town from the early 20th century, including from picture postcards.

Below and on the next page are bird's-eye views of the town. The one below is from a 1931 series by HENAU, and on the next page are two views—the top one from a postcard series produced before World War I (likely the F.K.Z. series mentioned below), and the lower one a view slightly to the left of the top one. All the pictures are looking in the same direction—the Catholic church appears on the horizon at the center (in the last one, on the horizon at the right), so that these were taken from just south of the center of town looking north/north-east. In the pre-World War I pictures, on the left, are the spires of the Russian Orthodox church. Note the predominantly wooden houses.

Ostrów-Łomżyński — Ogólny widok miasta

The Rynek—Market Square

In the center of town was the Rynek, or market square, where much of the town's business took place. The top picture is dated to 1914; the bottom one is likely from around the same time frame. Another picture appears in the World War I section. The Town Hall was later built in the Rynek area (1927).

Ostrów, gub. Łomż.

Targ czwartkowy

Ostrów-Łomżyński
Rynek

Pre-World War I

There are several postcards of Ostrow Lomzynski (the name of Ostrow Mazowiecka during the Imperial Russian era) from publishing house F.K.Z., probably from around 1910. On this page, the top one shows the book store of W. Paszkowski on Bialystok Street, the prior name for 3rd-May Street, the main street in the center of town. The lower one shows the villa of Wl. Kostecki on Wienikowska Street. Note the wooden houses to the left in the lower picture, which were more typical construction for the town.

Ostrów-Łomżyński
Ulica Białostocka
Księgarnia W. Paszkowskiego

Ostrów-Łomżyński
ulica Wienikowska
Wila p. Wł. Kosteckiego

Ostrów-Łomżyński
ulica Fabryczna

Fabryka wyrobów metalowych Kostecki Wiśniewski

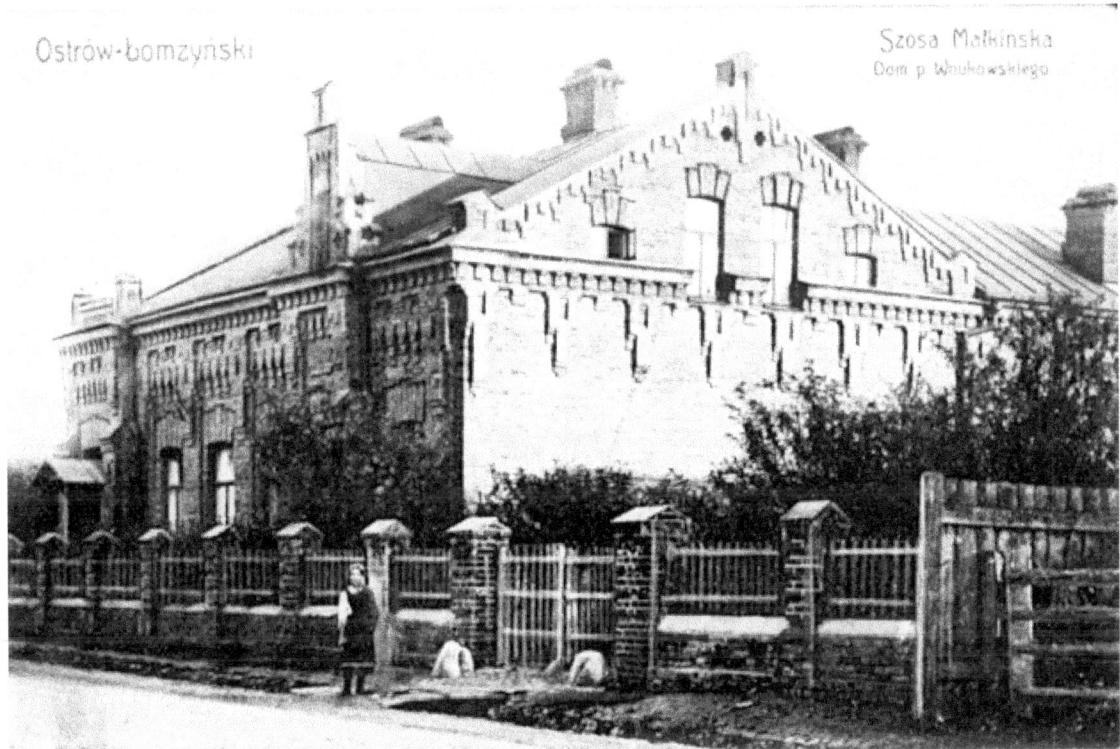

Ostrów-Łomżyński

Szosa Małkińska
Dom p Wnukowskiego

Top - metal factory of Kostecki / Wisniewski, on Fabryczna Street

Bottom—house of Wnukowski, on Malkinska Street

Warszawska Street

The top picture is from the F.K.Z. series.

The bottom one is probably from around the same time period.

The city pond, or Staw Miejski

The Russian Orthodox church of St. Nicholas. It was started in 1901 and completed in 1908. Like many other Russian Orthodox churches in Poland, it was torn down after World War I—in 1929-1930. The site bordered by Stare Brokowska, Jagiellonska and 3rd-May Streets was turned into Napoleon Park/Promenade Garden.

WORLD WAR I

German soldiers assembling in the Rynek, looking northeast—note the Catholic church in the left background. The photo is dated August 12, 1915. The Germans had entered and occupied the town two days earlier.

German soldiers in Ostrow—note the sign "Soldatenheim" (soldier's home) on the right

Between the Wars

3rd May Street / Swierczewski Street

From the 1931 HENAU series of postcards:

Above—Park Napoleon (which replaced the Russian Orthodox church)

Below—Gimnazium (high school)

Above: The Ratusz, or Town Hall, built between 1925 and 1927 in the Rynek area at the center of town

Below: The open space in front of the town hall, the corner of which can be seen in the left of the picture; on the right is 3rd-May Street

Ostrów.-Maz.

Młyn „Automat" ul. Lubiejewska.

The Jewish-owned steam mill "Automat" on Lubiejewska Street, described as the second largest in Poland and the largest enterprise in Ostrow. It was famous for its fine quality flour, reputedly the best in all of Poland.

Tejtel Family Businesses

One of the leading Jewish families in Ostrow Mazowiecka was the Tejtel family. The family owned and operated two of the major businesses in the town—a sawmill and lumber yard, and a brewery.

Sawmill and Lumber Yard

The family of Herszk (Hershel) Tejtel owned a sawmill and lumber yard on Szosa Rozanska (Rozanska Road). After Herszk Tejtel died in 1919, the property was managed by his brother Michel Tejtel and his son-in-law Josk Froimowicz, among others. After most of Herszk's children left for Palestine, the Froimowicz family ended up as the sole owners. The Froimowicz family - Fruma, Josk, and their two daughters - perished in the Holocaust.

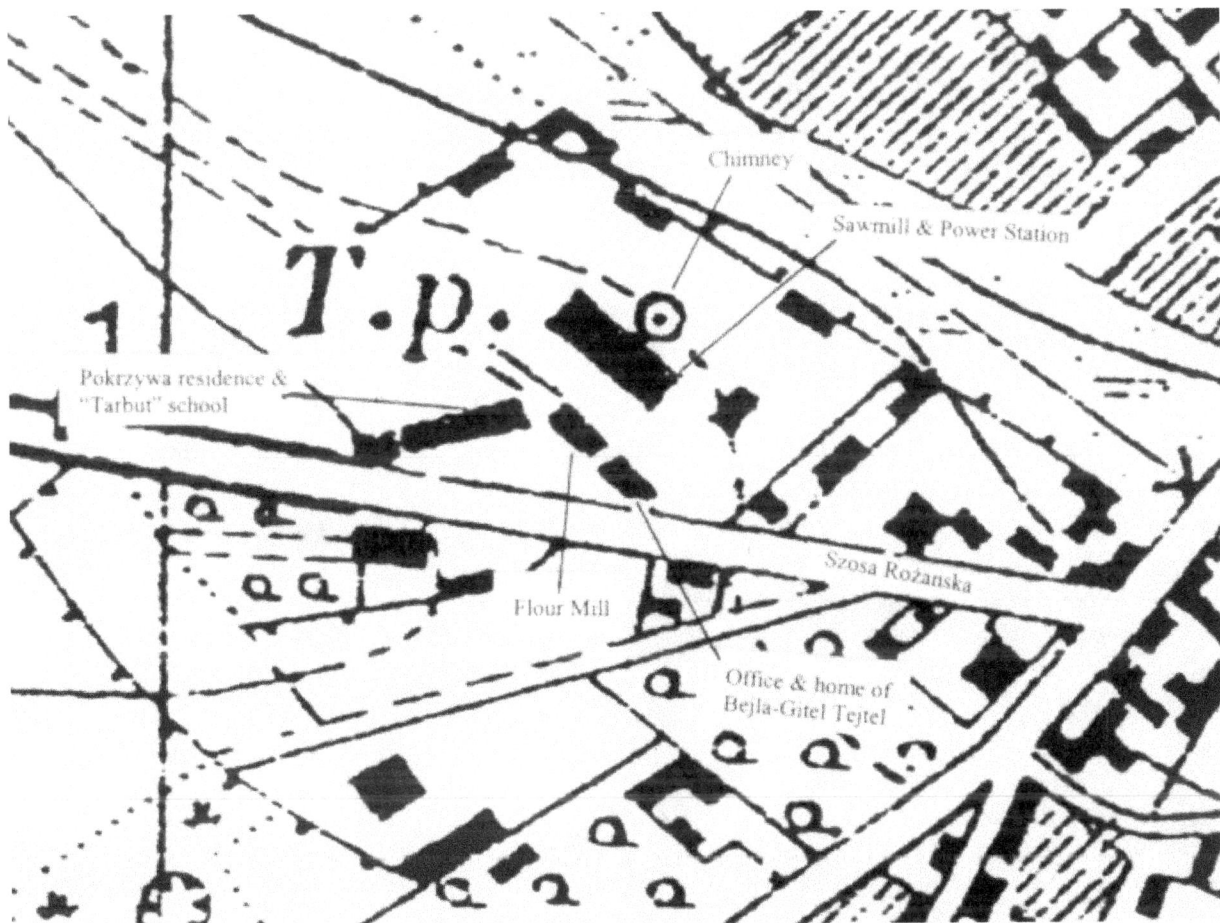

Outline of the property (using a 1933 map):

Bejla-Gitel Tejtel, the widow of Herszk Tejtel, lived with her younger children in a house at No. 4 Szosa Rozanska, which also served as the office for the lumber business. Next to her residence was a flour mill that later served as a carpentry workshop for Abram Jankiel Pokrzywa, who helped manage the business. The sawmill itself included an electrical power station, the first power station in Ostrow, which was added around 1920 following a fire. The sawmill's chimney was the tallest in the town.

The property was surrounded by a wooden fence. Just outside the fence, to the west of the property, was the Pokrzywa residence, No. 12 Szosa Rozanska, a former army barracks built in the late 19th century by Herszk Tejtel for the Russian army. The building also housed the "Tarbut" school during the 1920s and 1930s.

Photos on the following pages dating from around 1922, curtesy of Gerald Cook—reprinted with permission

The house on the left (A) was the residence of the Tejtel family - Bejla-Gitel (Herszk's widow) and her daughters Etka and Ides. The house in the middle (B) was the flour mill. On the right (C) is the "tartak," or sawmill, with its tall chimney partly visible.

In the foreground are (from left to right): Fruma Froimowicz with daughter Lodka; Michel Tejtel; Abram Jankiel Pokrzywa (a son-in-law of Herszk) with daughter Nechama; and Awigder Tejtel (a son of Herszk).

The sawmill ("tartak"), with its tall chimney, and the electrical power plant ("elektrownia"). In the foreground, left to right: Awigder Tejtel, Abram Jankiel Pokrzywa, Michel Tejtel.

View from Szosa Rozanska: To the right is the home of Bejla-Gitel Tejtel; in the center right is the flour mill; and on the left is the Pokrzywa family residence (the former barracks that also housed the Tarbut school)

View of Ostrow from the property. Note the height of the sawmill's chimney, and the Catholic church on the horizon (similar to the bird's-eye views shown earlier)

Tejtel Brothers Brewery

The brewery, a brick building situated on Warszawska Street, was founded in the late 19th century by Wolf (Arya Ze'ev) Tejtel (1844-1910) (the firm itself dated to 1854). After he died, the business was inherited by his sons and sons-in-law. According to an article in the 1960 yizkor book, it employed 50 people and was known throughout the region, with the person in charge of brewing—Icek Tejtel, a grandson of Wolf—having studied in Germany. During World War II, the building was turned into a jail and interrogation center. A monument now marks the site, which is occupied by a school.

The wording on the monument says:

"This place was sanctified by the martyr blood of Poles fighting for freedom during the hitlerite occupation of 1939-1944."

Label from a beer bottle produced by the brewery

Yeshiva Beis Yosef, on Batorego Street

What the building looks like in about 2005

Tarbut School, on Rozanska Road (a location in addition to the one next to the Tejtel sawmill property)

What the building looks like now (around 2005)

Train station on Lubiejewska Street

Nyski's shop

Prayer house on Szkolna Street, after being damaged on August 19, 1937

From the archives of the American Joint Distribution Committee—reprinted with permission

House on Warszawska Street (taken in 1995)

Old wooden houses on the former Stare Brokowska Street (taken in 1997)